Greenhouse Economics

This important book examines one of the most crucial issues in the modern world: climate change. Providing a refreshing interdisciplinary perspective, which pulls together strands of natural science, economics and ethics, *Greenhouse Economics* poses some serious questions and offers intelligent answers.

Themes covered include:

- How do we deal with uncertainty and ignorance?
- What role do science and economics play in policy formation?
- To what extent should individuals take responsibility for the society in which they and their descendants live?

By examining issues such as the Intergovernmental Panel on Climate Change reports, recent economic analyses, and ethical concerns in economics, *Greenhouse Economics* manages to provide an up-to-date and informative analysis of some of this important problem facing society.

This book will be of strong interest to students and academics in the field of ecological and environmental economics, while also being essential reading for all those for whom climate change is an important professional or personal concern. The interdisciplinary analysis will appeal to academics in a range of subjects such as geography, ethics and ecological studies, as well as being of interest to policy-makers.

Professor Clive L. Spash holds the Research Chair in Environmental and Rural Economics at the University of Aberdeen. He is head of the Socio-Economic Research Programme at the Macaulay Institute and President of the European Society for Ecological Economics.

Routledge Explorations in Environmental Economics
Edited by Nick Hanley
University of Glasgow

1 Greenhouse Economics
Value and ethics
Clive L. Spash

2 Oil Wealth and the Fate of the Tropical Rainforests
Sven Wunder

3 The Economics of Climate Change
Edited by Anthony D. Owen and Nick Hanley

4 Alternatives for Environmental Valuation
Edited by Michael Getzner, Clive Spash and Sigrid Stagl

Greenhouse Economics

Value and ethics

Clive L. Spash

Routledge
Taylor & Francis Group

LONDON AND NEW YORK

First published 2002
by Routledge, an imprint of Taylor & Francis
2 Park Square, Milton Park, Abingdon, Oxon OX14 4RN

Simultaneously published in the USA and Canada
by Routledge
270 Madison Ave, New York, NY 10016

This edition first published in paperback 2005

Routledge is an imprint of the Taylor & Francis Group

© 2002, 2005 Clive L. Spash

Typeset in Perpetua by
HWA Text and Data Management, Tunbridge Wells
Printed and bound in Great Britain by
MPG Books Ltd, Bodmin

British Library Cataloguing in Publication Data
A catalogue record for this book is available from the British Library

Library of Congress Cataloging in Publication Data
A catalog record for this book has been requested

ISBN 0–415–12718–1 (hbk)
ISBN 0–415–37244–5 (pbk)

To Edward, Glenn, Mark, Oliver, Simon, Hannah and members of other endangered species.

Sero medicina paratur cum mala per longas convaluerer moras.

Contents

List of figures   x
List of tables   xi
Acknowledgements   xiii
List of abbreviations   xv

1 Climate change: introducing some of the issues   1

Air pollution and the modern economy 2
Economic understanding of pollution 5
The scientific problem 6
A brief historical overview of developing awareness of the enhanced
    Greenhouse Effect 11
Values and ethical concerns 20
Conclusions 21

2 Scientific understanding of the enhanced Greenhouse Effect   25

Global climatic patterns 26
Sources and sinks of greenhouse gases 32
Greenhouse gas emission trends 40
Past and future trends in global climate 48
Conclusions 53

3 Impacts of global climate change   60

Regional impacts of greenhouse warming 63
Intertemporal impacts of global warming 76
Conclusions 87

4   Weak uncertainty: risk and imperfect information   97

The probability of the enhanced Greenhouse Effect 98
Measuring and predicting climatic change 107
The role of modelling 110
Conclusions 115

5   Strong uncertainty: ignorance and indeterminacy   120

Characterising future events 123
Economic use of weak uncertainty 128
How weak is weak uncertainty? 131
From weak to strong uncertainty 134
The changing perception of science 141
Conclusions 147

6   Calculating the cost and benefits of GHG control   153

The theory behind economic assessment 154
Studies using cost–benefit analysis 160
Conclusions 177

7   Loading the dice? Values, opinions and ethics   184

Inconsistency and disputed values 185
Strong uncertainty revisited 192
Conclusions 197

8   Dividing time and discounting the future   201

Discounting the future 203
Can the future be treated as less important? 209
Conclusions 215

9   Economics, ethics and future generations   221

Intergenerational ethical rules 223
Distinguishing basic and compensatory transfers 226
Harm and trade-offs 231
Rights versus consequences 233
Conflicting values and moral dilemmas 237
Conclusions 242

10 Science, economics and policy   **251**

Science and political economy 252
Choices and decisions 258
Redefining economic inquiry 265
Preferences, value and time 268
Concluding remarks 277

Glossary   283
Index   286

Figures

2.1a Global warming for GHGs added in 1970s   33
2.1b Global warming for GHGs added in 1980s   33
2.2   Monthly atmospheric CO_2, 1958–99   43
2.3   Annual CO_2 concentration at Mauna Loa   43
2.4   Annual cycle of atmospheric CO_2, 1999   44
2.5   Vostok temperature record   49
2.6   Global annual temperature anomalies, 1859–1999   52
2.7   Global monthly temperature anomalies,
      January 1979–December 1999   52
3.1   Long-term net cost of the enhanced Greenhouse Effect:
      a qualitative picture   87
4.1   Frequency distribution for temperature, 1856–1999   99
4.2a Hypothetical probability distribution   100
4.2b Hypothetical temperature variations   100
4.3a An increase in temperature mean   102
4.3b Hypothetical 1°C mean temperature rise   102
4.4a An increase in temperature variation   103
4.4b Hypothetical increase in variance   103
4.5a An increase in mean and variance   104
4.5b Hypothetical mean and variance shift   104
4.6   Double carbon dioxide scenarios   105
6.1   Marginal costs and benefits of reducing greenhouse gas emissions   155
8.1   Reducing the weight of future events   202
8.2   Weighting for 100 years of discounting   202

Tables

1.1 Some events in the development of scientific understanding of weather and climate 12

1.2 Events changing scientific perception of human–climate interactions 14

1.3 Events leading to a political agenda for the enhanced Greenhouse Effect 15

1.4 Emissions controls proposed in 1990 16

1.5 Events concerning the convention and protocol on climate change 17

2.1 Albedo of different surfaces 28

2.2 Land changes affecting global albedo 28

2.3 Annual particulate inputs to the atmosphere 30

2.4 Global CO_2 budget ($\times 10^{15}$ grams of carbon per year) 35

2.5 Sources of CO_2 by energy type 41

2.6 World energy demand 41

2.7 Summary of the principal greenhouse gases 53

3.1 Latitudinal temperature changes for three scenarios by year 2000 63

3.2 Regional scenarios for climate change 63

3.3 The arid nations 69

3.4 World trade in cereals: top ten countries, 1999 71

3.5 Time scales of processes influencing the climate system 77

3.6 IPCC 1990 'business as usual' sea level and temperature increases: 2030 and 2070 82

3.7 IPCC 1995 'best estimate' sea level and temperature increases to 2050 and 2100 82

3.8 Estimated sea level rise to the year 2100 85

5.1 Classifications of uncertainty, risk and ignorance 122

6.1 Double CO_2 equivalent GHG damages in Nordhaus 1991 161

6.2 Benefits of GHG control for China as weighted by CBA studies 170

7.1 Author weighting of impacts in CBA studies of GHG control for the US 193

7.2 Author weighting of benefits in CBA studies of GHG control at the world level 195

8.1 Positions defining economic and philosophic treatment of the future   216
10.1 Top twenty CO_2 emissions by country   255
10.2 CO_2 emissions by region, 1998   257

Acknowledgements

This book builds upon past research and continuing work on the inter-relationships between economics, environment and society. As a project extending over many years the book has changed and evolved. I have, for example, removed two earlier chapters on the mathematical modelling of the intergenerational transfers under the enhanced Greenhouse Effect, upon which I probably spent too much time and with too much faith in their potential. That such chapters were removed is also an indication of how my perception of both the subject and the audience I wished to address have changed. While lecturing on sabbatical in New Zealand the need to write about the economic approach for an audience lacking formal economic training became very apparent. Thus, this book draws upon my work at many different times and places, and because of its evolving nature some influences are more obvious than others. Here I would just like to mention a few of those who have aided my thinking.

Mick Common and Alistair Dow supplied early support for my interest in environmental economics. I thank Mick particularly for many insightful and stimulating discussions over the years which I'm glad to say we continue to have when we meet. Ralph d'Arge provided encouragement to nurture my initial ideas on economics and the enhanced Greenhouse Effect, and our joint work on intergenerational resource allocation, at the University of Wyoming, formed the foundations for the current book. A grant from the Scottish Economic Society, while I was lecturing at Stirling University, allowed me to complete preliminary survey work on public attitudes which probed into the potential for intergenerational compensation. This supported my theoretical and economic modelling-based concerns about the role of ethics in economics and the distinct moral character of transfers to meet the goals of distribution and compensation.

My interest in the need to address issues of uncertainty in economics was initially stimulated by Brian Loasby's lectures on methodology when I was an undergraduate. This interest was revitalised in the mid-1990s by an ecological economics conference where I met Silvio Funtowicz, whose work provided a new perspective. While a visiting professor at the University of Versailles, I was able to pursue these issues and discuss them with Martin O'Connor who provided me with useful references. In addition the work of Andy Stirling and of Brian Wynne gave support for my views on risk and uncertainty and I have benefited from listening to and discussing views with them. Besides Brian, I have also benefited from interactions with various current and former members of the Centre for the Study of Environmental Change (CSEC), in particular John Foster and Michael Jacobs during joint projects on environmental valuation.

Major thanks go to Alan Holland and John O'Neill of the Philosophy Department at Lancaster University. Their work on environmental values and valuation over the years has been of great interest. Listening to lectures by both John and Alan, and then being able to discuss and debate their ideas with them and others, has provided an opportunity to improve my understanding of philosophical concepts. Moral philosophy, like the classics, is too often regarded as irrelevant in a world driven by scientific knowledge and economic materialism where vocation takes a narrow meaning. The great relevance of ethics and civic virtue to applied environmental policy is perhaps becoming more apparent in some circles after two decades of political neglect in industrially developed countries. John has provided me with insight into the meaning of preferences and the importance of underlying values and virtues. Alan has raised several issues over the years, some of which have fallen on fertile ground and in the current context this is most directly the case with regard to intergenerational ethics. I still hope to learn much more from both of them.

In the execution of this work there are several other people to thank. Ian Moffat and John Harrison of the Environmental Science Department, Stirling University for reading and commenting on early drafts of the chapters on science and impacts. The Carbon Dioxide Information and Analysis Centre in the United States has been generous with data over the years and in particular Sonja Jones aided my requests. Gregg Marland of Oak Ridge National Laboratory was kind enough to provide some useful input and references to an early draft of the science chapter. Dale Rothman for discussions and who sent me some interesting readings. Anonymous reviewers and the editor of *Environmental Ethics* for comments and feedback on a paper on long-term environmental damages published in that journal. Anton Leist for among other things inviting me to a workshop to present and discuss my ideas on intergenerational damages with some critical thinkers in the area of economics and ethics. Various interactions with Dale Jamieson with regard to the enhanced Greenhouse Effect and intergenerational ethics, including becoming a co-author of a book chapter before we physically met! Michael Glantz for involving me in National Oceanic and Atmospheric Administration (NOAA) workshops debating how to address climate change from an interdisciplinary perspective including economics, ethics and social justice.

More generally, for their intellectual stimulation and support which has aided this research in many subtle ways, I wish to thank: Claudia Carter, Peter Earl, Jack Knetsch and Arild Vatn.

Thanks are also extended for the various permissions to reproduce figures and tables, and information adapted for use in my own tables and graphics.

Abbreviations

AOSIS	Alliance of Small Island States
BAU	business as usual
BP	before present
CBA	cost–benefit analysis
CCl_4	carbon tetrachloride
CETA	carbon emissions trajectory assessment
CFCs	chlorofluorocarbons
CH_4	methane
Cl	chlorine
CO	carbon monoxide
COP	Conference of the Parties
CO_2	carbon dioxide
CS_2	carbon disulphide
CSEC	Centre for the Study of Environmental Change
DICE	dynamic integrated climate economy
EC	European Community
EPA	Environmental Protection Agency, United States Government
FAO	Food and Agriculture Organisation, United Nations
GARP	Global Atmospheric Research Programme
gC	grams of carbon
GCM	general circulation model
GDP	gross domestic product
GFDL	Geophysical Fluid Dynamics Laboratory, USA
GHGs	greenhouse gases
GISS	Goddard Institute for Space Studies, USA
H	hydrogen
HFC	hydrofluorocarbon
ICSU	International Council for Scientific Unions
IEA	International Energy Authority
IG-BP	International Geosphere-Biosphere Programme

IIASA	International Institute of Applied Systems Analysis
IPCC	Intergovernmental Panel on Climate Change
MJ	megajoule
μm	micrometres
MT	million tonnes
MTOE	million tonnes oil equivalent
N	nitrogen
N_2O	nitrous oxide
NASA	National Aeronautical and Space Administration
NCAR	National Centre for Atmospheric Research, USA
NO_2	nitrogen dioxide
NO_x	oxides of nitrogen
NOAA	National Oceanic and Atmospheric Administration, USA
O	oxygen
O_2	diatomic oxygen
O_3	tropospheric ozone
OECD	Organisation for Economic Co-operation and Development
OH	hydroxyl radical
OSU	Oregon State University, USA
PCBs	polychlorinated biphenyls
PFC	perfluorocarbon
ppb	parts per billion
ppbv	parts per billion volume
ppm	parts per million
ppmv	parts per million volume
RICE	regional integrated climate economy
SAR	second assessment report (of the IPCC)
SBSTA	Subsidiary Body for Scientific and Technological Advice
SF_6	sulphur hexafluoride
SO_2	sulphur dioxide
TAR	third assessment report (of the IPCC)
UKMO	United Kingdom Meteorological Office (includes the Hadley Centre)
UN	United Nations
UNEP	United Nations Environment Programme
UNFCCC	United Nations Framework Convention on Climate Change
UV	ultraviolet
VAT	value added tax
WMO	World Meteorological Organisation
WTA	willingness to accept
WTP	willingness to pay
yr	year

1 Climate change

Introducing some of the issues

The central concern in this chapter is to provide a broad background picture of the scientific, political and economic issues relating to the enhanced Greenhouse Effect. This initiates the exploration of links between different disciplinary perspectives and some common problems they share. As the structure of the book shows, understanding complex environmental problems requires moving from scientific knowledge of physical relationships and impacts to socio-economic variables in order to comprehend the range of moral dilemmas faced and the limits to human understanding. This will then give insight into the different perspectives and languages being brought to bear on the issue, while allowing the substantive arguments to be identified.

The following pages explore the development of climate change as an international policy concern. Natural science has been at the fore of the debate, but as regulation of various emissions has moved onto the political agenda so economists have entered the debate. Here I begin to identify and describe how human-induced environmental change is linked to economic analysis and introduce themes which are explored in more detail by other chapters. As will be seen, seriously addressing the enhanced Greenhouse Effect challenges the approach to resource allocation of mainstream economics. A range of subjects arise which are relevant to all environmental policy issues: the objectivity of scientific information, asymmetry of costs and benefits over space (regional impacts) and time (intergenerational impacts); risk, uncertainty and ignorance; institutional power over information and policy; and the role of ethical judgement. Each of these areas is a major topic requiring research and posing serious challenges to the current conceptualisation of pollution as a technical problem which requires an engineered solution. Yet, as will be shown in this chapter, similar problems have been and continue to be posed by other pollution externalities. The difference in the case of the enhanced Greenhouse Effect is how the issues confront the analyst simultaneously, are non-separable and on a global scale.

This chapter sketches out some of the issues to be pursued later in the book and gives some context to the enhanced Greenhouse Effect in terms of economic and scientific approaches to pollution. In the next section the connections between developed industrial economies and pollution are drawn out. This is followed by a short introduction to the economic approach to pollution as an externality and critiques of this characterisation. Then the role of scientific knowledge and scientists is given a similar overview. The influence of science in society is a key concern which recurs throughout the book, and particularly the desire for scientific knowledge to be regarded as value free and separable from the political process. How the science of climate change has developed is then introduced in an historical briefing with key information summarised in several tables. A short precursor to some of the ethical concerns which will be raised later is provided before drawing concluding remarks. This introduction aims to provide the context within which the issues concerning the enhanced Greenhouse Effect fall.

Air pollution and the modern economy

The origins of this book lie in the early 1980s when I was working on the impacts of various forms of air pollution on the environment: primarily sulphur dioxide and nitrous oxides, as causes of acidic deposition in Europe and North America, and tropospheric ozone smogs resulting from car emissions. These problems provided lessons as to how pollution, and the environment in general, has been treated by business, politicians, academics and the public. They also raised serious questions about the (lack of) interactions between economics and natural science in policy formation. Natural science and socio-economic disciplinary fields largely avoided each other throughout the twentieth century. They also both have a tendency to ignore the political discourse in which they are entwined, wishing to be regarded as offering objective facts free from value judgements, e.g. the desire of the more recent reports of the Intergovernmental Panel on Climate Change (IPCC) to avoid discussing the meaning of 'dangerous anthropogenic impacts on climate change' because this is seen as a value judgement and part of the political process.

Perhaps this facade of political immunity is responsible for the dominant approach to pollution problems. For decades this has been to reduce the physical and political presence of pollution without addressing the underlying causes in the way economic and technological systems are being driven. Solutions have been offered and accepted without adequately reflecting upon their own eventual consequences. The environmental engineering and management approach could be summarised as 'dilution is the solution to pollution', a philosophy which is still prevalent in many quarters. Thus, pollution and environmental impacts have been transferred back and forth from one medium to another (air, land, oceans) and pushed across jurisdictional and ecosystem boundaries. Readily observable pollution incidents with immediate local damages (e.g. deaths) have been transformed into unobserved, long-term impacts spread internationally. Environmental threats have been transformed from high-frequency low-impact events to low-frequency high-impact events. This historical trend seems set to continue with new forms of 'pollution' which have the same economic and political causes but which redefine our understanding of the concept. Thus, the enhanced Greenhouse Effect and genetic bio-engineering can be seen as representing the latest (but undoubtedly far from the last) phases in this progress towards rapid globalisation of human-induced environmental change.

The last century of coal combustion in the UK provides an example. Coal burning for household heating and cooking was responsible for the infamous London smogs through which Sherlock Holmes struggled to find clues, and into which Jack the Ripper disappeared. These 'pea soup' smogs were finally brought to an end due to the high number of hospital admissions and deaths being recorded by the newly founded National Health Service in the early 1950s. In particular, during the London smogs of 1952–3, the death toll rose above 4,000, especially affecting the old and those with cardiac and respiratory disorders (Holdgate, 1980: 79). The Clean Air Acts of 1954 and 1962 restricted the zones where coal could be burnt while electricity produced by large coal-fired power stations was increasingly used for heating and cooking. Coal smogs were largely removed, although exceedance of World Health Organisation standards continued to occur in certain areas.

One result of the new power stations was to inject sulphur dioxide and nitrous oxides high into the atmosphere, where they were out of sight and out of mind. That was until the 1970s when Scandinavian scientists began to publicise the link between the changes in their forests and water ecosystems due to acidic deposition. A decade of dispute and research led to the more general acceptance that the long-range transportation of air pollutants from the UK and Germany to Scandinavia was possible, but there was no action by the major emitters. Emissions were given more serious attention by the German government as their own forests began to die and environmentalists began to successfully move into mainstream politics. The main impact on emissions in the UK was due to the changing political and economic fortunes of the coal industry with Conservative administrations determined to break the power of the mining unions. The availability of cheaper natural gas and a move away from heavy industry aided this political agenda. Thus, political and structural change was affecting emissions rather than any concern for environmental damages inflicted on others.

Acidic deposition remains a serious problem which has destroyed and is destroying ecosystems across Europe. In the late 1990s the Scandinavians were forced to issue health warnings against pregnant women eating fish due to the heavy metals released into the water by acidic deposition, which then accumulates in the body of the fish. The developing human foetus is particularly vulnerable to the toxic effects of these heavy metals. Of course decades of acidic deposition have also contaminated water supplies, in a similar fashion, and Scandinavian households in remote areas dependent upon ground water are at risk. The Norwegian and Swedish programmes for liming vast areas on a regular basis merely maintain a life line for ecosystems (similar to the geo-engineering options offered to counter climate change), which can only stand a chance of recovery if acidic deposition from burning fossil fuels in the United Kingdom and Germany are strictly curtailed. In the meantime ecosystems are degraded, biodiversity lost and once vibrant communities disappear as fish die and ecosystems degrade. However, attention has moved away from that ongoing environmental disaster and many seem to believe the problem has gone away because the media rarely seems to report on it anymore.

Tropospheric ozone is more frequently discussed because urban smogs are an international and seasonal phenomenon occurring in Athens, Los Angeles, London, Mexico City, Tokyo and Vancouver, to mention a few places. The brown nitrous oxide pollution hanging over a city turns to a blue ozone haze when stimulated by sunlight. When gases are trapped by the right weather conditions (e.g. an inversion in a mountain valley area) they can build up to high concentrations over several days. Ozone smogs often have a visible and directly observable presence. Health impacts can be serious for the young and old, and for others burning eyes and respiratory problems will result from high concentrations. While a focus on human health can often raise a more immediate reaction from the public this is only part of the picture. Wider damage also occurs to materials and ecosystems. Ozone affects plant growth and can contribute to loss of agricultural crops and forest decline (as has been notable and publicised in Germany).

Attempts to control the precursor emissions, coming largely from cars, have had limited impact. Many economists have tended to regard this as a failure by government to take into account economic incentives. The approach favoured by government administrations has been to adopt pollution standards, justified on scientific grounds, because these are meant to provide absolute protection (i.e. there is believed to be a threshold beyond which pollution impacts start to occur and below which damages are insignificant). However, regulation to meet scientifically pronounced thresholds is deemed economically inefficient because no account is given to the expected costs of pollution control in comparison to the expected benefits of avoiding damages. A controversial debate erupted on exactly these issues during the second international assessment of climate change (i.e. under IPCC Working Group III, to be discussed later).

In addition, direct regulation is also criticised by economists as ineffective because humans are regarded as acting primarily out of self-interest and therefore deemed to require financial incentives to change their behaviour (i.e. taxes or subsidies). The need for government intervention to adjust prices sits uncomfortably with the thrust of mainstream economics which favours a *laissez faire* approach. Ironically, the mechanisms of the market are meant to correct the failures of the market. These ideas seem to have moved to centre stage in negotiations on climate change regulation where the US has held sway and the idea of trading emissions is becoming enshrined under the Kyoto Protocol of the Framework Convention on Climate Change.

Economic understanding of pollution

Pollution is often seen as an activity involving a limited number of actors or agents and so a readily identifiable source and target. In economics the case of a smoky factory being sited near a laundry or a firm polluting a stream used by a farmer are typical examples. Thus, pollution is described as an activity by one agent which imposes negative consequences on another agent who has no control over the activity harming them, termed an externality. The aim of environmental economics is then to make all agents take account of the damages they impose on others, termed the need to internalise the externalities. Under a 'polluter pays principle', the factory should be charged for emitting smoke and the firm for putting waste in the stream. This charge should reflect the monetary amount of damages caused to the laundry or farmer per unit of pollution. This effectively places a price upon the environmental damages and so encourages polluters to reduce their use of the environment as a waste sink, which in turn means damages should be reduced. The avoidance of environmental damages is then described as the benefit of pollution control for society.

This particular economic approach appears in various IPCC reports. For example, while the report on regional impacts mentions legal and institutional strengthening, public participation and education, great emphasis is given to 'removing pre-existing market distortions (e.g. subsidies), correcting market failures (e.g. failure to reflect environmental damage or resource depletion in prices or inadequate economic valuation of biodiversity)' (Watson *et al.*, 1997: 6). However, the enhanced Greenhouse Effect challenges this model because rather than a few actors the entire population is liable to be affected. As is described in chapter 2, the responsible gases arise from numerous sources many of which are an integral part of modern industrial society. The focus of attention has been upon carbon dioxide caused by burning of fossil fuels: oil, coal and gas. However, other activities such as using artificial fertilisers, fridges, growing rice and raising cattle release nitrous oxides (N_2Os), chlorofluorocarbons (CFCs) and methane respectively. The idea that these are simple external effects which can be internalised by calculating an appropriate tax begins to lose credibility. In fact this characterisation had been questioned before the concern over the enhanced Greenhouse Effect took hold.

Kapp (1950) had criticised the concept of the externality as failing to recognise how economic systems operate. That is, given that firms are meant to maximise profits and individuals seek their own best interest, the pushing of damages onto others and avoiding the associated costs is to be expected as a normal and prevalent activity of the successful economic agent. This means terming pollution an externality is to engage in double-speak of Orwellian proportions. Pollution is internal to the economy and economic activity, and especially so if the system is as self-serving as mainstream economics assumes and describes. Profits are maximised by making use of all the 'free gifts of Nature' that are available, passing along costs to other agents (especially competitors) and avoiding as many waste disposal costs as possible. Similarly, the self-centred hedonistic consumer seeking to maximise their own welfare is directed to make use of all that is provided freely by others (whether wittingly or otherwise), avoid considering how their lifestyle may impact upon others (unless this gives them pleasure) and in fact actively get others to pay. Consumption and production at least cost for the individual agent can be achieved by avoiding as many costs as possible including pollution control costs.

Another theoretical argument against the simple story of externality theory was provided by work on incorporating the laws of thermodynamics into economics in the late 1960s, which lead to the concept of materials balance theory (Kneese, Ayres and d'Arge, 1970). The first law explains that matter like energy can neither be created nor destroyed. This means all material and energy production in an economy must produce an equal amount of waste material and energy, although in a qualitatively different form. Quantitative economic growth leads to qualitative degradation of the environment and hence a range of damages are self-imposed upon society due to additional consumption. Economic growth is then seen as a social process in which quality of life is eroded across a range of activities while the promise of more growth is meant to compensate for any social or environmental harm.

Thus taxes or tradable pollution rights to allow market transactions will fail to address the pervasive problem being conceptualised as 'externalities'. The inherently social character of consumption and production activities combines with the physical laws to portray a rather different picture of pollution than that found in mainstream economics. As Hunt and d'Arge (1973) explain, the individual agent is pushed by an 'Invisible Foot' to promote unintended harm and social misery. The activities of the Invisible Foot seem particularly strong in the consumer society of modern economies where consumption is a competitive activity driven by the desire to keep ahead of the 'Joneses'. This form of 'progress' is evident at both household and national government levels.

The scientific problem

The standard response of natural science to pollution problems is to construct models of expected outcomes and try to test them empirically. Such empiricism has been used effectively to support standards recommended to environmental agencies and legislators and is the key concern of ecotoxicologists. In essence the approach relies upon repeatedly doing the same action under controlled conditions to see if the same outcome results.

Thus, a given concentration or dose of a pollutant will be given to a subject or target and the response predicted from models based upon repeatedly doing so. For example, the health impacts of ozone smogs is predicted from exposing healthy young adults to low concentrations while monitoring how performance is affected during exercise. Models are used to extrapolate results to higher concentration, less healthy individuals, children and the aged. Alternatively, animal experimentation may be employed and the results transferred to humans on the basis of models.

The results from the dose-response approach are surrounded by a range of probable errors and uncertainties (Dickie, 2001). For example, the response of different individuals can vary widely for numerous unexplained and uncontrolled reasons, long-term impacts from low concentration exposure are neglected, actual concentration exposure (length, levels, frequency, mixture, time of day) can be difficult to reproduce but is known to be critical to response. Research extending the dose-response approach to the impacts of ozone smogs and acidic deposition on agricultural crops, and carbon dioxide (CO_2) on forests, have shown similar problems (Spash, 1997). For example, in trying to estimate the damage from ozone exposure to, say, potatoes the variety being exposed determines the response so no general dose-response function can be applied to all potatoes. Research budgeting has meant choosing a selection of varieties for study. The practices of farmers in growing their crops also changes the impact. In experiments all growing conditions are perfect to produce a healthy plant and then deviations from this ideal, due to exposure to a single pollutant, are analysed. In practice crops are grown under a range of environmental stresses (e.g. drought, pest invasion, lack of nutrients) and farmers have an impact on how crops respond (via irrigation, pesticides, insecticides and fertilisers). In addition, crops are exposed to multiple pollutants rather than one in isolation so response in the field can bear no relationship to the experimentally derived dose-response functions.

In terms of global climate change scientists use the experimental approach at different levels. Dose-response work is used directly to try and assess the impacts of temperature, water shortage and increased gas concentrations on plants and animals. More generally, modelling and empirical observation are employed to support theories about the impacts of emissions on global climate. In this latter case deviations in climate from that expected without human gas emissions are being predicted and evidence sought from global monitoring and historical records (discussed further in chapter 4).

The scientific approach also tries to predict the probability of making an error about the relevance of a functional relationship. This can be due to accepting an hypothesis (e.g. a dose-response model) as true when it is in fact false (a false positive), or rejecting the hypothesis as false when it is in fact true (a false negative). The way in which experimentation is conducted can accentuate the type of error. Thus, field experimentation, for example to test the hypothesis that genetically modified crops never transfer genes to other species, may be conducted to test that the hypothesis can (under some specified conditions) hold. Experimentation is conducted and evidence compiled to show how crops may be grown without gene transfer occurring rather than trying to achieve such transfer but then failing to do so. The risk of a false positive remains high and genes may be transferable, but the evidence was being compiled to show safety not danger. The body conducting an experiment becomes important because of the variety of ways in which experiments can be conducted, i.e. the type and range of relationships which are being investigated. This is an obvious reason why self-regulation and scientific evidence from vested interest groups is highly questionable. For example, large numbers of experiments have been conducted on genetically modified crops and this has been used to claim they are 'safe' in terms of gene transference, but the aim of those experiments was largely to investigate productivity improvements not gene transference.

The same empirical approach is being applied to the enhanced Greenhouse Effect. The models being employed are called general circulation models (GCMs) and were developed by atmospheric scientists to improve their understanding of how the atmosphere operates. That is, these models were not originally intended to predict global, and extrapolate regional, climate. Five GCMs have in the past tended to dominate the literature, each known by its associated research group: one from the UK produced by the Meteorological Office (UKMO), and four from the National Aeronautical and Space Administration (NASA) in the USA produced by the Goddard Institute for Space Studies (GISS), the National Center for Atmospheric Research (NCAR), the Geophysical Fluid Dynamics Laboratory (GFDL), and Oregon State University (OSU). One problem for these models has been their lack of detail on land formations and initial absence of any interactions with the oceans. As noted the models were aimed at studying the circulation of the atmosphere, but the application to global climate change has meant their former approach of ignoring two-thirds of the planet surface (the oceans) and regarding the rest as uniform blocks (no geographic description), on the scale of a country the size of France, was untenable. However, computing and modelling capacity is limited so a choice is still required as to the detail given to land, sea or air.

In the face of such potential for variability the scientific community has attempted to provide a consensus on the scientific understanding of the enhanced Greenhouse Effect, which is explored in chapter 2. As explained later in this chapter, international conferences, organisations and bodies of the United Nations (UN) have created a synthesis of information. Several large volumes have been produced over the past 30 years which attempt to cover the science in an objective way while trying to avoid the political implications of this work. Yet part of the scientific approach to pollution has been to determine thresholds and suggest emissions reductions. The result has been to describe various 'scenarios' while trying to avoid statements on the reductions required to avoid human-induced climatic change.

From a purely institutional perspective the international scientific bodies working on climate change are political bodies working within a political process, commanding power and authority, and elevating participants in terms of their international profiles and status. Various internal review procedures might be used to produce final documents and reports with varying results in terms of content and emphasis. The Intergovernmental Panel on Climate Change has become the most important body and employed the following process for its 1995 Second Assessment Reports (SAR), published in 1996. Government nominated experts were selected by government representatives to form the writing teams under three IPCC Working Groups: (I) science; (II) impacts, adaptation and mitigation; (III) economics and social dimensions. The texts these groups produce were then sent for comment by a peer community and hundreds of responses returned to the writing teams for consideration. The chapters of the full SAR were attributed to the authors, while a policymakers summary for each IPCC Working Group was meant to draw out key points. A 'Synthesis Report' was produced at a plenary meeting. As Grubb *et al.* (1999: 5) note: 'Since this represents a statement of what governments officially accept as a balanced account of the state of knowledge and reasoned judgement, its precise wording is subject to intensive negotiation between governmental delegations'. At the same time the IPCC has been precluded from making policy recommendations and is meant merely to be a source of internationally accepted knowledge.

The difficulties this raises can be seen in the artificial separation of socio-economics across working groups. Social factors such as population and energy use affect scientific predictions of Working Group I which therefore must rely upon assumptions concerning future political economy. The impacts reports of Working Group II, which were initially seen as listing physical consequences, have had to include more socio-economic research and this was compounded by the SAR remit expansion to adaptation and mitigation. The distinction between Working Groups II and III has been unclear. Indeed literature and topics which appeared under Working Group III in the SAR appear under Working Group II under the third assessment where the distinction between socio-economic and physical science seems less clear. Indeed there is some discernible tension within this institutional structure as to the meaning of 'objective' natural and social science versus relevant socio-economic analysis. More generally, the IPCC is embedded within an international debate covering a range of socio-eonomic (e.g. trade, globalisation, poverty, land ownership) and environmental (e.g. biodiversity loss, ozone depletion, urban air quality) issues.

In fact the institutional role of the IPCC has itself been given some attention by international political scientists (see Paterson, 1996). The IPCC grew from an international scientific community of climate change researchers dominated by geophysicists and meteorologists. Key figures have maintained a dominant role throughout all international assessments of climate change since the 1970s. Such influence must impact the direction of research and the areas seen as most useful to fund. At the same time the direction of international negotiations clearly influences the IPCC reports. For example, since the Kyoto Protocol raised the language of sustainable development this has begun to appear within the IPCC and has affected the Third Assessment Reports (TAR). The IPCC is therefore best viewed within the context of a series of historical events concerning climatic change research which are described later in this chapter.

A point to which I return in chapters 4 and 5 is the perception that information on complex environmental problems can conform to the scientific model of neutral information about objective facts. For example, combining hundreds of divergent opinions on a contentious international economic and political issue is far removed from 'objective' experimental science. As Paterson (1996: 154) has noted, the development of climatic research seems to show that: 'knowledge is something which is strenuously fought over, rather than something which acts in the background as a precursor to political action'. He goes on to argue that the success of GCM models, to the exclusion of other relevant climate models, data and related disciplines, has been due to their compatibility with broader political developments.

Questions must also be raised over the idea that there is a clear division of scientific fact from policy recommendation. The range of uncertainty relevant to environmental problems has in the past raised questions over the relevance of thresholds. Pollutants may be harmful for certain individuals even at low doses, they can bio-accumulate, they may cause impacts on the next generation rather than the individual being exposed, they can cause changes within the balance and structure of ecosystems. That is, the idea of a totally benign positive emissions level is often erroneous so that the actual decision is about the extent to which damages are acceptable rather than identifying an objective threshold at which the environment converts all chemicals and waste products to harmless substances.

Similarly, the debate over emissions reductions under the enhanced Greenhouse Effect concerns accepting that science is part of a discourse on policy. Climate scientists have been shown to hold specific policy beliefs on the need for action (Bray and von Storch, 1999). Hence there should be little surprise that the scientific community of the IPCC can clearly be seen as holding the normative belief that emissions must be reduced substantively. Calls for cuts have been made in the press by the IPCC Chair for its first decade, Bert Bolin, and Working Group I Chair, John Houghton, as well as other lead authors of IPCC reports, e.g. the petition to Kyoto by 11 European climate scientists for 20 per cent reductions. The absence of such statements from the IPCC SAR is due to its explicit politicisation and inclusion as a pre-negotiating document within a political process. In the first assessment a clear statement appeared on the level of CO_2 emissions reductions required to prevent atmospheric concentrations from continuing to increase (Watson *et al.*, 1990: 5): 'In order to stabilize concentrations at present day levels, an immediate reduction in global anthropogenic emissions by 60–80 per cent would be necessary'.

No such clear statement on CO_2 emissions reductions appeared in the SAR. In the meantime the language of stabilisation became associated in international negotiations with emissions levels rather than the more crucial atmospheric concentrations (which require emissions reductions). The drafting of the third assessment report involved strenuous attempts to avoid stating that any of the predicted events were dangerous because this was regarded as political territory which might imply the IPCC had an opinion about emissions reductions and was overstepping the scientific remit.[1] In contrast to the statement above calling for immediate action, the TAR policymakers summary states that in order to stabilise atmospheric concentrations (at whatever level): 'Eventually CO_2 emissions would need to decline to a very small fraction of current emissions' (IPCC Working Group I, 2001: 12). Of course the longer the delay the higher the atmospheric concentration and the greater the climate forcing so that average global sea level and atmospheric temperature will rise further.

A brief historical overview of developing awareness of the enhanced Greenhouse Effect

The potential of the enhanced Greenhouse Effect to add to the list of human-induced environmental problems became of increasing scientific and then public concern in the late 1980s and early 1990s. The enhanced Greenhouse Effect, like acidic deposition, concerns the long-range movement of chemicals through natural systems induced by the modern evolution of human activity. For those who had studied some atmospheric science and worked on air pollution control, the potential for significant environmental damage to persist unchecked could quickly be recognised as a real and present danger posed by the scale of economic activity. Perturbation of the Greenhouse Effect is easily understandable as one logical outcome of releasing a cocktail of chemicals into the upper atmosphere (the ozone hole being another). As discussed in more detail in chapter 2 and summarised in table 1.1, the science behind the Greenhouse Effect was established over a century ago. The main question has been the extent to which human impacts on the functioning of the atmosphere will have adverse consequences.

The importance of research and modelling of climate and the role of human interactions with climate only developed in the second half of the twentieth century (for more details on this historical development see chapter 2 of Paterson, 1996). In general, the opinion in the limited earlier literature was that CO_2 emissions would lead to global warming, with regional and seasonal variations, and this would benefit humans by delaying the next glaciation and improving agricultural production. In fact, during the technocentric optimism of the 1950s and early 1960s a common belief was that humans would be able to overcome the vagaries of Nature such as weather. As Patterson (1996: 24) notes, for example, President Kennedy addressed the UN General Assembly in 1961 proposing further international co-operation to eventually achieve 'weather control'.[2]

Such remarks were encouraged by the success of the World Meteorological Organisation (WMO) with data collection and co-ordination in order to understand and predict weather. A key event in this international co-operation and research was the International Geophysical Year which initiated experimentation and research worldwide. Data collection also aided the rejection of the hypothesis that human greenhouse gas (GHG) emissions were disappearing benignly into the oceans. Notably, the establishment of CO_2 monitoring at Mauna Loa in Hawaii produced conclusive evidence of an ever growing problem as concentrations were seen to rise year on

Table 1.1 Some events in the development of scientific understanding of weather and
climate

	Year	Comments
Fourier article	1827	Theory of the 'hothouse effect' of climate regulation establishing the atmosphere as a key determinant of global temperature
Tyndall article	1861	CO_2 and water recognised as radiative absorbers affecting climate
First International Meteorological Congress, Vienna	1873	Build-up to establishing International Meteorological Organisation
International Meteorological Organisation	1878	Formally established
Arrhenius article	1896	Double CO_2 leads to 5–6°C temperature increase; seen as positive consequence in his 1908 book
Callendar article	1938	Support for Arrhenius; empirical evidence linking increased CO_2 and global warming; seen as positive consequence
World Meteorological Convention	1947	Established World Meteorological Organisation under new United Nations
World Meteorological Organisation (WMO)	1951	Began operation replacing International Meteorological Organisation
International Geophysical Year	1957	Sponsored by WMO and International Council for Scientific Unions (ICSU)

year (see report of the data in chapter 2). This led to a meeting of the Conservation
Foundation on the subject in 1963 which concluded that a 3.8°C average temperature
increase would occur under a doubling of CO_2, and the first official government
acknowledgement occurred in the 1965 Report of the President's Scientific Advisory
Committee. Research into climate, especially in the US, was also stimulated by Cold
War concerns over the impacts of nuclear weapons and how their detonation might
initiate a never-ending 'nuclear winter'.

Only a limited understanding of natural systems is required to realise that reactions
to large-scale human pollution can be unexpected and far removed in time or space
from the original releases. Yet social scientists were slow to explore the consequences
of such pervasive activities as fossil fuel combustion. Instead, during the 1970s and
early 1980s, those showing concern for the impacts of rising CO_2 levels were primarily
natural scientists. During this period the damage from human industrial and mass
consumption activities became readily apparent, although economic analysis of these
issues remained a minority pursuit (Spash, 1999). In the area of climate change
research, until the late 1980s, the only economist showing any consistent concern
and attempting some analysis was Ralph d'Arge, who also presented the only economic
paper at the 1979 World Climate Conference.

In the 1970s, the United Nations through the WMO began to provide a focus for international efforts to co-ordinate environmental research on climate. In addition the UN organised several conferences following the major 1972 Stockholm meeting (which also raised the profile of acidic deposition problems). These explored the relationship between and fragility of human and natural systems with a particular emphasis on climate, see table 1.2. The culmination and synthesis of information from these meetings occurred in 1979 with the aforementioned first World Climate Conference where approximately 400 delegates from 50 countries were in attendance. The conference declaration emphasised the role of CO_2 in climate formation and the need for action to prevent adverse climatic changes. In the same year the US National Academy of Sciences was able to report on the state of climate modelling and confirm confidence in the prediction of a 1.5– 4.5°C temperature increase from a doubling of pre-industrial CO_2 concentrations in the atmosphere, expected sometime during the twenty-first century. However, the political and economic response took another decade and a series of extreme weather events (e.g. cyclones), droughts (especially that hitting the US in 1988) and high temperature years, which by the end of the 1980s made that decade the warmest on record.

General acceptance of human ability to enhance the Greenhouse Effect with adverse consequences has proven more difficult than might be expected. The scientific predictions changed little during the 1980s while the complexity of the models became greater and the role of other greenhouse gases besides CO_2 was recognised as equally important. More scientists, although far from all, did agree on global warming as the inevitable consequence of continued GHG emissions, and this group grew dramatically by the end of the decade. The Villach Conference of 1985 is credited with achieving a scientific consensus and its declarations on expected changes were widely quoted. The first report of the Intergovernmental Panel on Climate Change (IPCC) in 1990 was essentially the same (which is hardly surprising as it was compiled within a year). Towards the end of the 1980s sizeable reductions in emissions were being called for both by the scientific and policy communities (see table 1.3). For example, the 1988 Toronto Conference wanted 20 per cent reductions from then current levels at the time as a starting point.

By 1990 several nations were proposing unilateral reductions in CO_2 emissions and all European Community (EC) countries, except the UK, agreed on stabilisation of aggregate EC emissions. This informal EC agreement would have allowed Spain, Greece and Portugal to increase emissions. The US under the Bush administration remained opposed to emissions controls, while the Soviet Union was opposed to controls 'at the current time'. Divisions were clear between those proposing substantial reductions, up to 50 per cent, those proposing stabilisation of emissions (not atmospheric concentrations) at various levels, and those opposing any action. The positions being taken by various countries by the end of 1990 are reported in table 1.4.

Table 1.2 Events changing scientific perception of human–climate interactions

	Date	Comments
Revelle and Suess article	1957	Anthropogenic CO_2 going into the atmosphere not the oceans
Start of monitoring of CO_2 at Mauna Loa, Hawaii	1957	Keeling under supervision of Revelle as part of International Geophysical Year
US Meeting on consequences of CO_2 increases	1963	Conservation Foundation, double CO_2 lead to 3.8°C average temperature rise
Report of President's Scientific Advisory Committee	1965	Acknowledge possibility of anthropogenic climate change
Global Atmospheric Research Programme (GARP) and World Weather Watch	1967 1968	Established to improve scientific understanding and distribute data on weather; venture of WMO and ICSU
Study of Critical Environmental Problems	1970	One-month workshop in Massachusetts; Kellogg Chair Climate Effects group
Study of Man's Impact on Climate	1971	Conference at Wijk, Sweden; warming or cooling could result from CO_2 increase
UN Conference on the Human Environment	1972	Led to the establishment of United Nations Environment Programme (UNEP)
Physical Basis of Climate and Climate Modelling	1974	GARP Conference
UN World Food Conference	1974	
US Climatic Impact Assessment Program, six-volume report	1975	Project initiated 1973, assessing impact of supersonic aircraft on climate; first attempt at economic and social measures, 40 social scientists, General Chair Ralph d'Arge
Symposium on Long-term Climate Fluctuations	1975	International meeting organised by WMO, held at Norwich, UK
Panel of Experts on Climate Change	1975	Established by WMO
UN Water Conference	1976	
Workshop on comprehensive modelling of the atmosphere	1976	WMO backed, held at US National Oceanic and Atmospheric Administration
UN Desertification Conference	1977	
First World Climate Conference, Geneva	1979	Sponsors UN, WMO, ICSU; global warming predicted and seen as a negative consequence; d'Arge economic impacts
World Climate Programme	1979	Established by WMO to co-ordinate international research on climate
US National Academy of Science Report	1979	Double CO_2 lead to 1.5–4.5°C temperature increase

Table 1.3 Events leading to a political agenda for the enhanced Greenhouse Effect

	Date	Comments
Villach Conference	1985	Organised by WCP; inclusion of other GHGs in models; first international scientific consensus; double CO_2 or equivalent lead to 1.5–4.5°C temperature increase; call for economic and policy research and a Convention to regulate emissions
Villach and Bellagio Workshops on developing policies for responding to climatic change	1987	Organised by WCP; call for limitation and adaptation strategies
Montreal Protocol	1987	Initial regulation of CFCs to prevent stratospheric ozone depletion
US drought	1988	Half the states in US registered as drought stricken
Hansen, chief NASA climate scientist, statement to US Senate, Energy and Natural Resources Committee	1988	High degree of confidence in cause–effect relationship implicating human GHG emissions in climatic warming
Toronto Conference on the Changing Atmosphere: Implications for Global Security	1988	First major political treatment of the issue. CO_2 reduction by 20 per cent from 1988 levels by 2005
World Congress on Climate and Development	1988	Held in Hamburg; call for 30 per cent reduction by 2000 and 50 per cent by 2015; some dissenters
Intergovernmental Panel on Climate Change (IPCC)	1988	Established by WMO and UNEP; remit included assessing socio-economic consequences; Bolin chair
New Delhi Conference	1989	First conference on developing country perspective
Ministerial Conference on Atmospheric Pollution and Climatic Change	1989	Signatories to stabilise CO_2 by 2000 at levels set by the IPCC; Noordwijk Declaration, The Netherlands
Meeting of Small Island States	1989	Met in Maldives and produced Male Declaration

A movement was now underway for the development of a Convention to address the issue, but this also meant greater legal and political consideration. In December 1990 the UN established a negotiating committee for the Framework Convention on Climate Change (UNFCCC), following on from the Second World Climate Conference in November. This was the start of international negotiations which after seven years produced the Kyoto Protocol. Representation of national interests in negotiations would mean defensive diplomacy and a shift in the international debate. Governments generally withdrew from the level of emissions reductions initially proposed and began to produce measures well below those called for prior to the start of international negotiations. In fact reduction was replaced in many

Table 1.4 Emissions controls proposed in 1990

	Target		Proportion of 1990 world CO_2 emissions (%)
Emissions reduction proposals	%	*Date*	
Germany	25	2005	3.2
Italy	20	2005	1.8
Australia	20	2005	1.1
Netherlands	3–5	2000	0.6
Denmark	20	2000	0.3
	50	2030	
New Zealand	20	2000	0.1
Emissions stabilisation proposals	*Level*	*Date*	
Japan	1990	2000	4.4
UK	1990	2005	2.8
Canada	1990	2000	2.0
Italy	1990	2000	1.8
Belgium	1988	2000	0.5
Austria	1990	2000	0.3
Finland	1990	2000	0.3
Sweden	1988	2000	0.2
Norway	1990	2000	0.2
Switzerland	1990	2000	0.2
Ireland	1990	2000	0.1
No controls proposed			
USA			22.0
USSR			18.4

Source: *The Independent* newspaper, Monday 29 October 1990, cited by Harrison (1991).

quarters by 'stabilisation', which required only maintaining 'current' emissions rather than allowing them to grow exponentially. Similarly, 'prevention' of climate change was changed to 'mitigation' of impacts.

At the same time industrially developing countries became involved in the debate. These countries have been concerned that they should be compensated for emissions reductions and that the industrially developed nations accept responsibility for having degraded the global environment, putting their livelihoods at risk. The low-lying island states are particularly susceptible to sea level rise and have organised themselves into an association, the Alliance of Small Island States (AOSIS), which has lobbied for substantive emissions reductions, i.e. 20 per cent by 2005 for industrialised economies.

The last phase in the development of international events surrounding the enhanced Greenhouse Effect was to establish an international treaty, the UNFCCC (adopted May 1992, came into force March 1994), and mechanisms for its operation, the Kyoto Protocol (adopted December 1997, yet to come into force due to lack of

Table 1.5   Events concerning the convention and protocol on climate change

	Date	Comments
IPCC Working Groups established	1989	WG I: Science; WG II: Impacts; WG III: Responses
Second World Climate Conference	1990	IPCC First Assessment Report
IPCC WG I Report	1990	Most important, least original; claimed inclusive and consensus of leading scientists; certain that GHGs enhance Greenhouse Effect; 60–80 per cent emissions reduction needed to stabilise atmospheric CO_2
Alliance of Small Island States (AOSIS)	1990	Established at Second World Climate Conference
UN Resolution 45/212, Protection of global climate for present and future generations	1990	Established the Intergovernmental Negotiating Committee for a Framework Convention on Climate Change
IPCC Supplementary Science Report	1992	
UN Conference on Environment and Development	1992	25,000 attendees in Rio; Framework Convention on Climate Change initial signatories
IPCC Emissions Scenario Report	1995	
First Conference of the Parties	1995	Berlin
IPCC Second Assessment Reports	1996	WG I: Science; WG II: Impacts, Adaptation, Mitigation; WG III Economics and Social Dimensions
Third Conference of the Parties, Kyoto Protocol	1997	10,000 attendees in Kyoto; Protocol gives structure for addressing GHG emissions. 5 per cent reductions over 1990 levels. Requires ratification
Sixth Conference of the Parties	2000	The battle for ratification continues
USA withdrawal from Kyoto	2000	Initiative of incoming President Bush
IPCC Third Assessment Reports	2001	WG I: Science; WG II: Impacts, Adaptation, Vulnerability; WG III Mitigation

ratifying countries) (see table 1.5). In many ways the UNFCCC was a disappointment as momentum had been building for an agreement on actual reductions in GHG emissions. Instead the Convention merely expressed concern, proposed data gathering and delayed future action. The defining objective is given under Article 2:

> The ultimate objective of this Convention and any related legal instruments that the Conference of the Parties may adopt is to achieve, in accordance with the relevant provisions of the Convention, stabilization of greenhouse gas concentrations in the atmosphere at a level that would prevent dangerous anthropogenic interference with the climate system. Such a level should be achieved within a time-frame sufficient to allow ecosystems to adapt naturally

to climate change, to ensure that food production is not threatened and to enable economic development to proceed in a sustainable manner.

The Framework Convention was watered down by US opposition coming via the Bush (senior) administration. The US position had been clearly against quantified targets since 1991. Their then proposed 'comprehensive reduction strategy' actually meant allowing an increase of US emissions of CO_2 by 15 per cent because CFCs were already being phased out under the Montreal Protocol (Paterson, 1996: 54). A similar problem persists with the Kyoto Protocol, where, if gas emissions have fallen in some countries due to structural change (e.g. Eastern Europe), overall targets or even increased emissions can occur while maintaining an aggregate level of stabilisation. In effect no positive action or ethical responsibility for emissions reduction is then deemed necessary.

Under such an approach the sudden 'conversion' of Margaret Thatcher, in 1988, to an environmentally concerned politician demanding action on climate change, is more easily understandable. UK Conservative administration policy to close coal mines and remove the power base of the unions had already unintentionally lowered CO_2 emissions. Note, environmentalism was not then on the agenda, and, for example, funding for research into clean coal technologies was withdrawn in the administrations' first term. The Green credentials of the government could be easily boosted by employing the US argument on CFCs (the Montreal Protocol was hot on the agenda with a London new signatories session in March 1989). Under judicious choice of a base year for emissions reduction no further action or actual pollution control would be required.

The stated aim of the Kyoto Protocol is for an aggregate reduction of 5 per cent in CO_2 equivalent emissions over 1990 levels by Annex I countries (i.e. industrialised countries undertaking the commitment) at sometime between 2008 and 2012. While the Kyoto Protocol has been described as 'the most profound and important agreement of the late twentieth century' (Grubb, Vrolijk and Brack, 1999: xxxiii) the same authors note that:

> Given extensive flexibilities in the agreement, the specific commitments of the Protocol are modest in terms of both environmental and economic impacts: implementing the commitments themselves will neither halt global emissions growth, nor have a discernible impact on economic growth.

In addition, the Protocol will be unsustainable without US participation between 2000–4 (Grubb, Vrolijk and Brack, 1999: 276), and this is far from certain given business opposition, internal political divisions (e.g. Senate vs White House), and Presidential elections. In the latter regard the election of Bush (junior) immediately led to the US administration boycotting the Protocol, although the international response was perhaps more negative than they had expected. Even achieving the modest Kyoto commitments will be difficult for many countries because of the lack of positive action being planned. As the Director of long-term co-operation and policy analysis for the International Energy Agency has stated (Bourdaire, 1999: 37): 'Our projection indicates that unless substantial new policies to promote climate-friendly technologies are adopted to reduce CO_2 emissions, the Kyoto commitments will not be met by OECD countries in the period 2008 to 2012'.

Only during this decade of negotiation did the economics profession begin to pay serious attention to the enhanced Greenhouse Effect. Within that time frame global climate change has moved from being discussed by a handful of economic articles and half a dozen authors to being the focus of special issues in mainstream journals, the topic of hundreds of articles and books, and being discussed by thousands of economists (from Nobel laureates to humble undergraduates). Yet, the relevance of much of this work is highly questionable. As will be shown, there remain serious problems with assessing the monetary value of expected control cost and impacts (most controversially loss of life), and political debate has been caused over the economics in the SAR report of Working Group III. Under the TAR, Working Group III had a changed role and mainly covered mitigation measures which had previously been the remit of Working Group II. The debated issues under SAR Working Group III were then downplayed, qualified and merged into a broader discussion of impacts under Working Group II. The role of socio-economic analysis remains problematic. That is, the idea of physical impacts being objectively definable as separate from socio-economics has apparently failed. However, a similar step with regard to scientific prediction has yet to be taken despite the obvious reliance of scientific projections upon socio-economic scenarios (e.g. the IPCC itself uses such scenarios to inform Working Group I; Nakicenovic *et al.*, 2000). Despite the reshuffling of Working Group tasks, there still appears to be a belief among leading scientists of the IPCC that objective science leads to physical prediction and that socio-economic analysis is then conducted as a final stage (e.g. see Watson, 2001), although this has already broken down as a model.

In several other respects economic analysis also proves problematic. The approach taken to uncertainty is narrow and fails to adequately address surprise events and catastrophes, and the use of discounting to reduce distant values asymptotically to zero appears morally vacuous. Modelling of efficient regulatory approaches, such a tradable permits, persist in using unrealistic market models and ignoring institutional and political factors. Models attempting to investigate economic growth impacts fail to be related to the latest (if any) scientific knowledge and are too abstract for the policy purposes for which they are unfortunately being employed. Those policy purposes include arguing that only a small percentage of economic activity will be affected by a doubling of CO_2 and that adjustment costs for any substantive control of GHGs are lower the longer they are delayed. These arguments have aided those negotiating a delay in any action and wishing to avoid binding constraints.

Values and ethical concerns

Economics over the past century has managed to develop away from explicit consideration of politics, ethics and social relations. This has been part of the scientific project to define the subject as providing objective information. However, the project is exposed as misguided once simple models are applied to complex environmental issues. As will be discussed, the objective empirical approach is difficult to apply to the natural sciences, let alone those dealing with social relations such as economics.

In particular, the philosophical basis upon which modern economics is founded becomes questionable. The essence of the economic argument is that the best action is determined by comparing consequences. Emissions control of X per cent is estimated to cost \$C and will prevent so much harm or damages which are measured in terms of \$B benefits of that control. Harm is equated to good and compared. If current humans value the creation of future harm below an associated value of present benefits then they should proceed with the harm. That is, a harmful action is justified by creating enough good to compensate. Alternatively, if preventing harm requires too much in terms of lost good then the harm should be allowed to continue (\$B − \$C < 0). Harm and good are tradable items in a market economy.

In order to make such an approach operational all the consequences of emitting GHGs need to be taken into account in monetary terms. This means trying to define uncertain future events in great detail and then attributing exchange prices to those events. Controversy then arises over the values placed on the loss of human life, the distress of human migration and species loss. While these are difficult enough to consider another range of consequences are expected but fall beyond economic assessment, e.g. the diminishing scope for systems to operate independent of human management, and forced adaptation of cultures and societies. There is in addition a misunderstanding of the content and meaning of economic assessments. The range of values typically being assessed has been expanded from direct use of environmental attributes to indirect or passive use which includes being willing to pay for possible future use (option value) and the continued presence of an attribute regardless of any intended use (existence value). These indirect use values have been confused in the literature with valuing Nature or environmental entities on grounds that they are intrinsically valuable, i e. valued separately from how much somebody is prepared to pay. That human life is deemed intrinsically valuable is perhaps why there are such strong rejections of studies by some economists which attempt to place values on preventing the loss of life. Intrinsic value in Nature is more controversial but that controversy emphasises the limited scope within which economic assessments fall. As some environmental philosophers have been at pains to explain (regardless of the role of intrinsic values) some values are constituted by their non-tradability and incommensurability (O'Neill, 1993).

Another area of major concern is how humans discriminate across space and time. The former relates to a lack of action to aid other humans currently alive who already suffer a range of problems which climate change will make worse. Economics has tended to distance itself from issues relating to any inequity in the distribution of resources which is assumed to be a political question. The latter concerns the regard for future generations and any obligations the current generations has towards the future. Economics has used discounting procedures to turn such issues into a technical debate, but as chapter 8 explains this is flawed both theoretically and ethically. The impacts of deliberately inducing global climate change across both space and time raise questions of compensation which again economists have tried to avoid.

The arguments to be explored in chapters 9 and 10 concern these issues, the inseparability of science, economics and politics and the importance of ethics in all these areas. The discourse of science and economics tries to avoid this debate although it is at the heart of concerns about controlling the enhanced Greenhouse Effect. The negotiating language of the high per capita material consumption economies is about losing the perceived associated good from material throughput, that of developing industrial economies about achieving such throughput which is seen as good, and that of environmentalists about the harm to the poor unable to adapt to change, future humans forced to adapt, extinction of non-human species and loss of ecosystems' resilience, stability and functioning. In all this, the way in which the debate is dominated by a purely consequentialist rhetoric has been perpetuated through international negotiations and has resulted in the form of the Kyoto Protocol. That this is rhetorical can be seen in the continued neglect of energy efficiency which has consistently shown large benefits in terms of reduced resource consumption and environmental improvement. Apparently much of the economic discourse is merely being used to reinforce 'business as usual' while neglecting the moral discourse in which it implicitly participates. Yet this is symptomatic of a scientific discourse which predicts dramatic impacts on human and natural systems but refuses to directly discuss what is dangerous or harmful.

Conclusions

In recognising this latest air pollution problem the characterisation of pollution itself has become challenged along with the role of science and economics. The calls for better knowledge before action and assessing the costs and benefits of pollution control must been seen in context. Science persists in the rhetoric of a belief that there is an objective answer to such issues, that the public are ill informed and experts who have access to the 'truth' must help make decisions. Mainstream economics generally ignores the environment and characterises pollution as a minor aberration to an otherwise perfect system.

The enhanced Greenhouse Effect, like acidic deposition before it, has belatedly forced economists to pay attention to the environment, for a short time at least. Those in the mainstream sub-discipline of environmental economics struggle with fitting square pegs into round holes as they try to reduce environmental complexity to fit their models, and relegate the inherently social and ethical aspects of consumption and production. Effective communication between disciplines has been sorely lacking and despite on-going attempts to address the problem, such as the development of ecological economics, the divide persists.

The failure to communicate between IPCC Working Group Reports has been significant, although there has been some attempted redress under TAR through greater attention to the development of a variety of socio-economic scenarios meant to inform all reports (Nakicenovic et al., 2000). Initial dominance of the IPCC by meteorologists and geophysicists served to reinforce the separation between natural and social science approaches. Partially this divide has been due to a lack of interdisciplinary training and the belief that mono-disciplinary research can meaningfully address environmental issues. Thus, science is seen as providing objective facts upon which to act, while economics is meant to determine optimally efficient actions from human preferences (reflected in market prices). The unfortunate result is that neither has managed to communicate effectively with the general public on environmental (or other) issues. Both are apparently easily used within a political context to reinforce and negotiate pre-existing positions. However, there is little reason to dismiss all the information being supplied as without content or meaning; rather, that information must be understood within the context of its production.

As the IPCC enters the second decade of its existence there are some notable changes taking place. The reporting context is moving from natural science to socio-economics by giving greater emphasis to the provision of goods and services essential for sustainable economic development. This raises issues as to the commodification of the environment (e.g. see Vatn, 2000) and the meaning of sustainability and development. A more regional approach begins to move away from GCMs and raises questions as to socio-economic differences affecting the realisation and adjustment to impacts. The interaction with other environmental problems (such as biodiversity loss or land degradation) raises the pervasive character of human interaction with the environment and the social causes of damages. The need to address social trends, if predictions are to have any validity, means addressing future population structure and distribution, the path and type of economies expected and desired, and issues such as whether alternative technologies are going to be seriously placed on the agenda. The inclusion of more experts from industrially developing economies brings into the process different perspectives on all these issues and should raise equity and justice as concerns. The struggle to define vulnerability raises questions of the definition of damage or harm and reveals the impossibility of avoiding ethical judgements.

A key aim of this book is to provide an interdisciplinary perspective which pulls together science, economics and ethics. This might then give some insight into how human society in general and economics in particular has come to the point of discussing the optimal extinction of species and the extent to which current humans prefer more global climatic experimentation to reducing their rate of material consumption. The 'older' air pollution problems, mentioned in this chapter, show that failures in pollution control and policy go far beyond blaming an environmental agency or current government administration for ineffectiveness. The more serious questions concern how science operates and interacts with policy and business; how economic policy is studied, designed and justified; what role is played by the media in providing, controlling and ignoring information; whether and how the voice of the least powerful in society is allowed to enter the debate; and to what extent individuals should be expected to take responsibility for their actions and the values constituting the society in which they and their descendants live. The following chapters probe some of these questions more than others.

Notes

1   As this chapter underwent final writing the third assessment report of the IPCC was in production. Information indicated a similar approach to the SAR in terms of production of the reports. There was some indication of the beginnings of a change in direction with regard to several socio-economic subjects or at least greater awareness of alternatives. Policymakers summaries for each Working Group under the TAR had been approved and were available at the time of final work on this chapter and are cited where appropriate and relevant information has changed. Greater analysis of TAR therefore occurs in the final chapters of this book.

2   Such desires for total human management of climate still persist with technological optimists pushing for global 'engineering', also termed geo-engineering. Ideas include chemical seeding of the oceans to increase carbon uptake and spreading various substances in the upper atmosphere to increase backscatter of incoming radiation. This is put forward as the least-cost option to prevent global climate change despite the potential and unknown consequences of such deliberate attempts to manipulate the functioning of global systems.

References

Bourdaire, J.M. (1999) 'World energy prospects to 2020: issues and uncertainties', in *Energy: The Next Fifty Years*, edited by OECD, pp. 29–39, Paris: Organisation for Economic Co-operation and Development.

Bray, D. and H. von Storch (1999) 'Climate science: an empirical example of postnormal science', *Bulletin of the American Meteorological Society* **80**(3): 439–55.

Dickie, M. (2001) 'Environmental toxicology and health risk assessment in the United States: economic and policy issues', in *Evaluating the Impacts of Pollution: Applying Economics to the Environment*, edited by C.L. Spash and S. McNally, p. 42, Cheltenham: Edward Elgar.

Grubb, M., C. Vrolijk and D. Brack (1999) *The Kyoto Protocol: A Guide and Assessment*. London: Earthscan and Royal Institute of International Affairs.

Harrison, S.J. (1991) *Global Warming: Predicting the Uncertain*. Stirling: Department of Environmental Science, University of Stirling Climate Services.

Holdgate, M.W. (1980) *A Perspective of Environmental Pollution*. Cambridge, England: Cambridge University Press.

Hunt, E.K. and R.C. d'Arge (1973) 'On lemmings and other acquisitive animals: propositions on consumption', *Journal of Economic Issues* **7**(June): 337–53.

IPCC Working Group I (2001) *Climate Change 2001: Scientific Assessment; Summary for Policymakers*. Geneva: Intergovernmental Panel on Climate Change.

Kapp, K.W. (1950) *The Social Costs of Private Enterprise*. New York: Shocken.

Kneese, A.V., R.U. Ayres and R.C. d'Arge (1970) *Economics and the Environment: A Materials Balance Approach*. Washington, DC: Resources for the Future.

Nakicenovic, N., O. Davidson, G. Davis, A. Grubler, T. Kram, E.L. La Rovere, B. Metz, T. Morita, W. Pepper, H. Pitcher, A. Sankovski, P. Shukla, R. Swart, R. Watson and Z. Dadi (2000) *Emissions Scenarios: Summary for Policymakers*. Geneva: Intergovernmental Panel on Climate Change.

O'Neill, J. (1993) *Ecology, Policy and Politics: Human Well-Being and the Natural World*. London: Routledge.

Paterson, M. (1996) *Global Warming and Global Politics*. London: Routledge.

Spash, C.L. (1997) 'Assessing the economic benefits to agriculture from air pollution control', *Journal of Economic Surveys* **11**(1): 47–70.

Spash, C.L. (1999) 'The development of environmental thinking in economics', *Environmental Values* **8**(4): 413–35.

Vatn, A. (2000) 'The environment as commodity', *Environmental Values* **9**(4): 493–509.

Watson, R. (2001) *Future work program of the IPCC*. Geneva: Intergovernmental Panel on Climate Change.

Watson, R.T., H. Rodhe, H. Oeschger and U. Siegenthaler (1990) 'Greenhouse gases and aerosols', in *Climate Change: The IPCC Scientific Assessment*, edited by J.T. Houghton, G.J. Jenkins and J.J. Ephraums, pp. 1–40, Cambridge, England: Cambridge University Press.

Watson, R.T., M.C. Zinyowera, R.H. Moss and D.J. Dokken (eds) (1997) *The Regional Impacts of Climate Change: An Assessment of Vulnerability; Summary for Policymakers*. IPCC Special Report. Geneva: IPCC.

2 Scientific understanding of the enhanced Greenhouse Effect

The Greenhouse Effect refers to the phenomenon whereby carbon dioxide and other gases trap long-wave infrared radiation (heat) within the lower levels of the atmosphere. Those gases, such as carbon dioxide (CO_2), nitrous oxide (N_2O), certain chlorofluorocarbons (CFCs), methane (CH_4), tropospheric ozone (O_3) and water vapour, that are transparent to solar radiation but opaque to long-wave radiation, are termed greenhouse gases (GHGs). Increasing the concentration of greenhouse gases reduces the amount of long-wave radiation returning directly into space, causing reradiation of some of the heat energy back to Earth's surface, and so results in raised temperatures in the lower atmosphere. This process enhances the natural Greenhouse Effect.

The Greenhouse Effect is one of the better understood features of the atmosphere. In the early nineteenth century, the French mathematician Fourier speculated that certain atmospheric gases might prevent reradiation of heat, so warming the surface of the Earth (Jamieson, 1988). Since the work of John Tyndall, circa 1861, water vapour and carbon dioxide have been recognised as radiative absorbers affecting climate (Idso, 1982). Surface warming due to the greenhouse gases maintains a liveable climate, and their entire removal from the atmosphere (if possible) would reduce Earth's surface temperature by 33°C (Firor, 1989). However, the operation of this radiative balance mechanism has become a matter of concern because of the rate at which anthropogenic emissions of GHGs are increasing and the long residence times of some of these gases. Anthropogenic emissions of CO_2 from fossil fuel combustion were hypothesised as climate-altering at the end of the last century. Arrhenius (1896) estimated that a doubling of CO_2 would cause 4.9–6.1°C increase in continental surface air temperature depending upon latitude and season. He made calculations for reduced CO_2 levels and for increases by 1.5, 2.0, 2.5 and 3.0 times then present levels. While modern understanding is far more detailed, and the estimates of Arrhenius are at the upper end of current predictions (1.4°C–5.8°C under TAR), the general points from over a century ago remain correct. For example, Arrhenius noted warming would be greater in winter and in the higher latitudes, and also that these differentials would change with the amount of CO_2 in the atmosphere.

In this chapter the central factors understood to determine global climate balance are identified, and the main gases involved in the enhanced Greenhouse Effect are described in terms of sources, sinks and predicted trends. Relevant and useful work on economic aspects of environmental problems requires knowledge of their scientific aspects. Scientific information forms the basis from which an economic assessment of the Greenhouse Effect would have to evolve, and raises awareness of the physical constraints upon the operation of economic systems. In particular, this chapter aims to identify the role of anthropogenic emissions in building up the stock of GHGs and their connection to changing global climate.

The influence of socio-economic systems on global climate is characterised by the ability to alter climatic conditions. The concept of a 'normal' climate (discussed further in chapter 4) is required as a reference and can be regarded as the range and pattern of climatic conditions over a given period of time in the absence of anthropogenic forcing. In the next section a range of influences on climate are discussed, giving some perspective to the role of GHGs. The sources and sinks of greenhouse gases are then reviewed to further specify potential human ability for enhancing the Greenhouse Effect. Next, the actual trends in the major gases are presented to show the speed with which atmospheric concentrations are accumulating. This is followed by a presentation of knowledge on historical trends, changes and extremes of global climate which aims to provide a broader perspective from which to assess the significance of predicted changes under the enhanced Greenhouse Effect.

Global climatic patterns

Climate refers to the statistical collection and representation of weather conditions for a specific area and time interval, combined with a description of the external system or boundary conditions (O'Hara, 1990). The climatic pattern of the world is produced in a complex manner from the distribution of heating and cooling in the atmosphere and interactions between oceans, atmosphere and biosphere. Major mechanisms affecting climate change over time scales of 100–10,000 years are: ocean circulation, evolution of the atmosphere, volcanic activity, air–sea–ice–land feedback, solar variability, atmosphere–ocean feedback, and atmospheric autovariation (Goodess, Palutikof and Davies, 1992). If the concern for major mechanisms of climate change is extended to one million years then two additional factors would need to be considered, namely, orbital parameters and isostatic adjustment (involving movements in the Earth's crustal layer). In the following sections the central issues affecting climatic balance are outlined, while paying regard to the policy time horizon of the enhanced Greenhouse Effect, under four categories (based upon the work of Bryson (1974):

•   the intensity of solar radiation reaching Earth
•   the reflectivity or albedo of the earth–atmosphere or Earth's surface

- the transmittance of the atmosphere and
- infrared fluxes as controlled by gases and particulates.

Each of these areas forms a point of debate in the analysis of climate change, and 'new' findings relating to that science tend to be basically related back to these issues, e.g. the role of sulphates and whether trees are more reflective than farmland concern transmittance and albedo respectively. While the scientific detail changes, the basic arguments have remained the same for at least 30 years.

Solar energy

The solar energy reaching the upper atmosphere will vary with the distance between Earth and Sun, and the energy generated by the Sun. The Sun has gradually been increasing in temperature as its hydrogen supply has been consumed. In the time period during which higher life forms evolved (600 million years) the intensity of the Sun increased by 25 per cent (Sagan, Toon and Pollack, 1979). The impact of solar radiation on Earth's climate has been regulated in part due to the storage of atmospheric CO_2 by evolving life forms, which has also led to the creation of limestone and hydrocarbon deposits (Harrington, 1987: 1,317). These same hydrocarbon deposits are the source of fossil fuels (e.g. coal, oil, natural gas).

Wigley (1988) used observations of changes in solar irradiance over the past 300 years to estimate possible solar influences on climate. He concluded that this had caused fluctuations of $\pm 0.1°C$, relative to a hypothetical steady-state which would prevail in the absence of external forcing. The variation in the intensity of solar radiation reaching Earth (the solar constant) due to sunspot activity has been estimated at about 0.3 per cent (Rosenberg, 1986: 7). A dramatic reduction in sunspot activity (as occurred during the Maunder minimum 1654–1714) could offset some enhanced GHG forcing, but would fail to dominate the warming effect (Wigley, 1988: 223). Generally the intensity of the Sun is regarded as a constant over the time period within which the enhanced Greenhouse Effect is expected to arise (decades to a century) and impact (next millenia). Solar intensity is expected to remain approximately the same over the next several centuries.

Similarly, the distance between Sun and Earth is important to ice ages but of little contribution to understanding changes over decades or even millennia. James Croll (1875) linked Pleistocene (one-and-a-half to two million years before present) ice ages with variations in Earth's orbit. In the 1940s Milutin Milankovitch refined the theory and his calculations have been updated with increased precision and predictive validity. In general, this theory explains the ice ages in terms of the distribution of incoming solar radiation varying with Earth's orbital geometry (see Goodess, Palutikof and Davies, 1992 for more detail). Orbital forcing, the climate response and the linking cause–effect mechanisms are complex, involving all components of the earth–atmosphere system, e.g. oceans, atmosphere, biosphere. Orbital forcing could be either a driving or pacing mechanism of internal climate variability. There could in fact be important and irreversible impacts of the enhanced Greenhouse Effect upon the role of orbital forcing on climate (Goodess, Palutikof and Davies, 1992: 203). However, contrary to some popular statements, the operation of ice ages is in terms of thousands of years rather than the next 100 or so, with the transition to the next glaciation occurring in the next two millennia. This point is addressed again at the end of the chapter.

Reflectivity

The reflectivity of Earth's surface and atmosphere is affected by variations in land cover (e.g. desert, forest, snow), changes in surface characteristics of continents, cloudiness and turbidity. Some examples of the reflectivity of different surfaces are shown in table 2.1. As shown in table 2.2, Sagan *et al.* (1979) have calculated changes due to humanity in the type of land cover over the past millennia. The microclimates of numerous areas of Earth's surface are the direct result of human activities with

Table 2.1 Albedo of different surfaces

	Reflection of solar radiation (%)
Fresh snow	90 or more
Sandy desert	50
Alfalfa field	24
Coniferous forest	20
Dark dry soil	15
Wavy ocean	14
Dark wet soil	8
Calm ocean	7
Silt-laden river	7

Source: Rosenberg, Blad and Verma (1983: 42–9). Reprinted with permission. © 1983 John Wiley & Sons, Inc.

Table 2.2 Land changes affecting global albedo

Process	*Land change*	*Cumulative area* $(km^2 \times 10^6)$	*Present rate of change* $(km^2/yr \times 10^4)$
Desertification	Savanna to desert	9.0	6.0
Salinisation	Open field to salt flat	0.6	1.5
Temperate deforestation	Forest to field, grassland	8.0	Small
Tropical deforestation	Forest to field, savanna	7.0	10.0
Urbanisation	Field, forest to city	1.0	2.0

Source: Adapted from Sagan, Toon and Pollack (1979) table 2. Reprinted with permission. © 1979, American Association for the Advancement of Science.

about 15 per cent of continental surface dramatically modified. The cumulative effect on global climate during the past several thousand years is a potential 1°C drop in mean temperature and over the past 25 years about a 0.2°C drop. Future reflectivity changes due to such human intervention are expected to cause further declines in global temperature compensating for the enhanced Greenhouse Effect. However, at present rates all surface areas will have been converted to high reflectivity, preventing further reductions, by circa 2100. Indeed the UK Meterological Office (UKMO) has suggested that converting farmland to forestry in order to absorb CO_2 may reduce reflectivity and so increase warming (Hadley Centre, 2000).

Changes in reflectivity due to the enhanced Greenhouse Effect are expected to be significant. In a warmer world the area of snow and ice pack is reduced allowing further warming of the ground and oceans, a positive feedback. Simultaneously, faster rates of evapotranspiration would cause greater cloud cover reflecting more radiation back into space, a negative feedback. Thus, reflectivity is important to the understanding of how changes in climatic factors will be realised.

Transmittance

Transmittance is an important cause of global climate change operating over relatively short time frames. The climate of Earth is primarily determined by processes in the troposphere (lower atmosphere). The solar energy reaching the stratosphere (upper atmosphere) may, given the above discussion, be assumed to be fairly constant, but variations in the physical properties of the troposphere affect the transmittance of solar energy from the upper to the lower atmosphere.

A serious impact on transmittance can occur from volcanic activity, which creates particulates and aerosols. Large volcanic eruptions eject 100×10^6 metric tons of fine ash in a very short period of time (Bryson, 1974). Volcanoes can put vast quantities of dust and gas, particularly sulphur dioxide (SO_2), high into the atmosphere. Emissions remaining in the troposphere are washed or rained out within about ten days, but those reaching the stratosphere may persist for months or years. Rietmeijer (1990) reports that the erupting of El Cichon in 1982 injected ash into the stratosphere which persisted there for at least three years. Eventually particles either settle into the troposphere or are carried into the troposphere by injections from the stratosphere.

Measurements of the Agung 1963 eruption showed a decrease in the mean temperature of the tropics by 0.2°C for three years, with an ensuing rapid recovery (Harrington, 1987: 1,317). Tambora erupting in 1815 has been estimated to have ejected $100,000 \times 10^6$ m^3, ten times the size of Krakatau 1883, causing snow and frost in June and July of 1816 in northern Europe, 'the year without a summer' (Kerr, 1989). Large eruptions of volcanoes have been found to cool a hemisphere by 0.1–0.5°C causing cooling of 0.3°C on average which lasts two to three years. Sear *et al.* (1987) analysed five major northern hemisphere and four southern hemisphere eruptions and found the latter can affect both hemispheres and have the greatest cooling effect six to twelve months later.

An eruption's power over climate depends as much on the chemical composition of gases released as their quantity. Even tiny sulphuric acid droplets, derived from a volcano's gaseous sulphur, have lasting effects on the stratosphere. Observed temperature fluctuations around the mean trend are primarily caused by volcanic (e.g. sulphur) aerosols (Hansen *et al.*, 1981).

Volcanic activity is capable of explaining the cooling of the northern hemisphere apparent from the early 1940s into the early 1970s, about 0.5°C. More recently, the eruption of Mt. Pinatubo, The Philippines, in June 1991 has been attributed with a surface cooling of 0.4°C over two years, so obscuring the signal of the upward trend in global average temperatures (Houghton *et al.*, 1995: 12–13). This influence then disappeared, although the impact of such events on the popular perception of the enhanced Greenhouse Effect and related policy can be to encourage scepticism over predictions of global warming. That is, episodic volcanic-induced cooling can be perceived as evidence that global warming predictions are incorrect without regard to the various factors operating on climate. Indeed the concern in the early 1970s was for global cooling.

Anthropogenic particulate and aerosol emissions are also relevant to transmittance and have been increasing over the last century (e.g. slash-burn agriculture and forestry, soil erosion and fossil fuel combustion). Table 2.3 gives a breakdown of particulate emissions by source, and shows the enormous continuous inputs created by man as opposed to erratic volcanic activity. Human activity may double or triple the global average aerosol concentration in the boundary layer. The main effect of particulate loading of the atmosphere on transmittance is backscatter of incoming solar radiation. Small diameter background aerosols absorb radiation while large ones reduce global temperature, as do additions to the stratospheric sulphate layer. Human particulate emissions had been thought to leave climate unchanged due to the counterbalancing effects of the aerosols of different sizes (Harrington, 1987: 1,331). In contrast, volcanoes generally add to the large particles and to the stratospheric sulphate load, thus decreasing the temperature at Earth's surface. However, anthropogenic aerosols are now thought to also cause a substantial cooling effect.

Table 2.3 Annual particulate inputs to the atmosphere

	Volume of particulates (millions of metric tons)
Volcanoes	4
Human pollution	296
Slash/burn agriculture	40–60
Soil erosion (agriculture and construction)	100–250

Source: Bryson (1974: 758). Reprinted with permission. © 1979, American Association for the Advancement of Science.

Research in the early 1990s by the UKMO claimed that industrial emissions of sulphate aerosols were significant enough to cause a cooling effect which would reduce the predicted upward climate trend, of such groups as the IPCC, from 0.3°C per decade to 0.2°C per decade (Hadley Centre, 1995). Sulphate aerosols are in the atmosphere for only a short time and emitted largely by industry which means they accentuate regional climatic variations, i.e. creating cooling over large industrial areas (Carson, 1995). Such regional variations and differences in types of aerosols has meant that aggregating their impact for comparison with global average temperature changes over decades to centuries has proven highly problematic. While attributing a lowering of their previous (1990) global warming estimates as being partially due to the initial inclusion of sulphate aerosols, the IPCC 1995 report also cited the contribution from aerosols as 'probably the most uncertain part of future radiative forcing' (Houghton *et al.*, 1996: 24). As a result much attention has been focused upon trying to incorporate aerosols into climate models. Combined with improved ocean modelling, the result of including aerosols has been more accurate computer simulation of past climates and so greater confidence in predicting future trends. However, the Hadley Centre's revised model, as of the end of the 1990s, predicted a 3°C temperature rise over the next hundred years, which was above the IPCCs 1995 central estimate. Thus, the overall result of including anthropogenic aerosols along with other refinements in climatic modelling does not necessarily reduce global average temperature predictions. In addition, the role of sulphate aerosols in future should be reduced due to controls aimed at preventing damage from acidic deposition (arising from fossil fuel combustion) e.g. in the USA the 1990 Clean Air Act and in Europe the 1994 Second Sulphur Protocol. This implies that, where the climate forcing due to GHG emissions has been partially obscured by sulphate aerosols, in future the climate change signal should become stronger.[1]

Infrared fluxes

The surfaces of Earth absorb direct beam, short-wave, solar, diffuse solar (scattered by molecules of the atmosphere and suspended aerosols) and long-wave radiation emitted by the atmosphere. These large quantities of incoming radiation are disposed of by reflection and emission of radiation. There exists a balance between incoming and outgoing radiation for Earth as a whole and for any particular surface. (These radiation balances change with time of day and season of the year.) Earth as a whole must either dispose of the energy received from the Sun or heat up. However, specific regions may have either negative balances, e.g. the poles, or positive balances, e.g. the tropics. Alterations in the temperature differences between the equatorial regions and the poles can cause climatic changes throughout the globe.

The Sun emits radiation primarily in short-wave bands from 0.15–4.0 micrometres (μm), the ultraviolet to near infrared spectrum, with about 50 per cent of the total energy delivered in the range 0.4–0.7 μm. The earth and atmosphere emit long-wave radiation in the range 0.3–80.0 μm, the infrared bands, with maximum emissions about 10 μm. The 'atmospheric window' through which most reradiation occurs is in the range from 8–14 μm. Carbon dioxide (CO_2), nitrous oxide (N_2O), chloroflurocarbons (CFCs), methane (CH_4), ozone (O_3), carbon tetrachloride (CCl_4) and carbon disulphide (CS_2) all have absorption peaks within this range. Accumulation of these greenhouse gases thus tends to close the atmospheric window preventing the energy received from the Sun from being reradiated and thereby warming the troposphere. These gases have been accumulating rapidly and can persist, over long periods of time, in the atmosphere.

Sources and sinks of greenhouse gases

The balance of emission and absorption of a gas determines the concentration in the atmosphere, i.e. how much is added relative to that which is taken away. A sink is a reservoir which absorbs a gas released elsewhere in its cycle. A source is the pool from which a gas is released to another part of its cycle. The subsections which follow discuss in turn the sources and sinks of CO_2, N_2O, CFCs, CH_4 and O_3, while their growth potential is the topic of the next section.

Carbon dioxide has formed the central concern in the discussion of atmospheric pollution related to climatic change since at least the 1950s (Revelle and Suess, 1957). While CO_2 remains the most important single gas expected to cause increases in global temperature several other gases have been recognised as substantial sources of climate forcing (Marland and Rotty, 1985). Care must be taken to avoid confusion due to the practice of comparing the role of different GHGs by converting their concentration, accounting for different radiative properties and residence times, into the equivalent amount of CO_2; this is referred to as the 'equivalent CO_2 concentration'. As will be pointed out in later chapters, the tendency to regard CO_2 as the only gas of concern has lead to incorrect conclusions in economic assessments.

Background information is required on a host of gas species in order to understand the potential for anthropogenic impacts on global climate. Cumulative climatic effects of other GHGs are likely to be of comparable magnitude to that of CO_2 (Dowd, 1985: 767). Figure 2.1a shows warming due to the enhanced Greenhouse Effect during the 1970s for CO_2, CFCs, CH_4 and N_2O; the latter three are attributed with 35 per cent of the enhanced warming for that period. The IPCC estimated that GHGs excluding CO_2 accounted for 45 per cent of radiative forcing over the period 1980–90 (Watson et al., 1990: 7–8). In calculating these estimates ozone was excluded due to a lack of observational data. The IPCC's figures for percentage contribution of various gases in the 1980s show a similar pattern to those for the 1970s warming, as can be seen by comparing figure 2.1a with 2.1b. However, the growing importance of a range of CFCs is also evident.

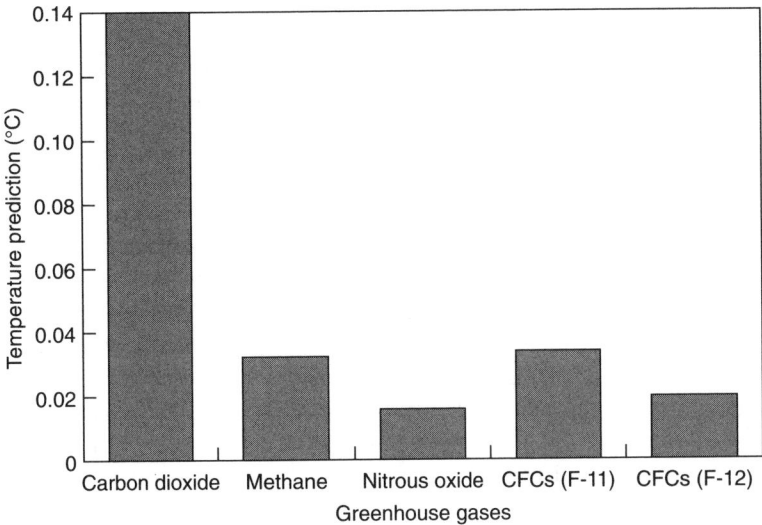

Figure 2.1a Global warming for GHGs added in 1970s
Source: After Marland and Rotty (1985: figure 3).

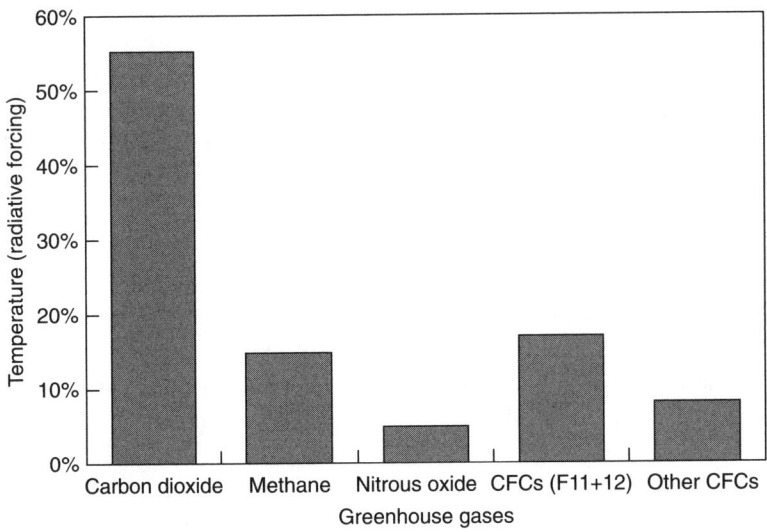

Figure 2.1b Global warming for GHGs added in 1980s
Source: Watson *et al.* (1990: 7–8).

Carbon dioxide

CO_2 is a product of complete combustion which industry has regarded as 'good' in comparison to toxic carbon monoxide (CO) from incomplete combustion (Henderson-Sellers, 1984). Fossil fuels can be ranked in order of their importance as sources of CO_2 going from coal, then oil and lowest natural gas. In the natural CO_2 cycle, sources are vegetative decay and atmospheric oxidation of methane, and sinks are biomass accumulation via photosynthesis and the solution of CO_2 in water bodies (most importantly the oceans). Increasing global concentrations are attributed to the burning of fossil fuels, deforestation, and increased oxidation of humus. During the decade up to the mid-1980s, annual global CO_2 emissions (mainly from fossil fuels) averaged 5.05×10^{15} grams of carbon per year (gC/yr) while the increase in the atmosphere was estimated at 2.73×10^{15} gC/yr (Rotty and Reister, 1986). The destruction of forests and humus oxidation was estimated to add a further $4–8 \times 10^{15}$ gC/yr (Woodwell, 1978). As can be seen in table 2.4, on the basis of these figures, a large amount of CO_2 is then unaccounted for by atmospheric uptake alone, suggesting other major sinks. Some debate has persisted since at least the 1970s as to where this CO_2 might be going and in earlier literature it was referred to as 'missing'. This epithet has disappeared although the issue persists (e.g. Grübler, 2000).

The oceans have been put forward as the only sink which appears large enough to account for the missing CO_2, although this proposition has been subject to challenge (Kerr, 1977). The oceans act as major distributors of heat around the Earth. Thus, changes from the present circulation could explain events such as the Little Ice Age. Deep ocean circulation and chemistry changes are thought to have a major role in the processes linking orbital forcing and climate response, i.e. amplifying glacial–interglacial climate change. There is also general agreement that atmospheric CO_2 concentrations are in some way controlled by marine productivity and ocean structure (Goodess, Palutikof and Davies, 1992: 46). However, only the top 100 m or so of the oceans mix freely. These surface waters are separated from the slowly circulating deep ocean by a layer with a steeper vertical temperature gradient than the water above and below it, a layer called the thermocline. The deep ocean exchanges with surface waters by only a few per cent every thirty years. Ocean uptake of CO_2 has been estimated at $2 \pm 0.5 \times 10^{15}$ gC/yr (Woodwell *et al.*, 1983: 1,085). Thus the contention of Kerr (1977) that oceans are too small a sink to absorb the required amounts of CO_2 seems to survive, while the strength of the sink remains unclear (Moore and Braswell, 1994b). A related concern is how far oceans will continue to absorb CO_2 in the future and whether they might become a source themselves under certain climatic changes.

A biotic sink is the remaining possibility. For example, as CO_2 increases, high-altitude subalpine conifers have shown evidence of increased photosynthetic rate leading to faster carbon storage in biomass (LaMarche *et al.*, 1984). However, theories

Table 2.4 Global CO$_2$ budget ($\times 10^{15}$ grams of carbon per year)

	Sources				Sinks						
	Emissions		Sink destruction		Atmospheric uptake		Ocean uptake		Forest regrowth		Unknown ?
Old estimate	5.05	+	6.0 ± 2.0	=	2.73					+	8.32 ± 2.00[a]
New estimate	5.05	+	1.0 ± 0.6	=	2.73	+	2.00			+	1.32 ± 0.60[a]
IPCC 1995[b]	5.50	+	1.6 ± 1.0	=	3.20	+	2.00	+	0.50	+	1.40 ± 1.50[c]

Notes: a Calculated by subtracting sum of sources from sum of other sinks.
 b Figures from Houghton *et al.* (1995: 18 table 1); error limits are given in the report for all sources and sinks, based upon a 90 per cent confidence interval.
 c Calculated by subtracting sum of midpoint estimates of sources from same sum for sinks; this is then attributed an uncertainty range of ±1.5.

that the 'missing' CO_2 was being absorbed by biota were largely dispelled because of deforestation and the burning of firewood (a major energy source in less industrially developed countries). Destruction of forests has, in the past, been cited as a rival to fossil fuel combustion as a CO_2 source (Adams, Mantovani and Lundell, 1977). Although calculations have reduced the estimated contribution, forests in general are a negative contributor to the absorption capacity. Detwiler and Hall (1988) estimate the tropics as a net source of 0.4–1.6 $\times$ 10^{15} gC. Net releases from non-tropical regions due to forest destruction, although significant in the nineteenth century, have now fallen to around zero. This allows a 'new estimate' of the CO_2 budget which reduces sink destruction as a source but adds oceans as a sink (see table 2.4). The considerably lower figure for the missing CO_2 is in line with Detwiler and Hall who calculated a median for 1980 as 1.2 $\times 10^{15}$ gC. The IPCC 1994 report goes beyond these calculations by including regrowth of northern hemisphere forests as a potential sink for 0.5 $\pm$ 0.5 $\times 10^{15}$ gC (Houghton *et al.*, 1995: 18), although higher emissions lead to the persistence of a similar amount of 'missing' CO_2. The 1995 report from the IPCC attributes the sink for this CO_2 as terrestrial although uncertain (Schimel *et al.*, 1996: 79).

Thus, while the global CO_2 budget has remained a mystery, the imbalance has been reduced and the deficit may be partially because of some miscalculations. In addition to recent downward revisions of the net additions of CO_2 from deforestation, atmospheric uptake has been revised upwards. One reason behind this revision is that preindustrial CO_2 concentrations may have been 270 ppm (parts per million) rather than 290 ppm, effectively increasing the calculated uptake of the atmosphere (Harrington, 1987: 1,325). Unfortunately, there appears to be a lack of consensus over the exact preindustrial concentration.[2]

As Moore and Braswell (1994a; 1994b) show, uncertainty over the processes absorbing CO_2 prevents prediction of how sinks for future emissions will evolve as other factors change, e.g. climate, land use, atmospheric concentrations. These uncertainties affect estimation of the atmospheric lifetime of CO_2, which is important for policy decisions on GHG control. Moore and Braswell (1994b: 7) state:

> The lifetime of a trace atmospheric constituent may be thought of as the amount of time required for some significant portion of an excess quantity of the gas to be removed chemically or to be redistributed to another part of the Earth system.

Care must be taken when comparing various estimates of gas lifetimes. The 1990 IPCC report gives 50–200 years as the time taken for atmospheric CO_2 to adjust to changes in sources or sinks (determined mainly by ocean uptake). The first reduction by 50 per cent takes 50 years, the next 50 per cent reduction (to 25 per cent) takes another 250 years, but the concentration never returns to its original value and instead maintains about 15 per cent of the initial emissions (Watson *et al.*, 1990: 8). So estimates of CO_2 lifetime have been given as 500 years where substantial decay is being considered (Wuebbles and Edmonds, 1988). Certainly the CO_2 emitted today will influence the atmospheric concentration for centuries into the future (Watson *et al.*, 1990: 5). Non-linear decay functions mean atmospheric lifetimes can increase with the concentration and Kasting (quoted in Nordhaus, 1994: 26) estimates a lifetime of 380 to 700 years for a tripling of CO_2 in comparison to the IPCC average of 120 years. In the 1994 IPCC report the point is made that defining a single atmospheric lifetime for CO_2 is impossible, in contrast to compounds destroyed chemically in the atmosphere, and that the timescales involved in CO_2 exchange range from annual to millennial (Houghton *et al.*, 1995: 42).

Nitrous oxide

Anthropogenic production of N_2O is due primarily to the combustion of fossil fuels, especially coal, and in the use of nitrogen fertilisers when denitrification of ammonia occurs. Other lesser sources include acidic deposition, sewage treatment, electric power transmission and forest clearing. The total anthropogenic contribution has been estimated to be approaching 50 per cent of the natural releases. Natural sources include bacteria in soils, oceans, estuaries and lakes, burning of vegetation, lightning and volcanoes (Marland and Rotty, 1985). The main sink for N_2O is photodissociation (breakdown by sunlight) in the stratosphere by oxygen producing nitrogen oxide and nitrogen dioxide.

Chlorofluorocarbons

Chlorofluorocarbons (CFCs) of type F-11 (CCl_3F) and F-12 (CCl_2F_2) accounted for 80 per cent of world production in the 1980s and are now regulated as Group I CFCs under international law arising from the Montreal Protocol and amendments. Such CFCs are part of a family of chemicals called halocarbons which are powerful greenhouse gases when containing fluorine, chlorine or bromine. The only source of CFCs is human industrial activity, i.e. they are completely synthetic. CFCs have been used as aerosol propellants, refrigerants, solvents, foam blowing agents, plastics and resins. There are several possible sinks for CFCs but the most important are the oceans, desert sands and chemical scavenging in the stratosphere (Gladwin, Ugelow and Walter, 1982). The largest sources of CFCs are associated with the industrial countries of the northern mid-latitudes, and tropospheric distribution shows the expected latitudinal gradient (National Research Council, 1984: 70).

The lifetimes of F-11 and F-12 in the atmosphere are 75 years and 110 years respectively (Wuebbles and Edmonds, 1988). During the long residence period in the troposphere, CFCs absorb infrared radiation from the surface of Earth thus contributing to global warming. On a molecular basis, CFCs are thousands of times more effective than CO_2 as contributors to the enhanced Greenhouse Effect (Forziati, 1982: 53); IPCC 1994 estimates placed CFCs at 10,000 times more effective

(Houghton *et al.*, 1995: 174). In the 1980s fears were raised that CFCs could well contribute as much to global warming as CO_2 by the year 2000 (Cumberland, Hibbs and Hoch, 1982). Their control, under the Montreal Protocol and its amendments, is discussed later in this chapter in the section on GHG emission trends. However, a side effect of regulation has been the development of substitutes, some of which are longer lasting in the atmosphere and more effective at climate forcing (Prather *et al.*, 1996: 92–3).

Ozone

Ozone's absorption band, at 9.6 μm, is where Earth's radiation is strongest and where CO_2 is more or less transparent. Ozone is formed from precursor emissions, i.e. other gases. The most important precursors for oxidant formation are non-methane hydrocarbons, nitrogen dioxide and nitric oxide (Benkowitz, 1983). Anthropogenic precursor emissions are most prevalent in and around urban areas, as evidenced by severe oxidant smogs. Hydrocarbons are produced during fossil fuel combustion and the evaporation of petrol, and oxides of nitrogen have the same sources as discussed above for nitrous oxides. The transportation sector has been identified as the primary source of anthropogenic tropospheric ozone precursor emissions in the USA (Benkowitz, 1983), and the same will generally be the case elsewhere. Attempts have been made to control the concentrations of this ozone in the lower atmosphere because it can adversely affect human health and plant growth and can damage materials.

The concentration of stratospheric ozone is maintained by a balance of processes that create and remove it. Ozone is created in a photochemical process that begins with the photolysis of diatomic oxygen (O_2). It is destroyed in several complex series of chemical reactions involving oxygen (O), hydrogen (H), chlorine (Cl) and nitrogen (N) compounds. Ozone is also removed from the stratosphere by large-scale transport processes between the upper and lower atmosphere (the tropopause).

In the 1970s human activities were identified as adding certain chlorine, nitrogen and other catalyst species to the stratosphere, upsetting the balance between production and destruction processes and leading to reductions in stratospheric ozone. The 'ozone hole' is the popular term used to describe a thinning of ozone in the stratosphere. Such thinning was first noted as the creation of a hole over Antarctica lasting for one month each year and growing (for a revealing history of the discovery process see Dotto and Schiff, 1978). The phenomenon signifies a general diminution of the stratospheric ozone layer which protects Earth's surface from the harmful effects of ultraviolet (UV) radiation. A 1 per cent decrease in total ozone is estimated to cause a 2 per cent increase in surface UV-B and so a 4 per cent increase in cases of human cancer (Firor, 1990: 35).

The oxides of nitrogen (NO_x) are the major chemical family responsible for such reductions. Significant quantities of NO_x can be added to the stratosphere by detonation of nuclear weapons, commercial fleets of supersonic aircraft and increasing concentrations of nitrogen dioxide (NO_2). While substantial stratospheric injections of NO_x are not expected (depending on such things as renewed French nuclear weapons testing in the South Pacific being held underground), release of CFCs and other halocarbons have been increasing. Chlorine and fluorine atoms released into the stratosphere by dissociation of CFCs act to destroy ozone. Stratospheric concentrations of chlorine are now more than twice the value associated with natural sources (National Research Council, 1984: 6).

CFC releases to date are expected to decrease total stratospheric ozone by several per cent. The resulting decreased absorption of radiation by stratospheric ozone tends to cool the stratosphere, reducing the infrared radiation emitted towards the earth, cooling the troposphere and ground (Forziati, 1982). The IPCC 1994 report estimated a dominant cooling from loss of ozone over the preceding 15–20 years (Houghton *et al.*, 1995: 29). However, estimating the radiative forcing due to ozone changes is more complex than for other GHGs due to its dependence upon the vertical distribution, which is difficult to estimate and measure.

Radiative cooling in the stratosphere is important because it influences photo-chemistry by reducing the rates for many reactions that destroy ozone. In addition, chlorine in the stratosphere depletes ozone by varying amounts at different altitudes; this affects the altitude at which ultraviolet heating is strongest, and so modifies the winds that blow at these heights (Firor, 1990: 29). These stratospheric winds help determine the distribution of chemicals and so where reactions and heating occur. Thus, the question of chemical perturbations to ozone must be considered in conjunction with the climatic alterations due to trace gases such as CO_2 (National Research Council, 1984).

Addition of NO_x to the upper troposphere, largely by subsonic commercial aircraft, leads to the production of ozone (in contrast to additions in the stratosphere which destroy ozone). This increase in tropospheric concentrations is further enhanced by a build-up of global concentrations of methane and other hydrocarbons. Excess tropospheric NO_x may produce substantial local concentration of tropospheric ozone and modest additions to the total amount of ozone in the atmosphere. Global mean radiative forcing due to increases in tropospheric ozone has been thought to be positive but relatively small. However, the IPCC 1995 report attributed a similar contribution since preindustrial times to radiative forcing (warming potential) as that from methane (compare Houghton *et al.*, 1996: 20; Prather *et al.*, 1996: 92). Ozone in the stratosphere is attributed with a cooling effect of only a quarter of this magnitude.

Methane

Senum and Gaffney (1989) attributed 30 per cent of then current greenhouse warming to the yearly rate of increase of methane. Sources include leaks from coal mines and pipelines, but most comes from organic material decaying with a lack of oxygen, e.g. municipal waste dumps, rice paddies, swamps, freshwater sediments, tundra, terrestrial debris on the continental shelves, enteric fermentation (in the intestines) of animals and termites. The main sink is removal by reactions with hydroxyl radical (OH), created by photo-induced reactions involving water vapour. Carbon monoxide (CO), emitted in industrial processes, fires and from automobile exhausts, also reacts with hydroxyl radicals. Thus, increasing CO reduces the sink for methane allowing a faster rate of build-up in the atmosphere.

Greenhouse gas emission trends

Out of the five gases discussed, O_3 is indirectly, and CO_2 and N_2O are directly, related to fossil fuel use so that energy policy and consumption trends are of direct relevance in forecasting future emissions rates. In the 1980s the level of CO_2 emissions was just over 18 grams of carbon per megajoule (gC/MJ) resulting from a mix of energy sources in which coal emitted 23.9 gC/MJ, oil 19.7 gC/MJ, natural gas 14.1 gC/MJ and alternative energy sources none (Rotty and Reister, 1986). Table 2.5 shows the relative importance of various energy sources in the 1990s and their contribution to atmospheric CO_2 accumulation. Natural gas has increased from supplying around 16 per cent of energy demand 20 years ago to current levels (see for comparison Hansen *et al.*, 1981: 964, table 2). Thus, the relative contribution of natural gas to CO_2 emissions has also grown. The central issue in changing emissions is the forecast for fossil fuel use, the relative price of coal and the viability of alternative energy sources (especially potential switch-over dates).

Throughout the last decades of the twentieth century IEA countries maintained the common objectives of expanding the use of coal as an 'alternative' fuel, and expanding the production of and international trade in coal to meet increased demand. At the European Summit in Venice, in 1980, a commitment was made to change from oil to coal (Stern *et al.*, 1984). The Organisation for Economic Co-operation and Development (OECD), as shown in table 2.6 predicted a central role for coal, and the International Energy Authority (IEA) has, for some time, seen coal as having great potential as an essential element in meeting future energy needs (OECD, 1982). The continued importance of coal has been reflected in IEA energy predictions: 'Despite perceived environmental drawbacks, world demand for coal and other solid fuels has been projected to continue to grow although its share of world energy requirements is expected to decline somewhat to just under 29 per cent' (International Energy Agency, 1993: 11). These expectations seem to have, at least so far, overestimated the relative role of coal while underestimating the potential of hydroelectricity and alternative energy sources. However, projections into the second half of the twenty-first century estimate use of coal for anything between 20 and 40 per cent of primary energy needs, but with a change in the method of use towards total conversion into gas, liquids and electricity (Grübler, 1999: 47).

Table 2.5 Sources of CO_2 by energy type

| | Energy consumption 1990–9[a] | | CO_2/unit of energy | Airborne CO_2 added |
	(Btu)	(%)	(Oil=100)[b]	(%)
Petroleum	152.20	40.1	100	46
Coal	84.77	22.4	130	34
Natural gas	86.89	22.9	76	20
Hydroelectric	27.29	7.2	0	0
Nuclear	25.25	6.7	0	0
Geothermal, solar, wind and wood	2.83	0.7	0[a]	0[a]
Oil shale	0.0	0.0	145	0
Total	379.23	100.0	–	100

Notes: a   Data source: International Energy Outlook (2001).
  b   Calculated from data in International Energy Agency (1998) CO_2 emissions from fuel combustion, table 3.
  c   Excludes wood; also note carbon from biomass is potentially high (150) but varies by product, e.g. solid, liquid or gas.

Table 2.6   World energy demand

| | Primary fuel percentage shares | | | |
	1971	1990	2000	2010
Oil	47.8	39.4	39.0	37.0
Natural gas	18.3	21.6	21.6	24.3
Coal/solid fuels	31.0	29.4	29.0	28.6
Nuclear	0.6	6.7	6.7	6.0
Hydro/other	2.2	2.8	3.8	4.1
Total (MTOE)	4865	7768	9129	11476
Carbon emissions (MT)	4062	5877	6829	8606

Source: IEA (1993: 57) adapted from table E. © OECD/IEA (1993).

World energy demand in the 1990s was predicted to be influenced by slower economic growth in the developed OECD countries, and faster economic growth in emerging economies due to rapid expansion of population, economic activity, industrialisation, road transportation and urbanisation, and the change to Western-style energy demand in the former Soviet Union. On this basis by 2010 OECD countries would be consuming 30 per cent more energy and 20 per cent more oil than in 1990 (IEA 1993: 9). Perhaps noteworthy is the fact that growth in actual fossil fuel demand as a percentage of total energy consumption outstripped the earlier 1982 OECD projections. While non-hydroelectric renewables, such as solar and wind, do have high projected growth rates their contribution to world energy requirements is expected to remain very small, especially in the next few decades.

The IPCC states that up to 2020, 'energy supply and conversion will remain dominated by relatively cheap and abundant fossil fuels' (IPCC Working Group III, 2001: 4).

If pollution problems are to be seriously tackled then economic activity will need to change fundamentally. That is, countries striving for industrial development will need to avoid the five times world average levels of per capita energy consumption found in North America, or even the two-and-a-half average European levels, which means de-coupling energy from economic growth (Imboden and Jaeger, 1999). In terms of positively changing patterns of energy consumption the turnover in capital stock provides a serious constraint and the incentive for 'business as usual'. This applies to energy production but also to the infrastructure of society (transport systems, housing, land use). The growing size of this capital stock locks society into a set development path.

Total world energy demand is projected to grow 66 per cent between 1995 and 2020 and boost CO_2 emissions by 69 per cent (Bourdaire, 1999: 31). Coal use is expected to remain large in North America, China and industrially developing countries. In general fossil fuels continue to dominate energy use until 2020, although oil and gas prices may rise 50 per cent at the end of the period (Lahidji, Michalski and Stevens, 1999: 9). Around 2020 the opportunities presented by infrastructure renewal could allow a transition to alternatives if governments act to provide institutional incentives. Oil and gas production is set to peak around 2050 and then decline rapidly (Lahidji, Michalski and Stevens, 1999: 12). Projections from the International Institute for Applied Systems Analysis (IIASA) show renewables emerging in all scenarios as the major source of energy in the long run (Grübler, 1999). In the interim period the rate of fossil fuel use will determine the extent, frequency and speed of perturbations to climatic chemistry.

Carbon dioxide

The natural concentration of CO_2 in the atmosphere is estimated at 200–250 parts per million (ppm) (Stern et al., 1984), but by circa 1880 concentrations had begun to increase and were around 280–300 ppm (Adams, Mantovani and Lundell, 1977: 54–6). Analysis of air trapped in ice shows the upward trend starting about 200 years ago (Neftel et al., 1985). There has since been steady growth with the level estimated at 358 ppm in 1994 (Schimel et al., 1996: 78). As of the year 2000 there had been a 31 per cent increase over preindustrial levels (IPCC Working Group I, 2001). Petit et al. (2000) note that the records from the Vostok ice core show present burdens of CO_2 and methane as being unprecedented during the past 420,000 years. Atmospheric concentrations are cumulative because of the potentially long atmospheric residence time. The relationship between carbon releases and fossil fuel use is shown in table 2.6; in 1991 estimated emissions were 6,188 million metric tons of carbon (Boden et al., 1994).

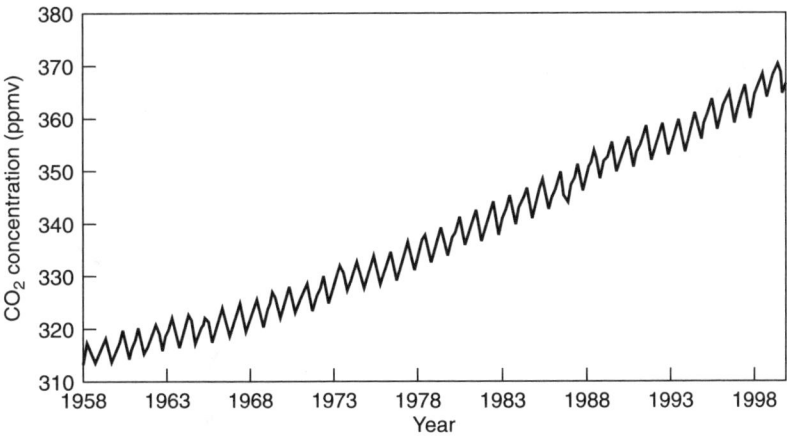

Figure 2.2 Monthly atmospheric CO_2, 1958–99
Data source: Keeling and Whorf (2000).

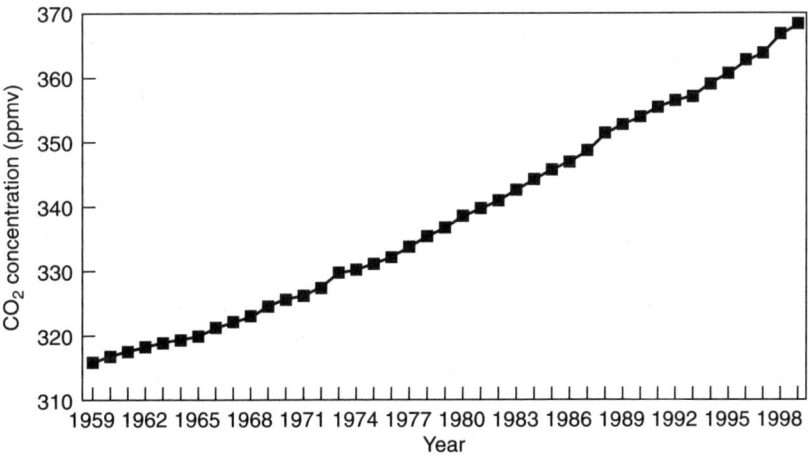

Figure 2.3 Annual CO_2 concentration at Mauna Loa
Data source: Keeling and Whorf (2000).

The longest sequence of CO_2 measurements is from Mauna Loa volcano in Hawaii and is shown in figure 2.2. The rate of growth of fossil fuel use is more or less directly reflected in the rate of increase of atmospheric concentrations (Rotty and Reister, 1986). The rate of CO_2 increase in the atmosphere was estimated at 0.7 ppm/yr during the 1960s (Bryson, 1974), increased during the 1970s and through the 1980s was running at 1.5 ppm/yr, i.e. 0.4 per cent per annum (Hansen, 1989: 7). The peak in the late 1980s was 2.0 ppm/yr, although this was followed by a drop to 0.5 ppm/yr, but the long-term average remained at 1.5 ppm/yr (Houghton *et al.*,

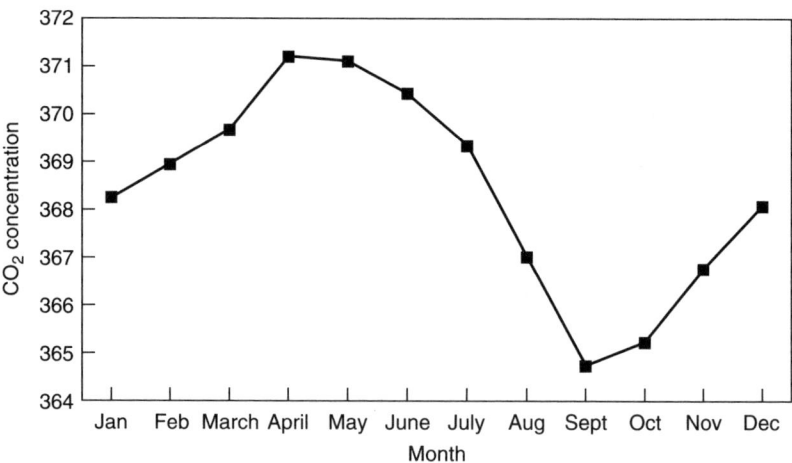

Figure 2.4 Annual cycle of atmospheric CO_2, 1999
Data source: Keeling and Whorf (2000).

1995: 42). The IPCC SAR raised this to 1.6 ppm/yr (Schimel *et al.*, 1996: 78) but the TAR returned to the former estimate while noting variability (IPCC Working Group I, 2001). In this regard, during the 1990s the increase varied from 0.9 ppm/yr to 2.8 ppm/yr. The variability was attributed largely to the impact of climate events, such as El Niño, on CO_2 uptake and release by land and oceans. Figure 2.3 illustrates the continual rise of the annual concentration of CO_2 in the atmosphere. The Hawaian record shows a 12.8 per cent increase in the mean annual concentration from 1959 to 1992 (Boden *et al.*, 1994: 8).

The smooth line in figure 2.3 is due to the removal of monthly variation in preference for annual averages. The fluctuations in figure 2.2 show the annual cycle in CO_2. This annual cycle is due to plants absorbing CO_2 in the spring as they grow and releasing it in the autumn as they die back. The annual biotic uptake and release is clearly visible in the record produced by Keeling and Whorf (2000) as shown in figure 2.4 for 1999 (note the record is for the southern hemisphere). This cycle has become more extreme, with the amplitude increasing by 20 per cent as measured in Hawaii and by 40 per cent in the Arctic, while spring uptake has also been occurring earlier and has shifted by a week since the 1960s (Keeling, 1996). These have been regarded as the first signs of the global impact of increased CO_2 on plant growth, and according to Keeling (1996: 146) could represent unprecedented changes in the terrestrial biosphere.

Energy scenario analysis for 1975–2000 shows CO_2 concentrations reaching 600 ppm by 2030 if pre-1973 growth rates were maintained (Rotty and Reister, 1986). Slowed growth of the world economy and increased oil prices push this date back to around 2075. However, rapid expansion of the world economy would triple or quadruple concentrations by the end of the next century, with the rate of increase growing after 2050. A high carbon release scenario causes a further doubling of CO_2 between 2050 and 2100 from 535 ppm to 1,040 ppm. A low scenario gives an increase from 503 to 690 ppm. The growth rate of CO_2 in 2100 would be 14 ppm/yr under the high scenario and 3 ppm/yr under the low scenario. A comparison with other studies suggests that a concentration of 540–600 ppm, double that of the early 1800s, would cause a 1.5–4.5°C increase in average world temperature. The temperature range given in the IPCC SAR 1995 report as their 'best estimate' was 1.0–3.5°C over the period from 1990 to 2100, approximately a third lower than their earlier reports (Houghton *et al.*, 1996: 6). This downward revisioning was reversed by the 2001 report which predicted a 1.4–5.8°C increase from 1990 to 2100 (IPCC Working Group I, 2001: 13). Note, these levels would be added on top of warming during the rest of the twentieth century, approximately 0.5°C.

According to analysts such as Rotty and Reister (1986), future emissions that are low enough to avoid large atmospheric CO_2 concentrations are only possible if reductions occur in factors such as growth rates of population, production of goods and per capita income. Hansen *et al.* (1981) estimated that CO_2 concentrations would be 390 ppm by the year 2000 and the accompanying surface temperature rise 0.5°C. While the temperature rise is consistent with observations the actual concentrations have been lower than this prediction, due to a drop in the rate of accumulation in the early 1990s to 0.6 ppm/yr before returning to 1.5 ppm/yr. The reasons for this short-term fluctuation are uncertain but regarded as insignificant in terms of the long-term trend (Houghton *et al.*, 1996: 15). Stabilisation of atmospheric CO_2, regardless of the level chosen (e.g. 350–750 ppm), will require anthropogenic emissions that eventually drop substantially below 1990 levels, e.g. even allowing for stabilisation at twice today's concentrations will mean dramatic future emissions control (Houghton *et al.*, 1995: 11). The reader should also note that even after stabilising CO_2 concentrations, climate forcing continues with global mean temperature rising for hundreds of years (Houghton *et al.*, 1996: 45).

Various scenarios for stabilising CO_2 concentrations in the atmosphere are reported in the 1995 IPCC report (Schimel *et al.*, 1996: 80–5). These scenarios '... were designed to account for inertia in the global energy system and the potential difficulty of departing rapidly from the present level of dependence on fossil fuels' (Schimel *et al.*, 1996: 83). The result is no scenario in which a return to concentrations of pre or early industrial levels are contemplated, but instead a range of increases from 60 to 260 per cent (450–1,000 ppm). The basic picture shows 'business as usual' in the short term leading to a penalty in terms of requiring higher and sharper emissions reductions later to achieve the same level of stabilisation. That is, cumulative emissions are what count. In general, for stabilisation in the 450–650 ppm range emissions need to be reduced by 30 to 60 per cent over 1990 levels, depending upon the amount allowed to accumulate before action, i.e. the longer the delay the larger the required sustained reductions later (Firor, 1990: 112; Schimel *et al.*, 1996: 80). The

SAR does note that 'Wigley *et al.* (1996) stress the need for a full economic and environmental assessment in the choice of pathway to stabilisation' (Schimel *et al.*, 1996: 83), which implies the inseparability of socio-economic and political factors from GHG prediction and climate science.

The IPCC emissions reduction predictions are perhaps a conservative estimate due to the political process within which science on complex environmental issues is embedded. For example, Walker and Kasting (1992) present a model where stabilising CO_2 at double preindustrial levels requires a 96 per cent reduction in emissions. While the IPCC's 1995 report is able to give clear executive summary statements on the percentage reductions required for stabilising methane and nitrous oxides this is absent in the case of CO_2. Instead the term 'substantially below 1990 levels' is employed. This contrasts with the 1990 IPCC report where immediate 60–80 per cent reductions in anthropogenic CO_2 emissions were stated as necessary to stabilise atmospheric concentrations (Watson *et al.*, 1990: 5). The later report states that (Houghton *et al.*, 1996: 25):

> Many different stabilisation levels, time-scales for achieving these levels, and routes to stabilisation could have been chosen. The choices made are not intended to have policy implications; the exercise is illustrative of the relationship between CO_2 emissions and concentrations.

This seems to belie the importance of the role IPCC has played in policy formation and deny the political aspect of science in GHG control; these are subjects to which we return in other chapters.

Nitrous oxide

Data on N_2O emissions from fossil fuel burning suggest coal is the major contributor followed by fuel oil and natural gas. Agricultural fertiliser is another important N_2O source. Between 1950 and 1980 global annual production of nitrogen in fertiliser increased 17 fold (Marland and Rotty, 1985: 1,033). Estimated climate forcing in the 1980s was for an increase in N_2O concentrations by one-third (then expected by 2000) to cause a $0.1°C$ increase in average global temperature, and a 100 per cent N_2O increase (expected by 2040) causing a $0.3°C$ temperature increase (Kelejian and Varichek, 1982). These levels of contribution seem unlikely given that the rate of increase in the 1980s was around 0.2–0.4 per cent per annum.[3] Atmospheric concentrations of N_2O are estimated to have increased by 17 per cent since 1750. The atmospheric lifetime of N_2O is approximately 120–150 years (Wuebbles and Edmonds, 1988; Prather *et al.*, 1996). In order to stabilise N_2O concentrations near current levels anthropogenic sources would need a more than 50 per cent reduction (Houghton *et al.*, 1995: 28).

Chlorofluorocarbons

Without increasing emissions the concentration of CFCs will increase for the next several decades because of the long time needed for atmospheric destruction processes to equilibrate with a steady input (Cicerone, 1989: 234). If CFCs F-11 and F-12 were to have increased at pre-1973 rates, i.e. 10 per cent per annum, by 1990 the temperature increase attributable to these two CFCs alone would have been 0.3°C and by 2000 0.7°C (Forziati, 1982: 52). As of 1980 the rate of increase of tropospheric abundance was 6 per cent per year (National Research Council, 1984: 77). Due to international controls this has since decreased and by the early 1990s was around 4 per cent per year for both F-11 and F-12.[4]

Under the Montreal Protocol (signed 1987, effective 1989, London amendment 1990) certain signatories have undertaken to reduce emissions of Group I CFCs, but the agreement is complex and allows industrially developing countries and the former Soviet Union to increase emissions. In the absence of the Protocol, Group I CFCs would have doubled over their 1986 levels by 2009. Under strict adherence to the original Protocol (i.e. a 50 per cent reduction in CFCs in industrially developed countries) and no increase in industrially developing countries' export of CFC-related products, emissions could range from a 20 per cent increase to a 45 per cent decrease from 1986 levels (Office of Technology Assessment, 1989).

Some of the uncontrolled substitutes for regulated halocarbons (such as CFC F-11 and F-12) are just as potentially effective as greenhouse gases and in the destruction of ozone. For example, chlorine is only one potential ozone catalyst; bromine is more effective and along with other halons is finding expanding use in fire extinguishers (Firor, 1990: 33). CFC F-22 is a substitute for CFC F-12 in air conditioning and refrigeration and has been growing rapidly in the atmosphere, at 10–14 per cent per annum. At this rate within 20–25 years a 1 ppb (parts per billion) increase in CFC F-22 is expected, leading to a 0.04–0.15°C mean global surface temperature increase, or even more (Ciborowski, 1989). Amendments to the Montreal Protocol have lead to regulation and/or phaseout plans for five CFCs, three halons and seven chlorinated hydrocarbons. However, a further eight perfluorinated compounds and 17 chlorinated hydrocarbons are unregulated recognised greenhouse gases. Some of these have very long atmospheric lifetimes (all perfluorinated compounds over 3,000 years) and large global warming potentials (thousands of times CO_2 and far stronger than CFCs) (Houghton *et al.*, 1995: 33; Prather *et al.*, 1996: 88–90).

Ozone

Detailed statistical analyses of measurements of total ozone between 1970 and 1980 indicated stability in the total-column abundance of ozone (the net amount of ozone above a unit area of Earth's surface). Since then downward trends in total-column ozone have been observed over much of the globe. Ozone in the stratosphere is under the simultaneous influence of a number of compounds including CFC-11, CFC-12 and N_2O (all of which reduce ozone), and NO_x from subsonic aircraft, CH_4 and CO_2 (which increase ozone). Large ozone reductions have been expected in the upper stratosphere and substantial increases in the lower and upper troposphere. Tropospheric ozone has been increasing at 0.7 per cent per annum (Harrington, 1987), but with wide regional variations. These changes may noticeably alter the dynamics of the upper atmosphere, and warm the troposphere.

Methane

Air bubbles trapped in ice indicate that the increase in methane began about 200 years ago, as with CO_2 (Stauffer et al., 1985). The atmospheric concentration of CH_4 has doubled over the last century after being constant for perhaps 20,000 years or more. The IPCC TAR estimates a 151 per cent increase since 1750 (IPCC Working Group I, 2001). Atmospheric observations have been supported by ice core measurements showing that the increase in concentrations from 1965–80 was dramatic compared to the past 100 years (National Research Council, 1984: 45). The lifetime of atmospheric methane has been increasing from 6.0–7.5 years in the 1970s (Khahlil and Rasmussen, 1987) to recent estimates of 11 ± 2 years (Houghton, Callander and Varney, 1992: 36); this is attributed to the depletion of OH radicals that remove CH_4 from the atmosphere. The trend in CH_4 appears to coincide with the changing trends of population and may be caused largely by industrial and agricultural activities associated with the production of food and energy (Khahlil and Rasmussen, 1987). The growth rate of atmospheric CH_4 is about 1.0–1.9 per cent per annum (Marland and Rotty, 1985: 1,033).

Past and future trends in global climate

So far this chapter has outlined influences on climate and how GHGs are forcing climate change due to human activity. In this section the meaning of expected forcing is placed in historical context. The use of past climate as a guide to the future requires that the same set of mechanisms which operated in the past will continue to act in the future, and the range of climate variability will be similar. Goodess et al. (1992) suggest using the last two million years record (Quaternary) as a guide to the next one million years. Climatic change over the past million years consists of periods of glaciation of 80,000–100,000 years in duration, followed by periods of interglacial warmth 10,000–15,000 years in duration.

Variations in temperature are clearly discerned in the Vostok ice core sample as shown in figure 2.5. An ice core of 2,200 m drilled at the Antarctic Vostok station in the 1980s contained accumulated ice dating back 160,000 years (Houghton and Woodwell, 1989). The deepest core so far recovered was completed in 1998, reaching a depth of 3,623 m and giving a climate record extending back 420,000 years (Petit *et al.*, 2000). Such ice cores contain snow and bubbles of air trapped at different depths and hence different times. The formation of snow incorporates ordinary water, H_2O, which contains a small fraction of molecules that have a heavier form of oxygen, ^{18}O, and a smaller amount of deuterium, a heavy form of hydrogen. These heavier molecules move relatively slowly and are incorporated into snowflakes at a different rate from common water molecules; this rate is dependent upon temperature (Firor, 1990: 68). Thus, temperature is closely associated with concentrations of deuterium and oxygen isotopes, allowing these concentrations to be measured and converted into temperature records, such as figure 2.5.

Past temperature changes, as discernible in the Vostok record, are associated with dramatic impacts; for example, at the peak of the last glaciation, 18,000 years ago, the ocean was 130 m lower than today. About 6,000 years ago Earth entered the hypsithermal or climatic optimum during which the mean temperature of Earth was approximately as it is now. As far as the glacial cycle is concerned, other things remaining the same, the world is slowly (over thousands of years) proceeding into the next glacial period. Glaciation, as discussed earlier, is due to complex rhythms in Earth's orbital parameters and accompanying internal climatic feedback mechanisms. An oscillatory rise to maximum ice volume over a 100,000-year period, followed by rapid collapse to zero volume, is predicted (Harrington, 1987: 1321–2).

Speculation as to the benefits of enhancing the Greenhouse Effect to avoid the next glacial period have overrated human control of such processes and understated the time horizons involved and the potential consequences. Goodess *et al.* (1992) have identified three possible patterns resulting from the interaction of the enhanced

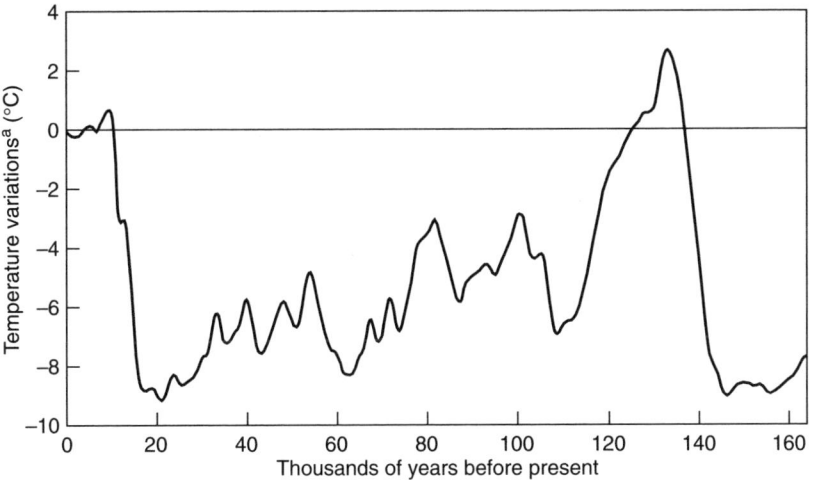

Figure 2.5 Vostok temperature record
Data source: Jouzel *et al.* (1994).
Note: a Variations from current temperature of 55°C.

Greenhouse Effect and orbital forcing. First, a short, 1,000-year period of enhanced global warming would be followed by a return to the 'normal' glacial cycle. Second, following the enhanced warming the next glaciation will be delayed and be less severe. Third, the enhanced warming will transform the relatively weak orbital forcing pattern so that future glaciations are prevented and an irreversible enhanced Greenhouse Effect results. Goodess *et al.* (1992: 105) regard the most likely scenario as a delay of the next glaciation by 5,000 years, from 55,000 to 60,000 years after present, and a reduction in its severity. Among the possible impacts of delayed glaciation would be sustained and enhanced sea level rise.

Mean global temperature has in the past been much warmer than at present: during the Holocene climatic optimum (5,000–6,000 BP) 1°C warmer, during the last interglacial warming (125,000 BP) 2°C warmer and during the Pliocene (3–4 million years BP) 3–4°C warmer (MacDonald, 1988). However, during the last 10,000 years, the Holocene, the mean temperature of the northern hemisphere varied by no more than about 2°C (Gates, 1983). During the last 1,000 years Earth was warmer around the eleventh century, and colder during the 'Little Ice Age' a few centuries ago (for more detail see Goodess *et al.*, 1992: 57). The variance during these periods has been estimated at about 0.5°C, and the rate of change 0.05°C per decade (Firor, 1989: 13). In recent years mean global temperature has been around 15°C.

Generally, forecasts of climatic warming have been conducted in terms of an 'effective doubling' of CO_2, that is, because a number of other gases contribute to the enhanced Greenhouse Effect, the radiative forcing equivalent to that under, for example, a doubling of CO_2 can be achieved much sooner and without CO_2 actually doubling itself. The best numerical models of the global atmosphere were consistently predicting a 1.0–4.5°C rise in mean temperature of the troposphere with a doubling of atmospheric CO_2 through the 1980s (Harrington, 1987: 1325) and in the 1990s. The date of such radiative forcing (i.e. equivalent to a doubling of CO_2) has formerly been estimated as soon as the late 2020s to 2060 (Hansen *et al.*, 1986: 207). A temperature rise of 2.5°C by 2100 is the slow-growth, no-coal phaseout, model seen as most likely in a review of the literature by Harrington (1987). This compares with a 2.0°C temperature rise from 1990–2100 predicted by the 1995 IPCC report under their best estimate emissions scenario, with an uncertainty range of 1.0–3.5°C (Houghton *et al.*, 1996) and the higher 1.4–5.8°C of the 2001 report (IPCC Working Group I, 2001).

Thus the enhanced Greenhouse Effect represents a potentially drastic temperature increase over a relatively short period of time. Earth's mean surface air temperature has already increased with estimates between 0.5–0.7°C since 1860 according to Abrahamson (1989), and 0.3–0.6°C since the late nineteenth century according to the IPCC SAR (Houghton *et al.*, 1996). The IPCC estimate was revised upwards to 0.4–0.8°C under TAR due to actual observations between 1995 and 2000 (IPCC Working Group I, 2001: 2). Hansen *et al.* (1986: 207) estimated the warming at most mid-latitude northern hemisphere land areas would be 0.5–1.0°C by 1990–2000, and 1–2°C by 2010–20. Towards the end of the twenty-first century the planet could warm up by 4.5°C (Smagorinsky, 1983). Within 100 years Earth would then be warmer than in several million years and certainly well beyond known human capabilities of adaptation. Even with less dramatic outcomes regional variability means areas becoming warmer and colder than the global mean, and impacts in terms of such factors as seasonal rainfall, and number of days at or above extreme temperatures.

The inherent variability of the climate creates background 'noise' in which it is difficult to discern GHG-induced climate changes. Some analysts predicted GHG warming would rise out of the noise level in the late 1980s and 1990s (Madden and Ramanathan, 1980). However, this underestimated the complexity of detecting the signal of the enhanced Greenhouse Effect from natural variability or noise of the climate system (due to the internal dynamics of the atmosphere and oceans). Emphasis was therefore placed upon determining the way in which the signal might manifest itself, i.e. the enhanced GHG fingerprint (see Santer, 1994). In the late 1990s there was such fingerprint evidence of global warming. For example, polar warming has been expected to be two to five times the global average (Stern *et al.*, 1984: 340), and should therefore be recognised relatively early. A temperature increase of 2–4°C appears to have occurred in the Alaskan Arctic during the last century (Lachenbruch and Vaughan Marshall, 1986). Such observational patterns linked to prediction are now accumulating. For other examples see the review by Mazza and Roth (1999) or evidence cited in the IPCC 2001 summary report (IPCC Working Group I, 2001).

Temperatures over the Northern Hemisphere steadily increased in the period from 1880–1940, decreased by 0.5°C between 1940 and 1970 (attributed to volcanic activity), and rose between the mid-1960s and 1980 yielding a warming of 0.4°C from the 1880s to 1980s (Hansen *et al.*, 1981).[5] The 1980s were 0.34°C warmer than earlier decades (Kerr, 1989: 127–8). By 1987 in the southern hemisphere seven of the eight warmest years on record had occurred in the 1980s, and in the northern hemisphere 1981 was the warmest year with 1987 a close second. In the southern hemisphere the warming had been most pronounced over Australia, southern South Africa, the tip of South America and Antarctica near Australia. In the northern hemisphere warming was strongest over Alaska, northwest Canada, the Greenland Sea, the Soviet Union (especially Siberia), parts of southern Asia, north Africa, and southwest Europe (Gribbin, 1988). Global (i.e. averaged across both hemispheres) annual temperatures since 1859 are shown in figure 2.6 as variations from the mean temperature for the period 1961–90 (Jones *et al.*, 2000).

As figure 2.6 clearly shows, unusually high global mean surface temperatures continued into the late 1980s and 1990s; by early 1995 the warmest years on record were 1990 and 1991. By 1999 the highest temperature on record was 1998 at 0.57°C above the 1961–90 reference period mean temperature (Jones *et al.*, 2000). By the end of the twentieth century the seven warmest years of the global record

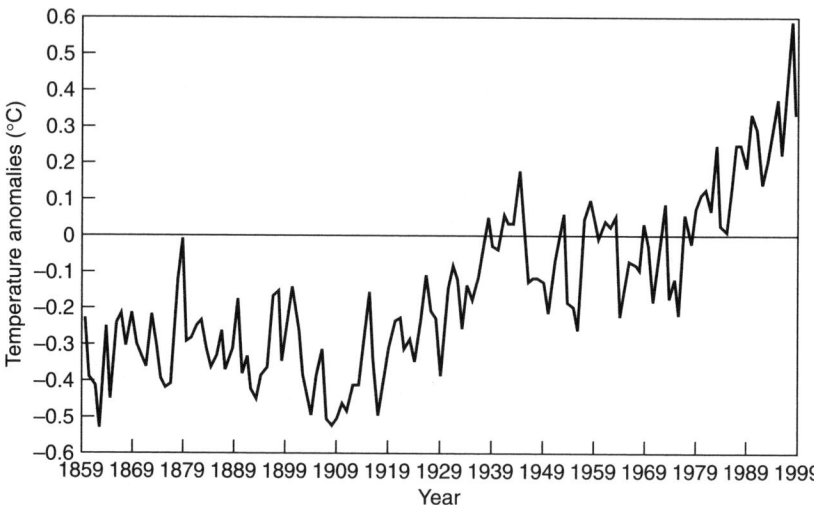

Figure 2.6 Global annual temperature anomalies, 1859–1999
Data source: Jones *et al.* (2000).

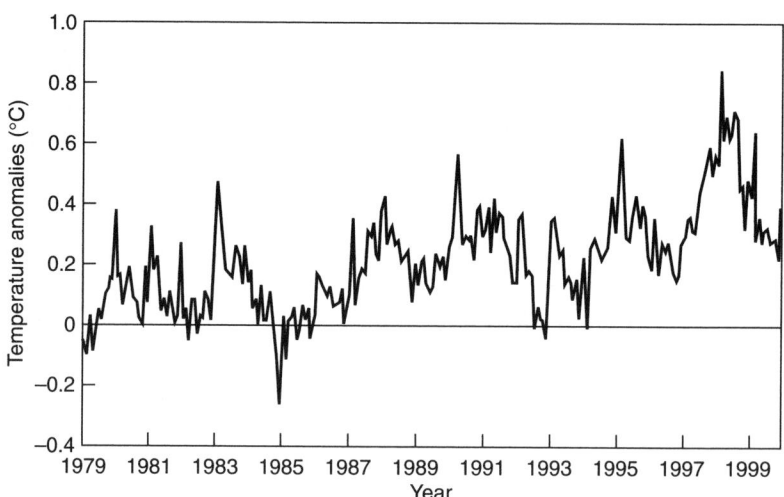

Figure 2.7 Global monthly temperature anomalies, January 1979–December 1999
Data source: Jones *et al.* (2000).

had all occurred in the 1990s and in descending order were: 1998, 1997, 1995, 1990, 1999, 1991 and 1994. The seasonal variation within these annual average changes is shown in figure 2.7 which gives the monthly global average temperatures as variations from the mean for 1961–90. This shows the divergence possible within the annual averages. For example, for 1998 the month of February was 0.84°C higher than the reference period and is clearly discernible as the peak value in figure 2.7.

Conclusions

Overall, the primary climatic control (solar irradiation of Earth), while subject to systematic variation due to changes in solar luminance and in the geometry of the Earth–Sun system, can be excluded from consideration as far as policy on the enhanced Greenhouse Effect is concerned. Although orbital forcing can be recognised as the major cause of glacial–interglacial cycles, the major influence on climate over the next 200 to 1,000 years will be anthropogenic greenhouse gases. The intensity of solar radiation reaching Earth is a constant within the next several centuries. The reflectivity of Earth is expected to have little or no effect on global climate itself but is important in determining the response of global climate to perturbations, e.g. via cloud formation. Volcanic activity is a potentially strong influence on hemispheric climate over short periods of time (a few years), but is unpredictable. The most influential climate control in the medium term (decades to centuries) is closing the 'atmospheric window' with greenhouse gases.

Table 2.7 summarises the information on greenhouse gases presented in this chapter. Ozone is excluded as it has been expected to have a relatively small temperature forcing role, but its importance in atmospheric chemistry and as a potential source of future warming (especially regional variations) should be remembered. The role of other GHGs besides CO_2 has tended to be neglected in

Table 2.7 Summary of the principal greenhouse gases

	Principal greenhouse gases			
	CO_2	CH_4	CFCs (F11 and F12)	N_2O
Main anthropogenic sources	Fossil fuel	Rice paddies, fossil fuel, cattle	Propellants, foams, fridges	Fossil fuel, fertiliser
Main sinks	Oceans and forests	Chemical scavenging	Stratospheric photodissociation	
Atmospheric lifetimes (years)	500[c]	9–13	75 and 110	120–50
Climate forcing (% of total change in temperature)[a]	55	15	17	6
Radiative index[b]	1	30	10,000	150
Atmospheric increase (% per year)	0.4	1.0–1.9	4.0	0.3

Source: the data are taken from various sources as referenced in the text.

Notes: a   Climate forcing is for 1980–90 taken from the 1992 IPCC report; other gases account for 7 per cent.
   b   The radiative index measures the current relative contribution to greenhouse warming per molecule.
   c   No single estimate possible as dependent upon sinks but figure here for significant stock removal.

policy debates and economic analysis, although the Kyoto Protocol does address five other gases not controlled by the Montreal Protocol (i.e. methane CH_4, nitrous oxide N_2O, hydrofluorocarbons HFCs, perfluorocarbons PFCs, and sulphur hexa-fluoride SF_6).

The extension of concerns to a range of GHGs has posed problems for scientists in modelling atmospheric chemistry. As noted in the 1995 IPCC report: 'The inclusion of methane and ozone in complex climate models will be a major challenge and will involve coupling GCMs to interactive tropospheric chemistry models' (Kattenberg et al., 1996: 349). The role of aerosols has also gained increasing attention but research has yet to address the effect of other anthropogenic forcing including indirect sulphate effects, soot, tropospheric ozone and aerosols from biomass. Control of acidic deposition if effective would reduce the dispersion of nitrous and sulphur oxides which can be expected to have further interactive impacts (e.g. reducing backscatter of incoming radiation).

The relative sizes of sources and sinks, trace gas abundance in the atmosphere and emissions trends are all changing over time, as is the mixture of gases contributing to climate forcing. Additional uncertainty surrounds the role of sources and sinks. For example, while table 2.7 shows forests as a CO_2 sink, global deforestation currently makes forests a net source of CO_2, and of greater concern is the potential for oceans to reduce their role as a carbon sink. While uncertainty is an essential aspect of the problem, there is consensus on many issues, including the serious threat human GHG emissions pose to atmospheric chemistry and climate. There is international acceptance of an average global warming due to anthropogenic GHG emissions and some sign that this is beginning to be realised. The susceptibility of economic and social systems to climatic change makes any such perturbations of grave concern. The greater controversy surrounds exactly how human-induced climatic change will be realised at the regional level and across time, and these are subjects to which I turn next.

Notes

1 As this chapter was in the final stages the IPCC Third Assessment Report was in production. While the main reports had yet to be released the policymakers summaries were available. The upward revision of IPCC estimates for climatic warming appeared to be based on exactly this reasoning.

2 Preindustrial concentrations of CO_2 are given below in the section on sources and sinks, with references. Estimates vary between 280–300 ppm with a 'natural' background concentration of 200–250 ppm.

3 The following range of estimates can be found in the literature: 0.2 per cent/yr National Research Council (1984: 69); 0.2–0.4 per cent/yr Marland and Rotty (1985: 1033); 0.2–0.3 per cent/yr IPCC (Houghton, Callander and Varney, 1992: 37) and Wuebbles and Edmonds (1988: 28).

4 Calculations based upon annual mean concentration and trends reported in Houghton, Callander and Varney (1992: 38) table A1.6.

5 This compares with the 1992 IPCC Report estimate of $0.3–0.6°C$ for the temperature rise over the preceeding century (Houghton, Callander and Varney, 1992: 5).

References

Abrahamson, D.E. (1989) 'Global warming: the issue, impacts, responses', in *The Challenge of Global Warming*, edited by D.E. Abrahamson, pp. 3–34, Washington, DC: Island Press.

Adams, J.A.S., M.S.M. Mantovani and L.L. Lundell (1977) 'Wood versus fossil fuel as a source of excess carbon dioxide in the atmosphere: a preliminary report', *Science* **196**(April): 54–6.

Arrhenius, S. (1896) 'On the influence of the carbonic acid in the air upon the temperature of the ground', *Philosophical Magazine and Journal of Science* **41**(251): 237–76.

Benkowitz, C.M. (1983) 'Characteristics of oxidant precursor emissions from anthropogenic sources in the United States', *Environment International* **9**(6): 429–90.

Boden, T.A., D.P. Kaiser, R.J. Sepanski and F.W. Stoss (1994) 'Trends '93: A compendium of data on global change', *CDIAC Communications* (Fall, no. 20): 8–10.

Bourdaire, J.-M. (1999) 'World energy prospects to 2020: issues and uncertainties', in *Energy: The Next Fifty Years*, edited by OECD, pp. 29–39 Paris: Organisation for Economic Co-operation and Development.

Bryson, R.A. (1974) 'Perspective on climate change', *Science* **184**(4,138): 753–60.

Carson, C. (1995) *Climate change: prediction and response.* Presented at a lecture to the Royal Society, Edinburgh, 11 May 1995.

Ciborowski, P. (1989) 'Sources, sites, trends, and opportunities', in *The Challenge of Global Warming*, edited by D.E. Abrahamson, pp. 231–8, Washington, DC: Island Press.

Cicerone, R. (1989) 'Global warming, acid rain, and ozone depletion', in *The Challenge of Global Warming*, edited by D.E. Abrahamson, pp. 213–30, Washington, DC: Island Press.

Croll, J. (1875) *Climate and Time in Their Geological Relations: A Theory of Secular Changes of the Earth's Climate.* Daldy, Ibister & Co.: London.

Cumberland, J.H., J.R. Hibbs and I. Hoch, (eds) (1982) *The Economics of Managing Chlorofluorocarbons: Stratospheric Ozone and Climate Issues.* Baltimore, MD: Johns Hopkins University Press.

Detwiler, R.P. and C.A.S. Hall (1988) 'Tropical forests and the global carbon cycle', *Science* **239** (January): 42–7.

Dotto, L. and H. Schiff (1978) *The Ozone War.* New York: Doubleday and Company.

Dowd, R.M. (1985) 'The greenhouse effect', *Environmental Science and Technology* **20**(8): 767.

Energy Information Administration (2000) *Annual Energy Outlook 2001 with Projections to 2020.* Office of Integrated Analysis and Forecasting, US Dept. of Energy, Washington, DC.

Firor, J.W. (1989) *The Straight Story About The Greenhouse Effect.* Presented at Western Economic Association International Meeting, Lake Tahoe, California, 18–22 June 1989.

Firor, J.W. (1990) *The Changing Atmosphere: A Global Challenge.* New Haven, CT: Yale University Press.

Forziati, A. (1982) 'The chlorofluorocarbon problem', in *The Economics of Managing Chlorofluorocarbons: Stratospheric Ozone and Climate Issues*, edited by J.H. Cumberland, J.R. Hibbs and I. Hoch, pp. 36–63, Baltimore: Resources for the Future, Johns Hopkins University Press.

Gates, D.M. (1983) 'An overview', in *CO₂ and Plants: The Response of Plants to Rising Levels of Atmospheric Carbon Dioxide*, edited by E.R. Lemon, pp. 7–20, Boulder, CO: Westview Press.

Gladwin, T.N., J.L. Ugelow and I. Walter (1982) 'A global view of CFC sources and policies to reduce emissions', in *The Economics of Managing Chlorofluorocarbons: Stratospheric Ozone and Climate Issues*, edited by J.H. Cumberland, J.R. Hibbs and I. Hoch, pp. 64–113, Baltimore: Resources for the Future, Johns Hopkins University Press.

Goodess, C.M., J.P. Palutikof and T.D. Davies (1992) *The Nature and Causes of Climate Change: Assessing the Long Term Future*. London: Belhaven.

Gribbin, J. (1988) 'Britain shivers in the global greenhouse', *New Scientist* **118**(June): 42–3.

Grübler, A. (1999) 'Global energy perspectives: 2050 and beyond', in *Energy: The Next Fifty Years*, edited by OECD, pp. 41–61, Paris: Organisation for Economic Co-operation and Development.

Grübler, A. (2000) 'Managing the global environment', *Environmental Science and Technology* **34**(7): 184–7.

Hadley Centre (1995) *Modelling Climate Change 1860–2050*. London: Meteorological Office.

Hadley Centre (2000) *Climate Change: An Update of Recent Research from the Hadley Centre*. Bracknell: Hadley Centre.

Hansen, J.E. (1989) 'The greenhouse effect: impacts on current global temperature and regional heat waves', in *The Challenge of Global Warming*, edited by D.E. Abrahamson, pp. 35–43, Washington, DC: Island Press.

Hansen, J.E., D. Johnson, A. Lacis, S. Lebedeff, P. Lee, D. Rind and G. Russell (1981) 'Climate impact of increasing atmospheric carbon dioxide', *Science* **213**(4,511): 957–66.

Hansen, J.E., A. Lacis, D. Rind, G. Russell, I. Furg, P. Ashcroft, S. Lebedeff, R. Ruedy and P. Stone (1986) 'The greenhouse effect: projections of global climate change', in *Effects of Changes in Stratospheric Ozone and Global Climate* **I**(August), edited by J.G. Titus, pp. 199–218, Washington, DC: US Environmental Protection Agency.

Harrington, J.B. (1987) 'Climate change: a review of causes', *Canadian Journal of Forest Resources* **17**(11): 1313–39.

Henderson-Sellers, B. (1984) *Pollution of Our Atmosphere*. Bristol, England: Adam Hilger.

Houghton, J.T., B.A. Callander and S.K. Varney, (eds) (1992) *Climate Change 1992: The Supplementary Report to the IPCC Scientific Assessment*. Cambridge, England: Cambridge University Press.

Houghton, J.T., L.G. Meira Filho, J. Bruce, H. Lee, B.A. Callander, E. Haites, N. Narris and K. Maskell, (eds) (1995) *Climate Change 1994: Radiative Forcing of Climate Change and an Evaluation of the IPCC IS92 Emission Scenarios*. Cambridge, England: Cambridge University Press.

Houghton, J.T., L.G. Meira, B.A. Callander, N. Harris, A. Kattenberg and K. Maskell, (eds) (1996) *Climate Change 1995: The Science of Climate Change*. Cambridge, England: Cambridge University Press.

Houghton, R.A. and G.M. Woodwell (1989) 'Global climatic change', *Scientific American* **260**(4): 36–44.

Idso, S.B. (1982) *Carbon Dioxide: Friend or Foe?* Tempe, AZ: IBR Press.

Imboden, D.M. and C.C. Jaeger (1999) 'Towards a sustainable energy future', in *Energy: The Next Fifty Years*, edited by OECD, pp. 63–94, Paris: Organisation for Economic Co-operation and Development.

International Energy Agency (1993) *World Energy Outlook*. Paris: Organisation for Economic Co-operation and Development.

International Energy Agency (1998) *CO_2 Emissions from Fuel Combustion*. Paris: International Energy Agency.

IPCC Working Group I (2001) *Climate Change 2001: Scientific Assessment; Summary for Policymakers*. Geneva: Intergovernmental Panel on Climate Change.

IPCC Working Group III (2001) *Climate Change 2001: Mitigation of Climate Change; Summary for Policymakers*. Geneva: Intergovernmental Panel on Climate Change.

Jamieson, D. (1988) *Managing the Future: Public Policy, Scientific Uncertainty, and Global Warming*. Boulder, CO: Department of Philosophy, Center for Values and Social Policy, University of Colorado.

Jones, P.D., D.E. Parker, T.J. Osborn and K.R. Briffa (2000) 'Global and hemispheric temperature anomalies: land and marine instrumental records', in *Trends: A Compendium of Data on Global Change*. Oak Ridge, TN: Carbon Dioxide Information Analysis Center, Oak Ridge National Laboratory, US Department of Energy.

Jouzel, J., C. Lorius, J.R. Petit, N.I. Barkov and V.M. Kotlyakov (1994) 'Vostok isotopic temperature record', in *Trends '93: A Compendium of Data on Global Change* ORNL/CDIAC-65, edited by T.A. Boden, D.P. Kaiser, R.J. Sepanski and F.W. Stoss, pp. 590–602, Oak Ridge, TN: Carbon Dioxide Information Analysis Center, Oak Ridge National Laboratory, US Department of Energy.

Kattenberg, A., F. Giorgi, H. Grassl, G.A. Meehl, J.F.B. Mitchell, R.J. Stouffer, T. Tokioka, A.J. Weaver and T.M.L. Wigley (1996) 'Climate models: projections of future climate', in *Climate Change 1995: The Science of Climate Change*, edited by J.T. Houghton, L.G. Meira, B.A. Callander, N. Harris, A. Kattenberg and K. Maskell, pp. 285–357, Cambridge, England: Cambridge University Press.

Keeling, C.D. (1996) 'Increased activity of northern vegetation inferred from atmospheric CO_2 measurements', *Nature* **382**(11 July): 146–9.

Keeling, C.D. and T.P. Whorf (2000) Atmospheric CO_2 records from sites in the SIO air sampling network. *Trends: A Compendium of Data on Global Change*. Oak Ridge, TN: Carbon Dioxide Information Analysis Center, Oak Ridge National Laboratory, US Department of Energy.

Kelejian, H.K. and B.V. Varichek (1982) 'Pollution, climate change, and consequent economic costs concerning agricultural production', in *The Economics of Managing Chlorofluorocarbons: Stratospheric Ozone and Climate Issues*, edited by J.H. Cumberland, J.R. Hibbs and I. Hoch, pp. 224–68, Washington, DC: Resources for the Future.

Kerr, R.A. (1977) 'Carbon dioxide and climate: carbon budget still unbalanced', *Science* **197** (September): 1352–3.

Kerr, R.A. (1989) 'Volcanoes can muddle the greenhouse', *Science* **245**(July): 127–8.

Khahlil, M.A.K. and R.A. Rasmussen (1987) 'Atmospheric methane: trends over the last 10,000 years', *Atmospheric Environment* **21**(11): 2445–2.

Lachenbruch, A.G. and B. Vaughan Marshall (1986) 'Changing climate: geothermal evidence from permafrost in the Alaskan Arctic', *Science* **234**(November): 689–96.

Lahidji, R., W. Michalski and B. Stevens (1999) 'The long-term future for energy: an assessment of key trends and challenges', in *Energy: The Next Fifty Years*, edited by OECD, pp. 7–28, Paris: Organisation for Economic Co-operation and Development.

LaMarche, V.C., D.A. Graybill, H.C. Fritts and M.R. Rose (1984) 'Increasing atmospheric carbon dioxide: tree ring evidence for growth enhancement in natural vegetation', *Science* **225**(September): 1019–21.

MacDonald, G.J. (1988) 'Scientific basis for the greenhouse effect', *Journal of Policy Analysis and Management* **7**(3): 424–44.

Madden, R.A. and V. Ramanathan (1980) 'Detecting climate change due to increasing carbon dioxide', *Science* **209**(4,458): 763–8.

Marland, G. and R.M. Rotty (1985) 'Greenhouse gases in the atmosphere: what do we know?', *Journal of Air Pollution Control Association* **35**(10): 1,033–8.

Mazza, P. and R. Roth (1999) *Global Warming is Here: The Scientific Evidence*. Washington, DC: The Atmosphere Alliance, Earth Island Institute.

Moore, B. and B.H. Braswell (1994a) 'The lifetime of excess atmospheric carbon dioxide', *Global Biogeochemical Cycles* **8**(1): 23–38.

Moore, B. and B.H. Braswell (1994b) 'Planetary metabolism: understanding the carbon cycle', *Ambio* **23**(1): 4–12.

National Research Council (1984) *Causes and Effects of Changes in Stratospheric Ozone: Update 1983*. Washington, DC: National Academy of Sciences.

Neftel, A., E. Moor, H. Oeschger and B. Stauffer (1985) 'Evidence from polar ice cores for the increase in atmospheric CO_2 in the past two centuries', *Nature* **315**: 45–7.

Nordhaus, W.D. (1994) *Managing the Global Commons: The Economics of Climate Change*. Cambridge, MA: MIT Press.

OECD (1982) *World Energy Outlook*. Paris: Organisation for Economic Co-operation and Development.

Office of Technology Assessment (1989) 'An analysis of the Montreal Protocol on substances that deplete the ozone layer', in *The Challenge of Global Warming*, edited by D.E. Abrahamson, pp. 291–304, Washington, DC: Island Press.

O'Hara, F.M. (1990) *Glossary: Carbon Dioxide and Climate*. Oak Ridge, TN: Oak Ridge National Laboratory.

Petit, J.R., D. Raynaud, C. Lorius, J. Jouzel, H. Delaygue, N.I. Barkov and V.M. Kotlyakov (2000) 'Historical isotopic temperature record from the Vostock ice core', in *Trends: A Compendium of Data on Global Change*. Oak Ridge, TN: Carbon Dioxide Information Analysis Center, Oak Ridge National Laboratory, US Department of Energy.

Prather, M., R. Derwent, D. Ehhalt, P. Fraser, E. Sanhueza and X. Zhou (1996) 'Other trace gases and atmospheric chemistry', in *Climate Change 1995: The Science of Climate Change*, edited by J.T. Houghton, L.G. Meira, B.A. Callander, N. Harris, A. Kattenberg and K. Maskell, pp. 86–103, Cambridge, England: Cambridge University Press.

Revelle, R. and H.E. Suess (1957) 'Carbon dioxide exchange between atmosphere and ocean, and the question of an increase in atmospheric CO_2 during the past decades', *Tellus* **9**(18): 18–27.

Rietmeijer, L. (1990) 'El Chicon dust a persistent problem', *Nature* **344**(6,262): 114–15.

Rosenberg, N.J. (1986) *A Primer on Climatic Change: Mechanisms, Trends and Projections*. Washington, DC: Resources for the Future.

Rosenberg, N.J., B.L. Blad and S.B. Verma (1983) *Microclimate: The Biological Environment*. New York: John Wiley & Sons.

Rotty, R.M. and D.B. Reister (1986) 'Use of energy scenarios in addressing the CO_2 question', *Journal of Air Pollution Control Association* **36**(10): 1,111–15.

Sagan, C., O.B. Toon and J.B. Pollack (1979) 'Anthropogenic albedo changes and the earth's climate', *Science* **206**: 1,363–8.

Santer, B.D. (1994) *The Detection of Greenhouse-Gas-Induced Climate Change*. Research Summary no. 29. Oak Ridge TN: Carbon Dioxide Information Analysis Center, Oak Ridge National Laboratory, US Department of Energy.

Schimel, D., D. Alves, I. Enting, M. Heiman, F. Joos, D. Raynaud and T. Wigley (1996) 'CO_2 and the carbon cycle', in *Climate Change 1995: The Science of Climate Change*, edited by J.T. Houghton, L G. Meira, B.A. Callander, N. Harris, A. Kattenberg and K. Maskell, pp. 76–86, Cambridge, England: Cambridge University Press.

Sear, C.B., F.M. Kelly, P.D. Jones and C.M. Goodess (1987) 'Global surface temperature responses to major volcanic eruptions', *Nature* **30**(6146): 365–7.

Senum, G.I. and J.S. Gaffney (1989) 'A re-examination of the topospheric methane cycle: geophysical implications', in *The Carbon Cycle and Atmospheric CO_2 Variations Archean to Present* **32**, edited by T.E. Sundquist and W.S. Broecker, pp. 61–9: American Geophysics Union.

Smagorinsky, J. (1983) 'Effects of carbon dioxide', in *Changing Climate: Report of the Carbon Dioxide Assessment Committee*, edited by N.R. Council, pp. 266–91, Washington, DC: National Academy Press.

Stauffer, B., G. Fischer, A. Neftel and H. Oeschger (1985) 'Increase of atmospheric methane recorded in Antarctic ice core', *Science* **229**: 1,386–88.

Stern, A.C., R.W. Boubel, D.B. Turner and D.L. Fox (1984) *Fundamentals of Air Pollution*. London: Academic Press.

Walker, J. and J. Kasting (1992) 'Effects of fuel and forest conservation on future levels of atmospheric carbon dioxide', *Global Planet Change* **5**: 151–89.

Watson, R.T., H. Rodhe, H. Oeschger and U. Siegenthaler (1990) 'Greenhouse gases and aerosols', in *Climate Change: The IPCC Scientific Assessment*, edited by J.T. Houghton, G.J. Jenkins and J.J. Ephraums, pp. 1–40, Cambridge, England: Cambridge University Press.

Wigley, T.M.L. (1988) *The climate of the past 10,000 years and the role of the Sun*. Presented at Secular Solar and Geomagnetic Variations in the Last 10,000 Years: NATO Advanced Research Workshop, Durham, England, 6–10 April, 1988, Kluwer Academic.

Wigley, T.M.L., R. Richels and J.A. Edmonds (1996) 'Economic and environmental choices in the stabilization of CO_2 concentrations: choosing the "right" emissions pathway', *Nature* **379**(18 January): 240–3.

Woodwell, G.M. (1978) 'The carbon dioxide question', *Scientific American* (January): 34–43.

Woodwell, G.M., J.E. Hobbie, R.A. Houghton, J.M. Melillo, B. Moore, B.J. Peterson and G.R. Shaver (1983) 'Global deforestation: contribution to atmospheric carbon dioxide', *Science* **222**(4,628): 1,081–6.

Wuebbles, D.J. and J. Edmonds (1988) *A Primer on Greenhouse Gases*. Washington, DC: GPO.

3 Impacts of global climate change

In this chapter a chain of relationships needs to be forged, so that the physical and socio-economic implications of the enhanced Greenhouse Effect can be more fully understood. The discussion in chapter 2 has outlined the link between human emissions of GHGs and the changes expected in average global temperatures. The next step requires an increasingly specific picture to be drawn which illustrates the range of climatic changes expected and their implications. This moves into the area of environmental impact assessment and socio-economic modelling.

Estimates of the impacts of climate change have most commonly been based upon changes in an assumed global equilibrium climate that is simulated (using GCMs) to result from an equivalent doubling of CO_2 (Watson et al., 1997: 2). In terms of understanding the impacts of environmental change due to the enhanced Greenhouse Effect global average temperature changes are of little use on their own. Predictions need to ideally include such factors as regional temperature patterns (mean, diurnal, seasonal), alterations in precipitation (amount, temporal and spatial distribution, storms, fronts), the frequency and severity of climatic events, changes in cloud cover and wind speeds, atmospheric pollutant formation and deposition, and so on. If this kind of information were available the next step would be to relate these parameters to specific ecosystems, their development and physical alterations in their functioning. Ecosystems will vary in their response depending upon their own characteristics such as nutrient levels, soil moisture and erosion, and bedrock type. Thus, climatic change would in turn influence soil moisture and erosion, insect and weed pests and plant pathogens.

These changes are directly relevant to human production systems, from agriculture to tourism, and so economic measures of welfare. Thus, economic analysis would be applied to the altering climatic circumstances founded upon scientific knowledge. In this way, an intricate chain of cause and effect relationships would be substantiated and analysed in order to predict the impacts of global climate change on human welfare. The tendency of scientific predictions to concentrate upon equilibrium changes is also common to economic assessment. This is despite the knowledge that both natural and social systems are characterised by change rather than equilibrium.

Enhancing the Greenhouse Effect is, for example, the initiation of a process of change rather than the shift from one stable equilibrium to another (as GCM models have tended to suggest). In this and other ways the deterministic, exact and idealised methodology of cause–effect impact assessment is often far from being either achievable or relevant. Much broader aims are therefore normally more appropriate.

In general, the goals of any impact assessment of climate change can be summarised as:

- increasing our basic understanding of climate–society interactions;
- identifying areas, populations or activities particularly sensitive to climate change;
- measuring and evaluating the impacts of particular climate fluctuations to aid mitigation or prevention of those impacts in future;
- improving the use of climate data in resource management;
- projecting future climatic impacts to improve long-term planning (Riebsame, 1989).

The UNEP has been particularly active in promoting understanding of this type; see Kates *et al.* (1985), Parry *et al.* (1988), Riebsame (1989), and Parry *et al.* (1991). A variety of methods are possible including: historical analysis of past climatic events and their impacts (e.g. the 1930s dust bowl in the USA, or the drought of 1988); top-down imposition of climatic variance on specific sectors globally (e.g. forestry or agriculture); or bottom-up understanding of the stability and resilience of particular ecosystems.

In order to try and restrict the complexity of the analysis particular regions may be selected, perhaps because they are deemed to be susceptible, politically important or representative in some respect. The aim of such case studies, given prevailing knowledge, is to aid the conceptualisation of interactions between society and climate, and identify mitigation and adaptation strategies, rather than to give accurate prediction of specific events. For examples, see Hulme *et al.* (1995) who analyse Africa, and the three regional case studies in Parry *et al.* (1991) – Brazil; Indonesia, Malaysia and Thailand; and Vietnam. Some governments have also commissioned national reports with similar aims such as Parry (1991) for the UK and Smith and Tirpak (1989) for the USA. National and regional studies are themselves subject to a range of uncertainties and context-specific factors. As will be shown in chapter 6, some influential economic analyses have focused upon US impact assessment and then extrapolated the results globally, and so produce considerable distortions in predicting expected economic losses. The IPCC concentrated upon impact assessment at the global scale until the late 1990s when a more regional approach was introduced (Watson *et al.*, 1997) and employed in the TAR of IPCC Working Group II (2001). Rather than gaining from the more socio-economic context specific country level this approach tries to offer broad predictions across large regions with common climatic and geographic features, i.e. Africa, the Polar regions, arid western Asia, temperate Asia, tropical Asia, Australasia, Europe, Latin America, North America and Small Island States.

In this chapter the expected results of climatic change will be described under two broad categories: spatial impacts and temporal impacts. The way in which the regional impacts are expected to and actually do materialise, influences international negotiations on the control of GHGs, and the timing, nature and extent of those controls. Unfortunately the impacts between and within nation states will be uneven and are likely to fall most heavily on those least able to adapt, i.e. the resource poor. Economics is notoriously bad at dealing with distributional issues because these tend to be regarded as political choices separable from resource efficiency. Thus, the optimal level of emissions reduction is discussed without considering who bears the costs and who gains the benefits. Yet these would seem to be crucial aspects of pollution control. For example, when those emitting pollution are the only ones to bear the cost of their emissions they may be regarded as in need of help, whereas when all the costs fall on others they are regarded as in need of prosecution.

Similarly, little serious attention has been paid by economists to the implications of temporal impacts, which bring forth questions over the ethical treatment of future generations. The lesson from economic externality theory, as discussed in chapter 1, is that costs will be externalised by self-absorbed businesses and individuals and this means pushing them on to others. Those others in this case include our descendants or the future unborn. Of course some, as long as they personally are left unaffected, regard future damages as something for the future alone to handle, as a senior Conservative politician in Margaret Thatcher's UK government told John Houghton after his Cabinet presentation (Houghton, 1997: 144). Politicians, scientists and economists all too often rationalise issues in a cold factual manner which excludes underlying ethical considerations, and economics has failed to help in this regard. How economics attempts to deal with, or in fact neglects, long-term issues is a central focus of chapter 8.

Thus, this chapter provides a general description of the expected extent and nature of spatial and temporal impacts. The aim is to lay the foundations for understanding how economic characterisations of the enhanced Greenhouse Effect might best proceed, and where they are likely to go astray. This organisation of the material subsumes discussions of events (such as sea level rise or agriculture damages) and case studies, in order to focus attention upon what are regarded here as the two key issues in general policy formation. Regional impacts are discussed concentrating largely upon the next hundred years, while the following section on temporal impacts takes the longer view.

Table 3.1 Latitudinal temperature changes for three scenarios by year 2000

Latitude		Global mean temperature scenario (°C)		
Belt	Range	I	II	III
		0.100	*0.425*	*1.200*
Polar	65°–90°	0.250	1.250	3.200
Higher mid	45°–65°	0.250	0.650	1.500
Lower mid	30°–45°	0.250	0.450	1.430
Subtropics	10°–30°	0.200	0.400	0.780

Source: Adapted from Kelejian and Varichek (1982: 235) table 7.4.

Table 3.2 Regional scenarios for climate change

	Temperature change (as a multiple of global average)		Precipitation change
	Summer	Winter	
High latitudes 60°–90°	0.5x–0.7x	2.0x–2.4x	Enhanced in winter
Mid latitudes 30°–60°	0.8x–1.0x	1.2x–1.4x	Possibly reduced in summer
Low latitudes 0°–30°	0.9x–0.7x	0.9x–0.7x	On average reductions but enhanced in areas where rainfall currently heavy

Source: After World Meterological Organization (1988: 9) table 1.

Regional impacts of greenhouse warming

The potential effects upon regional temperatures and climatic patterns can be quite different from global average temperature changes. Table 3.1 shows a relatively early example of prediction for GHG-induced temperature changes by latitudinal categories for three global average scenarios (Kelejian and Varichek, 1982). The temperature change categories are (I) the same as the last 30 years, (II) moderate warming and (III) large warming. This type of scenario modelling has been developed to predict latitudinal changes by season and with regard to precipitation, as in table 3.2. Precipitation changes are particularly important for rain-fed crops, which account for 80 per cent of global agricultural land use and 60 per cent of agricultural products (Riebsame, 1989: 11). The temperature changes in table 3.2 are taken from computer modelling results for the Northern Hemisphere, and are presented as multiples of global annual average temperature change. For example, a 1°C global annual average temperature rise is predicted to result in a 0.5°C–0.7°C temperature rise in high latitude summer temperatures. A qualitative assessment of precipitation changes is given which is supported by a number of studies.

The general picture gained from such modelling is one of far greater annual average changes in temperature towards the poles, and variable interregional changes. However, as table 3.2 shows, this difference between latitudes can disappear in summer. CO_2 is the main absorber of terrestrial radiation at high latitudes, while at the equator water vapour absorbs a large fraction. Thus, CO_2 plays a more effective role in the radiative balance of the high latitudes. This means the regional distribution of impacts is influenced by regional variations in water vapour and the mixture of GHGs prevalent in the atmosphere. As noted in chapter 2, these factors are changing over time due to anthropogenic gas emissions.

The next section gives a qualitative picture of the regional effects of global warming based on broad latitudinal zones. The IPCC has employed a top-down approach starting from general circulation models predicting changes at globally averaged and continental scales. This results in the authors having 'very low' confidence in their predictions at small-time and spatial scales (Kattenberg et al., 1996: 291). The outline of latitudinal impacts given here was structured around the conclusions of the workshops held in Villach, Austria (28 September–2 October 1987), and Bellagio, Italy (9–14 November 1987), under the auspices of the UN, World Meterological Organisation (WMO, 1988); for a summary see Jaeger (1989). The workshops were concerned with consensus predictions of climate change over the next hundred years and used scenarios for temperature increases per decade of 0.06°C, 0.30°C and 0.80°C. The main changes in understanding since these workshops have been in terms of the interactions between atmospheric and oceanic systems, and the role of aerosols in creating greater regional variability in climatic changes due to the enhanced Greenhouse Effect. A variety of other relevant literature and various IPCC reports are used to supplement and expand on the information presented. In the following sections broad geographical areas, such as arid regions, are identified as being particularly susceptible to the expected adverse effects of climate change. Sea level rise and agricultural susceptibility have formed a focus for much of the research on impacts and both are reviewed.

Impacts by latitude

In the Northern Hemisphere, above latitude 60° north, annual average temperature change is predicted at two to two-and-a-half times faster and greater than the global average. Maximum warming occurs in high northern latitudes in winter, although reduced warming, or even cooling, occurs in modelling simulations for the high-latitude southern ocean and part of the northern North Atlantic ocean (Kattenberg et al., 1996: 315). Withdrawal of summer pack ice could leave the Arctic ice-free around Spitzbergen and along the north Siberian coast. A positive feedback occurs as the duration of snow cover is reduced affecting albedo and causing further warming. Increased precipitation in the high-latitude regions of the Northern Hemisphere leads to greater run-off into the Arctic Basin. Increased precipitation and soil moisture in high latitudes during winter is a consistent prediction of models (Kattenberg et al., 1996: 315). The growth of Boreal forests would be stimulated. The rate of decay of organic material increases leading to additional emissions of methane and a further enhancement of the Greenhouse Effect. Melting of the permafrost in Alaska has been noted and tundra soils there now appear to be a net source of CO_2 (Mazza and Roth, 1999: 5). Most predicted short- to medium-term changes in this latitudinal range carry both negative and positive impacts on human activities so that neither can be identified as potentially dominant in the near future. For example, while opportunities for increased use of the Northeast and Northwest Passages should be beneficial for shipping this also has been raised as having potentially serious implications for national and international security.

The mid-latitude zone, from 30°–60°, is anticipated to warm more than the global average but less than the high latitudes. In model simulations, winter precipitation increases over Northern Europe and often also over Southern Europe (Kattenberg *et al.*, 1996: 337). Winter warming is predicted to be greater than summer, while summer rainfall decreases. Increases in floods are predicted for northern and Northwest Europe and droughts for Southern Europe (Watson *et al.*, 1997: 10). The main impacts are expected to be on unmanaged ecosystems, forests and agriculture. The reproductive success of many tree species would be reduced and both tree and plant mortality would increase. The extent and timing of forest dieback depends on the estimated sensitivity of the climatic response and actions taken to control GHG emissions.

Climatic variations altering rainfall patterns, and the length of growing seasons, will prevent subsistence agriculture in some regions (Henderson-Sellers, 1984). Precipitation may increase at higher mid-latitudes and decrease at lower mid-latitudes (Stern *et al.*, 1984: 340). Hansen *et al.* (1981) predict large regional climate variations and shifting precipitation patterns resulting in hot dry summers and wetter coastal areas for the continents. Bryson (1974) suggests that the changing static stability of the atmosphere will affect the latitude of subtropical anticyclones, and thus rainfall patterns.

Global agricultural studies, using double CO_2 equilibrium GCM scenarios, show lower-latitude and lower-income countries are more negatively impacted (Reilly, 1996: 429). The Villach workshop consensus report expected global food supplies, as a whole, to be maintained via adaptation based on agricultural research, except in the case of rapid warming. Negative effects on productivity in the lower latitudes (around 30°), due to greater evapotranspiration, may be balanced by positive effects in the higher latitudes (around 60°), due to a longer growing season. However, irrigated agriculture in the semi-arid areas of the mid-latitudes could be adversely affected, unless substantial offsetting irrigation developments are implemented. In addition, changes in regional agricultural production, as envisaged in North America, would require new infrastructure and abandoning some existing capital; they also have political implications where national boundaries are involved, and such adjustments suffer time lags of decades.

The semi-arid tropical regions, from 5°–35° north and south, already suffer from unevenly distributed seasonal average precipitation with high spatial and interannual variability. This latitudinal belt as a whole is expected to suffer reduced precipitation.

There has been a pronounced downward trend in precipitation since the early 1950s for this region, resulting in prolonged drought and aggravating the on-going desertification process. Future climatic changes could worsen these current problems.

In humid tropical regions global warming leads to a 5–20 per cent increase in rainfall. An increase in mean precipitation in the region of the Asian summer monsoon is consistently predicted by simulation models (Kattenberg *et al.*, 1996: 337). Water levels along coasts and rivers are increased by sea level rise, greater frequency of tropical storm surges, and rising peak run-off. Large areas of flooding and salinisation are likely to result. In addition, the spatial and temporal distribution of temperature and precipitation could change.

This broad qualitative picture provides a background within which sectors and key processes of change can be viewed. In particular, we can now add some more detail on expected sea level rise, changes in arid zones and the susceptibility of agricultural production. All of these have been implicated as among the areas of greatest concern.

Sea level rise

Average sea level has increased at 0.010–0.025 m per decade during the last century. Sea level rise is thus a current and continuing concern exacerbated because half of the global population inhabits coastal regions. During the twentieth century global average sea level rose between 0.1 and 0.2 m, according to tidal gauge data (IPCC Working Group I, 2001). An acceleration of sea level rise would occur as global warming melted land ice (mountain glaciers), caused thermal expansion of the oceans, and reduced the Greenland ice sheet. For example, Alpine glacier mass is predicted to have been reduced 95 per cent by 2100 (Watson *et al.*, 1997: 10). Changes in the Antarctic ice sheet are a major uncertainty discussed further under intertemporal impacts.

Estimates of sea level rise vary with the GHG emissions scenario, with a probable upper range of 0.90–1.70 m by 2100 (Thomas, 1986). The IPCC 1995 SAR estimates were much lower with best estimates of 0.38–0.55 m, because of lower predicted temperature changes, although the full range of projections was from 0.13–0.94 m and the 'business as usual' scenario predicted 0.50 m (Warrick *et al.*, 1996: 364). The TAR, despite higher temperature predictions, reduced estimates of glacial and ice sheet melt to a predicted rise of 0.09–0.88 m between 1990 and 2100, depending upon emissions scenario. A 0.50 m sea level rise, without adaptation or change in population, would put 92 million people at risk of flooding and a 1 m rise would increase this to 118 million, given current population distribution and density (Watson *et al.*, 1996: 9). Population growth would increase these figures dramatically.

Regional variations in sea level rise are expected due to variations in heating and ocean circulation changes. In addition, geological and geophysical processes cause vertical land movements and thus affect sea levels on local and regional scales. For example, in the British Isles uplift of the land as glaciers receded is responsible for ongoing rise in central northern Scotland of 3–6 mm per year; water loading, as the present continental shelf was flooded, creates a rate of depression of 3.8 mm per year in the south west; while neotectonic movements mean downwarping in the south east and uplift in the west (Goodess, Palutikof and Davies, 1992: 116). Thus, the impacts of general sea level rise can be dramatically different depending upon local circumstances.

Typical impacts of sea level rise would be beach and coastal margin erosion, loss of wetlands, increased frequency and severity of flooding, and damage to coastal structures and water management systems. Sea defence has been a long-term development for many low-lying industrialised countries, and some existing structures could be modified to accommodate up to a 1 m sea level rise at substantial but relatively small cost. These countries are generally able to adapt and are likely to only show serious concern as the 2 m mark is approached. For example, Goemans (1986) estimated the cost of protecting against a 1 m rise for the Netherlands, where extensive coastal protection already exists, at $4.4 thousand million. New sea defences in the UK to protect against up to a 1.5 m rise would cost around £5 thousand million, but still leave problems such as water logging of low-lying soils due to raised fresh groundwater levels (Parry, 1989: 35). In the USA the cost of maintaining shores under threat on the East coast has been estimated at ranging from $10–$100 thousand million, for a 1 m rise (Jaeger, 1989: 101). Primary impacts of a 1 m rise on the USA have been estimated to cause damages of $270–$475 thousand million, ignoring future development. These figures can be compared to a single storm event (Hurricane Andrew) which caused $20 thousand million in damages (Rogers, 1994: 185).

The impacts on industrially developed countries such as the USA are more serious as the rise becomes more extreme nearer the end of the century and into the following one. Park *et al.* (1986) have predicted a loss of 40–73 per cent of existing USA coastal wetlands by 2100. This might be reduced to 22–56 per cent if new wetlands were allowed to form on current lowland areas. A more extreme sea level rise of 5 m would flood 25 per cent of Louisiana and Florida, 10 per cent of New Jersey and many other lowlands throughout the world (Hansen *et al.*, 1981).

In contrast, industrially developing countries would generally suffer serious impacts from even a 1 m sea level rise or less. Flood disasters are particularly threatening for the delta regions of South Asia and Egypt and low-lying island communities. The UNEP has identified ten countries as most vulnerable to sea level rise: Bangladesh, Egypt, the Gambia, Indonesia, the Maldives, Mozambique, Pakistan, Senegal, Surinam and Thailand (Jacobson, 1990: 89). Egypt would have 12–15 per cent of its arable land area flooded, affecting 7.7 million people – 16 per cent of its population (Broadus *et al.*, 1986). In Bangladesh 8.5 million people would be affected (9 per cent of the nation's population) as a result of 11.5 per cent of the land area being flooded (Broadus *et al.*, 1986).

The Maldives are coral islands on average less than 1.5 m above sea level. Thus the population (177,000 people) could be totally displaced by even a small sea level rise and the encroachment of storm surges (Economist, 1986: 36). The Maldivians are in a situation typical of many low-lying island populations, e.g. Tokelau, the Marshall Islands, the Line Islands and Kiribati (Gribbin, 1990: 176). These islands along with the Bahamas have most of their land area below 3–4 m (Watson *et al.*, 1997: 13). Under a 1 m sea level rise, the Majuro atoll in the Marshall Islands would suffer erosion and land loss affecting 85 per cent of the area, while 12.5 per cent of Kiribati would be affected (Watson *et al.*, 1997: 13). Such island nations formed an international lobby group, the Alliance of Small Island States (AOSIS), which has actively pressed developed nations to control their GHG emissions (Grubb, 1995). In the negotiations leading to Kyoto they were demanding 20 per cent emissions reductions by 2005 as a starting point, but US opposition resulted in much weaker targets.

The ability of nations to adapt to sea level rise is determined by their capital resources and technical knowledge. Developed nations are therefore better equipped to respond, at least initially, to predicted sea level increases. Many less developed countries will find their current floods becoming worse with a direct impact in terms of human suffering, permanent dislocation and loss of life. As Jaeger (1989: 101) has stated: 'In developed countries, lowland protection against sea level rise will be costly. In developing countries without adequate technical and capital resources it may be impossible'.

Arid zones

The important arid zones of the world are found around latitude 30° north and south, where most of the large deserts are situated, e.g. the Sahara (north Africa), the Syrian desert and Arabia (west Asia), Death Valley and surrounding areas (USA), and the Australian deserts (Wallen, 1966). Only 12 nations are wholly arid while 27 nations have some territory within the arid zone but the larger part of their land area outside of it, as shown in table 3.3. The peripherally arid nations are those in this latter group for which aridity is significant only at the regional level.

Characteristically, the equilibrium of water, soil, geological and vegetative processes in arid lands is a delicate one, so that a slight shift in one aspect may initiate a disastrous chain of events (White, 1966). The scarcity and variability of rainfall are dominant elements in the complex of physical factors affecting arid lands. The natural limits of arid lands are set by climatic conditions influencing the surplus and deficit of water for plant growth. For example, under initial climate change, while cooler wetter New Zealand may gain agricultural productivity, Australia's relatively low latitude means particular vulnerability to impacts on its scarce water resources and crops growing near their temperature thresholds (Watson *et al.*, 1997: 10). High temperatures over long periods increase the energy available for evapotranspiration so that the potential water loss is greater than the amount available. Such high

Table 3.3 The arid nations

Description	No.	Area of nation arid or semi-arid (%)	Nations
Core	11	100	Bahrain, Djibouti, Egypt, Kuwait, Mauritania, Oman, Quater, United Arab Emirates, Saudi Arabia, Somalia, South Yemen
Predominately arid	23	75–99	Afghanistan, Algeria, Australia, Botswana, Cape Verde, Chad, Iran, Iraq, Israel, Jordan, Kenya, Libya, Mali, Morocco, Namibia, Niger, North Yemen, Pakistan, Senegal, Sudan, Syria, Tunisia, Upper Volta
Substantially arid	5	50–74	Argentina, Ethiopia, Mongolia, South Africa, Turkey
Semi-arid	9	25–49	Angola, Bolivia, Chile, China, India, Mexico, Tanzania, Togo, USA
Peripherally arid	18	<25	Berin, Brazil, Canada, Central African Republic, Ecuador, Ghana, Lebanon, Lesotho, Madagascar, Mozambique, Nigeria, Paraguay, Peru, Sri Lanka, former USSR, Venezuela, Zambia, Zimbabwe

Data source: Heathcote (1983: 9). © Longman Group Ltd. Reprinted by permission of Pearson Education Limited.

temperatures can intensify the chemical processes in a plant causing death. Extreme temperature may lead to crop failure, and also stress both animals and humans (Wallen, 1966). The swing from crop success to utter failure is quick and frequent and the greatest risk is in semi-arid areas.

Except for the USA, Australia and the desert oil-exporting nations, most arid or semi-arid nations have low levels of capital formation and/or technical expertise required to develop strategies to protect against drought or extreme variations in climate. A number of countries in areas prone to military conflict are dependent upon foreign water supplies and are therefore particularly sensitive to any reduction in domestic supplies, e.g. Cambodia, Eygpt, Iraq, Syria, Sudan (Watson, Zinyowera and Moss, 1996: 32). The predicted impacts on water resources in Latin America could be 'sufficient to lead to conflicts among users, regions and countries' (Watson *et al.*, 1997: 11). Water supply problems are exacerbated by aquifer depletion, urbanisation, contamination and land-use changes (e.g. deforestation). Sub-Saharan Africa appears most vulnerable to agricultural impacts and in recent decades has suffered more from severe famine and starvation than other regions; the area is also politically unstable. As Reilly (1996: 447) notes:

The region is already hot, and large areas are arid or semi-arid; average per capita income is among the lowest in the world and has been declining since

1980; more than 60 per cent of the population depends directly on agriculture; and agriculture is generally more than 30 per cent of gross domestic product.

Among the 19 countries classified as water-stressed, Africa has the most and is predicted to get more due to population growth and degradation of watersheds (Watson *et al.*, 1997: 6).

Agriculture

Agricultural impacts due to the enhanced Greenhouse Effect can be attributed to a CO_2 fertilisation effect, temperature/precipitation changes and inundation with associated salinisation of land due to sea level rise (Parry, 1990: 37). Assessing the economic impact of climate change on agriculture due to the first two causes typically follows the three idealised stages of modelling mentioned in the introduction to this chapter. First, the climatic alterations must be characterised and their agricultural-specific influences determined, e.g. precipitation, growing season, frequency and duration of extreme events. Second, these climatic predictions are linked to plant or animal science models, normally developed under experimental conditions, which describe the relationship between yield/output and environmental factors. Finally, changes in the yield, and ideally marketability, of the agricultural product, are fed into an economic model of the agricultural sector which may be linked to a model of the whole economy.

Most agricultural impact studies tend to concentrate upon crops, neglecting livestock losses or impacts, although these are also liable to be significant. For example, an increase in CO_2 from 340–700 ppm decreases nitrogen content of leaf material 10–30 per cent, which reduces the digestibility of the material lowering the weight gains for grazing animals (Parton, Ojima and Schimel, 1994: 135). Concentrating on crops alone can be misleading, as Maunder and Ausubel (1985: 95) show for the case of New Zealand where the value of sheep production is more important in terms of climatic monetary damages than the more climatically sensitive crop production, because crops accounted for only one sixth of the agricultural value of the wool industry. In general, livestock production will be affected by climatic change impacting grain prices, the prevalence and distribution of pests, the productivity of grazing and pasture, and direct effects on animal health (e.g. heat stress).

In terms of crops, some plants may benefit because an increase in CO_2 concentrations can boost plant growth. Plants of the C3 group (e.g. wheat, rice and soybean) are more responsive than C4 plants (e.g. maize, millet, sorghum and sugar cane) which include tropical crops mostly grown in Africa and most importantly maize. Pest plant species which are C3 weeds in C4 crops may benefit, particularly in tropical regions, while C4 weeds in C3 crops decline. The C3 group includes the more troublesome weeds for arable farming in north-west Europe (Parry, 1990: 30), but many of the world's worst weeds are C4 species (Reilly, 1996: 435). Rising CO_2

Table 3.4 World trade in cereals: top ten countries, 1999

	Importers			Exporters	
	100 million tons	*%*		*10 million tons*	*%*
Japan	278,133	10.7	USA	911,556	34.3
Mexico	135,928	5.2	France	348,590	13.1
Korea Republic	108,044	4.1	Australia	220,611	8.3
China	101,584	3.9	Canada	200,453	7.6
Egypt	96,637	3.7	Argentina	186,315	7.0
Brazil	90,783	3.5	Germany	100,775	3.8
Indonesia	85,986	3.3	China	75,525	2.8
Iran	84,386	3.2	Thailand	69,480	2.6
Italy	80,822	3.1	Ukraine	61,425	2.3
Russia	70,118	2.7	Vietnam	46,023	1.7
World	2,604,081	100.0	World	2,654,952	100.0

Source: Food and Agriculture Organisation of the United Nations (1993) table 38.

concentrations also improve plant water-use efficiency which can aid production in semi-arid regions where moisture limits growth. These changes have serious distributional consequences for agricultural production, but much depends upon field conditions, infrastructure and farming practices.

Evidence of the likely impacts was initially from glass-house experiments only (Parry, 1990), which substantially alter the growing environment raising questions as to their applicability under actual field conditions. Open-top chambers and some enclosed field experiments have since been conducted, but also alter the growing environment. Variations in experimental conditions are known to cause a wide range of responses. Meanwhile, few experiments have been conducted on perennials (tree fruits, coffee, tea, cocoa, bananas, grapes, many forage and pasture crops and other small fruits), especially the woody species (Reilly, 1996: 431).

The relative importance of different countries' production for world trade in cereals can be estimated from table 3.4. The dominant role of North America is clear with approximately 42 per cent of gross exports (this has been higher, e.g. 47 per cent in 1992) and the three largest European exporters accounted for a further 18.5 per cent (with the UK being the eleventh largest exporter at 1.6 per cent). According to Parry and Carter (1986: 270), climate impact studies generally agree that warming is detrimental to cereals in the main wheat-growing areas of Europe and North America, when agricultural adjustments are ignored. A 1°C increase in global mean temperature could reduce cereal yields by 1–9 per cent, and a 2°C increase could cause a 3–17 per cent decrease, holding precipitation constant. However, there is considerable room for variations in models, parameters, cultivars, GCM scenarios and overall economic modelling approaches which mitigate against any general conclusions.

Water stress is a major limiting factor for agricultural production world wide and therefore forms a central part in influencing crop losses or gains from rising concentrations of CO_2 and global warming. An increase in frequency, duration and severity of droughts in the Great Plains of the USA would lead to a more rapid depletion of the Ogallala aquifer (partial source of ground-water to eight western states). The semi-arid western and mid-western states in the USA have for some time been recognised as particularly susceptible to the effects of climate change on river systems (d'Arge, 1975). Large decreases in surface run-off (40–76 per cent) could accompany a 2°C temperature increase (Barbier, 1989: 24).

The effect of global warming due to a double CO_2-equivalent scenario on US agriculture in the western states has been estimated by Adams *et al.* (1988) to induce crop losses of $5.8 thousand million under the GISS model to $33.6 thousand million with the GFDL model (1982 US dollars), in the absence of technological adaptation or CO_2 fertilisation. Almost half of the consumers' surplus losses from climate change in the US fall on foreign consumers. Consumers in the US face slight to moderate price rises under most scenarios, but supplies are adequate to meet current and projected domestic demand. Adams *et al.* (1988: 348) note that climate change is not a food security issue for the US; even in the most extreme case their analyses indicate that the productive capacity of US agriculture will be maintained at a level that avoids major disruptions to the supply of the modelled commodities. However, as other authors have also found, exports experience major reductions. Rosenzweig and Daniel (1988: 6–22) predict declines in exported commodities of up to 70 per cent in some scenarios, assuming constant export demand. In the Adams *et al.* study, allowing crop yields to increase at the rate observed over 1955–87 ameliorates but fails to remove losses. Crosson (1989) has suggested history may be a poor guide in this respect because the environmental costs of agricultural production itself have been neglected but are rising, and the best land and most available water has already been brought into production. If, in addition to historical yield increases, demand is allowed to grow at population trend rates then losses actually increase despite supposed technological advances, $6.8 thousand million under the GISS model and $44.6 thousand million with the GFDL model. Another factor affecting the sensitivity of results is the CO_2 fertilisation effect which is shown to decrease losses with GFDL predictions and create gains under GISS; this is in the absence of demand growth and assumes double CO_2 concentrations although the climate scenario is due to all GHGs, i.e. a CO_2 equivalent scenario.

While arid regions of North America may suffer, the northern latitudes may simultaneously benefit from a longer growing season, and a shift northward and eastward in the agricultural belt. Agricultural adjustments could increase yields via the extension of winter wheat into Canada, a switch from hard to soft wheat in the Pacific Northwest due to greater precipitation, and an expansion of areas in fall-sown spring wheat in the southern latitudes due to higher winter temperatures (Rosenzweig, 1985: 380). Indeed Canadian scientists are generally optimistic about the consequences of the enhanced Greenhouse Effect upon their country, although believing others will suffer (Bray and von Storch, 1999). Kelejian and Varichek (1982: 262) believe the US to be slightly below optimal temperature for wheat and corn. They estimate a temperature increase of 1°C–2°C could cause a 22 per cent decrease in wheat and corn crops outside the US and a 5 per cent increase within the US. Such a negative effect on agriculture abroad would improve the position of US agricultural producers through exports. More generally, Oram (1985) points out that food-exporting countries would benefit substantially while grain reductions and higher prices cause food importers to suffer.

Higher temperatures tend to favour higher yields for cereal crops in regions where temperature limits the growing season. For example, in the central European region of the former USSR, wheat yields have been projected to increase a third under a double CO_2 scenario (Parry and Carter, 1986: 275). However, where cereal production is already drought prone, increased evapotranspiration and plant stress will lead to production declines. For example, a fifth to a third (depending on soil type) of the spring-sown wheat in Saskatchewan could be lost due to early-summer moisture stress. A 1°C increase in temperature and 10 per cent reduction in precipitation has been estimated to induce a 26 per cent reduction in corn and soybean yields and a 10 per cent reduction in wheat (Kokoski and Smith, 1987: 336). Smit *et al.* (1988: 512) reviewed several studies and concluded that a warmer climate could create a more favourable environment for wheat and grain corn in Canada, northern Europe, and the former USSR, and restrict opportunities in the US.

In the case of semi-arid regions of less developed countries the impact of climate on economic activities is severest in the agricultural sector of the desert and areas marginal to it, e.g. in Africa, the Sudan and Sahel. Oguirtoyirbo and Odiro (1979: 2) pointed out that areas marginal to the desert can give a false sense of security to their inhabitants during periods of successively wet years, but are highly vulnerable in periods of drought. Continued wet-year land use and livestock practices during droughts are a contributing factor to desertification.

Moderate, or worse, desertification has occurred in 80 per cent of the agricultural lands of the world's arid regions. Irrigated lands suffer waterlogging and salinisation, grazing lands lose plant cover, and rain-fed croplands are desertified by soil erosion. Those areas currently undergoing severe desertification are agricultural economies with the livelihood of their people being 27 per cent urban based, 51 per cent cropping based, and 22 per cent animal based. The population of the arid regions is approximately 700 million with 78 million living in areas where severe desertification has occurred. Among these people 50 million have been estimated as already suffering a loss in ability to support themselves and under pressure to migrate to overcrowded cities. The population of the moderately desertified portion of the arid lands is at least eight times that of the severely affected regions (Dregne, 1983: 19–21). Water quality, availability and sanitation are indeed much larger concerns with 1,300 million people worldwide suffering inadequate supplies of safe water and 2,000 million inadequate sanitation (Watson *et al.*, 1997: 3).

Climatic changes due to the enhanced Greenhouse Effect will be imposed upon the already fragile ecosystems of semi-arid regions. The prediction of reduced precipitation for the latitudinal zone from 5–35° north and south would, alone, aggravate the existing climatic problems of the arid regions. In addition, the temperature increase can be expected to add to crop and livestock stress and fatality. Agriculture is central to the economies of most non-oil exporting African countries, contributing 20–30 per cent of gross domestic product (GDP) in sub-Saharan Africa and 55 per cent of total African exports by value (Watson *et al.*, 1997: 7). The size and subsistence level of the population living in this region implies the possibility of a far greater cost than created by the expected shifts northward of agricultural production predicted for North America and Europe. A major factor in determining the impact of climate change on agriculture is the ability to implement agricultural adjustments. In this respect the industrially developed countries are better prepared to take advantage of any opportunities and handle negative impacts.

Climatic and soil resources have been estimated as unable to meet the food needs of the local populations over 22 per cent of the globe and for 11 per cent of the world population (Food and Agricultural Organisation (FAO) data reported in Parry, 1990: 3). The main areas in this susceptible category are: the Andean region, the Maghreb in north Africa, the mountain regions of south-west Asia, the Sahel and the Horn of Africa, the Indian subcontinent, and parts of mainland and insular south-east Asia. There are 65 low-income, food-deficit countries, with the greatest risk group being those who have failed to increase per capita food production in the past. Unfortunately, most of this latter group have extensive agricultural areas located in arid and semi-arid regions. As a result global climate change threatens to make a bad situation worse.

At the global scale, the failure of crops in one region may be balanced by productivity increases in other regions, as mentioned earlier for the mid latitudes. Newman and Picket (1974) suggested that generally an equilibrium climate obeys a law of conservation, born out by the history of global climatic variations. That is, whenever one large area gets too little precipitation, another gets too much. Thus, one strategy to respond to the problems of arid lands is to organise resource use to compensate for the inevitable shortages of production in one location by transfers of surpluses from other locations. While there have continued to be excess supplies of world food production this has failed to prevent 730 million people in industrially developing countries being denied enough energy from their diet to allow them an active working life (Dregne, 1983: 26) or 800 million from suffering chronic and seasonal malnourishment (Watson *et al.*, 1997: 4). As Sen (1986) has described, a lack of purchasing power and the incompatibility between non-monetary and monetary economic sectors can mean starvation even in the presence of food surpluses within a region, due to a misallocation of resources via the market system.

Overall studies on the impacts of climate change on agriculture have concentrated on a few principal grains important to North America and European farming sectors. Even these show the variability in predicted impacts on yield between countries, scenarios, methods of analysis and crops. Thus generalisation of the results across areas or climate change scenarios is difficult. Instead the IPCC 1995 report on agriculture identified vulnerability as a key concept while including a confidence level for their concluding statement on this subject.

> Vulnerability to climate change depends on physical and biological response but also on socioeconomic characteristics. Low-income populations depending on isolated agricultural systems, particularly dryland systems in semi-arid and arid regions, are particularly vulnerable to hunger and severe hardship. Many of these at-risk populations are found in Sub-Saharan Africa, South and Southeast Asia, as well as some Pacific Island countries and tropical Latin America (High Confidence).
>
> (Reilly, 1996: 430)

The IPCC 1997 special report on regional impacts emphasised 'concerns over the "potential serious consequences" of increased risk of hunger in some regions, particularly the tropics and subtropics' (Watson *et al.*, 1997: 4).

The response of unmanaged ecosystems

From the viewpoint of ecosystems functions, global climate can create stress which shows up in the composition of species rather than functional collapse. Species dynamics, and so biodiversity, can be more sensitive to stress than processes thus implying some notion of 'functional redundancy' (Schindler, 1990). This is similar to the concept of substitution amongst economic inputs to a production process and implies that the most vulnerable ecosystem functions are those for which few species are available to carry out that function. Thus the resilience of food webs, energy flows and biogeochemical cycles is dependent upon the degree of functional redundancy and by implication the extent of biological diversity (already in decline).

Biota face two major differences concerning their ability to adapt to climate change compared to the past 10 million years. First, the rate of change is predicted to be faster than flora and fauna have ever experienced; the NCAR model predicts warming 50 times faster than in the past (Schneider, Mearns and Gleick, 1992). Second, the response is required in a highly modified environment. The ability of organisms to adapt is limited by increasing human pressure on habitat, human predation of roaming wildlife and the creation of engineered physical barriers, e.g. reservoirs, roads, cities, farms and plantations. Terrestrial biota are confined to parks and reserves and are locked in by human populations. Thus, whether climate fluctuations are colder or warmer, they will change and stress natural ecosystems, bringing into question current conservation strategies and emphasising the importance of non-reserve habitat.

Climatic warming will affect both the latitudinal range within which species survive and also shift upwards the altitude at which current habitats occur (Peters and Darling, 1985). For example, under a double CO_2-equivalent scenario causing a 3°C warming, ranges would move hundreds of kilometres north in the Northern Hemisphere and altitude shift 500 m upward (Murphy and Weiss, 1992). A short climb in altitude corresponds to a major shift in latitude, e.g. 500 m elevation approximates to a 250 km altitude shift. In this way, some high elevation species may be 'squeezed out' as habitats are reduced to fragments on mountain summits.

A diverse range of influences on species mix will be introduced. As climate changes so will predation rates, parasitism, competitive interactions, reproduction rates, lethality (e.g. coral death) and the introduction of 'exotic' competitors. Shifting range means separation of species and communities dependent upon colonisation ability and the influence of both manmade and natural barriers to dispersal.

The impacts for marine ecosystems have received little attention. One exception is Alexander (1993) who describes the importance of continued sea ice to the arctic marine food chain. If sea ice were to melt marine mammals would lose ice floes on which they rest, travel and pup, and the effective growing season for phytoplankton, which supports the food chain, would be significantly shortened. The IPCC report on oceans notes the significant negative impact of increased temperature on coral which causes bleaching and is potentially irreversible. If temperatures rapidly reach 2°C (expected before 2100) then neither mitigation nor adaptation is deemed possible (Ittekkot, 1996: 283).

Overall the unpredictability of climate change impacts on unmanaged ecosystems raises considerable reason for concern, and Mendelsohn and Rosenberg (1994: 27) see this as the strongest justification for halting, or at least moderating, the emissions of GHGs. The impacts on unmanaged ecosystems will include: shifting their geographic location, changing the mix of species, and altering their ability to provide a wide range of benefits upon which societies rely for their continued existence (Watson *et al.*, 1997: 2). As climate forcing becomes more extreme so humans will be preoccupied with trying to adapt their own economic and social systems and those ecosystems they already attempt to manage. This may prove a short-sighted strategy as the degradation of ecosystems and functions reveal how susceptible human society is to unforeseen changes and the dangers of assuming systems are unconnected.

Intertemporal impacts of global warming

The literature on the enhanced Greenhouse Effect has largely focused upon the possible impacts within a hundred years. Initially attention was driven by the predictions of GCMs and these used an arbitrary equilibrium scenario of double CO_2 which might be achieved by mid-century and certainly within a century.

Table 3.5 Time scales of processes influencing the climate system

	Time scale	
	Minimum	*Maximum*
Turnover of capital stock responsible for emissions of GHGs (without premature retirement)	Years	Decades
Stabilisation of atmospheric concentrations of long-lived GHGs given a stable level of GHG emissions	Decades	Millennia
Equilibration of the climate system given a stable level of GHG concentrations	Decades	Centuries
Equilibration of sea level given a stable climate	Centuries	Centuries
Restoration/rehabilitation of damaged or disturbed ecological systems	Decades	Centuries
Changes such as species extinction or the reconstruction and re-establishment of some disturbed ecosystems	Infinite (irreversible)	Infinite (irreversible)

Source: Adapted from Watson *et al.* (1996: 4) box 2.

Most projections of IPCC scientific assessments have been for the years 2050 and 2100 (Denman, Hofmann and Marchant, 1996: 489). The 2001 report again appears restricted, arbitrarily, to 2100 with some side-remarks as to possibilities beyond that time horizon.[1] Yet major concerns are the processes of change rather than change at fixed points and for changes over timescales which are much longer. Somewhat paradoxically this is apparent from the 1995 IPCC report of Working Group II (on impacts). Table 3.5 reproduces their estimates of the timescales of processes influencing the climate system while adding those left implicit for the last category.

In fact the minimum times for some of the processes mentioned in table 3.5 are optimistic. A substantial turnover in the capital stock responsible for GHG emissions is only expected to start around 2020 making the minimum here decades (Lahidji, Michalski and Stevens, 1999: 9–10). Stabilisation of atmospheric concentrations is unlikely to occur within decades due to the slow response of governments to agree and enforce the substantial emissions reductions required. The prior assumption of a stable level of GHG emissions (at any level) is unlikely to be achieved in decades.

The debate on impacts thus falls into those expected to occur within the twenty-first century and those beyond. As the timescales show events are irreversibly being set in motion. That is, given the level of emissions reductions likely over the coming decades atmospheric concentrations will continue to increase and the chain of climate forcing events and resulting impacts will be set in motion into the distant future. The next section looks at the case for short-term gains from initial climate change which is followed by impacts in the medium to long term and an emphasis of the rate as well as timing and scale of change. A separate sub-section follows dedicated to impacts from sea level rise as temperature forcing becomes more extreme. Note, the range given for average global temperature change by 2100 under TAR is given as 1.4°C to 5.8°C from 1990, which on adding warming already achieved from preindustrial times to 1990 (about 0.5°C) gives expected warming of 1.9°C to 6.3°C by 2100.

The coming decades: a time of beneficial impacts?

While the regional impacts show the potential for negative consequences, for some regions, others may gain so that there appears to be a time during which aggregate benefits from continuing current levels of GHG emissions dominate costs. In the past an argument has been put forward in favour of deliberately increasing mean global temperature to reap the benefits of delayed glaciation and increased agricultural range. Callendar, who is normally cited with regard to making the connection between anthropogenic CO_2 emissions and increased temperatures, held this view.

> In conclusion it may be said that the combustion of fossil fuel, whether it be peat from the surface or oil from 10,000 feet below, is likely to prove beneficial to mankind in several ways, besides the provision of heat and power. For instance the above mentioned small increases of mean temperature would be important at the northern margin of cultivation, and the growth of favourably situated plants is directly proportional to the carbon dioxide pressure {Brown and Escombe, 1905}. In any case the return of the deadly glaciers should be delayed indefinitely.
>
> (Callendar, 1938: 236)

More recently, the same line of reasoning has been expressed by Crosson (1989) who suggests the costs of stopping warming should be weighed against the potential losses from doing so too soon.

Most obviously, society benefits from the use of fossil fuels and derived products, but Calendar and Crosson are pointing to potential benefits from actually enhancing the Greenhouse Effect. Indeed, there is some evidence for benefits from initial warming (although as noted in chapter 2 the glaciation argument is seriously flawed). In the 1970s an average global warming of 0.5°C was predicted to produce net benefits in terms of heating, agriculture, and water use, estimated to be approximately 16 per cent of the global economy at the time (d'Arge, 1975). Optimists can also look to emphasise various other benefits. For example, research suggests that Great Lakes fish may become more productive, with Walleye yields in Lake Michigan increasing 29–33 per cent, although trout may simultaneously decrease by 2–6 per cent (Mlot, 1989: 145). In fact, this mixture of gains and losses seems more typical, with the argument then being as to whether one outweighs the other (e.g. are the increases in Walleye in some sense preferable to the decrease in trout?).

Fitzharris (1996: 259) discusses the potential benefits from less sea and river ice and fewer icebergs. Shorter winters and the disappearance of icebergs and sea ice could benefit oil and gas exploration and extraction and reduce downtime; although an increased frequency of extreme waves will require redesign of coastal and offshore structures. Reductions in ice are also expected to save on the need for ice-breaking, e.g. in Russia and a lesser extent North America. Safer shipping channels include the potential for tourist ships and sightseeing around the Arctic and Antarctic, although, Fitzharris notes winter tourism will suffer elsewhere. Despite increases in precipitation the cover, depth and quality of snow will be reduced adversely affecting winter tourism (e.g. skiing) in most alpine countries. This is cited as costing the US ski industry $1 thousand million. Nordhaus (1994: 57) has countered this argument by pointing out that there could be gains for warm weather leisure industries such as camping.

Agricultural impacts have featured prominently in the work of those citing benefits from the enhanced Greenhouse Effect. Idso (1983) maintains that increased levels of atmospheric CO_2 will increase future well-being via crop fertilisation, supplying more food for a growing population. This is achieved if escalated CO_2 concentrations enhance crop productivity by simultaneously increasing rates of photosynthesis and reducing water use via decreased transpiration. According to Seneft (1990: 23) the range of projected yield increases extends from 16 per cent for corn to 60 per cent for cotton when the concentration of CO_2 is doubled (ceteris paribus), and, if combined with a 3.3°C global temperature rise, crop yields could increase by 56 per cent. Experimental work in hot houses by Kimball (1986) shows the following rise in yields for a doubling of CO_2: C4 plants 14 per cent, C3 grain crops 31 per cent, C3 non-agricultural plants 34 per cent, cotton 118 per cent. While these may represent potential benefits they would (as mentioned earlier) also themselves imply serious economic adjustments which some countries and regions will view unfavourably, e.g. agricultural production declining in one region and increasing elsewhere. Working Group II of the IPCC has pointed out that the full effects of changes in temperature and precipitation lag the effects of a change in atmospheric GHG composition by a number of decades and hence 'the positive effects of CO_2 precede the full effects of changes in climate' (Watson *et al.*, 1997: 3).

Thus, while benefits will accrue to some members of the current generation these are transitory and should not be overemphasised or unqualified. For example, much has been made of the CO_2 fertilisation effect mentioned above. However, the positive CO_2 fertilisation effect will only prove beneficial while CO_2 remains a dominant gas in climate forcing. If other gases become relatively more important, this benefit will diminish while negative impacts of global warming on crop yields increase. Erickson (1993) has criticised the claims made for the fertilisation effect on several grounds and these are discussed more fully in the next chapter as an example of scientific uncertainty. If only some of his arguments are correct there would be no fertilisation effect and, as economic models have predicted, economic gains become losses. For example, gains of $645 million become losses of over $2 thousand million for four US states in Easterling *et al.* (1992), and crop yield is negative in all countries without the fertilisation effect in Rosenzweig *et al.* (1992), while in Adams (1989) the US sees gains of $9.5 thousand million turn to losses of $6.5 thousand million using the GISS GCM model and losses of $10.5 thousand million become losses of $35.9 thousand million under the GFDL model.

Care also needs to be taken in classifying outcomes as positive or beneficial. For example, the growth in the marine instruments industry in order to facilitate research and monitoring of climate change is noted as a positive outcome in the 1995 IPCC report on oceans (Ittekkot, 1996: 282). In fact this is a cost of global climate change as are all the current research resources, time and energy which are being devoted to the subject.

Adapting to future climate change: faster and further

In general, predictions of climatic change beyond the next 100 years are scarce because the majority of evidence concerning global warming initially limited itself to an equivalent double CO_2 scenario. More recent reports (e.g. by the IPCC) have tended to restrict themselves to the time up to 2100 while acknowledging the commitment to climate change beyond this time period which will result from GHG emissions. However, there is, of course, no reason for global climate change to stop at CO_2 equivalent level, double CO_2 or in 2100. Indeed, past and continuing GHG emissions create a stock in the atmosphere making some global warming irreversible over coming centuries. A change in the IPCC scientific summary under TAR is the recognition given to some of the long-term influences of GHG emissions and the potential impact on sea level rise over 1,000 years (IPCC Working Group I, 2001: 17). Long-term sea level rise is discussed separately in the next section.

The lifetime of CO_2 in the atmosphere, biosphere and upper ocean combined is hundreds of years with some permanent increase (Houghton, Jenkins and Ephraums, 1990: 8). Emissions of GHGs prior to 1985 have already committed Earth to a warming of 0.9–2.4°C, of which about 0.6°C has been experienced. The warming yet to be experienced from those emissions is 0.3–1.9°C, and is unavoidable (Ciborowski, 1989). As shown in chapter 2, emissions of the principal GHGs are increasing at rates between 0.3 and 4.0 per cent per year. Within 50 years we are likely to create an irreversible increase of 1.5–5.0°C, and in the 10 years following that a further 1.5–5.0°C increase. As Cline (1992) reports, a sixfold increase in CO_2 has been estimated by 2250 and an eightfold increase by 2275 associated with central estimates of 7.5°C and 10°C respectively. Beyond this point the role of ocean uptake is hoped to be our saviour with CO_2 levelling out at 3.5 times pre-industrial levels in 750 years time, given that this is a stable equilibrating system. The implication is of continually rising temperatures and associated damages for at least the next 250 years followed by 500 years of 'stabilisation'.

In the absence of emissions reductions both the extent and rate of GHG increases can be expected to grow. The speed of change has been neglected because the focus has been on equilibrium modelling. However, the rate of temperature increase will presumably accelerate with emissions and atmospheric concentrations. The implications of the rate of this change has also been relatively neglected in impact assessment and economic studies despite being recognised as central to the ability of human and natural systems to adapt.

Abrahamson (1989: 10) estimated, given 'business as usual' gas emissions, that global warming is proceeding at between 0.15°C and 0.50°C per decade. The consensus projection among scientists for the rate of heating during the next few decades, accounting for all delaying factors, was 0.30°C per decade (Firor, 1989: 12–13) prior to the inclusion of sulphate aerosols in the models which might reduce this to 0.20°C per decade (Hadley Centre, 1995). Although, the mitigating role of aerosols was revised downwards by the IPCC TAR adding 2.30°C to their 2100 upper estimate.

Of course the average rate of change masks diurnal, seasonal, altitudinal and regional variations. The average increase in night-time daily minimum air temperatures was 0.20°C per decade between 1950 and 1993, compared with 0.10°C per decade for the increase in daily maximum air temperatures (IPCC Working Group I, 2001: 2). Global average temperatures of the lowest 8 km of the atmosphere have been estimated to be changing at only 0.05°C ± 0.10°C per decade, but at the surface are increasing at 0.10–0.20°C per decade (IPCC Working Group I, 2001: 4). Faster warming has been predicted at the poles and historical measurements on the Antarctic Peninsula show a warming of 0.56°C per decade for a total 2.50°C since 1945 (Vaughan and Doake, 1996: 328). The IPCC TAR predicts that nearly all land areas will warm more rapidly than the global average, especially at northern high latitudes in winter. In particular, warming in northern North America and northern and central Asia exceeds the global average by 40 per cent (IPCC Working Group I, 2001).

Assessing the expected timing of temperature increases from available sources becomes problematic because of the emphasis on the doubling of CO_2 or its equivalent. Thus dates have tended to be associated with temperatures expected from such a doubling. In the 1980s there were predictions of a temperature rise of 2°C as soon as 2010 if N_2O and CFCs were to grow at 2 per cent per annum. The best-guess scenario for the date of such a warming according to the EPA was 2040, and under some scenarios this was pushed back to 2070 (Marland and Rotty, 1985). In the 1990 IPCC report data could be gleaned for the next century on changes in temperature and sea level rise up to 2070 from 1990 and preindustrial levels, as shown in table 3.6. Constructing a comparable table from the 1995 IPCC report proved more difficult as shown in table 3.7. During the intervening period the process of producing the reports entered into the international political negotiating field, see chapter 1, and this appeared to affect the presentation (especially in policymakers summaries). Comparing tables 3.6 and 3.7 shows a clear moderation in the expected immediacy of rises in temperature and sea level. What remained clear was the large increase in temperature expected by the end of the twenty-first century, i.e. in the

Table 3.6 IPCC 1990 'business as usual' sea level and temperature increases: 2030 and 2070

	Range	Best guess
Warming by 2030		
From 1765	1.3°C to 2.8°C	2.0°C
From 1990	0.7°C to 1.5°C	1.1°C
Sea level by 2030		
From 1990	0.08 to 0.29 m	0.18 m
Warming by 2070		
From 1765	2.2°C to 4.8°C	3.3°C
From 1990	1.6°C to 3.5°C	2.4°C
Sea level by 2070		
From 1990	0.21 to 0.71 m	0.44 m

Data sources: Bretherton, Bryan and Woods (1990: 177); Warrick and Oerlemans (1990: 276).

Table 3.7 IPCC 1995 'best estimate' sea level and temperature increases to 2050 and 2100

	Range	Best guess
Warming by 2050		
From 1990	?	?
Sea level by 2050		
From 1990	0.07 to 0.39 m	0.20 m
Warming by 2100		
From 1990	1.5°C to 4.5°C	2.0°C
From late 19th century[a]	1.8°C to 5.1°C	?
Sea level by 2100		
From 1990	0.20 to 0.86 m	0.49 m
From 1890s[b]	0.30 to 1.11 m	?

Data sources: Warrick *et al.* (1996: 381, 384); Nicholls *et al.* (1996: 143).

Notes: a calculated by adding estimated past temperature change to predicted future range;
              b calculated by adding observed sea level rise for the last 100 years to predicted range.

order of 2°C over 1990 levels, while temperatures were generally regarded as already being 0.5°C warmer due to the enhanced Greenhouse Effect. This alone brings into question the ability of natural and human systems to adapt. Under the 2001 IPCC report the temperatures are higher and sea level rise slightly lower (IPCC Working Group I, 2001).

The need to consider the timing of impacts emphasises the speed as well as the extent of global climatic change and thus the time within which systems must adapt. As temperature continues to increase, any net benefits will diminish if only because of the large adaptation costs implied. Sub-sectors, activities and human infrastructure most sensitive to climate change include: agroindustry, energy demand, renewable energy supply, construction, transportation, flood mitigation, and infrastructure in coastal zones and permafrost regions (Watson *et al.*, 1996: 9). In fact the need for adaptation, as opposed to preventing climate change, has been internationally accepted. The UN Framework Convention on Climate Change recognises this by aiming for stabilisation of GHG concentrations to allow adaptation, see Article 2 quoted in full in chapter 1. The Convention goes on to discuss adaptation under Article 4 (e) which calls upon all parties to:

> Cooperate in preparing for adaptation to the impacts of climate change; develop and elaborate appropriate and integrated plans for coastal zone management, water resources and agriculture, and for the protection and rehabilitation of areas, particularly in Africa, affected by drought and desertification, as well as floods.

The discussion has clearly shifted from an earlier concern for preventing climate change to accepting some unspecified level of change which is meant to 'allow ecosystems to adapt naturally to climate change, to ensure that food production is not threatened and to enable economic development to proceed in a sustainable manner' (Article 2).

Agriculture will need to alter, and technological optimists may hold out faith in genetic engineering. However, thorough analysis of adaptive capacity has for some time been lacking for the agricultural sector (e.g. noted by Parry, 1990). The 1995 IPCC report argues that socio-economic factors will be a key determinant of agricultural adaptation rather than lack of technical options (Reilly, 1996). They also estimate the time frame within which most adaptive strategies (e.g. new crop adoption, irrigation equipment, variety development) have been adopted in the past as being in the order of decades, and for dams and irrigation systems 50–100 years. Climate change implies a different mix and range of cultivars, species and ecosystems. Thus, the extent to which human systems are perceived to suffer depends upon their perceived ability to adapt to the changing environment.

Agriculture and, particularly, forestry are more susceptible to serious declines if climatic change occurs rapidly (for reviews of impacts on forestry see Shands and Hoffman, 1987; Dale and Rauscher, 1994). For example, in North America each 1°C rise in temperature translates into a range shift of about 100–150 km, while the rate of northward dispersal of trees under past warming, shown by fossil records, is 10–45 km a century, with Spruce the fastest at 200 km (Roberts, 1989). That is, historical adaptation shows most of these trees would struggle to shift range in line with changes expected from a 0.5°C temperature rise over a century (i.e. 50–75 km). Table 3.7 shows the IPCC SAR best estimate for 2100 as 2.0°C which would be a challenge even for Spruce trees to match given associated range shifts. Under the current predictions almost all forest species in North America will expand into colder northern climates at slower rates than their current range becomes uninhabitable (Davis and Zabinski, 1992). In general the functioning and composition of forests will be significantly altered and some forests will completely disappear under a mean increase of as little as 1.0°C (Kirschbaum and Fischlin, 1996: 97).

Rainfall is the primary determinant of vegetative structure and trees only occur where annual rainfall exceeds 300 mm (Woodward, 1992). Boreal forests have been predicted to decline by 37 per cent for a 3°C warming (Emanuel, Shugart and Stevenson, 1985). An increase in the frequency of fires would cause a rapid alteration in forest structure in the US (Franklin *et al.*, 1992) and current species may fail to re-establish themselves in the aftermath due to the change in climatic conditions. Meanwhile unmanaged ecosystems will be forced to adapt or perish.

Future sea level rise: an example of commitment to extreme events

As far as terrestrial ecosystems are concerned, costs will escalate as the ability to adapt is restricted by the absolute size and increasing rate of sea level rise. An increase in the frequency of 6 m waves from 16 to 39 per cent of the time is predicted for the Beaufort sea due to warming melting ice (Fitzharris, 1996), and this raises the question of how large and general perturbations of the natural system will materialise. Increases in the frequency and extent of storm surges and extreme weather events will exacerbate the impacts of sea level rise. About 46 million people are living in areas currently at risk from flooding due to annual storm surges (Watson *et al.*, 1996: 9; Watson *et al.*, 1997: 5). Even moderate levels can have serious regional impacts. For example, several Chesapeake Bay islands and associated towns were washed away over the past 100 years due to a 30 cm local average sea level rise (Peters and Lovejoy, 1992: 9). In the longer term the major concern is for melting of the land ice in Greenland and Antarctica.

Studies suggest the rate of change of sea level will be relatively small in the first quarter of the twenty-first century compared to the last quarter, and this is true for a variety of underlying emissions scenarios, as shown in table 3.8. Non IPCC studies estimate the absolute rise at between two-thirds of a metre to over 3.5 m by 2100 (Thomas, 1986; Titus, 1989). Thomas (1986) gives a 2.3 m rise by 2100 as the upper limit. A more conservative scenario results in a sea level rise of 0.3 m by 2025, and 0.9–1.7 m by 2100, which is in line with the studies in table 3.8. In comparison, the IPCC reports give much lower estimates, as was shown in tables 3.6 and 3.7, predicting a sea level rise of less than a metre during the next century.

However, earlier IPCC best estimates have been noted by Goodess *et al.* (1992: 120) to underestimate actual sea-level rise over the past hundred years. The IPCC sea level rise results mainly from thermal expansion while the contribution from ice sheets is regarded as minor but 'a major source of uncertainty' which can make a very large difference in sea rise estimates (Warrick *et al.*, 1996: 364). They also note (p.381) that direct comparisons of these apparently low estimates with other studies (and previous IPCC reports) is complicated due to non-comparable assumptions

Table 3.8 Estimated sea level rise to the year 2100

Study	Scenario	Projected sea level rise at future dates (metres)				
		2000	*2025*	*2050*	*2075*	*2100*
Hoffman *et al.* (1986)						
	High	0.055	0.210	0.550	1.910	3.680
	Low	0.035	0.100	0.200	0.360	0.570
EPA (1983)						
	High	0.171	0.550	1.170	2.120	3.450
	Low	0.048	0.130	0.230	0.380	0.560

Source: After Titus (1989: 169) figure 12.2.

(e.g. emissions scenarios, concentrations, radiative forcing and climate sensitivity).

Whatever the level, much of the rise over the next hundred years has been determined already by past changes in radiative forcing (due to lags in the response of oceans and ice masses). This same delayed reaction means, even after any stabilisation in atmospheric concentrations of GHGs, that sea level will continue to rise for many centuries.

The Antarctic region may reduce sea level rise due to increased snow accumulation, as long as the ice sheets remain stable and avoid disintegration. The 1990 IPCC report cites predictions of Antarctica changes as increasing ice accumulation up to 100 years, reducing sea level rise by 10 cm, followed by relatively small positive contributions to sea level rise of 40 cm over 200 years and a further 30 cm rise over 300 years (Warrick and Oerlemans, 1990: 274). However, the West Antarctic Ice Sheet has been regarded as a special case and could disintegrate, although the IPCC reports have regarded this as unlikely before the end of the twenty-first century (Warrick and Oerlemans, 1990: 261; Warrick *et al.*, 1996: 364). By comparison with other sources these estimates appear conservative and neglect the increasing possibility of a disintegration of the West Antarctic Ice Sheet after 2100. Disintegration of Antarctic ice shelves appears to be on-going due to warming trends (Vaughan and Doake, 1996). The Larsen A Antarctic Ice Shelf took a dramatic step forward when it broke apart during a storm in January 1995. In February 1998 a third of the Larsen B Antarctic Ice Shelf (an area three times Manhattan Island) broke away (Mazza and Roth, 1999). The disintegration of such ice shelves has no direct impact on sea level as they are floating in the sea already, but indirect 'changes in the interconnected grounded ice will affect sea level in ways that cannot be predicted at present' (Warrick *et al.*, 1996: 397).

Hansen *et al.* (1981: 965) have predicted the relatively rapid disintegration of the West Antarctic Ice Sheet, which is grounded below sea level, if temperature in this vicinity were to increase by 5°C. Deglaciation could then require a century or less and cause a sea level rise of 5–6 m. They estimated a 2°C global warming would be sufficient to ensure a 5°C warming at West Antarctica. The IPCC TAR assumes greater stability (while noting the dependence on numerous assumptions) and suggests the West Antarctic Ice Sheet could add 3 m to sea level rise only over a millennium but give no associated temperatures (IPCC Working Group I, 2001: 17).

The rapid final disintegration of the 1,300 km² Larsen A Ice Shelf over 50 days in 1995 produced thousands of small icebergs in a plume 200km long (Vaughan and Doake, 1996). This raised serious questions over the understanding of the processes involved in the stability of these structures. In their review of the impacts of warming in the Antarctic, Vaughan and Doake (1996: 330) concluded:

> We have still, however, to determine the precise mechanisms whereby the atmospheric warming had such a catastrophic effect on the ice shelves of the Antarctic Peninsula but it is clear that ice shelves cannot survive periods of warming that last more than a few decades.

The Larsen B has since begun serious calving and is expected to disappear soon. This has led to the conclusion that after retreat beyond a critical limit ice shelves may disintegrate rapidly (Doake *et al.*, 1998).

Vaughan and Doake (1996) noted that other ice shelves are threatened by continued warming, although the Filchner-Ronne and Ross ice shelves, which may stabilise the West Antarctic Ice Sheet, are not immediately threatened because they estimated that a further warming of 10°C is required. If warming were to proceed in this region as over the last half century this would take about 200 years. Since the best estimate of the IPCC's SAR was at least four times that rate, and that of the TAR higher still, such destabilisation can be expected sooner than the authors suggest.

Due to delays in climate forcing the full effect of an equilibrium warming on sea level may take centuries. Polar warming of several times the global mean could create a positive feedback in which higher temperatures melt snow and ice reducing the albedo causing higher temperatures and so on (Stern *et al.*, 1984: 338–41). Greenland is potentially another major ice source for sea level rise representing about 5 m but is currently in balance between loss and accumulation; if, as is possible, future warming were to tip this balance collapse is estimated to take several hundred years (Grumbine, 1993). The Greenland ice sheet becomes a net contributor to sea level rise under a 1°C climatic warming (Warrick *et al.*, 1996: 377 table 7.5). Temperatures in Greenland are expected to be up to three times average warming. The IPCC TAR estimates that a 3°C rise in Greenland over a millennium would melt the ice sheet almost completely contributing 7 m to sea level rise, while 5.5°C sustained would allow Greenland itself to add a further 3 m. On the basis of current decadal temperature increases the 3°C rise in Greenland could be achieved as early as 2030 and certainly before 2100 (Grumbine, 1993).

As the IPCC TAR notes, thousands of years after climate has been stabilised ice sheets will continue to react to climate warming and so contribute to sea level rise

(IPCC Working Group I, 2001). Melting of land-based ice sheets over East Antarctica might occur over thousands of years with the potential to raise sea levels by 70 m (Hansen *et al.*, 1981), but East Antarctica is considered stable being an extremely large ice and land mass ringed by mountains. In the very long-term sea level is dominated by glacial and inter-glacial cycles, with the former having caused drops in the order of 130 m and the later rises of 6 m over present levels. The next glaciation is due in 55,000 years' time, if unaffected by the enhanced Greenhouse Effect. Interactions between the enhanced Greenhouse Effect and glacial cycles are discussed in chapter 2.

Clearly, the more extreme and rapid the temperature increases, the greater are the costs and the fewer are the benefits. Thus, not only will the damages of preceding generations' GHG releases be placed upon those in the distant future, but the cost of continuing to release those gases will escalate. Overall detrimental welfare effects can be expected to fall upon our descendants, as characterised in figure 3.1.

Conclusions

Past burning of fossil fuels has committed the Earth to substantial climatic change over the next century, while continued emissions of GHGs accelerate the potential for even greater warming. Overall the variability in climate and precipitation predicted from simulation models at the regional level is far greater than that at the global scale. In reviewing the available evidence for the 1995 IPCC report, Kattenberg *et al.* (1996: 344) concluded: 'Considering all models, at the 10^4–10^6 km^2 scale, temperature changes due to CO_2 doubling varied between $+0.6°C$ and $+7°C$ and

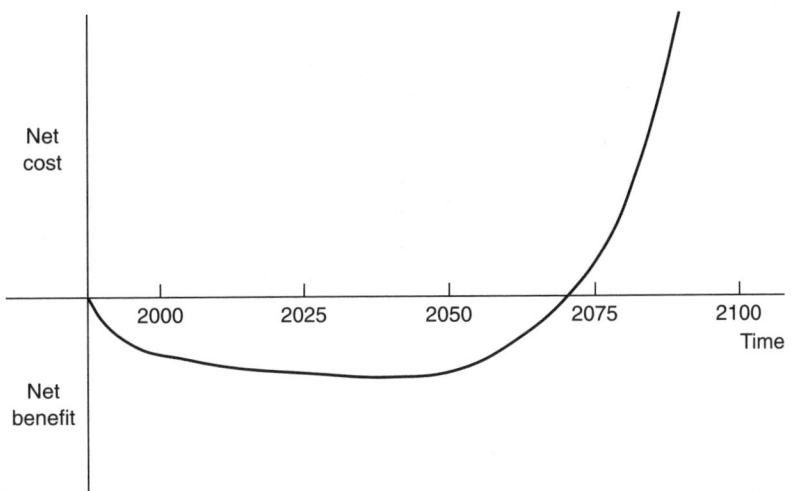

Figure 3.1 Long-term net cost of the enhanced Greenhouse Effect: a qualitative picture
Source: after d'Arge *et al.* 1982.

precipitation changes varied between −35 per cent and + 50 per cent of control run values, with a marked inter-regional variability'. The potential regional effects combine numerous positive and negative impacts. Global warming would alter precipitation patterns, evapotranspiration, and the length of growing seasons, affecting food supplies. The resulting impacts include changing crop and forest growing regions, raising sea level, spreading disease and pests, and reducing the number of animal species.

Thus, as has been previously recognised, the benefits or costs of induced climatic change will be unevenly distributed between nations (d'Arge, Schulze and Brookshire, 1982; Broadus *et al.*, 1986; Kosobud and Daly, 1987; Glantz, 1990; d'Arge and Spash, 1991). In particular, sea level rise and changes in semi-arid regions imply greater costs for the developing nations of the world. Even given imprecise regional projections, the general direction of change can be estimated from available information, i.e. most areas will be warmer and soil moisture will decrease in continental interiors. The impact will be pronounced in temperate and arctic regions where temperature increases are projected to be relatively large. Regions and populations at risk and susceptible to climate change can be identified. For example, in a regional analysis, Watson *et al.* (1997: 6) find that 'Africa is the continent most vulnerable to the impacts of projected changes because widespread poverty limits adaptation capabilities'. Similarly, an increase in the rate of sea level rise, storm surges and precipitation can clearly be identified as threatening populations and capital in low-lying areas both in developing and developed industrial economies (i.e. including cities such as Venice and London).

As is apparent from this brief review, economists need to be concerned with how climate change will affect the welfare of different economies, nations and groups. Even beneficial agricultural impacts will change the comparative advantage of producing nations and so affect world trade. Another aspect of work in this area is the impact of policy responses to climate change on world trade, e.g. carbon taxes. Strangely, some work in this area labels environmental policy as a potential source of trade tensions (Whalley, 1991), neglecting the fact that such policy is in fact aimed at removing impacts upon trade relations previously created by pollution. This distorted perspective arises because the polluted environment is assumed to be the status quo and the costs of policy intervention are considered while ignoring the benefits. Manne and Richels (1992) provide another example of providing policy advice in the total absence of discussion of the impacts of GHGs. In regard to benefits, a major policy problem occurs where they fall outside of the country incurring the costs of pollution control, the standard economic pollution externality. Adams and Crocker (1991: 310) have shown that improving air quality in the USA has international trade implications which actually benefit non-US citizens by increasing their consumers' surplus. Thus, in order to recognise the full trade impact of global climate change, economic analysts must avoid concentrating upon the potential for carbon taxes to fall heavily on industrially developed countries and go beyond the comparative safety of analysing pollution control costs using pre-existing economic models. This requires discussing the potential benefits from avoiding damages to foreign traders due to perturbation of global environmental systems.

Imposing negative changes on industrially developing countries raises the problem of how the market system will respond to the required redistribution, as well as ethical concerns for redistribution and compensation (d'Arge and Spash, 1991). A further issue concerns compensation for the imposition of these changes. If, say, the outcome of global climate change was that the industrially developed North was made better-off by more than the industrially developing South was made worse-off, no actual compensation is required under 'the potential compensation test', as applied in modern welfare economics, because on aggregate the world is a better place. Such ethical concerns are an integral part of the issue and are discussed further in chapters 7 and 9.

The North–South divide is set to play an important role in the ability to adapt. The major Northern Hemisphere food-exporting and capital-intensive countries are in a better position than the low-income, food-importing developing countries. The wealthier northern nations, while facing substantial changes in types of crops cultivated, water distribution and areas of available land, are more able to adapt. In general, these countries have surplus land available for production, stocks of produce, advanced agricultural research and development facilities, efficient market support and information systems and extensive water management structures (Barbier, 1989: 25). In broad terms, if adaptation raises costs and reduces supplies in the food-exporting North, the food-importing South is likely to suffer the most.

Wealthier nations with better endowments of fertile soils, less arid and semi-arid land, and that are further inland and/or above sea level will be tempted to ignore less fortunate regions. Population migration will undoubtedly occur as land is lost to rising seas and storm surges, and agricultural productivity is reduced in semi-arid regions. Some groups are particularly vulnerable, such as those in Latin America living in shanty towns established in flood-prone areas and on unstable hillsides; or low-income rural populations dependent upon traditional agriculture and marginal lands in tropical Asia, where the 1,600 million population is principally rurally based (Watson *et al.*, 1997: 11, 15–16). More generally, the evidence from GCMs shows that the number of areas of the globe which benefit from enhancing the Greenhouse Effect declines as the climate forcing increases in size and rate.

The intertemporal asymmetry of impacts is also apparent as initial benefits to regions, from slight climate change, turn into very large economic costs, as this continues. As the IPCC TAR recognises, some gases will persist for centuries at substantial levels, and several centuries after the stabilisation of GHGs, global mean surface temperature continues to increase and sea level to rise due to thermal expansion (IPCC Working Group I, 2001). The expected consequences of changes in unmanaged ecosystems, sea level rise, agricultural and forestry suggest substantial and widespread negative impacts by the time a 2°C increase in average global temperature is achieved. Those who have contended that human-induced warming could be beneficial appear to be concerned with the period well before this temperature is reached while ignoring the temporal and spatial distribution of impacts and changing frequency of extreme events. For example, in Europe more droughts are expected in the south and more river floods in the north and north-west. An issue discussed in the next chapter is the concentration on changing means to the exclusion of extremes. While the IPCC has lately become aware of the importance of highlighting changes in extreme events, many (such as thunderstorms, tornadoes, hail and lightning) are excluded from climate models (IPCC Working Group I, 2001: 15).

Clearly, complex environmental problems, such as the enhanced Greenhouse Effect, which extend over long periods of time, are shrouded in uncertainty and challenge the idea of an objective consequential approach to impact assessment, outlined as the idealised approach in the introduction to this chapter. As a result the range and extent of impacts due to climate change can only be broadly outlined with wide variation in the confidence and precision placed upon the occurrence of specific events. This leaves us with a rough sketch of many possible events rather than a detailed picture of the type and timing of exact impacts.

The possibilities of events beyond double CO_2 levels and beyond 2100 are both highly relevant to emissions reduction and adaptation strategies. That these possible futures are uncertain is true, just as all the predictions in the IPCC reports and elsewhere are uncertain. In fact uncertainty is endemic to economics and policy. The problem for developing socio-economic understanding lies in how such uncertainty is addressed. Here there is an identifiable crisis at the heart of modern approaches to policy and the expectations placed upon science and economics. How uncertainty has been and should be addressed is the topic of the next two chapters.

Note

1   Model sensitivities to climate forcing are still based upon such equilibrium doubling. That is, models are often calibrated on the basis of equilibrium simulations of double CO_2 equivalent.

References

Abrahamson, D.E. (1989) 'Global warming: the issues, impacts, responses', in *The Challenge of Global Warming*, edited by D.E. Abrahamson, pp. 3–34, Washington, DC: Island Press.

Adams, R.M. (1989) 'Global climate change and agriculture: an economic perspective', *American Journal of Agricultural Economics* **71**: 1272–9.

Adams, R.M. and T.D. Crocker (1991) 'The economic impact of air pollution on agriculture: an assessment and review', in *Towards Sustainable Agricultural Development*, edited by M.D. Young, pp. 295–319, London: Belhaven.

Adams, R.M., B.A. McCarl, D.J. Dudek and J.D. Glyer (1988) 'Implications of global climate change for western agriculture', *Western Journal of Agriculture Economics* **13**(2): 348–56.

Alexander, V. (1993) 'Arctic marine ecosystems', in *Global Warming and Biological Diversity*, edited by R.L. Peters and T.E. Lovejoy, pp. 221–32, New Haven, CT: Yale University Press.

Barbier, E.B. (1989) 'The global greenhouse effect: economic impacts and policy considerations', *Natural Resources Forum*: **13**(1): 20–32.

Bray, D. and H. von Storch (1999) 'Climate science: an empirical example of postnormal science', *Bulletin of the American Meteorological Society* **80**(3): 439–55.

Bretherton, F.P., K. Bryan and J.D. Woods (1990) 'Time-dependent greenhouse-gas-induced climate change', in *Climate Change: The IPCC Scientific Assessment*, edited by J.T. Houghton, G.J. Jenkins and J.J. Ephraums, pp. 173–93, Cambridge, England: Cambridge University Press.

Broadus, J.M., J.D. Milliman, S.F. Edwards, D.G. Aubrey and F. Gable (1986) 'Rising sea level and damming of rivers: possible effects in Egypt and Bangladesh', in *Effects of Changes in Stratospheric Ozone and Global Climate* **IV**, edited by J.G. Titus, pp. 165–89, Washington, DC: US Environmental Protection Agency.

Bryson, R.A. (1974) 'Perspectives on climate change', *Science* **184**(4,138): 753–60.

Callendar, G.S. (1938) 'The artificial production of carbon dioxide and its influence on temperature', *Quarterly Journal of the Royal Meteorological Society* **64**: 223–40.

Ciborowski, P. (1989) 'Sources, sites, trends, and opportunities', in *The Challenge of Global Warming*, edited by D.E. Abrahamson, pp. 231–8, Washington, DC: Island Press.

Cline, W.R. (1992) *The Economics of Global Warming*. Harlow, Essex: Longman.

Crosson, P. (1989) 'Greenhouse warming and climate change: why should we care?', *Food Policy* (May): 107–18.

Dale, V.H. and H.M. Rauscher (1994) 'Assessing impacts of climate change on forests: the state of biological modeling', in *Assessing the Impacts of Climate Change on Natural Resource Systems*, edited by K.D. Frederick and N.J. Rosenberg, pp. 65–90, Dordrecht, The Netherlands: Kluwer Academic Publishers.

d'Arge, R.C., W.D. Schulze and D.S. Brookshire (1982) 'Carbon dioxide and intergenerational choice', *American Economic Association Papers and Proceedings* **72**(2): 251–6.

d'Arge, R.C. and C.L. Spash (1991) 'Economic strategies for mitigating the impacts of climate change on future generations', in *Ecological Economics: The Science and Management of Sustainability*, edited by R. Costanza, pp. 367–83, New York: Columbia University Press.

d'Arge, R.C. (1975) *Economic and Social Measures of Biologic and Climatic Change*. Washington, DC: US Department of Transportation, Climate Impact Assessment Program.

Davis, M.B. and C. Zabinski (1992) 'Changes in geographical range resulting from greenhouse warming: effects on biodiversity in forests', in *Global Warming and Biological Diversity*, edited by R.L. Peters and T.E. Lovejoy, pp. 297–308, New Haven, CT: Yale University Press.

Denman, K., E. Hofmann and H. Marchant (1996) 'Marine biotic response to environmental change and feedbacks to climate', in *Climate Change 1995: The Science of Climate Change*, edited by J.T. Houghton, L.G. Meira, B.A. Callander, N. Harris, A. Kattenberg and K. Maskell, pp. 482–516, Cambridge, England: Cambridge University Press.

Doake, C.S.M., H.F.J. Corr, H. Rott, P. Skvarra and N.W. Young (1998) 'Breakup and conditions for stability of the northern Larsen Ice Shelf, Antarctica', *Nature* **391**(19 February): 778–80.

Dregne, H.E. (1983) *Desertification of Arid Lands*. Chur, Switzerland: Hardwood Academic Publishers.

Easterling, W.E., P.R. Crosson, M.S. Rosenburg, M.S. McKenney and K.D. Frederick (1992) 'Methodology for assessing regional economic impacts of and responses to climate change: the MINK study', in *Economic Issues in Global Climate Change*, edited by J.M. Reilly and M. Anderson, pp. 168–99, Boulder, CO: Westview Press.

Economist (1986) 'Catastrophe at Chernobyl' (3 May 1986).

Emanuel, W.R., H.H. Shugart and M.P. Stevenson (1985) 'Response to comment: climate change and the broadscale distribution of terrestrial ecosytem complexes', *Climate Change* **7**: 457.

EPA (1983) *Projecting Future Sea Level Rise*. Washington, DC: US Environmental Protection Agency, Government Printing Office.

Erickson, J.D. (1993) 'From ecology to economics: the case against CO_2 fertilization', *Ecological Economics* **8**(2): 157–76.

Firor, J.W. (1989) *The Straight Story About The Greenhouse Effect*. Presented at Western Economic Association International Meeting, Lake Tahoe, California, 18–22 June 1989.

Fitzharris, B.B. (1996) 'The cryosphere: changes and their impacts', in *Impacts, Adaptations, and Mitigation: Scientific-Technical Analyses*, edited by R.T. Watson, M.C. Zinyowera and R.H. Moss, pp. 241–65, Cambridge, England: Cambridge University Press.

Food and Agriculture Organisation of the United Nations (1993) *FAO 1993 Yearbook: Trade and Commerce*. Vol. 46. Rome FAO.

Franklin, J.F., F.J. Swanson, M.E. Harmon, D.A. Perry, T.A. Spies, V.H. Dale, A. McKee, W.K. Ferrell, J.E. Means, S.V. Gregory, J.D. Lattin, T.D. Schowalter and D. Larsen (1992) 'Effects of global climate change on forests in Northwestern North America', in *Global Warming and Biological Diversity*, edited by R.L. Peters and T.E. Lovejoy, pp. 244–57, New Haven, CT: Yale University Press.

Glantz, M.H. (1990) 'Assessing the Impacts of Climate: The Issue of Winners and Losers in a Global Climate Change Context'. Paper prepared for the Conference on Adaptive Responses to Sea Level Rise, Miami, Florida, 27 November 1989–1 December 1990.

Goemans, T. (1986) 'The sea also rises: the ongoing dialogue of the Dutch with the sea', in *Effects of Changes in Stratospheric Ozone and Global Climate* **IV**, edited by G. Titus, pp. 47–56, Washington, DC: US Environmental Protection Agency.

Goodess, C.M., J.P. Palutikof and T.D. Davies (1992) *The Nature and Causes of Climate Change: Assessing the Long Term Future*. London: Belhaven.

Gribbin, J. (1990) *Hothouse Earth: The Greenhouse Effect and Gaia*. London: Black Swan.

Grubb, M. (1995) 'The Berlin climate conference: outcome and implications', *FEEM Newsletter* **2**: 15–20.

Grumbine, R.W. (1993) *Survey of Physical Processes Affecting Sea Level*. MIT, Unpublished manuscript.

Hadley Centre (1995) *Modelling Climate Change 1860–2050*. London: Meteorological Office.

Hansen, J.E., D. Johnson, A. Lacis, S. Lebedeff, P. Lee, D. Rind and G. Russell (1981) 'Climate impact of increasing atmospheric carbon dioxide', *Science* **213**(4,511): 957–66.

Heathcote, R.L. (1983) *The Arid Lands: Their Use and Abuse*. Harlow, Essex: Pearson Education.

Henderson-Sellers, B. (1984) *Pollution of Our Atmosphere*. Bristol, England: Adam Hilger.

Hoffman J.S., J. Wells and J.G. Titus (1986) 'Future global warming and sea level rise', in *Iceland coastal and river symposium*. Edited by G. Sigbjarnarson. Reykjavik, Iceland: National Energy Authority.

Houghton, J. (1997) *Global Warming: The Complete Briefing*. Cambridge, England: Cambridge University Press.

Houghton, J.T., G.J. Jenkins and J.J. Ephraums (eds) (1990) *Climate Change: The IPCC Scientific Assessment*. Cambridge, England: Cambridge University Press.

Hulme, M., D. Conway, P.M. Kelly, S. Subak and T.E. Downing (1995) 'The impacts of climate change on Africa', CSERGE Discussion Paper no. GEC 95–12, University of East Anglia.

Idso, S.B. (1983) 'Carbon dioxide and global temperature: what the data show', *Journal of Environmental Quality* **12**(2): 159–63.

IPCC Working Group I (2001) *Climate Change 2001: Scientific Assessment; Summary for Policymakers*. Geneva: Intergovernmental Panel on Climate Change.

IPCC Working Group II (2001) *Climate Change 2001: Impacts, Adaptation, and Vulnerability; Summary for Policymakers*. Geneva: Intergovernmental Panel on Climate Change.

Ittekkot, V. (1996) 'Oceans', in *Impacts, Adaptations, and Mitigation: Scientific-Technical Analyses*, edited by R.T. Watson, M.C. Zinyowera and R.H. Moss, pp. 267–88, Cambridge, England: Cambridge University Press.

Jacobson, J.L. (1990) 'Holding back the sea', in *State of the World 1990: A Worldwatch Institute Report on Progress Towards a Sustainable Society*, edited by L.R. Brown, pp. 79–97, New York: W.W. Norton and Company.

Jaeger, J. (1989) 'Developing policies for responding to climate change', in *The Challenge of Global Warming*, edited by D.E. Abrahamson, pp. 96–109 Washington, DC: Island Press.

Kates, R.W., J.H. Ausubel and M. Beherian (eds) (1985) *Climate Impact Assessment: Studies in the Interaction of Climate and Society*. Chichester: John Wiley & Sons.

Kattenberg, A., F. Giorgi, H. Grassl, G.A. Meehl, J.F.B. Mitchell, R.J. Stouffer, T. Tokioka, A.J. Weaver and T.M.L. Wigley (1996) 'Climate models: projections of future climate', in *Climate Change 1995: The Science of Climate Change*, edited by J.T. Houghton, L.G. Meira, B.A. Callander, N. Harris, A. Kattenberg and K. Maskell, pp. 285–357, Cambridge, England: Cambridge University Press.

Kelejian, H.K. and B.V. Varichek (1982) 'Pollution, climate change, and consequent economic costs concerning agricultural production', in *The Economics of Managing Chlorofluorocarbons: Stratospheric Ozone and Climate Issues*, edited by J.H. Cumberland, J.R. Hibbs and I. Hoch, pp. 224–68, Washington, DC: Resources for the Future.

Kimball, B. (1986) 'Influence of elevated CO_2 on crop yield', in *Carbon Dioxide Enrichment of Greenhouse Crops*, edited by H.Z. Enroch and B.A Kimball, pp. 105–15, Boca Raton, FL: CRC Press.

Kirschbaum, M.U.F. and A. Fischlin (1996) 'Climate change impacts on forests', in *Impacts, Adaptations, and Mitigation: Scientific-Technical Analyses*, edited by R.T. Watson, M.C. Zinyowera and R.H. Moss, pp. 95–129, Cambridge, England: Cambridge University Press.

Kokoski, M.F. and V.K. Smith (1987) 'A general equilibrium analysis of partial-equilibrium welfare measures: the case of climate change', *American Economic Review* **77**(3): 331–41.

Kosobud, R.F. and T.A. Daly (1987) 'Global conflict or cooperation over the CO_2 climate impact', *Kyklos* **37**(4): 638–59.

Lahidji, R., W. Michalski and B. Stevens (1999) 'The long-term future for energy: an assessment of key trends and challenges', in *Energy: The Next Fifty Years*, edited by OECD, pp. 7–28, Paris: Organisation for Economic Co-operation and Development.

Manne, A.S. and R.G. Richels (1992) *Buying Greenhouse Insurance: The Economic Costs of CO_2 Emissions Limit*. Cambridge, MA: MIT Press.

Marland, G. and R.M. Rotty (1985) 'Greenhouse gases in the atmosphere: what do we know?', *Journal of Air Pollution Control Association* **35**(10): 1033–8.

Maunder, W.J. and J. Ausubel (1985) 'Identifying climate sensitivity', in *Climate Impact Assessment: Studies of the Interaction of Climate and Society* **SCOPE 27**, edited by R.W. Kates, J.H. Ausubel and M. Berberian, pp. 85–105, Chichester: John Wiley & Sons.

Mazza, P. and R. Roth (1999) *Global Warming is Here: The Scientific Evidence*. Washington, DC: The Atmosphere Alliance, Earth Island Institute.

Mendelsohn, R. and N.J. Rosenberg (1994) 'Framework for integrated assessment of global warming impacts', in *Assessing the Impacts of Climate Change on Natural Resource Systems*, edited by K.D. Frederick and N.J. Rosenberg, pp. 15–44, Dordrecht, The Netherlands: Kluwer Academic Publishers.

Mlot, C. (1989) 'Great lakes fish and the greenhouse effect', *BioScience* **39**(3): 145.

Murphy, D.D. and S.B. Weiss (1992) 'Effects of climate change on biological diversity in Western North America: species loss and mechanisms', in *Global Warming and Biological Diversity*, edited by R.L. Peters and T.E. Lovejoy, pp. 355–68, New Haven, CT: Yale University Press.

Newman, J.E. and R.C. Picket (1974) 'Global climate and food supply variations', *Science* **186**: 887–81.

Nicholls, N., G.V. Gruza, J. Jouzel, T.R. Karl, L.A. Ogallo and D.E. Parker (1996) 'Observed climate variability and change', in *Climate Change 1995: The Science of Climate Change*, edited by J.T. Houghton, L.G. Meira, B.A. Callander, N. Harris, A. Kattenberg and K. Maskell, pp. 133–92, Cambridge, England: Cambridge University Press.

Nordhaus, W.D. (1994) *Managing the Global Commons: The Economics of Climate Change*. Cambridge, MA: MIT Press.

Oguirtoyirbo, J.S. and R.S. Odiro (1979) *Climate Variability and Land Use: An African Perspective*. Presented at WMO World Climate Conference, Geneva, 12–23 February 1979.

Oram, P.A. (1985) 'Sensitivity of agricultural production to climatic change', *Climatic Change* **7**: 129–52.

Park, R.A., T.V. Armentaro and C.L. Cloonan (1986) 'Predicting the effects of sea level rise on coastal wetlands', in *Effects of Changes in Stratospheric Ozone and Global Climate* **IV**, edited by J.G. Titus, pp. 129–52, Washington, DC: US Environmental Protection Agency.

Parry, M.L. (1989) 'The potential impact on agriculture of the greenhouse effect', in *The Greenhouse Effect and UK Agriculture*, edited by R.M. Bennett, pp. 24–46, Reading: Centre for Agricultural Strategy.

Parry, M.L. (1990) *Climate Change and World Agriculture*. London: Earthscan.

Parry, M.L. (1991) *The Potential Effects of Climate Change in the United Kingdom*. London: HMSO, Department of the Environment.

Parry, M.L. and T.R. Carter (1986) 'Effects of climatic changes on agriculture and forestry: an overview', in *Effects of Changes in Stratospheric Ozone and Global Climate* I, edited by J.G. Titus, pp. 257–98, Washington, DC: US Environmental Protection Agency.

Parry, M.L., T.R. Carter and N.T. Konijn (eds) (1988) *Assessment of Climate Impacts on Agriculture*. Dordrecht, The Netherlands: Reidel.

Parry, M.L., A.R. Magalhaes and N.H. Ninh (1991) *The Potential Socio-Economic Effects of Climate Change: A Summary of Three Regional Assessments*. Nairobi, Kenya: UNEP, World Climate Impacts Programme.

Parton, W.J., D.S. Ojima and D.S. Schimel (1994) 'Environmental change in grasslands: assessment using models', in *Assessing the Impacts of Climate Change on Natural Resource Systems*, edited by K.D. Frederick and N.J. Rosenberg, pp. 111–41, Dordrecht, The Netherlands: Kluwer Academic Publishers.

Peters, R.L. and J.D. Darling (1985) 'The greenhouse effect and nature reserves', *Bioscience* **35**(11): 707.

Peters, R.L. and T.E. Lovejoy (eds) (1992) *Global Warming and Biological Diversity*. New Haven, CT: Yale University Press.

Reilly, J. (1996) 'Agriculture in a changing climate: impacts and adaptation', in *Impacts, Adaptations and Mitigation of Climate Change: Scientific-Technical Analyses*, edited by R.T. Watson, M.C. Zinyowera, R.H. Moss and D.J. Dokken, pp. 427–67, Cambridge, England: Cambridge University Press.

Riebsame, W.E. (1989) *Assessing the Social Implications of Climate Fluctuations: A Guide to Climate Impact Studies*. Nairobi, Kenya: UNEP, World Climate Impacts Programme.

Roberts, L. (1989) 'How fast can trees migrate?', *Science* **243**: 735–7.

Rogers, P. (1994) 'Assessing the socioeconomic consequences of climate change on water resources', in *Assessing the Impacts of Climate Change on Natural Resource Systems*, edited by K.D. Frederick and N.J. Rosenberg, pp. 179–208, Dordrecht, The Netherlands: Kluwer Academic Publishers.

Rosenzweig, C. (1985) 'Potential CO_2 induced climate effects on North American wheat producing regions', *Climatic Change* **7**: 367–89.

Rosenzweig, C. and M.M. Daniel (1988) 'Agriculture', in *The Potential Effects of Global Climate Change on the United States* **2, National Studies**, edited by J.B. Smith and D.A. Tirpate, pp. 367–417, Washington, DC: US Environmental Protection Agency.

Rosenzweig, C., M.L. Parry, G. Fisher and K. Frohberg (1992) *Climate Change and World Food Supply: A Preliminary Report*. University of Oxford: Environmental Change Unit.

Schindler, D.W. (1990) 'Natural and anthropogenically imposed limitations to biotic richness in freshwaters', in *The Earth in Transition: Patterns and Processes of Biotic Impoverishment*, edited by G.W. Woodwell, pp. 425–62, Cambridge, England: Cambridge University Press.

Schneider, S.H., L. Mearns and P.H. Gleick (1992) 'Climate-change scenarios for impact assessment', in *Global Warming and Biological Diversity*, edited by R.L. Peters and T.E. Lovejoy, pp. 38–55, New Haven, CT: Yale University Press.

Sen, A. (1986) *Poverty and Famines: An Essay on Entitlement and Deprivation*. Oxford, England: Clarendon Press.

Seneft, D. (1990) 'Greenhouse effect may not be all bad', *Agricultural Research* **38**(October): 20–3.

Shands, W.E. and J.S. Hoffman (eds) (1987) *The Greenhouse Effect, Climate Change, and US Forests*. Washington, DC: The Conservation Foundation.

Smit, B., L. Ludlow and M. Brklacich (1988) 'Implications of a global warming for agriculture: a review and appraisal', *Journal of Environmental Quality* **17**(4): 519–27.

Smith, J.B. and D.A. Tirpak (1989) *The Potential Effects of Global Climate Change on the United States*. Washington, DC: US Environmental Protection Agency, GPO.

Stern, A.C., R.W. Boubel, D.B. Turner and D.L. Fox (1984) *Fundamentals of Air Pollution*. London: Academic Press.

Thomas, R.H. (1986) 'Future sea level rise and its early detection by satellite remote sensing', in *Effects of Changes in Stratospheric Ozone and Global Climate* **IV**, edited by J.G. Titus, pp. 19–36, Washington, DC: US Environmental Protection Agency.

Titus, J.G. (1989) 'The cause and effects of sea-level rise', in *The Challenge of Global Warming*, edited by D.E. Abrahamson, pp. 161–95, Washington, DC and Covelo, CA: Island Press.

Vaughan, D.G. and C.S.M. Doake (1996) 'Recent atmospheric warming and retreat of ice shelves on the Antarctic Peninsula', *Nature* **379**(25 January): 328–31.

Wallen, C.C. (1966) 'Arid zone meteorology', in *Arid Lands: A Geographical Appraisal*, edited by E.S. Hills, pp. 53–76, London: Methuen.

Warrick, R. and J. Oerlemans (1990) 'Sea level rise', in *Climate Change: The IPCC Scientific Assessment*, edited by J.T. Houghton, G.J. Jenkins and J.J. Ephraums, pp. 257–81, Cambridge, England: Cambridge University Press.

Warrick, R.A., C. Le Provost, M.F. Meier, J. Oerlemans and P.L. Woodworth (1996) 'Changes in sea level', in *Climate Change 1995: The Science of Climate Change*, edited by J.T. Houghton, L.G. Meira, B.A. Callander, N. Harris, A. Kattenberg and K. Maskell, pp. 358–405, Cambridge, England: Cambridge University Press.

Watson, R.T., M.C. Zinyowera and R.H. Moss (1996) 'Technical summary: impacts, adaptations, and mitigation options', in *Impacts, Adaptations, and Mitigation: Scientific-Technical Analyses*, edited by R.T. Watson, M.C. Zinyowera, R.H. Moss and D.J. Dokken, pp. 19–53, Cambridge, England: Cambridge University Press.

Watson, R.T., M.C. Zinyowera, R.H. Moss and D.J. Dokken (1996) *Impacts, Adaptations and Mitigation of Climate Change: Scientific-Technical Analyses*. Cambridge, England: Cambridge University Press.

Watson, R.T., M.C. Zinyowera, R.H. Moss and D.J. Dokken (eds) (1997) *The Regional Impacts of Climate Change: An Assessment of Vulnerability; Summary for Policymakers*. IPCC Special Report. Geneva: IPCC.

Whalley, J (1991) 'The interface between environmental and trade policies', *The Economic Journal* **101**(March): 180–9.

White, G.F. (1966) 'The world's arid areas', in *Arid Lands: A Geographical Appraisal*, edited by E.S. Hills, pp. 19–30, London: Methuen.

WMO, World Climate Programme (1988) *Developing Policies for Responding to Climate Change*. Villach, Austria and Bellagio, Italy, World Meteorological Organization.

Woodward, F.I. (1992) 'A review of the effects of climate change on vegetation: ranges, competitions and composition', in *Global Warming and Biological Diversity*, edited by R.L. Peters and T.E. Lovejoy, pp. 105–23, New Haven, CT: Yale University Press.

4 Weak uncertainty

Risk and imperfect information

As should be apparent from chapters 2 and 3, the Greenhouse Effect itself is a scientifically well-founded phenomenon, but questions arise as to the extent of and speed with which human enhancement of that effect is taking place, and with what consequences. There is a positive global warming trend, and a general consensus that atmospheric CO_2 has increased due to fossil fuel combustion. The increasing atmospheric concentration of the cocktail of greenhouse gases is known to be changing atmospheric chemistry. However, beyond these 'facts', there are problems with establishing a trace-gas-cause climate-change-effect relationship. The imprecision of prediction grows as more detail is attempted in the description of the impacts of global climate change, as the move is made from physical to socio-economic concerns, from global to regional or local, and the further into the future events are predicted to occur.

The aim of this and the next chapter is to explore and question the way in which such uncertainties are standardised and characterised. Different types of uncertainty should be recognised, especially because public debate often interprets risk and uncertainty as meaning the same thing and referring to unknowable outcomes (strong uncertainty), while the professional debate by economists and scientists tends to restrict attention to known events which are uncertain (weak uncertainty). The concepts to be discussed in this chapter are grouped under weak uncertainty and concern the realm of normal science and standard economics. The realm of weak uncertainty is in specifying the probabilities of future events. Weak uncertainty can be contrasted with strong uncertainty where knowledge is actually lacking due to partial ignorance and because outcomes are indeterminate. These are topics to which I return in chapter 5.

In the current chapter, the weak uncertainty approach is outlined in the context of global climate change using a characterisation of mean temperature increases as an example. This raises the need for filling in gaps in our knowledge and improving estimates of future changes and their probability. The extent to which different types of uncertainty pertain to the measurement and prediction of climate change is discussed. Modelling is seen as necessary to help inform prediction and the nature of that modelling in science and economics is then analysed. This leads to a concern for the role of scientists and economists in the policy debate, and the way in which their models are reported as 'factual'.

The probability of the enhanced Greenhouse Effect

If standard scientific methodology and burden of proof are followed, an intricate chain of cause–effect relationships is required to establish the nature of potential outcomes from increased GHGs. A key controversy has been the extent to which anthropogenic additions to the atmospheric concentration of GHGs will raise Earth's surface temperature. Much of the debate centres upon the role of feedback mechanisms', e.g. whether or not increased temperatures will lead to greater cloud cover and so backscatter of incoming radiation, which causes cooling. If a range of climate change scenarios could be agreed upon then the physical results for other aspects of the global biosphere would need to be calculated in order to derive predictive consequences. Calls for a rigorous scientific proof of human-induced changes due to the Greenhouse Effect involve evidence of increasing concentrations of trace gases being linked directly to specified changes in climate, which in turn are estimated to cause physical damages: for example, the prediction of an increased probability of hurricanes in the southern US followed by the realisation of that probability in specific weather patterns and resulting loss of man-made capital. The physical events would therefore be linked to economic models which require their own calculation, estimation and abstraction, creating associated errors and so adding to the potential inaccuracies of the predictions. An increased frequency of hurricanes may fail to cause damages (by occurring off-shore) or the damages may be minimal from the standard economic viewpoint (being unrelated to human utility).

The probability density function

In trying to observe whether climatic change is underway only the initial step of the above process of proof has been undertaken with any rigour. This step emphasises changes in climatic variables predicted as a result of increasing greenhouse gases, most obviously increased global mean temperature. Figure 4.1 takes actual temperature data (Jones *et al.*, 2000), as used in figure 2.6, and expresses this in terms of the frequency with which given anomalies have occurred. The anomalies are measured as variations from the mean temperature for the period 1961–90. Data have been divided equally into four 36-year periods to show how the distribution has been shifting. Thus, the last period (1964–99) has a range of observations from −0.23 to +0.59°C while the first period (1856–91) ranges from −0.53 to 0.0°C. This distribution of observed global temperatures implies an increasing probability of above average or relatively warm climatic conditions.

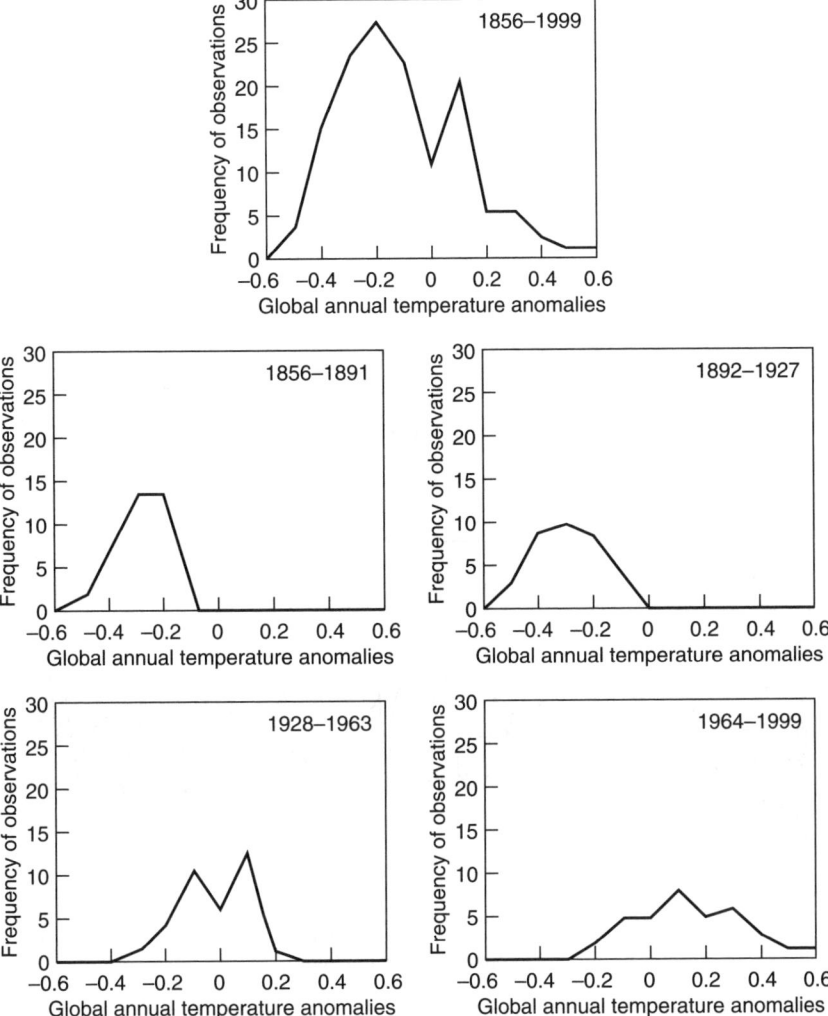

Figure 4.1   Frequency distribution for temperature, 1856–1999
Data source: Jones *et al.* (2000).

The dominant weak uncertainty approach takes such information and fits it within a probability density function. If the climatic variables of concern for the prediction of global climate change are assumed to be continuous and random, showing a distribution that is normal then some of the problems surrounding their expected range can be easily explained. This approach is illustrated below and can be found in Fukui (1979), Hare (1979; 1985), Parry and Carter (1986) and Riebsame (1989: 6–7). For example, the estimation of average temperature in the Northern Hemisphere might be the variable

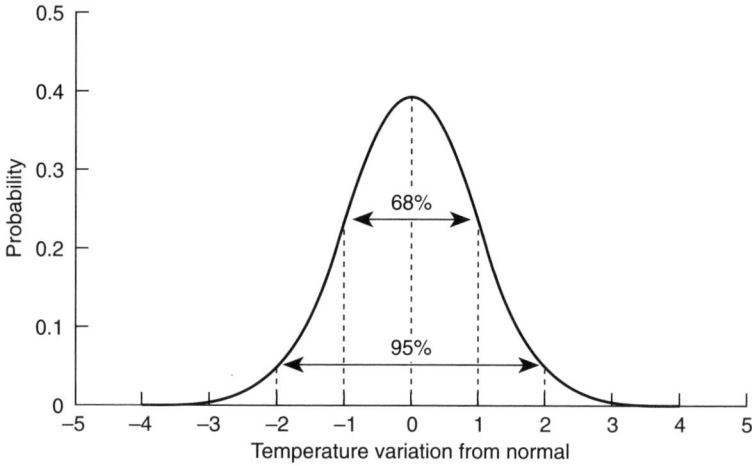

Figure 4.2a Hypothetical probability distribution

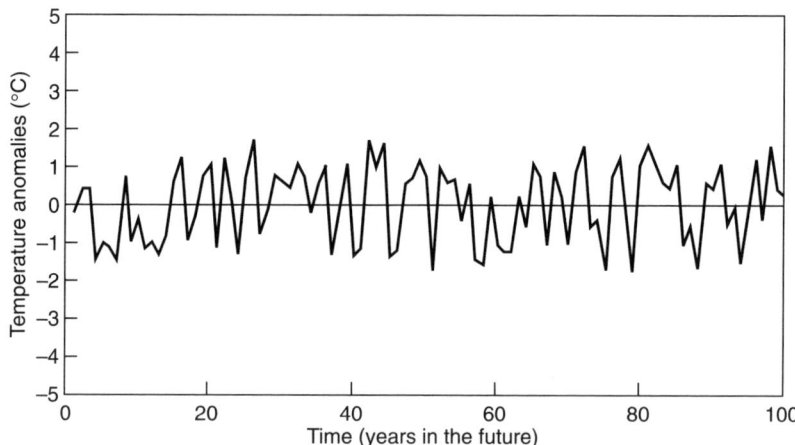

Figure 4.2b Hypothetical temperature variations

which is to be predicted. In figure 4.2a the variation of temperature from usual is characterised as a Gaussian distribution. The mean in figure 4.2a is zero and the standard deviation one, giving what is called a standard normal distribution.

The concept of a usual, typical or normal temperature is derived from observations over time. A time series data set for a given period (e.g. observations of temperature over the past 100 years) gives the average or mean temperature which will be used as a reference value or status quo. As new observations are collected they can be compared to this status quo to test whether there is evidence for global warming. Thus, imagine the year is 2100 and a set of data has been collected over the past 200 years, the results could be displayed as in figure 4.2b which provides a set of hypothetical observations for the period 2000–2100. In order to test whether global warming has been occurring this data might be compared to the average temperature from 1900–2000. Interest is then focused upon the probability of variations from the norm as experienced in the twentieth century, which can be shown by expected temperature deviations from the mean; in this way the mean becomes the zero reference point, as was shown previously for actual data in figure 4.1.

On the basis of the particular normal distribution in figure 4.2a, the expected values of temperature variations can be specified; that is, approximately 68 per cent of the temperatures, shown in figure 4.2b, fall within ±1°C of the mean, 95 per cent within ±2°C and over 99 per cent within ±3°C. Alternatively, the probability of some threshold temperature of interest might be expressed: for example, the chance of a temperature greater than 2°C can be specified as just over 2 per cent. As mentioned in chapter 2, the mean temperature of the Northern Hemisphere has varied no more than 2°C in the past 10,000 years, which would suggest a smaller standard deviation than the 1°C used in the hypothetical data of figures 4.2a and 4.2b.

Increasing mean temperature

Much attention in the literature has focused upon the double CO_2 scenario and its impact on temperature. The lower range of estimates give an increase of 1.5°C, thus a 1°C change might be observed in the near future. If this were the only change, the mean rise in temperature would then shift the normal distribution as shown in figure 4.3a, resulting in the chance of temperatures above 2°C becoming approximately 16 per cent (from just over 2 per cent in figure 4.2a). Such a change would be related to observations like those in figure 4.3b. That is, halfway into the next century a sudden increase in mean temperature might be observed. Currently, actual mean temperature has been estimated to have increased by 0.6°C. However, confirming that the mean temperature has in fact shifted is difficult because of the considerable area of overlap with the original probability density function. Thus, observed high temperatures could merely be part of normal variability and might be evened out by low temperatures in future years. In order for greater confidence to be expressed in the hypothesis that a shift in mean temperature has occurred, more observations above the original mean temperature are required.

Even a marked and consistent shift, as illustrated in figure 4.3b, can take decades to be substantiated. In this regard the nature of the transition from current norm to the higher mean is an important indicator of change. However, the nature of this change is unknown, and in fact neglected by equilibrium models (such as GCMs, and those in economic applications). There may be a smooth transition, a sudden shift (as in figure 4.3b) or a 'surprise'.

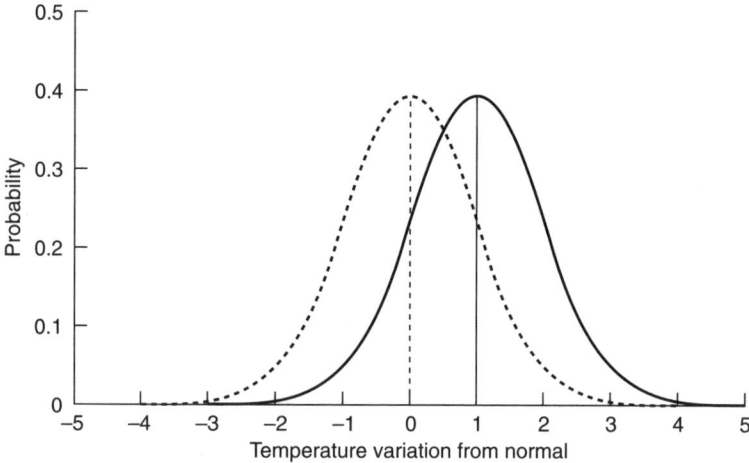

Figure 4.3a An increase in temperature mean

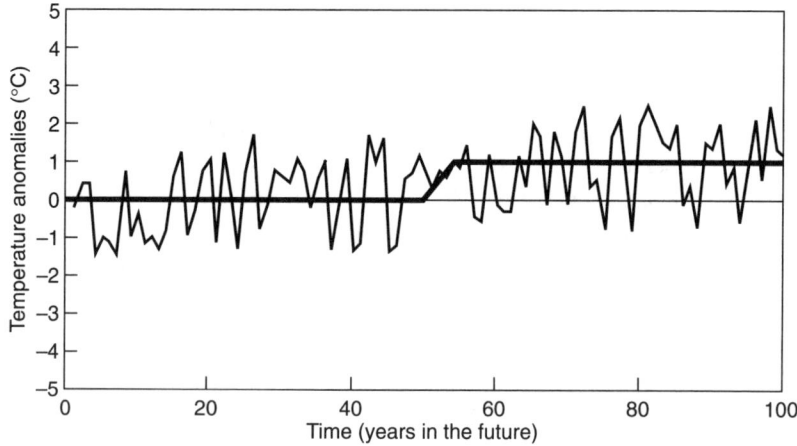

Figure 4.3b Hypothetical 1°C mean temperature rise

The importance of variability

Yet the picture is still more complicated, even though the restrictions of the normal probability density function are maintained. One complication is that the concentration on a shift in mean ignores the likely change in the variability of climatic factors. Concern has been expressed that temperature, precipitation, sea level and other variables will become more erratic, i.e. higher highs and lower lows will occur. Hence, the Small Island States are concerned about storm surges as much as mean sea level rise. An increase in variability can happen independently of a change in

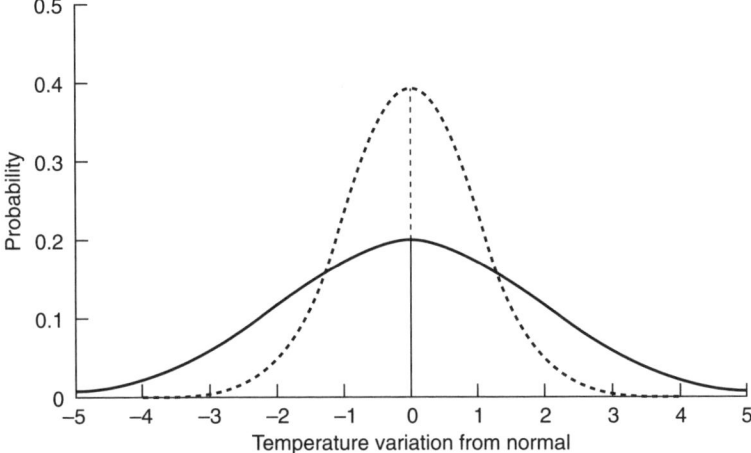

Figure 4.4a An increase in temperature variation

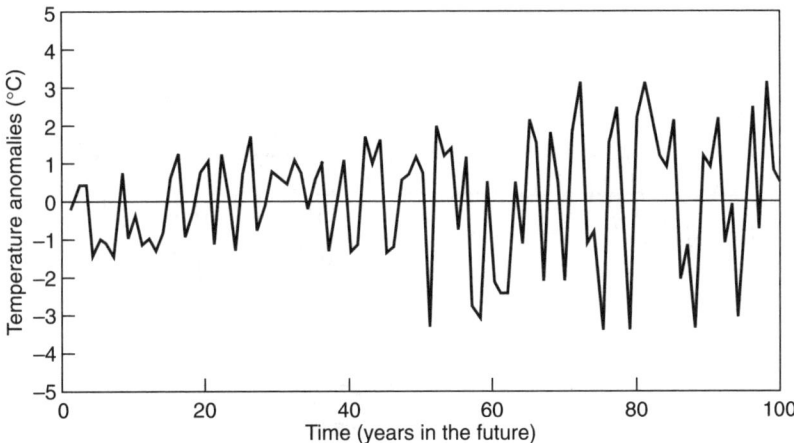

Figure 4.4b Hypothetical increase in variance

mean, as shown in figures 4.4a and 4.4b for temperature. In this case increasing the variability, while holding the mean constant, by doubling the standard deviation, results in the probability of a greater than 2°C temperature again becoming 16 per cent. Merely concentrating on mean temperature observations would ignore this change, i.e. a change in variance may fail to be detected if attention is focused upon the trend in mean values. Consider another example: in the case of rainfall, the result of climatic warming might be increased years of drought and years of flood but the average amount of rainfall would be the same as when neither of the extremes occurred. There is an increased risk of both excessive and deficient rainfall which an average would conceal.

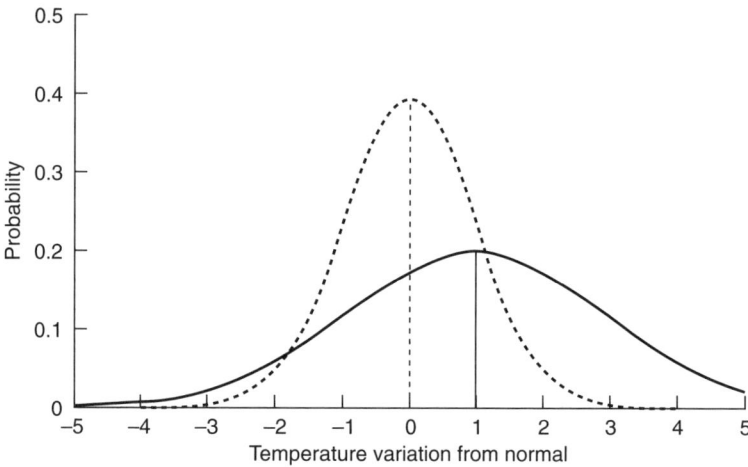

Figure 4.5a An increase in mean and variance

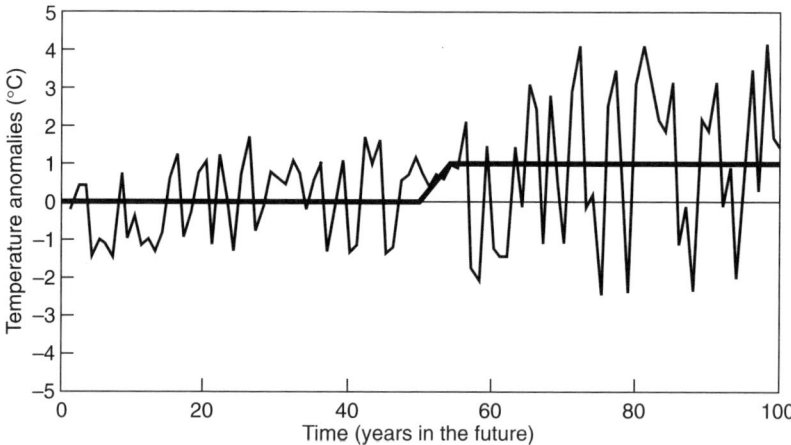

Figure 4.5b Hypothetical mean and variance shift

The relevance of variability seems to be easily neglected while the concentration upon averages can influence the policy debate. For example, Rowlands (1995. 242) notes the impact of the 1988 hot summer in North America in raising concern over global warming policy at that year's international conference in Toronto and Congressional hearings in Washington DC. The subsequent cold winters then eradicated memories of that hot weather, and dispelled fears of global warming until the next hot summer. The policymakers' misconception of the role of variability can be gleaned directly from transcripts of Congressional hearings. There Senator Ford is found asking Dr Hansen to explain why winters in the Ohio River area were, in his experience, more severe, as if this were counter-evidence to a global warming hypothesis (Hansen, 1988: 80). A decade or even a few years of colder temperatures

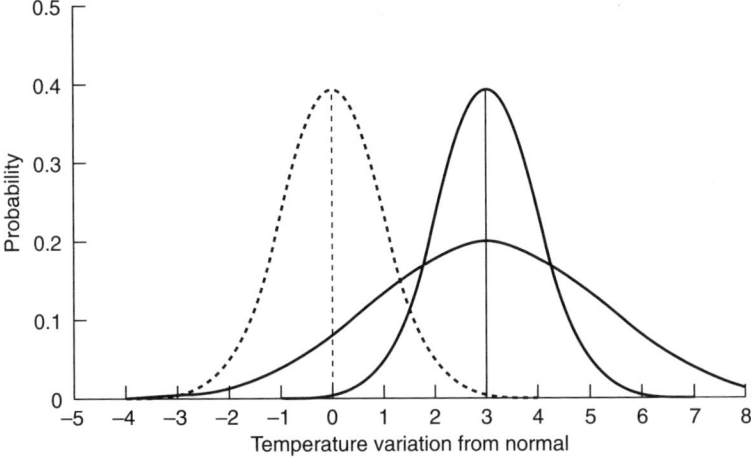

Figure 4.6 Double carbon dioxide scenarios

could have a dramatic political impact on the support for action on climatic change due to oversimplistic perceptions of what is possible.

Of course, a change in both the mean and variance of a climatic variable is another prospect. An increase in annual average temperature could result in greater fluctuations between years and a generally warmer climate. This kind of change is shown in figures 4.5a and 4.5b, where the probability of a temperature greater than 2°C is now 31 per cent. An interesting point to note here is that, despite the shift in mean temperature, the frequency with which years below the previous norm occur is also 31 per cent. Thus, a generally warmer world can include colder years than currently occur on average and, if variability increases, extreme cold years become even more likely.

Thresholds, niches and critical values

Another complication is evident in a paper by Fukui (1979) who points out the importance of critical ranges of rainfall for agricultural crops and illustrates this with a normal distribution. This role of critical values can be generalised to other variables and their relationship to individual species or entire ecosystems. Thus, in figure 4.2a the range of temperatures between ±2°C could be critical for a given species, i.e. temperatures above or below 2°C of current mean temperature will cause that species to die out. Now, if the warming under double CO_2 equivalent is 3°C (possible by 2050), and variability is unchanged, the probability of temperature being within the necessary species survival range falls from 95 per cent to 16 per cent. This is shown in figure 4.6. If, in addition, variability also increases, then the probability improves to 30 per cent. Thus, survival of species in the next century will be crucially dependent upon the mix of changes in mean and variability and the range of climatic variability within which a species can survive. Timing of events is also crucial for species and ecosystems (e.g. cold winters, rain in spring, summer sunshine). The range or niche can also change and may be reduced by, say, increasing stress due to habitat loss or greater parasitism due to warmer climates. Knowledge of the changing vulnerability of species is an example of the complications involved in assessing the impacts of climate change.

How useful is the probability approach?

In summary, the probability approach appears to provide some insight into aspects of climate change and be a useful characterisation of the weak uncertainty imposed by climate change. For example, the concentration on mean temperature changes can be exposed as misleading despite common use in economic studies, policy discussions and the media. However, the reduction of unknown futures to risk must also be recognised as an extreme simplification. The probability approach as a description of imperfect knowledge gives the perception that the concern of scientific research is to increase the confidence level with which possible future states of the climate and their implications are predicted. The job of scientists is then to define the possible future states and the probability of their occurrence.

According to this view, defining frequency distributions for the main variables is the key to convincing the still sceptical of the dangers, or otherwise, of global warming. Hence IPCC Working Group I (2001: 17) calls for the improvement of 'methods to quantify uncertainties of climate projections and scenarios'. IPCC Working Group II (2001: 17) calls for further research 'to reduce uncertainties' and although recognising the need for multiple metrics emphasises risk assessment, quantification and monetary valuation. Thus, the areas in which our knowledge is currently deficient are to be identified and that deficiency removed by further research. Economists also often voice such an opinion. For example, while discussing the economic costs of CO_2 reductions, Manne and Richels (1992: 1, 86) express a belief in the resolution of scientific uncertainty and better information leading to better decisions. Similarly, Adger and Fankhauser (1993: 117) regard more scientific research on costs and impacts as the best response to 'a high level of uncertainty', and state that 'all uncertainties can be resolved', although action may be necessary before then. IPCC Working Group III (2001) also believes in the 'reduction of scientific uncertainty' (p. 11), and in particular 'developing decision analytical frameworks for dealing with uncertainty' (p. 13). So next, let us look at issues relating to the measurement and prediction of climatic change to see how far the gaps in knowledge conform to this perception.

Measuring and predicting climatic change

Standard concerns over the impact of information on prediction can be relate to two areas: first, the ability to measure variables with minimal error, and second, imperfect knowledge about systems and how they change over time. In this section, the first area is shown to be concerned largely with estimable risk, while the second moves into the area of strong uncertainty. In order to see how these information issues relate to the enhanced Greenhouse Effect, the two main sources of information for confirming human-induced global warming GCMs and actual climate observations are considered. In doing so the main problem, as outlined in the probability approach above, is to be regarded as finding evidence for climatic variations which show as substantial differences between reference periods.

In assessing the accuracy of observational data on temperature Harrison (1991) has suggested four points be considered. First, the measurement of temperature and sea level are subject to errors. Second, the span of the climatological record is at best about 200 years and for many areas less than 50 years in terms of reliable direct measurement, which is very short in terms of estimating unusual disturbances. Third, the extent of background variations is unknown, so that the observed trends may be incorrectly attributed to humans or expected trends may fail to show because of environmental variation. Fourth, environmental systems are best described as complex networks rather than simple cause–effect relationships. These points are worth considering in turn.

Measuring variables

Examples of measurement error can certainly be found easily enough and are associated with specific confidence ranges given along with any climatic data. For example, measurement from land-based weather stations can suffer cumulative observation errors depending upon the calibration of thermometers, observer diligence, maintenance of thermometer shelters, local topography and the proximity of features such as urban areas or open water. Harrison points out that the result is accuracy within $\pm 0.5°C$ at any individual station, but he neglects to mention that as long as errors are consistent trends in temperature would be unaffected. Local measurement errors can also be specified and corrected.

Whether temperature, precipitation, gas concentration or some other climatic variable, repeated observation can allow identification of influencing factors. For example, the Mauna Loa site measuring CO_2 is considered one of the best locations because local influences are minimal and can be observed and excluded from the records. The methods and equipment used to obtain the Mauna Loa measurements have remained essentially unchanged since the late 1950s when the monitoring programme was initiated (Keeling and Whorf, 2000). Where equipment has changed and practices altered over time the number of factors affecting measurement comparability increases. In such cases figures are recalibrated to match the impacts of different techniques. Thus, repeating a measurement with different equipment allows for comparison and estimation of bias. The ability to observe from repeated experience means probability functions can be constructed and precise error estimates calculated.

Observational evidence

While observational data is indeed a short time series for prediction this fails to recognise the availability of alternative data sources. The composition of the atmosphere estimated from ice core samples has given a climate record extending back 420,000 years (Petit *et al.*, 2000) with a resolution of a few decades (Jouzel *et al.*, 1994). The changing terrestrial vegetation has left a record in lake bottoms and bogs which allows analysis of climates back to a 100,000 years ago (Boulton, 1994). Research in recent decades has reconstructed detailed records of climate cycles extending up to 500,000 years ago from high resolution ocean sediment cores, land-based sediments, pollen records, ice cores and coral reef sea level records (Goodess, Palutikof and Davies, 1992: 20). Tree rings can be used to reconstruct variability in complex climatic factors, e.g. precipitation, stream flow, warmth and humidity (LaMarche, 1978). Other principal sources of historical climates are glacier fluctuations, fossil beetle remains and fluctuating snowlines and treelines. Collation and cross comparison of existing observational records can also improve data sources. For example, during the 1990s the observational global average monthly temperature measurements were extended back from 1881 to 1856 (compare Vinnikov, Groisman and Lugina, 1994; Jones *et al.*, 2000). This is an area in which scientific research has been successfully reducing the imprecision of the basis for climatic comparisons, and looking for repeated experiences.

Fingerprints, signal and noise

The evidence for greenhouse warming from climate observations suffers the problem of discerning a signal from the background noise. Watts (1982: 447–8) has summarised several features of Earth's climate history which show the difficulty of observing changes in climate as being 'abnormal':

    (i)   the globe is currently experiencing unusually warm temperatures compared to the last million years;

    (ii) warmer centuries than the 1900s have occurred as frequently as cooler ones since the beginning of human history;

    (iii) the variance of Northern Hemisphere climate has been 1°C since the ancient Greeks to the present temperature;

    (iv) within this 2°C range are the Little Ice Age (fifteenth to sixteenth centuries) and current high temperatures;

(v) the rate and magnitude of greenhouse warming over the next century could equal or exceed historical human experience of climatic warming.

The observed changes in the twentieth century were faster than previous records show but generally remained within historical bounds. Thus, this year's Ethiopian drought, or last year's flooding in Bangladesh, are difficult to identify as results outside of 'normal' climatic variations, at the present time.

The US Department of Energy funded an attempt to detect early signs of anthropogenic climate change (Santer, 1994). The identification of variables which are expected to show a clear link between past GHG levels and climate change would provide what has been termed an enhanced Greenhouse Effect 'fingerprint'. Describing and separating GHG signals from noise of natural background variability is a key task. This noise is solely due to the internal dynamics of the atmosphere and ocean, and unrelated to the effect of GHG concentrations on climate variability. Noise could easily mask climate change. As shown earlier, extreme cold years can occur even in a warmer world without signifying warming has failed to materialise, and conversely severe droughts with a low frequency of occurrence, perhaps every 300 years, can be mistaken for global warming. A fingerprint might show up as theoretical predictions of the pattern of surface air temperature, under a double CO_2 equivalent scenario, which differs from any dominant natural variability pattern identifiable from observations or theoretical models of current and historical climates. The aim is then to find these distinct variables and patterns and try to collect data with sufficient accuracy to provide evidence of GHG-induced climate change. Thus, modelling uncertainty and measurement risk become relevant to the fingerprint exercise.

Feedbacks, complexity and prediction

There is a danger in simplifying systems knowledge and, most relevantly here, failing to accept limits to our ability to understand complexity. For example, feedback mechanisms can either amplify a small change via a positive feedback, or pacify the same change via a negative feedback; treating the systems in a simplified way can therefore lead to the misinterpretation of observational data. This problem relates most seriously to predicting future climate as opposed to defining past norms.

During the 1970s the concern amongst climatologists was as much for global cooling as global warming. The emission of CO_2 was seen to be an important influence upon the operation of the Greenhouse Effect but the outcome was disputed, specifically due to the relative strengths of various feedback mechanisms. In a survey of 24 climatologists, conducted in the late 1970s, 35 per cent expected cooling of between 0.05 to 1.20°C by the year 2000 and the same per cent expected warming of between 0.25 to 1.80°C, with the remaining 30 per cent predicting a status quo of −0.05 to +0.25°C (National Defense University 1978, cited in Kelejian and

Varichek, 1982). Bray (1991) attempts to pour derision on all concerns over the susceptibility of climate to human influence by quoting several eminent scientists who published warnings of global cooling between 1973 and 1976. This concern for cooling was supported by observation of a cooling trend in the decades after the Second World War, now attributed to volcanic activity, which then reversed itself in the late 1970s. Extrapolating trends to the future from relatively short time period data is highly likely to give erroneous forecasts. The implication is that scientists (like everybody else) can be too ready to simplify complex issues, in which case large-scale, irreversible schemes, recommended to solve media-inflated issues, should be avoided. However, the underlying relevance of human impacts on the atmosphere, which has been of consistent concern, is in danger of being written off as just another media 'event'. In addition, outlining a range of scenarios from cooling to warming need only signify honesty about strong uncertainty rather than incompetence as a scientist. The attitude of critics is that there is only one correct scenario and if you back the wrong one you deserve ridicule. This simplistic view of prediction shows the importance of expanding the conception of uncertainty and debating the role of both science and economics.

The experience of the 1970s also signifies one of the main limitations of observational data which is in terms of telling where climate is heading. More generally, there is in principle no reason to expect the past to be a good guide to the future in regard to human perturbation of climatic systems. Looking at, say, the 1930's drought in the US as an analogy for likely impacts in a warmer world may be a useful exercise (see Crosson, 1993), but the way in which systems change in the future due to GHG releases may bear little or no relationship to the processes responsible for historical droughts (and social responses would also be different). The rapid change in atmospheric gases which has occurred this century has no direct historical or paleoclimatic precedent. Paleoclimatic data, from sources such as tree rings or ice cores, while providing a reference norm, are useless for predicting regional and seasonal climate patterns or the rate of change over the coming centuries. The global experiment is unrepeatable. Thus, in order to predict climatic changes, a theoretical model is required and for the natural scientists that means using GCMs. In addition, social scientists have their own models, which attempt to characterise potential futures.

The role of modelling

Scientific models of climate change

One of the main sources for predicting the impacts of global warming is climate simulation modelling using GCMs. While these models tend to be in broad agreement at the global level, significant differences arise between models as results are examined on successively smaller scales, eventually focusing on subcontinental regions. GCMs treat the world as uniform blocks, ignoring topographical and meteorological variations within these blocks. For example, a typical grid might represent as a single average all of Greece, including the Aegean Sea, or an entire region such as Mexico including mountains, plains and deserts. Of the five individual GCMs which have dominated the literature the most detailed grid size has been OSU (4° latitude by 5° longitude), but such high horizontal resolution has only been achieved by simplifying the atmospheric model (two rather than nine layers), although the ocean model is multi-layered (Goodess, Palutikof and Davies, 1992: 77–80). Clearly there are restrictions on the detail which GCMs can obtain and different groups of scientists and modellers decide on the areas in which their models will have the greatest resolution, e.g. oceans, atmosphere or regional scale.

GCMs were designed for basic research in the atmospheric sciences, and thus have drawbacks in their modelling of other systems, e.g. the oceans and biota. As commonly cited, the role of oceans as modelled in GCMs has typically lacked detail. Oceans are known to be both an important sink for CO_2 and a heat sink, but their size in these roles is unclear. For example, the amount of biomass stimulation due to CO_2 enrichment could play a significant role in continued CO_2 uptake by phytoplankton. Within the atmospheric system the exact role of each trace gas is unknown, and their interactions are complex. While source inventories for CO_2 are reasonably well defined, those for CH_4 and N_2O are vague, and the budget for CO_2 still remains a point of debate.

Yet GCMs are extremely complex, typically solving 200,000 equations on each run, using computers that perform half a billion operations each second. Current examples have developed from using single averages as representative of conditions everywhere to including realistic wind development; cloud formation, precipitation and disappearance; air flows over mountains; moisture exchange with the ocean surface; soil moisture accumulation and evaporation; and snow and ice fluctuations by season and altitude (Firor, 1990: 76). Despite the potential for model variations, results from comparative studies show the results from different GCMs often agree well with each other, and with historical temperature data, over large scales (global, hemispherical, zonal). More than 100 independent studies have given estimates of average global warming within the 1.5°C to 4.5°C range, for a scenario indicating a doubling of CO_2 equivalent, with values near 3°C tending to be favoured (MacDonald, 1988: 437).

The process of GCM construction seems to create a scientific consensus and internal validity. A central issue has been the role of feedback mechanisms which could be either stabilising or destabilising depending on the relative dominance of alternative mechanisms. For example, albedo could be reduced in a warmer world, as the area of snow and ice cover is reduced, leading to further warming. Alternatively, a warmer world may increase cloud cover, cause greater backscatter of incoming solar radiation, and so reduce tropospheric temperatures. The scientific consensus, as witnessed by the dominant warming predictions of GCMs, is that the positive feedbacks will dominate negative feedbacks (Crosson, 1989: 109) and this has been reconfirmed by the IPCC reports (Houghton, Jenkins and Ephraums, 1990; Houghton *et al.*, 1996; IPCC Working Group I, 2001).

Yet, as far as greenhouse economics is concerned, there are problems with the type of data GCMs generate. In order to assess economic impacts variance is more useful than means, and regional impacts more useful than global. Where the concern is for scales below the regional extent for which an average is estimated, adopting the average value can be misleading. Two models can have precisely the same average for a regional variable but still give significant spatial differences for that variable within the region. Thus, GCMs have been regarded as inadequate for quantitative prediction even at the level of a multi-state region, let alone a particular state, county or city (Grotch, 1988: 253). The aim has therefore been to link these with regional atmospheric models with correspondingly scaled ecological, hydrological and mesoscale ocean models, although, the IPCC 1995 report warned that: 'Regional modelling techniques, however, rely critically on the GCM performance in simulating large-scale circulation patterns at the regional scale, because these are a primary input to both empirical and physically based regional models' (Kattenberg *et al.*, 1996: 345).

The degree of expected error multiplies dramatically as predictions move from global to continental to country to state levels, because GCMs currently treat the world as uniform blocks, ignoring topographical and meteorological variations within these blocks. Yet the more detailed predictions are those required for rigorous proof of the Greenhouse Effect. In addition, questions must be raised about the process of internal validation without reflection upon external concerns. There are, quite simply, unknown factors which scientists are unable to estimate, but about which they are forced to make judgements.

Socio-economic models

In the estimation of socio-economic impacts of climatic change another set of judgements is introduced. Even with 'perfect knowledge' from the scientific models the prediction of future states of the world would be dependent upon the estimation of such factors as population growth, technology and the nature of demand for products. Thus, imperfect information in relation to the implications of the enhanced Greenhouse Effect must consider knowledge about socio-economic effects. For example, while forests are regarded as a physical sink for CO_2, global deforestation currently makes this a net source of that gas. The unknowns pertaining to the socio-economic outcomes of global climate change, while dependent upon the scientific knowledge of physical effects, also feed back upon the physical systems. Thus, the interrelationship of the physical and socio-economic variables increases the inability to predict future events in accordance with the principles of weak uncertainty.

In the face of such complexity economists attempt to simplify the problem by holding factors constant and considering one issue at a time. However, as Kelejian and Varichek (1982: 225) have pointed out, the sum of the partial effects can be completely different from a combined effect occurring simultaneously. They gave the following example: annual increases of CFCs by 10 per cent, CO_2 by 5 per cent, and N_2O by 2.5 per cent as a sum of partial effects on wheat production in the US would be +0.4 per cent. In contrast, the total combined effect of these pollutants being simultaneously released was estimated to be −13.1 per cent.

The practice of analysing the effects of change in only a part of an economy, partial equilibrium analysis, is common in economics. For example, the study of western US agriculture by Adams *et al.* (1988) is typical of this methodology. The successful application requires ignored sectors to be relatively benign in terms of the variables under analysis. Thus, this approach can be misleading if relative prices in secondary sectors are changed by the relevant climatic variables, because all benefit estimates calculated on the basis of stability in those prices are brought into question. This problem can be extended as a critique of regarding inherently dynamic systems as static. Yet the extent to which changes in other sectors affect the results and at what stage such exogenous factors become significant is unclear. In a comparison of partial equilibrium and general equilibrium analyses of climate change, Kokoski and Smith (1987) found very divergent descriptions of the economic impacts where such a large-scale change in environmental conditions affects production activities. Thus, the results of many studies, such as those on agricultural impacts, are brought into question, along with the partial methodology for conducting environmental economic assessments of the enhanced Greenhouse Effect.

Paradoxically, the variations in environmental and socio-economic conditions around the world mean local information is critical for understanding the implications of climate change, e.g. local evaluation of probable species extinction. This would mean assessing national and international risks and potential costs and benefits largely on the basis of induction from numerous local and regional studies (Frederick and Rosenberg, 1994), i.e. partial equilibrium analysis.

In contrast, others have approached the issue from the level of global aggregates, often favouring abstract neo-classical modelling. Continuing efforts are aimed at global cost–benefit analysis of the enhanced Greenhouse Effect. Amongst these attempts that of Nordhaus has been noteworthy.[1] For example, Rowlands (1995: 138) refers to the earlier work by Nordhaus as a prescription to the US administration to avoid co-operative action which commanded significant respect and currency in that country. Others have noted the influence of this work in supporting the US position in international negotiations against emission reduction. The work also exemplifies several points with regard to economic modelling and the treatment of uncertainty.

In his summary volume, Nordhaus (1994), an optimisation model is presented which is purposefully designed to run on a personal computer; this is a stark contrast with the scientific input to the issue which employs Cray supercomputers to run GCMs. While GCMs are, as has been pointed out, still criticised for being too abstract and simple, Nordhaus rejects complex models in favour of 'transparency'. On the surface this appeal seems reasonable because of the tendency for excessive detail in modelling leading to results that are extremely precise but precisely wrong. Unfortunately, the transparency is rhetorical and the outcome is similar to previous models by Nordhaus in that the management of quantitative uncertainty and value-commitments are concealed (Funtowicz and Ravetz, 1994: 203).

The optimisation model approach requires 'developing' the scientific information to obtain 'highly simplified aggregate relationships' (Nordhaus, 1994: 23). Despite this bringing into question any policy relevance of the model or its predictions, Nordhaus claims these studies suggest avoiding a massive effort to slow climate change. This is particularly interesting given the assumptions made in constructing the model on both the physical science and economic sides, which are briefly considered next. Various other problems have been noted in Nordhaus's work (e.g. see Ayres and Walters, 1991; Daily *et al.*, 1991; Funtowicz and Ravetz, 1994) and are discussed further in chapter 6.

The scientific assumptions appear to go beyond mere simplification. The deep ocean is assumed to be an infinite carbon sink while the 'missing sink' for CO_2 is ignored. Price (1994) calculates that the unrealistic assumptions about ocean uptake of carbon used by Nordhaus result in the benefits of CO_2 control being under-estimated, at low discount rates, by a factor of four. Climate change is represented by global mean surface temperature, although a better range of variables for impact assessment are precipitation, soil moisture, sea level rise and measurement by seasonal patterns, rate of change and variance (rather than mean). Most attention is paid to CO_2 on the basis that it contributes 80 per cent of global warming (p. 15), although the IPCC only attributed 55 per cent of warming to this gas at the time (Houghton, Callander and Varney, 1992); methane and nitrous oxides are considered to be external to the Nordhaus model. With little explanation a mixture of 1990 IPCC scenarios was chosen for the no action base case; thus CO_2 and N_2O are 'business as usual', CFCs are phased out under the IPCC accelerated policies scenario, and methane emissions occur at the low-level scenario.

Next consider some of the economic assumptions. These include all countries having competitive industries, producing perfect substitutes, with identical Cobb–Douglas production functions,[3] all of which apparently has no effect on major conclusions (Nordhaus, 1994: 8), although one result would be no need for international trade. World estimates of damages are extended from estimates for the US economy, and regional distributions are largely ignored. Impacts are restricted to agriculture, coastlines, energy and 'other' and then bounded in model runs by the percentage of GNP these sectors are judged to contribute to the economy, e.g. agriculture is valued at 2.52 per cent of 1981 GNP ignoring the value of the related food sector. A change in the value of any sector due to increasing relative scarcity or cross-sectoral impacts are ruled out by assuming constant relative prices. The overall outcome is to recommend an optimal policy which leads to a 3.1°C global average temperature rise by 2100.

The way in which uncertain future events are characterised is also particularly revealing. The main treatment of uncertainty is the considerable effort put into sensitivity analysis. There is discussion of difficult-to-calibrate catastrophic scenarios '... which might be equivalent to the damages from a major war, or from a half century of Communist rule' (Nordhaus, 1994: 115). Rather than unknown surprises, such 'catastrophes' are then treated as known threshold events, at which large losses of GNP occur. That is, it is assumed that the states can be known, can be avoided and while large are bounded. There is considerable optimism concerning the ability to assess the risk of future events and the belief is expressed that many of the uncertainties are ones which can be resolved by further study or at least by the passage of time (Nordhaus, 1994: 169).

Overall this type of approach seems to present political argument as the outcome of an objective scientific modelling process. There are clearly a set of implicit values behind the work. For example, the idea of preserving Nature at the expense of economic growth is termed 'ultraconservative'. Nature is described as exogenous and to be regarded as threatening with the potential to 'deal us a nasty hand'. The emphasis is upon a specific model of political economy which is, however, never explicitly described. This study is indicative of more general issues concerning environmental assessment in economics, which is the subject of chapter 6, but also raises the problem of how economics has limited its view of uncertainty.

Conclusions

The approach to characterising uncertainty in relationship to climatic futures under the enhanced Greenhouse Effect has relied upon standard probability theory. This has the ability to show the importance of changing the frequency of events at different extremes and how thresholds may be exceeded or unusual climatic events become more common. Yet a sole emphasis on this approach to uncertainty neglects how knowledge and the ability to understand are limited.

Problems arise in the application of standard risk assessment and probability theory because of the complexity of climate change and its possible consequences. For example, the current size, age and species composition of many ecosystems are unique and have been strongly affected by human activities. Hence, strong uncertainty pertains to ecosystems functions in addition to risk. Biological systems vary over time and space due to physical factors to which they are related in a non-linear fashion. In order to study the effect of changes in atmospheric chemistry upon biological systems, data analysis must be based upon fluxes, variances, extreme events and 'noise', rather than concentrations, smoothed means and steady states (Williamson, 1992: 32).

A search for evidence about the implications of GHG emissions has led to modelling exercises to reduce strong uncertainty. Reliance for prediction has concentrated on simulation models (e.g. GCMs) as opposed to historical analogue because global temperatures are expected to occur at unprecedented rates. This need for artificial scenarios is a recognition of indeterminacy and partial ignorance. However, the extent to which models are then expected to provide answers seems to ignore their limitations. For example, the Northern Hemisphere, having most of the land area, is liable to heat more rapidly than the Southern Hemisphere, with most of the oceans; the result could change the general circulation of the atmosphere but would fail to be recognised by GCM models working on steady-state calculations, i.e. assuming shifts from one stable equilibrium to another (Firor, 1990: 78). A feature of non-linear systems is that small changes in a forcing variable can lead to abrupt and large changes in a dependent variable. Examples are the disruption of the El Niño systems or the North Atlantic Gulf Stream. The El Niño is an unusual warming of the water in the Equatorial Pacific appearing every three to five years and having a strong influence on weather patterns. The late 1990s saw intense El Niño causing extreme weather events in the Americas, Australia and Africa (May, 1997). Similarly, small changes in regional transportation of heat by oceans (a major heat reservoir) can have large but unpredictable impacts on local climate. The interactions between climate, atmosphere and oceans are areas of strong uncertainty (see on-going scientific research by Christiansen *et al.*, 2000). In this regard concern has been expressed for any disruption of the Gulf Stream which transports heat to the British Isles.[2] As the UK government's chief scientific officer has stated: 'The possibility that this might be significantly reduced, much less turned off, is an awesome prospect' (May, 1997: 5).

The idea that uncertainty can be reduced, and even eradicated, by more research, seems common amongst both natural scientists and economists. However, several points can be raised against such a prognosis: the persistence of weak uncertainty due to measurement errors; the persistence of strong uncertainty due to differences in the interpretation of given 'facts'; the methodological problem that evidence can only disprove but never prove a theory; the existence of irreducible ignorance; the lack of any single metric for damage assessment; and the persistence of unknown cause–effect relationships. The type of work being produced by economists exemplifies how implicit value-loaded boundaries are drawn in terms of designating which knowledge is employed. While the social aspect of economic knowledge may be deemed to make it implicitly subjective, a similar methodological problem also faces natural scientists. That is, how environmental problems are characterised is seen to be determined by assumptions which restrict the focus of any given research.

The alternative to trying to define risk states is to accept that global systems are inherently unpredictable so that many different outcomes are equally likely. Strong uncertainty must then be regarded as a property of the system rather than a failure of scientific method which can be removed in the long term or by increased research budgets. Yet the main approach to uncertainty being put forward by both scientists and economists limits itself to weak uncertainty and fails to discuss the meaning or content of strong uncertainty.

Notes

1   The faith of Nordhaus in the potential of neo-classical modelling is witnessed by his stating that: 'Our future lies not in the stars but in our models' (Nordhaus, 1994: 6).
2   The heat being delivered amounts to 27,000 times the total power-generating capacity of the UK. Increased precipitation in the region flowing into the North Atlantic would reduce surface water salinity. This less dense water would fail to sink as easily so changing the fluid dynamics, impacting deep ocean circulation and the Gulf Stream.
3   A particular type of production function of the form:

$$Q = b_0 x_1^{b1} x_2^{b2} \ldots x_n^{bn}$$

Where Q is output, x are factors of production (e.g. capital, labour) and b are parameters. The name derives from the authors Cobb and Douglas who introduced it in an article published in the *American Economic Review* in 1928. The function has been widely used in economics especially in the form where the parameters add to one.

References

Adams, R.M., B.A. McCarl, D.J. Dudek and J.D. Glyer (1988) 'Implications of global climate change for western agriculture', *Western Journal of Agriculture Economics* **13**(2): 348–56.

Adger, N. and S. Fankhauser (1993) 'Economic analysis of the greenhouse effect: optimal abatement level and strategies for mitigation', *International Journal of Environment and Pollution* **3**(1–3): 104–19.

Ayres, R.U. and J. Walters (1991) 'The greenhouse effect: damages, costs and abatement', *Environmental and Resource Economics* **1**(3): 237–70.

Boulton, G.S. (1994) *The spectrum of recent climatic change and its reflection in the biosphere.* Presented at The Royal Society of Edinburgh, 2 February 1994.

Bray, A.J. (1991) 'The ice age cometh: remembering the scare of global cooling', *Policy Review* **58**: 82–4.

Christiansen, H.H., L.E. Mortensen, T. Nielsen, T.L. Rasmussen and O. Humlum (2000) *Linking Land and Sea at the Faroe Islands: Mapping and Understanding North Atlantic Changes.* Copenhagen: University of Copenhagen.

Crosson, P. (1989) 'Greenhouse warming and climate change: why should we care?', *Food Policy* (May): 107–18.

Crosson, P. (1993) 'Impacts of climate change on the agriculture and economy of Missouri, Iowa, Nebraska, and Kansas (MINK) region', in *Agricultural Dimensions of Global Climate Change,* edited by H.M. Kaiser and T.E. Drennen, pp. 117–35, Boca Raton, FL: St Lucie Press.

Daily, G.C., P. R. Ehrlich, H.A. Mooney and A.H. Ehrlich (1991) 'Greenhouse economics: learn before you leap', *Ecological Economics* **4**: 1–10.

Firor, J.W. (1990) *The Changing Atmosphere: A Global Challenge.* New Haven, CT: Yale University Press.

Frederick, K.D. and N.J. Rosenberg (eds) (1994) *Assessing the Impacts of Climate Change on Natural Resource Systems.* Dordrecht, The Netherlands: Kluwer Academic Publishers.

Fukui, H. (1979) *Climatic Carriability and Agriculture in Tropical Moist Regions.* Presented at World Climate Conference, Geneva, 12–23 February 1979.

Funtowicz, S.O. and J.R. Ravetz (1994) 'The worth of a songbird: ecological economics as a post-normal science', *Ecological Economics* **10**(3): 197–207.

Goodess, C.M., J.P. Palutikof and T.D. Davies (1992) *The Nature and Causes of Climate Change: Assessing the Long Term Future*. London: Belhaven.

Grotch, S.L. (1988) *Regional Intercomparison of General Circulation Model Predictions and Historical Climate Data*. Washington, DC: Department of Energy.

Hansen, J.E. (1988) *Testimony to US Senate*. Presented at Committee on Energy and Natural Resources, Washington, DC, 23 June 1988, Alderson Reporting Company.

Hare, F.K. (1979) *Climatic Variation and Variability: Empirical Evidence from Meteorological and Other Sources*. Presented at World Climate Conference, Geneva, 12–23 February 1979.

Hare, F.K. (1985) 'Climatic variability and change', in *Climate Impact Assessment: Studies of the Interaction of Climate and Society* **SCOPE 27**, edited by R.W. Kates, J.H. Ausubel and M. Berberian, pp. 37–68, Chichester: John Wiley & Sons.

Harrison, S.J. (1991) *Global Warming: Predicting the Uncertain*. Department of Environmental Science, Stirling: University of Stirling Climate Services.

Houghton, J.T., B.A. Callander and S.K. Varney (eds) (1992) *Climate Change 1992: The Supplementary Report to the IPCC Scientific Assessment*. Cambridge, England: Cambridge University Press.

Houghton, J.T., G.J. Jenkins and J.J. Ephraums (eds) (1990) *Climate Change: The IPCC Scientific Assessment*. Cambridge, England: Cambridge University Press.

Houghton, J.T., L.G. Meira, B.A. Callander, N. Harris, A. Kattenberg and K. Maskell (eds) (1996) *Climate Change 1995: The Science of Climate Change*. Cambridge, England: Cambridge University Press.

IPCC Working Group I (2001) *Climate Change 2001: Scientific Assessment; Summary for Policymakers*. Geneva: Intergovernmental Panel on Climate Change.

IPCC Working Group II (2001) *Climate Change 2001: Impacts, Adaptation, and Vulnerability; Summary for Policymakers*. Geneva: Intergovernmental Panel on Climate Change.

IPCC Working Group III (2001) *Climate Change 2001: Mitigation of Climate Change; Summary for Policymakers*. Geneva: Intergovernmental Panel on Climate Change.

Jones, P.D., D.E. Parker, T.J. Osborn and K.R. Briffa (2000) 'Global and hemispheric temperature anomalies: land and marine instrumental records', in *Trends: A Compendium of Data on Global Change*. Oak Ridge, TN: Carbon Dioxide Information Analysis Center, Oak Ridge National Laboratory, US Department of Energy.

Jouzel, J., C. Lorius, J.R. Petit, N.I. Barkov and V.M. Kotlyakov (1994) 'Vostok isotopic temperature record', in *Trends '93: A Compendium of Data on Global Change* ORNL/CDIAC-65, edited by T.A. Boden, D.P. Kaiser, R.J. Sepanski and F.W. Stoss, pp. 590–602, Oak Ridge, TN: Carbon Dioxide Information Analysis Center, Oak Ridge National Laboratory, US Department of Energy.

Kattenberg, A., F. Giorgi, H. Grassl, G.A. Meehl, J.F.B. Mitchell, R.J. Stouffer, T. Tokioka, A.J. Weaver and T.M.L. Wigley (1996) 'Climate models: projections of future climate', in *Climate Change 1995: The Science of Climate Change,* edited by J.T. Houghton, L.G. Meira, B.A. Callander, N. Harris, A. Kattenberg and K. Maskell, pp. 285–357, Cambridge, England: Cambridge University Press.

Keeling, C.D. and T.P. Whorf (2000) 'Atmospheric CO_2 records from sites in the SIO air sampling network', in *Trends: A Compendium of Data on Global Change*. Oak Ridge, TN:

Carbon Dioxide Information Analysis Center, Oak Ridge National Laboratory, US Department of Energy.

Kelejian, H.K. and B.V. Varichek (1982) 'Pollution, climate change, and consequent economic costs concerning agricultural production', in *The Economics of Managing Chlorofluorocarbons: Stratospheric Ozone and Climate Issues,* edited by J.H. Cumberland, J.R. Hibbs and I. Hoch, pp. 224–68, Washington, DC: Resources for the Future.

Kokoski, M.F. and V.K. Smith (1987) 'A general equilibrium analysis of partial-equilibrium welfare measures: the case of climate change', *American Economic Review* **77**(3): 331–41.

LaMarche, V.C. (1978) 'Tree ring evidence of past climatic variability', *Nature* **276**(November): 334–8.

MacDonald, G.J. (1988) 'Scientific basis for the greenhouse effect', *Journal of Policy Analysis and Management* **7**(3): 424–44.

Manne, A.S. and R.G. Richels (1992) *Buying Greenhouse Insurance: The Economic Costs of CO_2 Emissions Limit*. Cambridge, MA: MIT Press.

May, R. (1997) *Climate Change*. London, Office of Science and Technology.

Nordhaus, W.D. (1994) *Managing the Global Commons: The Economics of Climate Change*. Cambridge, MA: MIT Press.

Parry, M.L. and T.R. Carter (1986) 'Effects of climatic changes on agriculture and forestry: an overview', in *Effects of Changes in Stratospheric Ozone and Global Climate* **I**, edited by J.G. Titus, pp. 257–98, Washington, DC: US Environmental Protection Agency.

Petit, J.R., D. Raynaud, C. Lorius, J. Jouzel, H. Delaygue, N.I. Barkov and V.M. Kotlyakov (2000) 'Historical isotopic temperature record from the Vostok ice core', in *Trends: A Compendium of Data on Global Change*. Oak Ridge, TN: Carbon Dioxide Information Analysis Center, Oak Ridge National Laboratory, US Department of Energy.

Price, C. (1994) *Emissions, Concentrations, and Disappearing CO_2*. Bangor: University College of North Wales.

Riebsame, W.E. (1989) *Assessing the Social Implications of Climate Fluctuations: A Guide to Climate Impact Studies*. Nairobi, Kenya: UNEP, World Climate Impacts Programme.

Rowlands, I.H. (1995) *The Politics of Global Atmospheric Change*. Manchester, England: Manchester University Press.

Santer, B.D. (1994) *The detection of greenhouse-gas-induced climate change*. Research Summary no. 29. Oak Ridge, TN: Carbon Dioxide Information Analysis Center, Oak Ridge National Laboratory, US Department of Energy.

Vinnikov, K., P. Groisman and K.M. Lugina (1994) 'Global hemispheric temperature anomalies from instrumental surface air temperature records', in *Trends '93: A Compendium of Data on Global Change* ORNL/CDIAC-65, edited by T.A. Boden, D.P. Kaiser, R.J. Sepanski and F.W. Stoss, pp. 615–27, Oak Ridge, TN: Carbon Dioxide Information Analysis Center, Oak Ridge National Laboratory, US Department of Energy.

Watts, J.A. (1982) 'The carbon dioxide queston: a data sampler' in *Carbon Dioxide Review 1982*, edited by W.C. Clark, pp. 431–69, Oxford: Clarendon Press.

Williamson, P. (1992) *Global Change: Reducing Uncertainties*. Stockholm, Sweden: International Geosphere-Biosphere Programme.

5   Strong uncertainty
Ignorance and indeterminacy

A repeatedly stated aim of the scientific community addressing the enhanced Greenhouse Effect is to reduce, evaluate and quantify uncertainties. This is reflected in calls for risk–benefit analysis and similar deterministic quantitative approaches. However, contradictory messages appear across reports and within single documents. Such approaches sit uneasily with the recognition that: 'Because of the uncertainties associated with regional projections, of climate change, the report necessarily takes the approach of assessing sensitivities and vulnerabilities of each region, rather than attempting to provide quantitative predictions of the impacts of climate change' (Watson *et al.*, 1997: vii). The scenarios which informed the IPCC work under the TAR were explicitly stated to be 'equally valid with no assigned probabilities of occurrence' (Nakicenovic *et al.*, 2000: 4). However, the TAR then used a classification of 'subjective' probabilities with precisely defined quantitative confidence levels (see IPCC Working Group I, 2001: 2). There is an obvious discrepancy between the different approaches to uncertainty, resulting in inconsistent statements.

In the last chapter the way in which uncertainty pervades the issue of predicting climate change was explored from the perspective of weak uncertainty. That approach concentrates upon a specific characterisation of missing knowledge as 'objective risk'. The idea of strong uncertainty was also introduced and discussed as being relevant to both scientific and economic modelling and prediction. The aim in the current chapter is to further elucidate the distinction between different types of uncertainty, their relevance to climate change and implications for research and policy. This requires a more in-depth explanation of the classification already introduced before moving on to the issues raised by strong uncertainty.

Risk can be defined as the case where the set of all future events are known but the occurrence of any one event is only a potential. Thus, tossing a fair (evenly weighted) coin would be regarded as leading to two events, either heads or tails, with a known probability of 50:50. In common use risk is associated with harm or negative outcomes, but under environmental risk assessment or economic decision analysis the outcomes could all be beneficial, neutral or harmful or any mixture of the three.

The standard theory of decision-making under uncertainty modifies the normal economic assumption of perfect knowledge to account for risk. That is, rather than being certain as to the outcome of their choices, the decision-maker (e.g. consumer, producer, civil servant or politician) still knows all future possible outcomes but only the probability (density function or distribution) of their occurrence. This allows the calculation of every possible outcome and the expected value (or utility) of each choice, also called the probability weighted average. Additional weightings can be added to account for the attitude of the decision-maker towards risk, i.e. risk neutral, risk averse or risk taker. The original economic decision model can be maintained by using the expected values instead of the known ones. This theory assumes that 'objective' probabilities are associated with events or outcomes.

Empirically observable and repeatable events, such as a coin toss, allow the construction of what are termed 'objective' probabilities or risks of an event occurring. That is, anybody could repeatedly toss the coin and count the number of heads and tails and would find the same probability of their occurrence. However, as Loasby (1976: 8) states, 'the notion of an objective probability distribution carries a strong (but unstated) implication about the nature of the world, namely that it generates all the necessary (and quite unambiguous) frequency distributions from a stable population of events'. As already shown in chapter 4, this is not the case for global climate change and, as Loasby notes, is indeed a generally implausible requirement. As also explained in the last chapter, the past provides no assurance of the future.

Accepting that 'objective' probabilities are absent means moving to what economists term 'uncertainty', which is in fact still only a limited, although problematic, adjustment. In the absence of an ability to estimate a probability distribution from observation (i.e. 'objective' probabilities) an appeal may be made to 'subjective' probabilities as an alternative. The assumption is now that probability functions are undefined although all states of the world or future outcomes are still known. The solution to this problem for mainstream economists is to allow the use of probabilities placed by the decision-makers themselves upon the likelihood of an event. In practice various methods are employed to obtain such 'subjective' probabilities. This new adjustment makes the move from 'objective risk' to 'subjective risk', but neither has addressed what is commonly understood as uncertainty. Thus, economists (and scientists) tend to restrict themselves to discussions of weak uncertainty.

Keynes (1988), amongst others, argued that the terms risk and uncertainty should be regarded as strictly separate.[1] However, in common use the terms are often interchanged so that employing the term 'uncertainty' in such an unusually restrictive way (i.e. excluding risk) can create confusion; the temptation is always to slip back into common usage. Therefore, here, risk is included under weak uncertainty while the term strong uncertainty is applied to the more Keynesian concepts, as shown in table 5.1.

Table 5.1 Classifications of uncertainty, risk and ignorance

	Sub-categories	Explanation
Weak uncertainty	Objective risk	Known outcomes and their probabilities; termed 'risk' by mainstream economists; probabilities given by natural world
	Subjective risk	Known outcomes only; termed 'uncertainty' by mainstream economists; probabilities assessed from human preferences
Strong uncertainty	Partial ignorance	Unknown outcomes
	Indeterminacy	Unpredictable outcomes

Strong uncertainty then refers to the admission of a lack of knowledge about potential outcomes. The coin may land on its edge or disappear between the floor boards. Such strong uncertainties are often excluded from calculation because they are regarded as so unlikely as to be of negligible significance, in which case, we are truly surprised when they occur. They often relate to events which have been excluded by assumption. Thus, partial ignorance is an inevitable part of modelling where situations are simplified and vision restricted in order to aid understanding. Strong uncertainty requires that allowing for surprise events and admitting knowledge about future possible events is always incomplete. This is particularly relevant to complex systems (such as those forming climate, or economies) where choice cannot be assumed to be fully informed (contrary to the simple coin toss, and assumptions of positive economics).

As Loasby (1976) has explained, choice within complex systems provides the basic subject matter of economics. Thus, what he terms 'partial ignorance' becomes central to economics because the subject concerns the study of the unintended social repercussions of human actions. As a result the problem of how to describe and deal with a lack of knowledge in the sense of ignorance opens up a much wider debate. The concept of ignorance raises the idea of an irreducible lack of knowledge which is never removed by research and is in fact endemic to scientific knowledge. As a result ignorance is revealed due to events external to an individual's or group's models, disciplinary focus or world view and this can force a changed of perspective.

In addition, the concept of an 'indeterminacy' of outcomes is also relevant. While the concept of an indeterminate future may appear similar to a state of partial ignorance there are additional distinct features. Indeterminacy will arise due to a lack of knowledge and an inability to comprehend all existing knowledge, but also because of the social context within which knowledge is applied. Social context varies and involves customs, culture, institutions and socio-economic systems. The importance of indeterminacy is explained later in this chapter.

First in the following section five events are used to characterise the range and type of uncertainty confronting society due to the enhanced Greenhouse Effect. This draws upon chapter 3 but aims to focus the reader's mind on how some of the issues have been debated, judged or neglected. The way in which weak uncertainty has been used to address such issues is then discussed with specific focus on the insurance risk model. This shows flaws in the economic approach which are then explained in greater detail. The need to move away from the weak uncertainty characterisation is explained and the alternative explanation using strong uncertainty described. The current conception of scientific and technological research as removed from social processes is highlighted as false. Knowledge about natural and socio-economic systems is then placed within a common context of choice where humans simplify, assume and guess.

Characterising future events

This section considers how relatively near, future generations could be affected by global warming.[2] Below, five events caused by the enhanced Greenhouse Effect are identified from the literature presented in chapter 3 so as to characterise the type and range of impacts which might occur around the year 2100. Such events form the basis for economic cost–benefit analysis, which is discussed in the next chapter, as well as the case for concern over distant future people. The resulting ethical issues, which will be discussed in chapter 9, include questions over compensating future generations for harm due to enhancing the Greenhouse Effect. The framing and characterisation of impacts is therefore central to the entire debate over policy responses.

Agricultural impacts

Researchers have estimated that doubling carbon dioxide equivalent levels will cause annual welfare losses of $33 thousand million due to lost US crop production.

This compares to a $40 thousand million loss in the US mainly to agriculture from the drought in 1988 (Wilhite, 1990). Nordhaus (1991) associates a double CO_2 equivalent world with much lower losses of $9.7 thousand million and possibly gains of $10.6 thousand million (1982 prices); his figures were selected from amongst those of an EPA study which gave a much wider variety of scenarios and outcomes under a double CO_2 equivalent. The original research was done for the EPA by Adams *et al.* (1988), as discussed in chapter 3. They reported losses of $5.9 thousand million using the GISS global circulation model and $33 thousand million under the GFDL model, without a CO_2 fertilisation effect; with fertilisation these figures became those selected by Nordhaus. However, Adams *et al.* also reported losses of up to $44.6 thousand million if increasing demand was included with technological progress but without a fertilisation effect. The IPCC has noted the failure of studies to account for changes in agricultural pests and climatic variability (Watson *et al.*, 1996: 9). For this and other reasons faith in the extent to which fertilisation benefits will actually occur has been brought into question (see: Daily *et al.*, 1991; Erickson, 1993; Wolfe and Erickson, 1993).

Even accepting full fertilisation, Cline (1992) has recognised errors in the fertilisation calculations as employed by Nordhaus and adjusted the EPA figures for a $2 \times CO_2$ equivalent scenario accordingly. This requires recognising that rather than 600 ppm (double CO_2) the appropriate concentration of CO_2 is 442 ppm (double CO_2 equivalent); as a result central estimate losses with the fertilisation effect are $17.5 thousand million (1990 prices) or $13 thousand million (1982 prices); this excludes any demand increase. In addition, Cline (1992: 32) gives the figure of $95 thousand million for the long-run annual loss, i.e. a beyond $2 \times CO_2$ equivalent figure. Note that, according to Cline (1992: 74), a $2 \times CO_2$ equivalent warming of 2.5°C is exceeded before 2050, by when temperature is predicted to have risen by 3.1°C. On this basis losses of $33 thousand million per annum by 2100 seem conservative.

However, the process of estimating cause–effect relationships between agricultural crops and an enhanced Greenhouse Effect is fraught with difficulties. Erickson (1993) has pointed out a series of problems with the research being used to predict increased agricultural yields from CO_2.

- The results from experiments measure changes in crop dry matter which ignores the difference between economic yield and plant growth.
- Negative feedback mechanisms are ignored, such as greater stomata resistance increasing leaf temperature and so impairing radiation use.
- The experimental conditions rather than field conditions are idealised; this ignores the normal limiting factors to growth. For example, phosphorous deficiency can prevent any CO_2 fertilisation effect.
- Water stress is a key factor determining plant response and is inadequately taken into account. For example, water stress at key times can affect the marketability of products, flooding can damage crops directly, and a greater frequency of extreme events cause ongoing stress.
- Research into combined impacts is lacking. For example, there are no studies on increased CO_2 in association with water stress and higher temperatures, although this is a typical scenario under climate change.
- The need for increased fertiliser applications and other complementary inputs in order to benefit from CO_2 fertilisation is neglected.
- Managerial ability to grow crops in the field under new conditions diverges from that of expert plant scientists in an experimental situation.
- The role of non-CO_2 gases in changing climate parameters is ignored, e.g. temperature and water stress will then increase faster than predicted.
- CFCs are depleting the stratospheric ozone layer and UV-B damage is therefore expected, but models have yet to take this into account in association with climate change.
- The role of other air pollutants on crops is neglected, but is known to be important, e.g. crop losses due to tropospheric ozone.

- Pests, diseases and weeds are predicted to have a greater impact on crops in a warmer world. Erickson cites work showing 32–4 per cent losses in North America and 45–6 per cent in Africa.

In summary, a standard experimental approach to developing dose-response functions grows plants under ideal environmental circumstances excepting the one factor being studied (e.g. CO_2 levels). Thus, the simultaneous impact of multiple factors is ignored (e.g. nutrient deficiency, precipitation, pollutants, pests). Transferring results to actual farm conditions results in numerous variations. Extrapolation from limited experimental data on a small range of crop species creates considerable room for error and potential inaccuracy when estimating aggregate environmental impacts on agriculture across large regions, let alone nationally or globally (for a detailed discussion see Spash, 1997). As the IPCC note:

> 'Major uncertainties result from the lack of reliable geographic resolution in future climate predictions, difficulties in integrating and scaling-up basic physiological responses and relationships, and difficulty in estimating farm sector response and adaptation to changing climate as it varies across the world. Thus, while there will be winners and losers stemming from climate impacts on agricultural production, it is not possible to distinguish reliably and precisely those areas that will benefit and those that will lose.
>
> (Reilly, 1996: 429)

Sea level rise

The Maldives are a group of islands off the coast of Africa. They are only a few metres above sea level and will be totally submerged due to rising sea levels, forcing the 177,000 inhabitants to lose their homes and be relocated.

As Gribbin (1990: 176) points out the 2,000 atolls which constitute the Maldives at no point rise more than 2 m above current sea levels. The upper bound of IPCC estimates for sea level rise are around 1 m by 2100, but storm surges at this level could easily inundate such low-lying islands. As shown in a previous chapter, table 3.8, other studies place the upper range at 3.5 m in 100 years.

Bangladesh currently suffers from severe annual floods. As sea level rises and monsoon rains increase, 11 per cent of Bangladesh will be flooded all year affecting 8.5 million people.

The estimate given here is based upon Broadus et al. (1986) for a 1 m or less average sea level rise. The UNEP has estimated that 15 million Bangladeshis are threatened by total inundation from a primary rise of 1.5 m, and a secondary increase up to 3 m would flood 20 per cent of the land area dislocating a further 8 million people (Jacobson, 1990). These estimates are calculated on the basis of a static population size and density, both of which are growing. These displacements would be part of a more general shift in population due to sea level rise during the next century. Asduzzaman (cited by Hayes, 1993: 129) estimates 80 million refugees from sea level rise alone.

Forced migration and droughts in arid zones

As global warming becomes a predominant trend 50 million people living in the arid areas of the Third World will be forced off their land by persistent droughts.

This kind of outcome is more speculative and is normally mentioned in general terms. As discussed by Keyfitz (1992) the poor are set to suffer most, be least able to adapt, and the problem of forced migration will be exacerbated by population growth. Where agricultural zones shift, the migratory pressures will increase on the rural poor. The impacts of changing climate will be severest for industrially developing countries which have half or more of their population engaged in agriculture and population density which is closely linked with soil fertility. Barbier (1989) has discussed such dislocations without quantification. Woodwell (1990: 128–9) mentions hundreds of millions of people being displaced by sea level rise in the next century and additional countless millions becoming migrants due to aridity and biotic impoverishment.

Human migration in response to chronic crop failures, regional flooding or drought is cited by the 1995 IPCC report as 'difficult to quantify or value in monetary terms' (Watson, Zinyowera and Moss, 1996: 36). However, Adger and Fankhauser (1993) produced a highly speculative figure of $4.3 thousand million for a doubling of CO_2 (based upon Fankhauser, 1995). These numbers from Fankhauser are meant to largely exclude impacts from sea level rise as coastal populations are assumed to be protected. In order to produce the financial number Fankhauser (1995: 49–51) borrows money estimates, only covering relocation costs, from Cline (1992) and Ayres and Walter (1991). He admits costs of hardship and stress are 'almost impossible to assess', but speculates they are a larger amount than the 'pure economic losses'; although they too are welfare impacts and no less pure in economic terms. The borrowed migration numbers of 2.7 million per year are based on a percentage 'guesstimates' for the US, also from Cline, which is then applied globally. How the 2.7 million per year becomes the figure for all impacts under double CO_2 is unclear, i.e. the 2.7 million is a flow rather than a stock. If this is meant to be a constant flow then after about 18.5 years the 50 million migration mark would be reached.

Catastrophic surprise

The West Antarctic ice sheet could totally melt causing an average sea level rise of 6 m.

During the last interglacial 132,000 years ago the temperature was 1°C warmer and sea level approximately 6 m higher (Goodess, Palutikof and Davies, 1992: 109). The melting of the West Antarctic ice sheet is discussed by Revelle (1983) and Schneider and Chen (1980). The latter estimate an 8 m sea level rise. The IPCC has reported that this event is unlikely under typical scenarios (Warrick and Oerlemans, 1990: 261). As Warrick *et al.* state (1996: 364):

> Concern has been expressed that the West Antarctic Ice Sheet might 'surge', causing a rapid rise in sea level. The current lack of knowledge regarding the specific circumstances under which this might occur, either in total or in part, limits the ability to quantify the risk. Nonetheless, the likelihood of a major sea level rise by the year 2100 due to the collapse of the West Antarctic Ice Sheet is considered low.

Such a catastrophe is seen to represent a positive and increasing risk of occurrence with continued warming. This is a characteristic treatment of an unquantifiable irreversible event as a low positive risk (weak uncertainty) rather than a case of strong uncertainty, i.e. partial ignorance or indeterminacy.

Collapse of the West Antarctic Ice Sheet would initially release about two million cubic km of ice causing a 5–6 m sea level rise prior to the remaining half of the ice sheet, which is below sea level, beginning to float (Revelle, 1983: 442). This is estimated to take a minimum of 300 years, starting from the middle of the next century, giving a 2 m rise per 100 years, or perhaps 500 years with a 1.1 m rise per 100 years. However, warming might thin the Ross and Filcher-Ronne ice shelves enough in the next 100 years to make the process irreversible (Titus, 1989: 188). The implications are dramatic, systems appear to have non-linear characteristics and knowledge is extremely limited. As Warrick *et al.* (1996: 396) state:

> Of all the terms that enter the sea level change equation the largest uncertainties pertain to the Earth's major ice sheets. Relatively small changes in these ice sheets could have major effects on global sea level, yet we are not even certain of the sign of their present contribution.

As discussed in chapter 3, the understanding of ice shelves and sheets and their disintegration is poor and rapid collapses of ice shelves in the late 1990s raised some alarm while bringing into question scientific knowledge of the issue.

Judgement in assessment

A central issue in trying to assess the probability of future events is determining what is at risk and when in the future it will be at risk. These five events indicate how different experts attribute varying likelihoods to the occurrence and characteristics (i.e. magnitude, speed and timing) of future events related to the enhanced Greenhouse Effect. Thus, even given a particular set of outcomes or states of the world, assessing the unknown probability of a state being realised as a subjective risk will result in widely varying responses depending upon who is asked for their opinion. The way in which knowledge is collected and used to form such opinions is crucial to how the issue is perceived. In addition, how the issue is framed in terms of which aspects are regarded as relevant and how different information is considered will determine the scope of perceived dangers.

Economic use of weak uncertainty

Attractions of the risk analogy

The essence of wanting to limit trace gas emissions is to avoid a state of the world in which an uncontrollable threat to human life support systems is created. The potential outcomes involved in the case of global climate change have been perceived by the international community to include extremely large damages, such as outlined by the five events above. This is also evidenced by the final statement of the 1988 Toronto conference on the issue which included representatives of 46 countries and 15 international organisations: 'Humanity is conducting an unintended, uncontrolled, globally pervasive experiment whose ultimate consequences could be second only to a global nuclear war' (Environment Canada, 1988: 1).

The military analogy has also been used by Daily *et al.* (1991) to compare the policies required to reduce the risk of damages due to global climate change to those implemented over the last 40 years to protect the world from a third world war. In the decade of the 1980s, the US alone is estimated to have spent $1,500 thousand million to protect against an enemy whose probability of attack in the previous quarter of a century was given as less than 3 per cent. In contrast, climatologists in the 1980s were cited as giving the chances of unprecedented climate change as 50 per cent.

Introducing risk in this way can appear attractive because it allows for the inclusion of risk aversion. This can lead to the conclusion that reducing GHG emissions is desirable even if the expected costs of doing so are known to exceed the expected benefits. The reasoning is based upon social decision-making being risk averse. For example, assume the costs of reducing GHG emissions by 75 per cent are known to be $1 trillion. The benefits of reducing GHG emissions might range from $0.25 trillion to $10 trillion, with an expected value of $0.8 trillion. If risk aversion is operating there can be a logical preference for incurring the certain loss of $1 trillion (the 'certainty equivalent') rather than the expected loss of $0.8 trillion, with the potential for higher losses.

Thus, GHG control could be regarded as an insurance premium against known but only potential future states of the world, where the probability of those states occurring is known or knowable. This would be consistent with an expected utility framework, and could justify a safe minimum standard approach. That is, once a threshold with a safe margin has been chosen, the economy could be 'safely' allowed to emit GHGs. So even environmentalists might wish to welcome the insurance analogy and the weak uncertainty characterisation of the enhanced Greenhouse Effect.

Greenhouse Effect insurance

Manne and Richels (1992: 1) conduct a more detailed analysis of the enhanced Greenhouse Effect as if it were a case of deterministic risk where policymakers can act 'as though they were purchasers of greenhouse insurance'. The extent to which the policy outcome is removed from an 'objective' scientific approach to economic analysis is apparent in the role of belief in their following statement:

> Depending on one's views of control costs, a case can be made either for or against emission cuts. The issue is similar to purchasing an insurance policy. If one believes that there are great risks from global warming and that the insurance premium is negligible, there is little reason to delay. This is the attractiveness of 'no regrets' strategies, such as costless conservation. The problem becomes more complex when there are price tags attached to limiting the emission of greenhouse gases. If the insurance premium is expensive, it may be worthwhile to pursue alternatives to immediate cutbacks on emissions.
>
> (Manne and Richels, 1992: x)

In fact, Manne and Richels, and others, are wrong in this analogy because insurance does nothing to prevent the chances of damage, but merely arranges for compensation after a harmful event has occurred. The error here is to regard endogenous risk as exogenous, a point discussed further below; but for now another aspect of this approach is relevant.

In a fragmented world, risk aversion leads to a risk externality; that is, the risk is placed upon 'others' who are often unable to respond (e.g. future generations, the resource poor, non-humans), rather than leading to GHG control. Action at a global government level is implied to correct both an international and intergenerational pollution and risk externality. Interestingly, Chichilnisky and Heal (1993) claim that insurance markets (rather than GHG control) can cope with climate change risks. Their explanation neglects missing future markets (e.g. inability to communicate with future generations) and is limited to the geographical distribution of damages. They argue that there are efficiency gains to be made by selling 'Arrow securities' and mutual insurance contracts when facing ignorance.

However, their argument depends upon ignorance being defined as weak uncertainty about the distribution of damages, so that a probability can be assigned to each frequency distribution. As they state:

> A typical probability distribution of this type might state for example that there is a 10 per cent chance that 90 per cent of the population will be harmed by global warming, a 25 per cent chance that 50 per cent of the population will be harmed, and so on.
>
> (Chichilnisky and Heal, 1993: 69)

In effect they accept a wider concept of uncertainty (besides risk) and then reduce it to a 'secondary probability distribution'; the result is a probability of a probability of a damage. Individuals or communities then buy and sell securities which pay if the 'correct' secondary probability distribution occurs. Why this secondary probability is any easier to specify than the primary one is unclear. The authors themselves note some difficulties when they state that:

> In practice of course, probability distributions are not observable, and we cannot condition contracts on unobservable events. So conditioning on a probability distribution means conditioning on frequency distributions with that probability distribution in a sampling sense.
>
> (Chichilnisky and Heal, 1993: 71)

The method and meaning of the sampling sense and indeed this explanation remains unclear.

The distributional assumptions of this insurance risk model should also be noted. First, impacts are never mutually harmful; there is a gainer able to compensate the loser by transfers. Second, there is no consideration of the equity or ethics in asking, for example, Bangladeshis to buy insurance from the US to cover themselves against the threat of GHG emissions created historically by the US and other industrially developed economies. In fact, the position of the less industrially developed countries is carefully avoided by the authors giving the example of the US, as sceptic, trading securities with the EC, as concerned party. Third, the moral hazard issue is relegated to a footnote, but would be extremely important because, were such a market feasible and perfect, the insured have an incentive to increase their GHG emissions regardless of the consequences. Those who cannot afford the insurance premiums would be double losers. Fourth, the lower limits of insurance premiums, which allow entry into the market, are ignored and will depend upon the insurer's willingness to risk bankruptcy. Fifth, the possibility of insurer's bankruptcy is neglected.

Such an oversimplified characterisation of ignorance and catastrophic events using weak uncertainty is typical of the mainstream economic approach to modelling the enhanced Greenhouse Effect. This is also symptomatic of the general economic modelling approach under Pareto optimal resource allocation. For example, the model in Heal (1984), also used by Chichilnisky and Heal (1993), assumes two states of the world: economically favourable and unfavourable, where a future climate catastrophe occurs. The movement between these two states is from one equilibrium system to another with a positive probability of no change occurring. The probabilities sum to one so that all relevant outcomes are assumed known and included.

How weak is weak uncertainty?

The mainstream economic approach to unknown aspects of the world has tried to emulate the natural sciences in as far as potential future states are reduced to probabilistic events. However, knowledge about climatic systems prevents either future states and/or their associated probabilities being defined. In this regard, there are several limitations to the weak uncertainty approach for dealing with the policy implications of the enhanced Greenhouse Effect. These shortcomings are more generally relevant to the economic theory of imperfect information and the treatment of uncertainty.

The range of issues affecting the applicability of weak uncertainty go from establishing systems behaviour through to the social psychology of the individual. The concept of a probability density function (as discussed in the last chapter) is often an inappropriate characterisation of uncertainty. The assumptions required to establish future states via cause–effect relationships mean systems behaviour can be excessively simplified. Simplification is an essential part of understanding but must be recognised as creating partial ignorance. In moving science and technology forward at a rapid pace modern society is creating new and unpredictable futures so that how partial ignorance is addressed becomes a central concern. An appeal to subjective probabilities to avoid some of these issues raises another set of issues including how these numbers are produced, by whom and what their value content is? Attitudes to risk vary and psychological research shows an extensive range of behaviour, much of which diverges from that under risk assessment models. The psychological importance of appealing to risk assessment as a decision support raises questions over their false precision, i.e. using a bad tool because that is the accepted method and fending off critiques with the quip that 'there are no better alternatives'. All these factors combine to make the characterisation of uncertainty as weak a highly misleading approach. Thus there should perhaps be little surprise that endogenous and exogenous risks are confused or treated as identical for analytical convenience. The following subsections give more attention to each of these points.

The probability density function

There are difficulties in adopting probability density functions to characterise climate change uncertainty. The variable of concern, say temperature or rainfall, might have a probability density function which is different from the normal distribution, and may be non-random. Climate shows periodic and quasi-periodic cycles which describe non-random behaviour (Hare, 1979). More generally, the probability of many events under the enhanced Greenhouse Effect is unobservable because the events are unique and cannot be evaluated as frequency events, e.g. the melting of the West Antarctic Ice Sheet, sea level rise, disruption of El Niño or the Gulf Stream.

Cause–effect relationships

A cause and effect relationship is required to determine both the actions relevant to a decision and the outcomes to be included in the set of possible future states. This is a difficult task for global climate change, even if climate and socio-economic systems were deterministic with regular, and therefore predictable, behaviour. A search for a single specific cause of a climatic event can be futile. Small disturbances can result in large effects, e.g. from positive feedback amplification, while every link in the loop is both cause and effect (Berger, 1990). Note, this difficulty applies to even the apparently most scientifically tractable problem of crop response to GHGs.

Excluding alternatives

Uncertainty is always reduced to weak uncertainty as if there were no case of a simple lack of knowledge nor a danger of the exclusion of relevant alternatives (the two of which may interact). For example, the developers of CFCs had no idea that their product would deplete the stratospheric ozone layer; this was an unknown potential which was never remotely considered or relevant to them. Similarly, the detection of the stratospheric ozone hole was hampered by the programming of software which rejected what was regarded as satellite data so far from expected models as to be in error. Partial ignorance is a design feature of the way in which technology and science proceed.

Subjective probabilities as concepts of value

In order to make exclusive use of the weak uncertainty model, probabilities are required in association with all future states of the world. As explained earlier, an action leading to an event may be recognised as a possible (uncertain) state but without a probability being attached to the outcome. The probability itself may be unknown or non-existent. This may be because the event of concern is unique and therefore no frequency distribution can be estimated, e.g. the melting of the West Antarctic Ice Sheet.

An appeal to subjective probabilities means that individuals could be asked to give their estimates of the probability of an event and this information would then form the basis of a probability density function (or an expected frequency distribution). These density functions are then taken to form the prior belief of individuals before additional information is gathered allowing revision. This framework is that of Bayesian analysis and rejects the notion that strong uncertainty exists.

The underlying intuition is that rational individuals act as if they knew a probability distribution. The individual need only make rough subjective judgements about the likelihood of damages to enable their attitude to risk to be described as a loss of utility associated with damage-causing events. Subjective probabilities can, for example, be inferred from the willingness to pay for insurance. This ability to create probability density functions neglects their meaning and worth as concepts of value.

The derivation of a subjective probability function begs the question: whose subjective probabilities? For example, the general public might be argued to be the relevant constituency in a democracy, but asked the probability of, say, sea level rise flooding the Maldives by 2100 would draw a blank. The appeal to the general public might seem rather pointless given their presumably ill-informed background on such specialist topics. If some group of experts were convened this would still leave room for disagreement while forcing a consensus might exclude divergent viewpoints. The information conveyed by such expert-derived probabilities is very different from the frequency observed probability, as explained next.

Divergent perceptions of risk

The problems of using subjective probabilities then relate to the meaning of risk as a concept and the divergence of perceptions of risk amongst different groups. The general public has been observed to reject very low-probability, high-loss risks which experts judge to be acceptable (Freeman, 1993: 260). Thus, experts could vastly underestimate the potential welfare costs that these risks impose upon people. The public is worried by the potential meltdown of nuclear power stations despite continuous reassurance from the power industry and nuclear experts of the low risk. Here the concept of weak uncertainty which the nuclear industry is talking about diverges from the concept of strong uncertainty perceived as relevant by the general public.

Jaeger (1996) makes a related point concerning risk paradoxes, of which he gives two examples. First, probabilities close to zero are treated in practice in different ways despite appearing identical in expected utility terms, i.e. when the outcomes are weighted by their probability and utility. So in some cases probabilities close to zero are treated as zero, e.g. as train accidents have historically been viewed, and in others create extreme concern, e.g. nuclear power station meltdown. Context and culture will also play a role in such divergence, and the mix of attitudes can also change over time for various reasons, e.g. public perception of train accidents in the UK since privatisation. Second, Kahneman and Tversky (1979) have shown that choices with identical outcomes and probabilities are treated differently if they are losses as opposed to gains. Amongst other implications this affects the economic use of willingness to pay and accept as welfare measures (Knetsch and Sinden, 1984; Knetsch, 1997).

False precision and 'objective facts'

The use of probability estimates can give a false sense of precision and the results of illustrative examples may be misinterpreted as conveying scientific 'facts'. Thus, probabilities may be given to two or more decimal places despite their speculative character. Probability density functions make the production of such precision straightforward although the meaning may be lacking, e.g. specifying the subjective probability of the West Antarctic Ice Sheet melting as 1.34 per cent. The highly uncertain and unpredictable is apparently converted to a precise prediction.

More generally, the conception of 'facts' as central to an issue can give a false sense of objectivity to decision-making where the 'facts' are taken to 'speak for themselves'. That is, a belief is engendered in an underlying objectivity which can be discovered and which should direct environmental management and, indeed, society. Whether ecological or technological such 'facts' result in social regulation which should be openly debate rather than dictated. As noted in chapter 4, and will be seen again in chapter 6, economists call for further research to obtain 'true' costs and benefits while the search for scientific facts is meant to resolve uncertainty. These points are addressed again in the context of the meaning and implications of strong uncertainty.

Exogenous and endogenous risk

Related to the conception of 'objectivity' is the discussion of climate change risk as if it were exogenous. The extent to which the Greenhouse Effect is enhanced is driven by the release of GHGs, and the extent to which these releases occur is a human choice. The risk is endogenous and therefore fundamentally different from observing the frequency of events beyond our control. As Chichilnisky and Heal (1993) point out, but without much analytical consequence, this is in contrast with most economic models of resource allocation under uncertainty. Probabilities may be subjective and modified in a Bayesian sense in an Arrow–Debreu model, but the frequency of harmful events is assumed to be beyond control. Similarly, classical insurance risk models assume such events are exogenous. Once the risks are taken to be endogenous (i.e. within the control of the decision-maker) the entire range of social perspectives on responsible action becomes relevant. The type of uncertainty no longer fits neatly into the weak uncertainty characterisation and the role of economists and scientists seems less clearly divided upon value versus fact specialisms.

From weak to strong uncertainty

Scientists, and engineers, have built up assumptions of well-defined and deterministic processes when dealing with the unknown on the basis of well structured mechanical problems (e.g. aircraft, aerospace, nuclear plants). In fact even '...these systems have often shown themselves to be less well-defined than analysts and designers thought, exhibiting surprising properties – such as exploding – which indicate that the system was less determined by controlling forces than the analyst recognised' (Wynne, 1992: 113). The approach has been extended to badly structured problems, non-mechanistic environmental systems and the global scale. For global environmental problems, such as the enhanced Greenhouse Effect, the limitations of available knowledge are more serious. Contrary to technological artefacts these systems cannot be designed, manipulated and reduced to within the boundaries of existing analytical knowledge. Thus, pragmatic factors, such as what can be measured, dictate the structure of resulting knowledge.

There is no surprise then in finding that the OECD (1995) publication on the economic appraisal of environmental projects and policies, which is subtitled 'A practical guide', concludes: 'The treatment of uncertain risk looms large in environmental appraisal. Converting uncertainty into risk is essential to make the problem tractable' (OECD, 1995: 150). Such apparent pragmatism ignores the theoretical straightjacket into which uncertainty is being squeezed. A warning then seems appropriate: 'Those who reject theory for pragmatism are liable to find themselves unwitting adherents of bad theory' (Loasby, 1976: 21).

Ignorance

Besides the design of limits to models merely to make them manageable, limitations arise for a number of reasons related to a basic lack of knowledge: ignorance about a particular system, ignorance about the behaviour of a class of systems, and the indeterminate nature of some complex systems (which can become chaotic at various points). This means that even where the behaviour of such systems might be modelled in probabilistic terms the relevance of this analysis is limited temporally and spatially.

All the models of the behaviour of complex systems, such as environmental and economic systems or their interactions, are imprecise and limited in their scope. The discussion in chapter 4 implied a stable equilibrium around the current mean of a climatic variable (e.g. temperature) and that the process of climatic change could be described by a shift to a new stable equilibrium. However, the process of human-induced climatic change could equally lead to a long path of alterations without creating the conditions for order and stability, which may in any case fail to represent climatic systems.

Ignorance also pertains to sources of utility which must be identified to assess economic impacts. Thus, there are elements, substances and organisms on the planet which have yet to be utilised directly by humans. This can be viewed as partial ignorance over future use patterns. For example, losses in biodiversity due to global climate change can cause future losses of which present humans are ill-equipped to guess; species properties may be unknown or presently of no economic value. In addition, many of the features of Nature that are directly utilised in economic processes are dependent on features of Nature that are indirectly utilised. Current biomass depends on an ecological infrastructure which enables flows into human systems but is ignored itself. For example, stratospheric ozone can be depleted by CFCs so allowing higher levels of UV-B radiation to reach the surface of the planet; this would in turn affect the marine biota at the base of the food chain on which harvested species of fish depend. Partial ignorance becomes particularly important when society builds commitments around the knowledge base.

Indeterminacy

The problem posed by complex systems cannot be avoided even by removing oneself to a desert island, a favourite economic example for clarifying basic principles. As Loasby (1976: 1–2) notes:

> Even Robinson Crusoe had to operate within a complex natural system, the future states of which could not be predicted with confidence; how much more difficult then to predict the future states of a system which is driven in part by the acts of other decision-makers similarly placed. Choice within a complex system cannot be fully informed; neither can the study of a complex system from outside. Partial ignorance is intrinsic to the problems of choice which economists claim to investigate.

Yet here Loasby is combining a lack of knowledge about the future with the indeterminate nature of complex natural and social systems, i.e. where the behaviour of others is a determining factor. While the two may be connected a distinction is also worthwhile.

An important aspect of indeterminacy is recognised by Loasby as being linked to choice, a matter at the heart of economics, e.g. consumer choice, decision-making, choices under weak uncertainty. 'If knowledge is perfect, and the logic of choice complete and compelling, then choice disappears; nothing is left but stimulus and response' (Loasby, 1976: 5). In order to be meaningful in terms of a reasoned action choice must be neither random nor predetermined, and be able to make a difference (if there is no difference choosing is meaningless). Choice and determinacy are incompatible and the future unpredictable. As Loasby (1976: 5) summarises: 'If choice is real, the future cannot be certain; if the future is certain, there can be no choice'. Thus, indeterminacy is at the heart of economics.

The importance of treating indeterminacy as a distinct concept from ignorance is emphasised by Wynne. Thus, he argues that when trying to draw causal links the difficulties that arise have less to do with lack of problem definition (unknown states) and more to do with '... a combination of genuine constraints laid down in a determinate fashion, and real open-endedness in the sense that outcomes depend on how intermediate actors will behave' (Wynne, 1992: 117). This social indeterminacy is readily apparent from the discussion of choice, and has serious implications for the implementation of policy. For example, technical solutions determined to solve a problem only do so under specific social conditions, i.e. if actors make the 'right' choices.

There is always an element of indeterminacy in classifying empirical evidence under one theory or model or another. Concepts of sameness and difference in Natural relations are never fully determined solely by Nature but open to social commitment. This social commitment is part of the scientific culture of a discipline and often operates subconsciously on choices. As Wynne (1992: 123) states:

> scientific knowledge is not fully determined by 'the facts' – what 'the facts' are has to be actively read into nature to some extent. In other words, social mechanisms of closure around particular logical constructions have to occur in order to complete the otherwise incomplete logical construction. This is a further, more subtle and pervasive sense in which indeterminacies exist in the basis of authoritative natural knowledge about environmental risks.

Thus, normative choices which are meant to be 'external' to the scientific process actually influence 'internal' choices about inferences, sameness and difference relations in theoretical models and what is then regarded as problematic.

Models in science and economics: revisited

As discussed with regard to economic and scientific models in chapter 4, the understanding of the enhanced Greenhouse Effect clearly shows choices about what is to be included and excluded. Here this process of judgement has been argued to be a normal part of the process of learning and understanding. However, this process also means 'facts' are dependent upon the theory by which they are classified, judged, measured and selected.

Thus, for example, the form of experimental research on crop responses depends upon accepted scientific theory and, as has been explained, can influence or even determine the result. Experimental design, in aiming to achieve the desired scientific requirements of a controlled experiment, holds other factors constant which are then by assumption excluded from consideration. Testing one hypothesis requires accepting others and there is no definable end to this process of testing hypotheses, i.e. the assumptions in one hypothesis test are the hypothesis in the next, so new assumptions are required (Loasby, 1976: 19). If results are theoretically inconvenient the lack of a definitive test soon becomes apparent as a range of standard arguments appear: the experimental results were unreliable, discrepancies between empirical results and theory are only assertions and empirical anomalies will disappear if understanding or measurement methods were improved. The standard of evidence required for accepting and rejecting evidence depends upon the associated theory and how well the results conform with scientific or economic opinion.

In, for example, the work of Callendar (1938) presented to the Royal Society his evidence on climatic warming excluded the higher temperatures observed in the arctic. A commentator remarked that these temperatures were ten times those at middle and low latitudes and were inexplicable in terms of CO_2 releases. In his reported response, Callendar agreed 'that the recent rise in arctic temperatures were far too large to be attributed to change of CO_2' and that '[o]n account of their large rise he had not included the arctic stations in the world temperature curve' (Callendar, 1938: 239). He undoubtedly believed he was erring on the side of caution in reporting his results. Today higher than global average arctic temperatures are seen as a key signal of the impact CO_2 has on climate via the enhance Greenhouse Effect.

This is not a particular criticism of Callendar; scientific knowledge proceeds by externalising some of the significant uncertainties. Thus, 'scientists, like wise examination candidates, are careful not to attempt certain questions' (Loasby, 1976: 3). As Wynne (1992: 115) states:

> The conventional view is that scientific knowledge and method enthusiastically *embrace* uncertainties and exhaustively pursue them. This is seriously misleading. It is more accurate to say that scientific knowledge gives prominence to a *restricted agenda of defined uncertainties* – ones that are tractable – leaving aside a range of other uncertainties, especially about boundary conditions of applicability of the existing framework of knowledge to new situations.

Of course economics is no less guilty of ignoring the way in which it operates and selecting only the evidence which proves compatible with theory.

A major concern in this regard has been the gap between economics and ecology, see Dale and Rauscher (1994: 79–81). Holling *et al.* (1995) suspect many economists ignore ecological information despite the accumulated body of evidence from natural, disturbed and managed ecosystems. In particular they identify four key features, common to the function and structure of many ecosystems, which they believe economists should bring into their subject. Their points can be summarised as follows:

- Ecosystem change is episodic rather than continuous and gradual. For example, uncommon events (e.g. hurricanes) can unpredictably reshape structure at critical times or in vulnerable locations.
- Scaling up from small to large is a non-linear process. Thus, spatial attributes vary with scale rather than being uniform.
- Ecosystems exhibit multiple equilibria, an absence of equilibria and are destabilised by forces far from equilibria. The movement between such states maintains structure and diversity. This contrasts with the conception of ecosystems as single equilibrium systems with functions operating to maintain the stable state.
- Recognising that ecosystems have multiple features, which are uncertain and unpredictable, requires management and policies to be flexible, adaptive and experimental at scales compatible with those of critical ecosystem functions.

A belief in the near equilibrium definition of ecological resilience, as found in mainstream economics, focuses upon efficiency of function with emphasis upon resistance to disturbance and speed of return to equilibrium. This contrasts with ecological case studies and the inductive formation of ecological theory which focus attention upon the 'existence of function' where instabilities can flip a system from one domain of stability to another. In this case the resilience of a system is determined by the ability to absorb disturbance before the system changes its structure by changing the variables and processes that control behaviour (Holling *et al.*, 1995: 48–51).

Implicit social regulation and control

Social and behavioural control is intertwined with the way risk is analysed and standardised. That is, social behaviour must be reorganised in order to conform to the implicit assumptions of social behaviour embedded in standardised models. For example, nuclear power stations are built upon the premise of human control-lers acting in response to certain signals in a given order and within a given amount of time. In order to operate such a power station humans must conform to the requirements of the system. A nuclear power station may be regarded as having an objective risk of meltdown, but whether this is sited in Afghanistan, China, France, Germany, Indonesia, Iraq or Russia would generally be accepted as making a difference due to institutional, social and cultural differences, i.e. the assessment of performance is indeterminate and requires assumptions about specific types of social control. 'Thus an inherent contradiction exists between such standardising tendencies and the realistic appreciation of the diverse and more open-ended situational forces and factors which defy such reductionist and deterministic treatment' (Wynne, 1992: 119). If social systems fail to conform to the definition of risk, and related regulations, then greater flexibility is necessary. The possible paths Wynne identifies for social control include following the determinate discourse from technology (as is current), following one from Nature, or finding 'socially flexible technologies'.

One response to ecological complexity and the interactions between components is the imposition of constraints upon economic systems to avoid undue environmental stress. This requires policy decisions at the scale of the function being considered, e.g. global atmospheric regulation. The process of setting such constraints will, however, mean that specialists have a central role in the formation of information inputs to any decision. Thus, the premises upon which a specialist decides what is important, where research time and effort should be expended and how modelling should proceed all have implications which go far beyond the perception of research as increasing confidence by refining the probabilities of given outcomes, i.e. risk analysis under weak uncertainty. That is, the conception that research on the enhanced Greenhouse Effect is fundamentally based upon the need to fill agreed-upon factual gaps in understanding is itself only a belief, as are the choice of gaps upon which research ends up focusing.

The belief in such a foundational truth may also imply social norms because acknowledging boundary conditions can be used to require human behavioural change to avoid passing thresholds. For example, Friends of the Earth Scotland (1995) has argued for the concept of 'environmental space', which calls for the definition of physical constraints required for the region to be sustainable (based upon input–output type analysis), which then implies limits on individuals (e.g. per capita carbon dioxide emissions allowed) but is presented as a scientific fact. Martinez-Alier (1994) has raised a similar concern related to the limitations of ecological planning and gives the example of prescriptions on carrying capacity. As he states (Martinez-Alier, 1994: 29):

> precisely because of uncertainties about the future and the inevitability of choices being made between differing social, species, and ecosystem options, a so-called ecological rationality is not an indisputably better base for policy decisions than the usual economic rationality.

The danger here is that the decision process is removed to the realm of the objective 'scientific' manager who reveals the truth and conveys the 'facts' as uncontestable commandments.

Norgaard (1994: 66–7) critically explains such a scientific approach as the acquisition of knowledge whereby individual minds investigate the parts and processes of Nature, which he refers to as an atomistic-mechanistic view. This view is seen to be premised upon unchanging parts and relations allowing knowledge to be regarded as universal over space and time. Variations in natural and social systems are then regarded as due to differences in the proportions of parts and the strength of relations, rather than being an indication of fundamental differences. 'Thus, the idea of underlying universal truths could be maintained across diverse environments and cultures' (Norgaard, 1994: 67). This methodology leads in turn to the separation of facts from values and what is termed logical positivism (see Gordon, 1993). While the logical positivist approach is flawed (e.g. in rejecting non-empirical knowledge) it still remains dominant in public beliefs and institutional structures. Thus, the 'professional' natural scientist and neo-classical economist participate in public decision-making through this dominant belief pattern, which they then reinforce.

A powerful lobby amongst economists has for some time been eager to treat economics as methodologically scientific with an emphasis upon empiricism to confirm an objective reality, i.e. following logical positivism (see Hutchinson, 1938). This view of economics as a science requires a belief in an objective truth and the ability of economists to reveal this truth. In the environmental economics literature this begins to appear in statements and approaches which suggest the 'correct' picture is being presented by the economic analysis. This lobby has tended to refuse to accept the idea of strong uncertainty and must logically do so if they wish to defend an absolute truth because there can be no absolute truth discoverable by research if we accept our own irreducible ignorance.

The changing perception of science

Knowledge and belief

There is a concern amongst some scientists that the type of media coverage given to issues such as global warming encourages 'bad science'. 'Bad' in this context refers to the lack of a notion of objectivity in the conduct of science. This objectivity might be seen as the conduct of repeatable experiments to test well-constructed hypotheses. For such a methodology issues of belief and subjectivity are non-scientific issues, and if such issues come to the fore the scientist is guilty of 'bad' science. Hence Harrison (1991: 4) has stated:

> A scientific community under financial siege has been all too eager to jump on a global warming bandwagon and there is a suspicion that objectivity has, in some cases, been sacrificed. Published conclusions have not always been supported by rigorous scientific arguments, but have degraded into conjecture.

Yet the notion that there is a rigorous scientific methodology of relevance to climate change is itself open to question. The extreme objectivity position seems to be closely associated with a belief in an ultimate truth (i.e. moral or theological), a concept which is again highly contestable. In the case of Christian scientists such as Harrison or Houghton this is clearly religious.

This leads the scientific community into a dilemma because 'good' scientists cannot admit they start from prior beliefs which are subject to their own personal experience and self-reflection and which influence their conduct of research. Idso (1984), a global warming sceptic, regards scenario development in relation to the enhanced Greenhouse Effect as being influenced more by the psychological disposition of the protagonists than science. Indeed, the preceding sections have shown how when modelling climatic systems, as well as their impacts on socio-economic systems, many apparently arbitrary restrictions are set in place by the analyst. This is recognised by climatologists as a problem when they make policy recommendations.

> So many other features of the system are excluded from examination that it becomes reasonable to suspect that the discussion – especially if it concludes that we must take action – is not an accurate forecast of the future but rather an artefact determined by the study's particular selection of which parts of the overall system to consider. Until this suspicion is overcome, no amount of warning about the need for early action is likely to be heeded.
>
> (Firor, 1990: 73)

The problem here is that, outside of the objective science school of thought, overcoming this suspicion is impossible. There is, however, the potential for individuals to be persuaded and convinced of the dangers pointed out by the forecasts, through a process of open discussion and debate on the limitations of the models. Firor misunderstands the problems with the knowledge base, in which he has so much faith, and that this goes beyond converting everyone to belief in scientific objectivism. As Wynne notes:

> The very considerable amount of scientific work which has gone into the modelling of environmental risk systems over the past few decades cannot, therefore, be taken as reassurance that even the main dimensions of environmental harm from human activities have been comprehended. To understand this requires not only intense and open examination of the scientific evidence and competing interpretations in an area of interest; it also requires reflexive learning at a deeper level, about the nature and inherent limitations in principle of that knowledge, however competently produced.
>
> (Wynne, 1992: 113)

Yet when such debate is seen to be possible scientists are encouraged to disengage for fear of becoming advocates.

A notable exception to the 'good science' position is the case of Dr Hansen, Director of the Goddard Institute at NASA. Hansen created considerable controversy in the late 1980s and was regarded as being blunt and forthright in his statements concerning the enhanced Greenhouse Effect (Newton and Dillingham, 1994). In giving evidence at US government hearings he was seen to be acting as an advocate. Yet, on reading them, his remarks appear to be carefully worded judgements made on the basis of many years' work in the area of climate modelling (see Hansen, 1988). He was apparently being attacked for opening up a previously closed scientific debate for public scrutiny.

Much of the scientific community appears loath to see colleagues take such an open position, and try to avoid phrasing themselves in terms of their opinions or beliefs. Interestingly, the lead scientific author of the IPCC reports, John Houghton, was more open about the Christian beliefs underlying his concern for Nature and future generations when he published an introductory text on global warming. His open confessions of the importance of his beliefs in motivating his research and the values he associates with that work are highly unusual. Yet, according to the introduction to the second edition, while being 'surprised' or finding confessions of religious belief 'startling' in a scientific context, most peers accepted them as useful background information. That is, Houghton's beliefs were, he believes, accepted as arguments of why systems operate and seen as separable from the scientific quest for how they operate. Even with the apparent support of his colleagues, Houghton notes the need he felt to revise the specific chapter covering his Christian beliefs and, for the second edition, states that: 'I have been somewhat more objective and less personal – which I felt was more appropriate for student readers from a wide range of disciplines, for whom the edition is particularly suited' (Houghton, 1997: xv).

In general, economists can far more easily be identified with positions based on strong uncertainty resulting in advocacy, even though, as noted in chapter 4, some then try to disguise this in a veil of 'objective' modelling. The role and importance of personal belief is clear in statements by Crosson (1989), for example. When discussing impacts on agriculture he finds 'no persuasive reason to believe that on balance they will be negative' prior to a doubling of CO_2 equivalent. After that point:

> I think it is likely, although neither I nor anyone else can now prove it, that at some point the amount of warming and associated changes in climate would begin to sharply increase the economic and environmental costs of world production, not only in agriculture but in other sectors as well.
>
> (Crosson, 1989: 115)

Crosson is, however, guilty of a relevant methodological flaw in his statement. The hypothesis that warming due to the enhanced Greenhouse Effect will result in net damages to economic systems can never be proven. The evidence in favour of the hypothesis can increase so none may doubt its truth, but there will always be the possibility of an alternative hypothesis and counter-intuitive evidence. For example, accepting that all swans are white is held true only until a black swan is discovered on arrival in Australia. Only white swans may have been observed for hundreds or thousands of years by Europeans, but this cannot preclude the existence of the black swan. If we stop GHG emissions no climatic change may occur because the theory was incorrect, and if we go ahead and climatic change does occur the cause may be other factors of which we remain unaware.

In most daily life the world around us is accepted on the basis of beliefs (or social commitments) which are so common that to question them would make most people regard you as mad (pity the philosopher). Yet the point here is quite serious, because science plays a central role in the formation of those beliefs in modern society and especially so when confronting complexity and strong uncertainty. Scientific methodology has also been important in influencing economics. Thus, the basis upon which society is being formed and reformed, and information is accepted as valid, is intertwined with modern faith in science and technology. Where that faith is lacking the scientists or industrialists pushing technological solutions are seen as biased and their information suspect. Hence public concern, from nuclear power to genetically modified organisms, and the distinct change in the perception of science from the technological optimism of the 1950s.

Post-normal science

The type of uncertainty that complex problems such as the enhanced Greenhouse Effect confront us with is strong, not weak. Does this make the enhanced Greenhouse Effect a very different problem from that repeatable experiment in controlled conditions around which scientific objectivity was classically formulated? Some may fear that accepting the role of partial ignorance in epistemology and the need for belief in science means all is conjecture. On the contrary, a clearer picture is required of the process by which information is accepted as valid and on what grounds.

Funtowicz and Ravetz (1990; 1992a; 1992b; 1993; 1994a) have been conducting a constructive analysis of how society might proceed beyond the postmodern temptation to be nihilistic, while avoiding the modernist temptation (prevalent in the models discussed here) to claim a single optimal answer. Their recommendations are for opening up the process of knowledge validation because:

> The nature of policy debates involving science has been transformed by the success of non-expert stakeholders in contributing to the assessment of quality. Previously only subject-speciality peers could assess quality in connection with refereeing or peer-review. But when science became used in policy, it was discovered that laypersons (e.g. judges, journalists, scientists from another field, or just citizens) could master enough of the methodology to become effective participants in the dialogue.
>
> (Funtowicz and Ravetz, 1994b: 203–4)

One response to the call for more participation is to incorporate this within existing models and frameworks. Jaeger (1996) has suggested conflict resolution techniques be used to obtain consensus subjective probabilities. Interviews are to document individual attitudes and opinion, while focus groups document social processes of attitude formation. The aim is to assess the acceptability of new policy options. More than this, Jaeger wants tools of co-operative risk management to foster standards of justice when attempting to blend individual probabilities and utilities into socially acceptable decisions. This moves beyond standard expected probability theory because the role of debates in modifying preferences is seen as central to co-operative risk management in order to overcome social dilemmas (Jaeger, 1996: 15). The aim then becomes agreeing standards for what is a fair way of sharing risks, and regarding scientific input as sharing knowledge about plausible consequences of various actions. However, the reversion to producing 'subjective probabilities' seems reminiscent of the attempts by economists to reduce catastrophic unique events to known risks. The response to the need for opening up debate cannot be to then curtail the outcomes in the most effective way possible by returning to the very models which denied the need for debate in the first place.

Consensus is also unlikely to be a part of an open process of debate about understanding of science and would be counterproductive. As Wilenius and Tirkkonen (1997) point out, attempting to create unanimity, on issues such as climate change, is likely to appear unnatural, and to lead to a loss of vital information and the suppression of viewpoints. Their use of modified Delphi techniques to address climate change policy options in Finland aimed to get researchers communicating with policymakers. Developing such techniques beyond expert groups is even more challenging but necessary.

A new methodology for science is appropriate to deal with strong uncertainty and, as Funtowicz and Ravetz (1993) recognise, it must be based upon assumptions of unpredictability, incomplete control and a plurality of legitimate perspectives. They regard an extended peer review approach as particularly relevant where systems uncertainties or 'decision stakes' are high and the research goals are issue-driven (as opposed to a core science approach motivated by curiosity). While critical of determinism when facing complex environmental problems, this approach does recognise the role core science has played in human society. Scientific success through the extension of laboratory experience has given many advantages in terms of health, safety and general comfort of living for many. As discussed, this experimental work isolates a part of natural systems and keeps it unnaturally pure, stable and reproducible, e.g. work on the CO_2 fertilisation effect on crops.

Unfortunately, as Funtowicz and Ravetz (1993) point out, while the successes of the normal scientific approach may be unstable, the method has become dominant over all other ways of knowing, e.g. commonsense experience, inherited skills of living. As has been shown above, a result is that public decision-making must at least appear to be scientific. The method of science is therefore adopted by those wishing to lead the policy debate, such as economists. The inability of science to provide experimentally derived theories to explain and predict the enhanced Greenhouse Effect has lead to the development of mathematical models and computer simulations which are essentially untestable. So the case made by Funtowicz and Ravetz seems particularly relevant to the enhanced Greenhouse Effect and can be summarised by two quotes:

> Now scientific expertise has lead us into policy dilemmas which it is incapable of resolving by itself. We have not merely lost control and even predictability; now we face radical uncertainty and even ignorance, as well as ethical uncertainties lying at the heart of scientific policy issues.
>
> (Funtowicz and Ravetz, 1993: 741–2)

> We would be misled if we retained the image of a process where true scientific facts simply determine the correct policy conclusions. However, the new challenges do not render traditional science irrelevant; the task is to choose the appropriate kinds of problem-solving strategies for each particular case.
>
> (Funtowicz and Ravetz, 1993: 744)

This latter argument implies that a new methodology for classifying problems and applying methods will need to be developed. However, further insight can be offered on the place of wider debate in this package.

Indeterminacy and the need for social discourse

Wynne (1992: 116–17) has provided a complementary analysis to that of post-normal science with a different classification of uncertainty. Funtowicz and Ravetz have described normal science as operating effectively when both the size of the decision stakes and scale of system uncertainties are small, while post-normal science is relevant when both are large. In contrast, Wynne rejects a scale going from risk to ignorance in such a two-dimensional space in preference for the relevance of different concepts of uncertainty being determined by the conditions placed upon knowledge. He has observed that the implied objectivity and independence of the two factors (i.e. systems uncertainties and decision stakes) is misleading. Focusing on the social context, he argues that apparently technical applied science questions are actually subject to assumed indeterminacy; such questions seem 'normal' only because the surrounding context is artificially assumed to be constant and effectively unimportant. He interprets 'decision stakes' as social commitments, and argues a two-way connection. First, the social commitments influence the way that lack of knowledge is expressed by any party (i.e. either as weak or strong uncertainty). Second, social commitments are themselves indeterminate and conditional because they depend to some extent upon unknown aspects of systems and their interactions. For example, while the stakes (or social commitments) are certainly high under continued emissions of GHGs, they are also indeterminate due to unpredictable interactions between natural and social systems.

This leads to three broad prescriptions in order to address partial ignorance and indeterminacy. First is the need to recognise the existence of ignorance and indeterminacy, and then to understand their complex social character, even within the domain of scientific knowledge. Second is the need to shift away from 'end-of-pipe' solutions towards considering upstream industrial processes, e.g. product design, research and development. This will broaden the range of explicitly recognised uncertainties which society is adopting as new products and technologies are introduced and old ones reassessed. Third, there is a need for social discourse on scientific information. The exaggeration of the scope and power of scientific knowledge is institutionalised and creates '... a vacuum in which should exist a vital social discourse about the conditions and boundaries of scientific knowledge in relation to moral and social knowledge' (Wynne, 1992: 115).

Thus, despite differences in approach and explanation of risk, uncertainty and ignorance, Funtowicz and Ravetz and Wynne come to a similar key conclusion about addressing the issue. 'The most important need is surely to develop "regulatory" cultures which successfully encourage greater public debate on the social benefits, costs and indeterminacies of different products and processes, as well as on conventional environmental strategy questions' (Wynne, 1992: 124).

Conclusions

An idealised scientific inquiry into the enhanced Greenhouse Effect might require very strong standards of proof, and pursue a research project in orderly stages. However, the very nature of scientific progress implies that Earth will be experiencing its consequences long before rigorous science has been able to convince sceptics of its existence. This is in part because of the modern state of scientific knowledge which persists in hiding beliefs and reasons for commitment to a body of knowledge. Scientific progress requires a willingness to accept some ideas which cannot be established conclusively because they lie beyond evidence or logic, while accepting that both evidence and logic are necessary for the scientific endeavour. Popper is quoted in Loasby (1976: 27) as stating:

> I am inclined to think that scientific discovery is impossible without faith in ideas which are of a purely speculative kind, and sometimes quite hazy; a faith which is completely unwarranted from the point of view of science, and which, to that extent, is 'metaphysical'.

Economics has adopted much from the natural sciences in methodological terms and follows the process of attaining knowledge by restricting its visions while denying the blinkers are on. Treatment of uncertainty in economics is perhaps best summarised by Loasby (1976: 9):

> When someone says he is uncertain, what he usually means is not just that he doesn't know the chances of various outcomes, but that he doesn't know what outcomes are possible. He may well be far from sure even of the structure of the problem he faces. This normal state of partial ignorance is simply not defined in the theory of decision-making under uncertainty, in which 'uncertainty' acquires an esoteric meaning. This meaning serves to hide from the layman the fact that the economist, faced with a very awkward problem, has succeeded, as so often, not in solving it, but in denying the legitimacy of its existence.

Neither economics nor science is currently addressing the key aspects of uncertainty – namely, partial ignorance and indeterminacy.

Once some areas of ignorance which cannot be easily placed into the framework of weak uncertainty are accepted, the process of assessing the validity of new knowledge must become open, rather than restricted to objective scientific and economic analysis. Where altering the potentialities of systems causes changes which are, in principle, unpredictable the appropriate response is to maintain options (Faber,

Manstetten and Proops, 1992). This implies accepting the importance of different views on the same problem, questioning current knowledge, and emphasising criteria of flexibility and reversibility.

Scientific and economic knowledge must be placed explicitly within its social, moral and cultural perspective. This requires recognising that research communities are secluded and create closure and internal validity around particular constructs. Broadening the social circle of discussion is essential when deploying such knowledge in society. This allows questioning of the methodology, epistemology (commitments and expectations), definitions of boundaries between Nature and culture, and the boundaries between objective determinism and human responsibility. If the process of creating scientific knowledge denies this openness then the extent to which it 'naturalises' and limits our moral, cultural and policy horizons will remain hidden (Wynne, 1992: 127).

The level of social commitment determines the scale of the problem at hand and so the type of uncertainty which is relevant. In previous human history climate change has made whole regions uninhabitable, forced mass migrations and encouraged exploration beyond known boundaries (Niedercorn, 1983). The belief that such potential futures can be neglected as irrelevant to current decisions (as in the case of surprise when our fair coin lands on its edge) seems to depend heavily upon faith, in this case in the power of technology. That is, much of society is heavily committed to one perspective on the issue due to the scientific and technological nature of modern economies.

The fundamental question is whether society can and will act today to address changes or problems which loom in the future, rather than whether scientists are able to provide conclusive proof of future risks (Lee and Kromer, 1987). An important aspect of that decision in international negotiations focuses upon different values. In economics this is the debate over the costs of controlling GHGs versus the benefits of that control.

Notes

1 Keynes developed these ideas between 1906 and 1911. Although book publication was delayed until 1921 his ideas received wide attention from 1911 onwards. Some authors cite Knight (1921) as the source of the division of risk and uncertainty, but Keynes' work clearly predates this by a decade.

2 The emphasis is placed upon the intertemporal impacts of enhancing the Greenhouse Effect because they are the most neglected but most threatening. However, from the discussion in chapter 3 the uneven regional distribution of impacts is also of obvious concern and should be remembered. Many of the ethical issues and matters of compensation, which will be raised later in the book, apply equally to both. In addition, the issues are often interconnected and inseparable, e.g. resource-rich regions amongst current generations benefiting while resource-poor regions amongst future generations suffer.

References

Adams, R.M., B.A. McCarl, D.J. Dudek and J.D. Glyer (1988) 'Implications of global climate change for western agriculture', *Western Journal of Agriculture Economics* **13**(2): 348–56.

Adger, W.N. and S. Fankhauser (1993) 'Economic analysis of the greenhouse effect: optimal abatement level and strategies for mitigation', *International Journal of Environment and Pollution* **3**(1–3): 104–19.

Ayres, R.U. and J. Walters (1991) 'The greenhouse effect: damages, costs and abatement', *Environmental and Resource Economics* **1**(3): 237–70.

Barbier, E.B. (1989) 'The global greenhouse effect: economic impacts and policy consider-ations', *Natural Resources Forum*: **13**(1): 20–32.

Berger, W.H. (1990) 'The Younger Dryas cold spell: a quest for causes', *Palaeogeography, Palaeoclimatology, Palaeoecology: Global and Planetary Change Section* **89**(3): 219–37.

Broadus, J.M., J.D. Milliman, S.F. Edwards, D.G. Aubrey and F. Gable (1986) 'Rising sea level and damming of rivers: possible effects in Egypt and Bangladesh', in *Effects of Changes in Stratospheric Ozone and Global Climate* **IV**, edited by J.G. Titus, pp. 165–89, Washington, DC: US Environmental Protection Agency.

Callendar, G.S. (1938) 'The artificial production of carbon dioxide and its influence on temperature', *Quarterly Journal of the Royal Meteorological Society* **64**: 223–40.

Chichilnisky, G. and G. Heal (1993) 'Global environmental risks', *Journal of Economic Perspectives* **7**(4): 65–86.

Cline, W.R. (1992) *The Economics of Global Warming*. Harlow, Essex: Longman.

Crosson, P. (1989) 'Greenhouse warming and climate change: why should we care?', *Food Policy* (**May**): 107–18.

Daily, G.C., P.R. Ehrlich, H.A. Mooney and A.H. Ehrlich (1991) 'Greenhouse economics: learn before you leap', *Ecological Economics* **4**: 1–10.

Dale, V.H. and H.M. Rauscher (1994) 'Assessing impacts of climate change on forests: the state of biological modeling', in *Assessing the Impacts of Climate Change on Natural Resource Systems*, edited by K.D. Frederick and N.J. Rosenberg, pp. 65–90, Dordrecht, The Netherlands: Kluwer Academic Publishers.

Environment Canada (1988) *The Changing Atmosphere: Implications for Global Security*. Presented at Environment Canada, Toronto, Ontario, 27–30 June, 1988.

Erickson, J.D. (1993) 'From ecology to economics: the case against CO_2 fertilization', *Ecological Economics* **8**(2): 157–16.

Faber, M., R. Manstetten and J.L.R. Proops (1992) 'Human kind and the environment: an anatomy of surprise and ignorance', *Environmental Values* **1**: 217–41.

Fankhauser, S. (1995) *Valuing Climate Change: The Economics of the Greenhouse*. London: Earthscan.

Firor, J.W. (1990) *The Changing Atmosphere: A Global Challenge*. New Haven, CT: Yale University Press.

Freeman, A.M. (1993) *The Measurement of Environmental and Resource Values: Theory and Methods*. Washington, DC: Resources for the Future.

Friends of the Earth Scotland (1995) *The Environmental Space for Scotland: Interim Summary (draft)*. Edinburgh: Friends of the Earth Scotland.

Funtowicz, S.O. and J.R. Ravetz (1990) *Uncertainty and Quality in Science for Policy*. Dordrecht, The Netherlands: Kluwer Academic Publishers.

Funtowicz, S.O. and J.R. Ravetz (1992a) 'The good, the true and the postmodern', *Futures* **24**(10): 963–76.

Funtowicz, S.O. and J.R. Ravetz (1992b) 'Risk management as a post-normal science', *Risk Analysis* **12**(1): 95–7.

Funtowicz, S.O. and J.R. Ravetz (1993) 'Science for the post-normal age', *Futures* **25**(7): 739–55.

Funtowicz, S.O. and J.R. Ravetz (1994a) 'Uncertainty, complexity and post-normal science', *Environmental Toxicology and Chemistry* **13**(12): 1,881–5.

Funtowicz, S.O. and J.R. Ravetz (1994b) 'The worth of a songbird: ecological economics as a post-normal science', *Ecological Economics* **10**(3): 197–207.

Goodess, C.M., J.P. Palutikof and T.D. Davies (1992) *The Nature and Causes of Climate Change: Assessing the Long Term Future*. London: Belhaven.

Gordon, S. (1993) *The History and Philosophy of Social Science*. London: Routledge.

Gribbin, J. (1990) *Hothouse Earth: The Greenhouse Effect and Gaia*. London: Black Swan.

Hansen, J.E. (1988) *Testimony to US Senate*. Presented at Committee on Energy and Natural Resources, Washington, DC, 23 June 1988, Alderson Reporting Company.

Hare, F.K. (1979) *Climatic Variation and Variability: Empirical Evidence from Meteorological and Other Sources*. Presented at World Climate Conference, Geneva, 12–23 February 1979.

Harrison, S.J. (1991) *Global Warming: Predicting the Uncertain*. Stirling: Department of Environmental Science, University of Stirling Climate Services.

Hayes, P. (1993) 'North–south carbon abatement costs', in *The Global Greenhouse Regime: Who Pays?*, edited by P. Hayes and K. Smith, pp. 101–43, London: Earthscan.

Heal, G.M. (1984) 'Interaction between economy and climate: a framework for policy design under uncertainty', in *Advances in Applied Microeconomics*, edited by V.K. Smith and A.D. White, pp. 151–8, Greenwich: JAI Press.

Holling, C.S., D.W. Schindler, B.W. Walker and J. Roughgarden (1995) 'Biodiversity in the functioning of ecosystems: an ecological synthesis', in *Biodiversity Loss: Economics and Ecological Issues*, edited by C. Perrings, K.-G. Mäler, C. Folke, C.S. Holling and B.-O. Jansson, pp. 44–83, Cambridge, England: Cambridge University Press.

Houghton, J. (1997) *Global Warming: The Complete Briefing*. Cambridge, England: Cambridge University Press.

Hutchinson, T.W. (1938) *The Significance and Basic Postulates of Economic Theory*. London: Macmillan.

Idso, S.B. (1984) 'A review of recent reports dealing with the greenhouse effect of atmospheric carbon dioxide', *Journal of Air Pollution Control Association* **34**(5): 553–5.

IPCC Working Group I (2001) *Climate Change 2001: Scientific Assessment; Summary for Policymakers*. Geneva: Intergovernmental Panel on Climate Change.

Jacobson, J.L. (1990) 'Holding back the sea', in *State of the World 1990: A Worldwatch Intstitute Report on Progress Towards a Sustainable Society*, edited by L.R. Brown, pp. 79–97 New York: W.W. Norton and Company.

Jaeger, C.C. (1996) 'Risk management and integrated assessment'. Darmstadt: Darmstadt University.

Kahneman, D. and A. Tversky (1979) 'Prospect theory: an analysis of decision under risk', *Econometrica* **47**(2): 263–91.

Keyfitz, N. (1992) 'The effects of changing climate on population', in *Confronting Climate Change: Risks, Implications and Responses,* edited by I.M. Mintzer, pp. 153–61, Cambridge, England: Cambridge University Press.

Keynes, J.M. (1988) *A Treatise on Probability*. London: Macmillan.

Knetsch, J.L. (1997) 'Reference states, fairness, and choice of measure to value environmental changes', in *Environment, Ethics and Behaviour: The Psychology of Environmental Valuation and Degradation*, edited by M.H. Bazerman, D.M. Messick, A.E. Tenbrunsel and K.A. Wade-Benzoni, pp. 13–32, San Francisco: The New Lexington Press.

Knetsch, J.L. and J.A. Sinden (1984) 'Willingness to pay and compensation demanded: experimental evidence of an unexpected disparity in measures of value', *Quarterly Journal of Economics* **99**(3): 507–21.

Knight, F. (1921) *Risk, Uncertainty and Profit*. Boston, MA: Houghton Mifflin.

Lee, J.C. and P.J. Kromer (1987) 'Forestry research needs and strategies', in *The Greenhouse Effect, Climate Change and US Forests*, edited by W.E. Shands and J.S. Hoffman, pp. 295–302, Washington, DC: The Conservation Foundation.

Loasby, B.J. (1976) *Choice, Complexity and Ignorance: An Inquiry into Economic Theory and the Practice of Decision-Making*. Cambridge, England: Cambridge University Press.

Manne, A.S. and R.G. Richels (1992) *Buying Greenhouse Insurance: The Economic Costs of CO_2 Emissions Limit*. Cambridge, MA: MIT Press.

Martinez-Alier, J. (1994) 'Ecological economics and ecosocialism', in *Is Capitalism Sustainable?*, edited by M. O'Connor, pp. 23–36. New York: Guilford Press.

Nakicenovic, N., O. Davidson, G. Davis, A. Grubler, T. Kram, E.L. La Rovere, B. Metz, T. Morita, W. Pepper, H. Pitcher, A. Sankovski, P. Shukla, R. Swart, R. Watson and Z. Dadi (2000) *Emissions Scenarios: Summary for Policymakers*. Geneva: Intergovernmental Panel on Climate Change.

Newton, L.H. and C.K. Dillingham (1994) *Watersheds: Classic Cases in Environmental Ethics*. Belmont, CA: Wadsworth.

Niedercorn, J.H. (1983) 'The origins of the ancient Sumerians: ecological crisis and repeated migrations over twenty millennia', *Man, Environment, Space and Time* **3**(1): 37–52.

Nordhaus, W.D. (1991) 'To slow or not to slow: the economics of the greenhouse effect', *Economic Journal* **101**: 920–38.

Norgaard, R.B. (1994) *Development Betrayed: The End of Progress and a Coevolutionary Revisioning of the Future*. London: Routledge.

OECD (1995) *The Economic Appraisal of Environmental Projects and Policies: A Practical Guide*. Paris: Organisation for Economic Co-operation and Development.

Reilly, J. (1996) 'Agriculture in a changing climate: impacts and adaptation', in *Impacts, Adaptations and Mitigation of Climate Change: Scientific-Technical Analyses*, edited by R.T. Watson, M.C. Zinyowera, R.H. Moss and D.J. Dokken, pp. 427–67, Cambridge, England: Cambridge University Press.

Revelle, R. (1983) 'Probable future changes in sea level resulting from increased atmospheric carbon dioxide', in *Changing Climate: Report of the Carbon Dioxide Assessment Committee*, edited by N.A.o.S. National Research Council, pp. 433–47, Washington, DC: National Academy Press.

Revelle, R. and H.E. Suess (1957) 'Carbon dioxide exchange between atmosphere and ocean, and the question of an increase in atmospheric CO_2 during the past decades', *Tellus* **9**(18): 18–27.

Schneider, S. and R. Chen (1980) 'Carbon dioxide warming and coastline flooding: physical factors and climatic impact', *Annual Review of Energy* **5**: 107–40.

Spash, C.L. (1997) 'Assessing the economic benefits to agriculture from air pollution control', *Journal of Economic Surveys* **11**(1): 47–70.

Titus, J.G. (1989) 'The cause and effects of sea-level rise', in *The Challenge of Global Warming*, edited by D.E. Abrahamson, pp. 161–95, Washington, DC: Island Press.

Warrick, R. and J. Oerlemans (1990) 'Sea level rise', in *Climate Change: The IPCC Scientific Assessment*, edited by J.T. Houghton, G.J. Jenkins and J.J. Ephraums, pp. 257–81, Cambridge, England: Cambridge University Press.

Warrick, R.A., C. Le Provost, M.F. Meier, J. Oerlemans and P.L. Woodworth (1996) 'Changes in sea level', in *Climate Change 1995: The Science of Climate Change*, edited by J.T. Houghton, L.G. Meira, B.A. Callander, N. Harris, A. Kattenberg and K. Maskell, pp. 358–405, Cambridge, England: Cambridge University Press.

Watson, R.T., M.C. Zinyowera and R.H. Moss (1996) 'Technical summary: impacts, adaptations, and mitigation options', in *Impacts, Adaptations, and Mitigation: Scientific-Technical Analyses*, edited by R.T. Watson, M.C. Zinyowera and R.H. Moss, pp. 19–53, Cambridge, England: Cambridge University Press.

Watson, R.T., M.C. Zinyowera, R.H. Moss and D.J. Dokken (1996) *Impacts, Adaptations and Mitigation of Climate Change: Scientific-Technical Analyses*. Cambridge, England: Cambridge University Press.

Watson, R.T., M.C. Zinyowera, R.H. Moss and D.J. Dokken (eds) (1997) *The Regional Impacts of Climate Change: An Assessment of Vulnerability; Summary for Policymakers*. IPCC Special Report. Geneva: Intergovernmental Panel on Climate Changes.

Wilenius, M. and J. Tirkkonen (1997) 'Climate in the making: using Delphi for Finnish climate policy', *Futures* **29**(9): 845–62.

Wolfe, D.W. and J.D. Erickson (1993) 'Carbon dioxide effects on plants: uncertainties and implications for modeling crop response to climate change', in *Agricultural Dimensions of Global Climate Change*, edited by H.M. Kaiser and T.E. Drennen, pp. 153–78, Delray Beach, FL: St Lucie Press.

Woodwell, G.M. (1990) 'The effects of global warming', in *Global Warming: The Greenpeace Report*, edited by J. Leggett, pp. 116–32, Oxford, England: Oxford University Press.

Wynne, B. (1992) 'Uncertainty and environmental learning: reconceiving science and policy in the preventive paradigm', *Global Environmental Change* (June): 111–27.

6 Calculating the costs and benefits of GHG control

Impact assessment by the IPCC has been described by the heads of the WMO (Obasi) and UNEP (Dowdeswell) as establishing a common base of knowledge about 'potential costs and benefits of climate change including the evaluation of uncertainties, to help Conference of the Parties (COP) determine what adaptation and mitigation measures might be justified' (Watson *et al.*, 1997: v). As discussed in the last two chapters, the scientific community has been concerned to evaluate the weak uncertainty associated with potential consequences from the enhanced Greenhouse Effect. The economic approach encapsulated within cost–benefit analysis attempts to formalise assessment of potential pros and cons of a policy or environmental change using monetary valuation.

Economics has been regarded as making a contribution to the understanding of environmental problems in two ways. First through analysis of those human welfare impacts which are signalled through markets and the price mechanism. These are recognised as changes in the level and distribution of costs and benefits. Second, as a method of producing institutions for the control of pollution which minimise control costs while achieving given environmental standards (e.g. taxes, subsidies, tradable permits). While the two areas are usually assumed separable they are connected because any pollution control policy requires a set of institutional mechanisms which have their own associated implications for human welfare. In both cases monetary valuation of change is used as the key signal of success or failure, i.e. benefits should exceed costs and policy instruments should be efficient or at least cost-effective.

As noted in the last chapter, how an environmental problem is characterised varies with belief and perception of the degree to which society is committed to a given path. Faced with the threat of global climate change, society has normally been regarded as having three options:

- do nothing and conduct 'business as usual'
- prepare to adapt as sea level and temperature rise, or
- reduce emissions of GHGs.

The first implies the enhanced Greenhouse Effect is either unimportant or beneficial. The second and third options take the problem seriously enough to warrant action, and can be carried out simultaneously. Note, the international discourse has moved from discussing prevention to mitigation, and thus implicitly accepts an unspecified amount of human-induced climate change.

Adaptation would include measures such as strengthening sea defences, changing cropping patterns, population migration, increasing irrigation and altering land use patterns. A policy solely relying on adaptation implies that all future consequences will remain within the boundaries of human adaptability and physical impacts can be offset by *expost* reaction. Risk aversion under weak uncertainty, irreversible damages and preparing for 'surprise' events under partial ignorance all argue in favour of controlling GHGs. However, to the extent that global climate change is already irreversibly underway society has no choice but to adapt and this option has been slowly getting more attention (for examples see Rosenberg *et al.*, 1989; Reilly, 1996; Peake, 1998; Tol, Fankhauser and Smith, 1998; Fankhauser, Smith and Tol, 1999).

The control option with reduction of GHG emissions at source remains the policy most commonly studied by economists and is the subject of this chapter. This approach may be recast as achieving stabilisation of a given level of atmospheric concentrations by cutting sources and increasing sinks rather than just cutting GHG emissions. As will be seen the benefits of control have proven most controversial and yet the methodological problems and ethical issues which arise are equally applicable to cost assessment. Similarly, the methodological issues and many of the problems in economic assessment, which will be discussed here, are also relevant to the evaluation of adaptation options.

In the next section some of the economic theory relating to pollution control is critically explained. The main part of the chapter then reviews various attempts at monetary valuation of the impacts of enhancing the Greenhouse Effect and controlling for GHG emissions. A short historical overview leads into the studies covering both costs and benefits. These studies include the work of Ayres and Walters, Cline, Fankhauser, Nordhaus and Tol. Some analysts prefer to work solely on the costs of pollution control, sometimes assuming a given standard will be politically set. Such cost-effectiveness studies are reviewed with reference to the work of Barker, Ekins, Manne and Richels, Nordhaus and others. The overall aim is to show how monetary assessment has been conducted and raise some of the areas of controversy which are pursued further in the next chapter.

The theory behind economic assessment

Climate forcing could be reduced by cutting CO_2, CH_4, CFCs, N_2O or other trace gas emissions, and/or increasing the sinks for these GHGs (e.g. increasing CO_2 absorption by reforestation). A stream of consequences are associated with adopting such actions and these can be classified as costs and benefits. Optimal levels of GHG

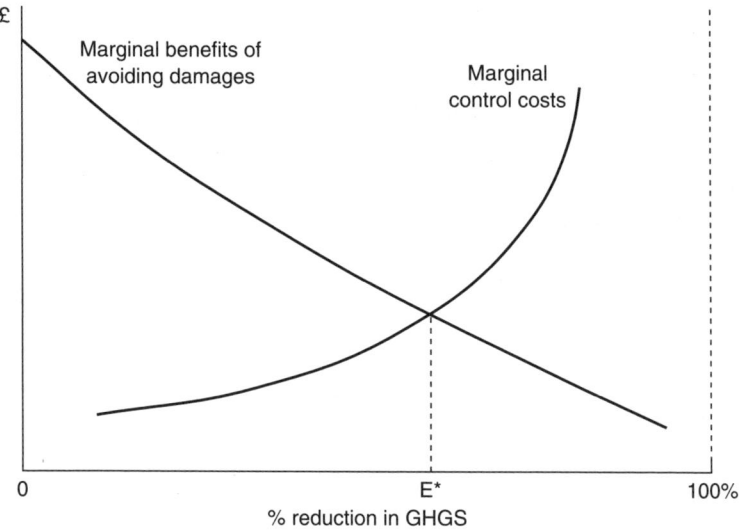

Figure 6.1 Marginal costs and benefits of reducing greenhouse gas emissions

reductions are meant to be deduced from an examination of how pollution-control costs and the benefits of avoiding damages vary with the level of reduction. However, as explained in the last chapter, such a model in fact describes the outcome which is consistent with the assumptions and constraints of the model, rather than a 'best' outcome.

Control costs are normally assumed to rise with the reduction in emissions, and be higher the quicker a given reduction is attempted. Conversely, the marginal benefits of reducing GHGs are assumed to fall with the level of control because fewer damages are avoided per unit of GHG reduced. The 'optimal' level of control is defined as occurring when the marginal benefits of GHG reductions, in present value terms, are just equal to marginal control costs.[1]

Figure 6.1 gives a standard graphical representation of this static equilibrium model. Marginal pollution control costs are shown as rising with the level of emission reduction while marginal benefits fall. The emission reduction E* is the optimal target. If the assumptions concerning control costs and benefits are correct this analysis implies that the optimal reduction in GHGs will be less than 100 per cent. This is because the output associated with GHG production is valued more highly the scarcer it becomes. That is, the products from the petro-chemical industry, energy use in buildings, agro-chemical energy intensive farming and the fossil fuel intensive transportation system are all regarded as creating welfare for humans which is valued and would in part need to be sacrificed under a strict reduction of GHGs. Thus, pollution control costs can include impacts from lost production, and this will be particularly relevant where input substitution is limited, e.g. where there is no alternative to the use of fossil fuels in the production of a good or service. Emissions are usually partially separable from production so that they can be controlled without cutting output but instead raise production costs, e.g. placing scrubber units on power plants or catalytic converters on cars. This theoretical model has proven attractive as an explanation of why positive levels of pollution are necessary evils. However, the discussion of GHG emission reduction immediately exposes some weaknesses of the approach in terms of the characterisation of the cost and benefit functions and their relationship to human well-being.

Control costs with respect to GHG control have been classified by Boero, Clarke and Winters (1991), cited by Perman (1994), as comprising the following three categories:

- negative costs due to correcting market failures, i.e. gains in gross domestic product (GDP)[2]
- ongoing costs relating to diverting resources from other uses, e.g. curtailed energy use or forgone output
- short-term transitional costs such as scrapping capital prematurely or creating unemployment because of structural changes in the labour market.

As Perman (1994) notes, most studies concentrate upon the second cost category, ignoring the third, while the first remains controversial, i.e. appearing in some studies and being ignored by others.

The first cost category above has been termed 'secondary benefits' or more popularly 'no regrets' strategies. These are basically actions that society should be undertaking now in any case but which also reduce GHG emissions. That is, there can be 'secondary benefits' to the control of GHG emissions and these must be included as a reduction of the net costs of pollution control. For example, curtailing the use of fossil fuels would reduce other air pollution problems and their associated damages. Improving energy efficiency is another common example, discussed further below. The result of these gains would be to reduce pollution control costs, e.g. the cost function would shift or rotate downwards. However, the question remains as to why no action has been taken to obtain these gains before. The implication is that production and consumption processes are far less efficient than commonly assumed and institutional barriers may prevent efficiency gains. This in turn questions the applicability of the simple model which ignores institutional structures.

The benefits function is based upon microeconomic demand theory and welfare measures (see Hanley and Spash, 1993: chapter 2). These measures are constructed assuming smooth continuous functions, and that price (or quantity) changes represent a small fraction of an individual's income. If there are catastrophic or irreversible events then the functions will no longer be smooth or continuous. If climate change is characterised by major impacts rather than marginal changes then the assumptions underlying welfare measures will break down and money values will no longer relate uniquely to welfare (e.g. Willig conditions[3] fail, marginal utility of money changes).

In particular, Pareto and Kaldor-Hicks tests of welfare economics are designed to judge the relative positions of individuals after a marginal change and rely upon the fact that other relevant things have remained the same, i.e. the assumption of *ceteris paribus*. The range and scale of impacts under the enhanced Greenhouse Effect clearly violate this condition (Brown, 1988), and more generally this brings into question the relevance of partial equilibrium analysis.

Most discussions of monetary value forget (or dismiss) the fact that cost–benefit analysis (CBA) techniques were developed for small-scale projects and that their theoretical basis (as measures of human welfare) lies in demand for consumer goods. The *ceteris paribus* assumption might make sense for adding or removing a unit of a product from the bundle of goods a consumer purchases, but the extensions beyond this theoretically sound region of analysis soon violates required conditions. In the case of large-scale, long-term changes the assumptions simply fail to hold. A serious GHG reduction programme would alter the technological base of the economy, e.g. developing alternative energy sources, new transportation systems and lifestyles. The basis for comparison of winners and losers is then no longer identifiable. This affects both benefit estimation and cost analysis.

Baseline scenarios in cost studies provide the basis of comparison for calculating costs, but are dependent upon an artificial distinction between 'business as usual' and policy intervention. As Hourcade *et al.* (1996: 281–2) note, multiple baseline scenarios make cost assessments non-comparable. The multiple feedback mechanisms between development patterns (population growth, energy use, transport systems, consumption patterns) and economic variables mean assumptions about one determines the treatment of the other. For example, costs vary with assumptions about energy production, such as the role of nuclear power or biomass, and this impacts the level of baseline GHG emissions, as well as other factors. The assumptions about different GHG emissions affect damages while those about energy production affect control costs. In addition, programmes undertaken for one reason may be justified under another if there is some advantage, e.g. expansion of nuclear power may be sold (quite literally) as removing GHG emissions while this expansion would have occurred with or without the threat of climate change. This latter problem is particularly relevant as carbon trading from baseline scenarios moves on to the political agenda. Thus, for example, a forest which would be planted or exist without GHG control is not an additional cost of that control.

Besides these concerns, E^* in figure 6.1 is an impractical policy goal because no authority can accurately estimate marginal benefit or control cost functions. This is often taken to mean that monetary calculations to obtain CBAs of controlling GHGs could, at the very best, and in the absence of other problems, only be one input to a larger process of information gathering. This then raises questions as to the exact nature of the decision-making process into which this information is to be fed and how the information is used relative to other information. One concern here is the ability for institutional capture of information (see Hanley and Spash,

1993: 160–3). The institutes producing CBA studies must be questioned for their own impartiality and the extent to which vested interests can determine outcomes. For example, nobody would really expect a study funded by an electricity generating industry with heavy investments in coal-fired power stations to argue in favour of large carbon taxes. CBA has also been a popular tool for use within government bureaucracies because of the power wielded by the Treasury. Thus, financial information flows can become dominant without regard to the assumptions upon which that information is based or the partial ignorance within which it is constructed, e.g. economics addresses resource efficiency and positively excludes a range of other policy goals such as equity, fairness, justice and moral rights. Yet these other considerations are impossible to exclude from the analysis and, as will be shown below, dominate a debate which is being presented as objective, free of value judgements, and solely concerned with efficient resource allocation.

An overview of monetary valuation of GHG control

The earliest example of a CBA of climate change is d'Arge (1975). This study, initiated in 1973, brought together 40 economists from across the US to evaluate the impacts on climate of emissions into the upper atmosphere due to jet aircraft. The economic assessment was the final stage which built upon five scientific research reports (the natural stratosphere of 1974, propulsion effluents in the stratosphere, the stratosphere perturbed by propulsion effluents, the natural and radiatively perturbed troposphere, and the impacts of climatic change on the biosphere). The primary concern was for the threat posed by proposed new fleets of supersonic jets, such as Concorde, on the chemistry of the stratosphere, although subsonic jets on long-haul flights were also implicated. Thus, the research was commissioned by the US Department of Transport. At this time climatic change was acknowledged to be capable of either heating or cooling the troposphere, and both scenarios were analysed. In most other respects little has changed concerning the approach to valuation and in some areas the report surpasses more recent work. Decision analysis was put forward as a useful but imperfect tool along with CBA. A range of sectors were addressed including world agriculture (corn, cotton, wheat and rice), US forestry, US water resources, world marine resources, world health, and US urban impacts (wages, housing, household expenditure, fossil fuel demand, public expenditures). In addition, specific sections of the report addressed, without valuation, possible social (family and community) and political impacts. This report certainly appears far more coherent than that on economics under the second assessment of the IPCC (Bruce, Hoesung and Haites, 1996).

Economic research on climate change largely disappeared until the late 1980s and then the major expansion of interest in the area was during the early 1990s. At the First World Climate Conference in 1979 the only presentation addressing economic impacts was by d'Arge (1979). An edited volume relating to climate change issues was produced by Resources for the Future (Cumberland, Hibbs and Hoch,

1982), and a section of the American Economic Association meetings discussed the subject with papers being duly published (d'Arge, Schulze and Brookshire, 1982; Lave, 1982; Nordhaus, 1982). In general, environmental economics and policy analysis were minority pursuits at this time, and interest in the enhanced Greenhouse Effect was dominated by scientific research.

Key aspects of the economic debate were, however, developing. The work by d'Arge followed a traditional CBA approach but also emphasised the intergenerational problems raised by such analysis, including the asymmetry of costs and benefits and the ethics of discounting. In contrast Nordhaus applied optimisation theory without questioning the applicability of standard assumptions, and so disregarded equity and ethics. Indeed the gap between these models and the reality they are addressing is a major methodological problem (Lawson, 1997). This division of economists, between those with deep faith in the models and those questioning theoretical constructs, continues to be apparent and relevant to the policy advice being offered.

Pachauri and Damodaran (1992) have described economists as following one of two distinct theories as to the correct behaviour for dealing with climate change. One is a strategy of 'acting then learning' to allow experimentation, foresight, cost-effective prevention and the adjustment of investment decisions. This position favours actions which, even without the enhanced Greenhouse Effect, offer major benefits. The alternative is 'learning then acting', requiring all uncertainties be resolved before any action is taken and favouring research and new technologies. This is characterised as the 'wait and see' school and Nordhaus (1991c), Manne and Richels (1990), and Peck and Teisburg (1993) are all described as being biased towards this approach in their work (Pachauri and Damodaran, 1992: 251).

In the early 1990s numerous studies appeared relating to the enhanced Greenhouse Effect and the literature on this subject continues to grow. In 1991 both the *Economic Journal* and *American Economic Review* published commissioned papers on climate change issues. There was, however, little or no follow-up to these articles in mainstream journals and no replies were printed. Yet the arrival of climate change on the political stage firmly placed it on the economic research agenda. Economic approaches to climate change have clearly been driven by the international political process. The initial phase was one of deciding on whether action was necessary and once this was largely accepted the debate moved to how soon action and what type of action was required. Thus, CBA studies have given way to papers on the costs of action and flexible economic instruments as promoted under the Kyoto Protocol, e.g. tradable permit schemes.

A variety of economic approaches have been applied to the economic impacts from climate change. These range from country-specific studies (Ingham and Ulph, 1991) to world models (Manne and Richels, 1990; Nordhaus, 1998), and analyses include partial equilibrium (International Energy Agency, 1989), general equilibrium (Bergman, 1991; Cameron, 1993) and input–output (Symons, Proops and Gay, 1994). Thus, the analysts can choose their approach. However, the modelling community is fairly small and interconnected, so that models and model attributes tend to be shared. This means apparently independent studies by different authors may indeed be fundamentally related. For example, work by Nordhaus (1991b; 1991c) has been used as the basis for the CETA (carbon emissions trajectory assessment) model of Peck and Teisberg (1992; 1993). Both Peck and Richels are affiliated with the US Electric Power Research Institute and the control cost model of the former is based upon that of the latter. Similarly, Demeritt and Rothman (1999) show how all the benefit assessments up to 1996 derived some of their key damage estimates from one study, i.e. Smith and Tirpak (1989). These links are important because of the way in which scientific replication of results lends validity and results from different studies are reported as converging on a specific policy conclusion as if this were confirmation of an underlying truth rather than an artefact of the model and its assumptions.

The main focus has been the control cost of CO_2 reductions (see surveys in Ayres and Walters, 1991; Hoeller, Dean and Nicolaisen, 1991; Nordhaus, 1991a; Hourcade *et al.*, 1996). In comparison, there have been relatively few studies attempting to account for the benefits of control and these have often proven most controversial (e.g. Ayres and Walters, 1991; Nordhaus, 1991b; Cline, 1992a; Nordhaus, 1994; Fankhauser, 1995; Tol, 1995). Controversy also surrounded the IPCC Second Assessment Report on economics and specifically the chapter on the benefits of preventing global climate change (Pearce *et al.*, 1996). This created considerable debate over the basis for the monetary valuation of human life. The authors of this chapter rejected the critical policymakers summary of their work and sought to formally distance themselves from that summary (Grubb, Vrolijk and Brack, 1999: 304). This has undoubtedly contributed to the focus upon cost-effectiveness of policy instruments to achieve predetermined standards. The Third Assessment of the IPCC appear to have tried ignoring the issues raised by the debate over the benefits of control on the basis of meeting given political emissions reductions, although the same problems can arise under cost estimation. Some limited initial attempts at obtaining new benefit estimates have been reported (e.g. sea level rise in the US; Yohe, Neumann and Ameden, 1995), but there appears to be no comprehensive research agenda.

In the following sections a selection of CBA and cost-effectiveness studies are reviewed in order to illustrate some of the key issues and controversies. This is followed by a closer look at how value judgements are implicit in economic assessment. As will be shown, the impossibility of reducing value conflicts to objective facts raises questions both for economics and science as to how complex environmental problems should be analysed and discussed in the public arena.

Studies using cost–benefit analysis

At the start of the 1990s the work of Nordhaus was almost alone in trying to formally model the costs and benefits of climate change on the economy. The particular estimates of Nordhaus are important because of their implication in supporting the US negotiating stance at the international level. *The Economist* (27 October 1990) ran a leader referring to the work of Nordhaus as 'the best (though magnificently simplified) cost–benefit analysis' on the issue and regarded the estimates as 'hard-nosed calculations'. Rowlands (1995: 138) notes that the lack of systematic studies of the benefits of GHG control has resulted in the verdict of Nordhaus against co-operative action commanding 'significant respect and currency in the US debate'. Controversy over the calculations occurred very quickly with both critiques and re-estimations. Most notable amongst the latter were the article by Ayres and Walters (1991) and the study by Cline (1992a; 1992b).

The initial work by Nordhaus (1991b; 1991c; 1992) divided the US into three sectors by susceptibility to climate change:

- very susceptible, such as agriculture
- medium susceptibility, such as construction
- unsusceptible, such as finance.

In 1981 these sectors were attributed by Nordhaus with 3 per cent, 10 per cent and 87 per cent of US gross national product (GNP) respectively.[4] The economic benefits of emissions reductions in the high and medium sensitivity sectors is small at only 0.25 per cent of GNP, or $6.23 thousand million for double CO_2 equivalent, because they account for a low proportion of total GNP. The work assumed that impacts would occur in 2050 and that the composition of world GNP at that date would be the same as that of US GNP in 1981. The marginal benefits from emissions reduction, given under three scenarios, using a discount rate 1 per cent above growth and 1989 dollars, are shown in table 6.1 (Nordhaus, 1991c: 927).

Nordhaus excludes undesirable effects of global warming on non-marketed resources such as biodiversity and species loss, human health, non-commercial recreation, and ecosystem damages. These are impacts he views as too difficult to value. Instead he relies upon his 'judgement' (Nordhaus, 1991b: 148), that this is no more than seven times the estimated value of 0.25 per cent of GNP. He states, '… my hunch is that the overall impact upon human activity is unlikely to be bigger than 2 per cent of total world output' (Nordhaus, 1991c: 933). In effect the overall

Table 6.1 Double CO_2 equivalent GHG damages in Nordhaus 1991

Damage scenario	$/ton	GNP (%)
Low estimate	1.83	0.25
Medium guess	7.33	1.00
High guess	14.64	2.00

Source: Nordhaus (1991c).

Note: 1989 US dollars, discount rate 1 per cent above growth rate.

loss for a doubling of CO_2 equivalent is a guess on the basis of 'an adjustment' which is 'purely *ad hoc*'.

An impact of 0.25 per cent loss of GNP resulting from a 3°C temperature rise associated with a doubling of CO_2 equivalent is argued to require 'very little CO_2 abatement' (Nordhaus, 1991b: 149). That is, his preferred estimate of benefits is outweighed by the estimated control costs. In calculating costs of emissions reductions the lowest cost methods are assumed to be employed. Nordhaus argues that these costs will depend upon the speed required, and that marginal control costs increase steeply beyond a 10 per cent emissions reduction. Reforestation is excluded because of the assumed high marginal cost of $100/ton of CO_2 removed. The medium control option (assuming a discount rate 1 per cent above the growth rate) is described as an 11 per cent reduction in GHGs split between CFCs at 9 per cent, and CO_2 at 2 per cent (Nordhaus, 1991c: 935).

Such minimalist recommendations and the approach by which they are derived have been criticised as misleading and biased by various authors (Ayres and Walters, 1991; Daily *et al.*, 1991; FitzRoy, 1992; Pachauri and Damodaran, 1992; Funtowicz and Ravetz, 1994; Price, 1994). Criticisms of this work note problems in both cost and benefit estimation. On the cost side, energy conservation is argued to achieve GHG reductions at no cost or even producing a gain, while other secondary benefits which have been excluded might prove substantial. On the benefit side, the estimates are regarded as too low, inaccurate and unrepresentative. On the methodological front, the approach is regarded as questionable because of the way it purports awareness of uncertainty but then actually neglects its importance. Several of these issues are dealt with in turn here and in some detail because most remain relevant to work since, and monetary valuation currently ongoing.

The costs of reducing GHGs are argued to be negative over some range, because society is better off with fewer of the substances generating GHGs regardless of climate change. There are two reasons for this conclusion. First, market distortions (e.g. oligopoly, government subsidies) are argued to result in excessive and inefficient use of energy. This is part of the first category of costs noted earlier in this chapter, i.e. negative costs (gains in GDP) due to correcting market failures. Second, profitable opportunities for energy conservation exist but are currently ignored, e.g. due to myopia on the part of individuals and institutions, and lack of information. Ayres and Walter (1991: 255) note that the economic expectation that all efficiencies will be exploited fails because, internally, large firms are bureaucratic, hierarchical, rule driven central planners rather than competitive, profit maximising and price driven.

Cutting energy demand and increasing energy conservation would reduce the largest source of GHGs. Ayres and Walter (1991) provide case-study evidence for Italy and the US to support these general arguments. If some GHG emissions can be cut at no net cost to society, then, *ceteris paribus*, a higher optimal level of emission reduction is required. According to the IPCC many studies show that energy efficiency gains of 10–30 per cent are feasible within two to three decades at little or no cost, via technical conservation measures and improved management practices (Watson, Zinyowera and Moss, 1996: 41). In addition, efficiency gains of 50–60 per cent are also cited as being technically possible for many countries within the same time frame. Cline (1992a: 63–5) estimates 20–25 per cent of carbon emissions could be cut back at zero cost via improved energy efficiency.

Net costs are also reduced if cutting GHG emissions has environmentally beneficial side effects. For example, a carbon tax would mean coal facing a higher tax rate than either oil or natural gas due to its relatively high carbon content by weight. Reduced coal use would reduce SO_2 emissions and so mean lower acidic deposition. Similarly, CFC reductions would help reduce stratospheric ozone depletion. Ayres and Walters (1991) claim that the indirect benefits of reduced air pollution for industrialised countries is between $20 and $60 per ton of CO_2. Secondary benefits would also accrue if the strategy to reduce GHG concentrations involved afforestation. This could generate a stream of non-market amenity benefits, depending on the type of forest planted. In fact, a decade ago the UK Forestry Commission started to include carbon absorption benefits in its investment appraisals of new tree planting (Whiteman, 1991). As with some other aspects, Nordhaus (1992: 64) was apparently aware of the potential for environmental gains reducing costs and some market imperfections in the energy market maintaining excessive consumption, but these considerations were excluded from the calculations.

The estimates of the benefits of cutting GHGs in the work of Nordhaus also appear excessively conservative. The susceptibility attributed to different sectors is highly questionable. The financial and service sectors seem to be excluded on the basis that they will avoid direct physical damages. However, there are many repercussions from human-induced climate change. For example, an economy may be affected by the size and balance of foreign investment. Thus, capital flight might be expected from countries under threat of or suffering damages. Alternatively, a country may lose substantial GNP due to foreign investment losses while the domestic economy (GDP) remains unaffected, at least initially. This would feed back into financial institutions which find their overseas capital under water, their foreign crops failing on an unprecedented scale or a foreign economy in crisis due to climate change impacts. There is already some concern in the insurance industry about the increasing frequency of extreme weather events (Pearce, 1995). Financial institutions are in fact susceptible to a range of damages due to the enhanced Greenhouse Effect, e.g. the insurance industry, property investment, long-term capital investment (see Dlugolecki, 1996).

The estimates for the US economy were extended by Nordhaus to the world level without structural adjustment, i.e. implicitly assuming all countries have the same economic structure as the US. Nordhaus (1992: 44) claims 'on average high income countries have less than 5 per cent of their GDP originating in agriculture'. However, for example, in Western Europe those countries with more than 5 per cent in agriculture include Finland, Greece, Iceland, Ireland, Portugal and Spain.

Direct agricultural production ignores the importance of the food sector which includes restaurants, fast-food outlets, cafés, hotels, the wine and drinks industry, supermarkets and so on. Such broad generalisation also ignores the fact that the countries expected to suffer most are those with a low income and high dependency on climate-sensitive food production, e.g. the 20 African countries with 30–60 per cent of GDP in agriculture (see GDP figures in Cantor and Yohe, 1998: 22–9).

Of course, GDP in such countries may be relatively small so that the global loss in GDP is also relatively small. Yet this is more a reflection of the failure to account for distributional inequity and the inadequacy of the measure than the irrelevance of the problem. In this latter regard note should be taken that GDP is a widely criticised measure of economic well-being because it ignores non-monetary welfare (e.g. ecosystems functions, biodiversity, aesthetics) and informal economic activity (e.g. housework, or the 'black' economy), is boosted by disasters (e.g. clean-up of oil spills), and is generally concerned with material throughput rather than quality of life. If concern were really being expressed for human well-being a multiple index with independent categories would seem more appropriate rather than conversion of all values into income and expenditure flows.

Excessive aggregation (as under the GDP studies) means losing sight of who suffers and who gains. Treatment of the regional impacts of global climate change is a major concern both within and between nation states, as explained in chapter 3. Developing industrial economies are more susceptible to global warming with a large dependence upon climate sensitive production, a limited ability to adapt, and a sizeable population of subsistence farmers (d'Arge and Spash, 1991). Population growth rates seem set to exacerbate damages. FitzRoy (1992) has argued that the benefits of reducing global warming are underestimated by Nordhaus because climate change combined with soil erosion in food-producing regions would reduce world food supplies at a time when the world population will have doubled. Declining water levels in major world aquifers would also aggravate this situation. Nordhaus (1992: 46) relies entirely upon the CO_2 fertilisation effect to argue that net benefits will be produced in the agricultural sector. Even if this were true, a presentation in terms of net GNP gains neglects the uneven distribution of gains and losses.

In presenting their critique Ayres and Walters concentrate on sea level rise. Their revised calculation includes: increasing the area of land loss by a factor of 10, a higher value for that land in less industrially developed economies (e.g. Egypt and Bangladesh), and the cost of resettling refugees forced to move as a result of sea level rise. Even without attempting to include other market or non-market effects, these revisions in damages from global warming are stated to be 10 times greater than the comparable damage scenario estimates given by Nordhaus. This can be seen by roughly calculating the total damages in the two papers. The estimated total sea level rise impact over 50 years (excluding migration) are just over $264 thousand million in Nordhaus (1991c: 932) compared with $1,750 to $2,000 thousand million in Ayres and Walters (1991). The major difference here is in terms of the value of land lost which was estimated at just over $77 thousand million in the former and $1,500 thousand million in the latter.

In recalculating the benefits of preventing just sea level rise, Ayres and Walters (1991: 245) raised the annual damages giving the range as 2.1–2.4 per cent of gross world income. The lower limit of quantifiable damages is then given as $30–$35 per ton of CO_2 equivalent excluding secondary benefits, non-market impacts and improved energy efficiency. If we include the 'ad hoc' adjustment for non-market impacts used by Nordhaus the loss of world income would be 3.85–4.15 per cent.

Further criticisms of the calculations relate to the construction of the model by Nordhaus. This assumed a resource-steady state and a linear relationship between greenhouse damages and emissions. The former implies a constant level of CO_2 emissions over time, which is clearly unrealistic (see chapter 2). The latter results in assuming that damages remain constant regardless of the concentration of CO_2. Damages in fact rely upon the increasing atmospheric concentration of GHGs and the resulting radiative forcing. As Fankhauser (1995: 60) notes, a ton of CO_2 added to a small atmospheric stock is expected to add less damage than a ton added to a large stock (i.e. high concentration). The atmospheric lifetime of a GHG may also increase with concentration as available sinks are removed. Thus, non-linear relationships would then be appropriate when considering GHG damage functions and the benefits of GHG control. However, the situation is further complicated by rapid changes in climate, causing sharp discontinuities, threshold effects and irreversibilities.

Cline (1992a; 1992b) offers a far more comprehensive estimation of impacts increasing the number of detailed categories from just three (agriculture, sea level, energy) to fourteen. The more extensive range of categories and emphasis on long-term damages is probably due to a better understanding of the science than many economists (see Cline, 1991). Whereas Nordhaus attributed over 70 per cent of damages to sea level rise and only 6 per cent to agricultural losses, Cline's figures gave 11 and 28 per cent respectively. He also introduced significant levels of damages in water supply and human mortality and morbidity contributing around 10 per cent each to total damages, and forest damage and species loss at around 5 per cent each. A very different conclusion from that of Nordhaus is also found on the basis of extending the damage estimates and time horizon. Rather than claiming only modest action is required he suggests 'an aggressive program of international abatement' (Cline, 1992a: 1–2). The damages are again built upon the US economy and the numbers are highly speculative in the same vein as the work of others. His best-guess estimate for a double CO_2 equivalent warming of 2.5°C is a loss of $60 billion or 1 per cent of US GDP in 1990 dollars, which is estimated at seven times that of Nordhaus (Cline, 1992b: 61). The main contributions are clarifying the need for much higher damage estimates, refining the different impact categories and, perhaps most importantly, extending the time frame from 50 to 300 years.

There is clearly no reason to restrict attention to an arbitrary point such as a doubling of CO_2 and Cline therefore gives long-term estimates as well. His baseline projections give a CO_2 concentration eight times the pre-industrial level by 2275 (Cline, 1992a: 23). The damage function is non-linear. The central estimate is that damages reach 6 per cent of GDP with a 10°C warming and under the pessimistic scenario losses rise to 20 per cent of GDP. In the first 30 years (of which 10 have now gone) forestry is the main means of reducing concentrations. By 2100 carbon reductions of 80 per cent are required with taxes of $100 to $250 per ton. Even an 'aggressive' emissions reduction programme would be unable to avoid 2.5°C of warming because stabilisation of radiative forcing would only be achieved by 2100. This also means that for each decade in which policymakers delay action, an additional 0.25°C in long-term warming is added (Cline, 1992a: 27).

Discounting is crucial to the outcome of long-term impacts, but far from the only issue creating a divergence in study results (contrary to some commentaries). Even with a 5 per cent rate, incorporating only a small probability of catastrophe is required to justify 'aggressive' action (Cline, 1992a: 6). The study showed the estimates of Nordhaus to be on the conservative bottom end of the scale in terms of possible damages. However, despite Cline's work the debate has remained largely based in that conservative zone and concentrates upon the double CO_2 scenario with 2.5°C equilibrium warming and a 50 cm sea level rise.

Fankhauser (1995) also presents a more comprehensive assessment than Nordhaus, and borrows largely from Cline in terms of designating his 10 main damage categories. Probability distributions are applied to model damage estimates in an attempt to formalise the treatment of uncertainty. The characteristic of the probability density function then becomes important and this is argued to be skewed to the right, even without catastrophic events, i.e. a severe damages outcome is more likely than a moderate one. This work has added significance as it formed a large part of the controversial chapter 6 of the IPCC's Second Assessment addressing monetary valuation of damages (Pearce *et al.*, 1996).

Compared to Cline the estimates in Fankhauser downplay the relative roles of impacts on agriculture, energy consumption and leisure while raising the importance of species and ecosystem loss, and sea level rise. In terms of GNP the impact on the world is 1.4 per cent which is stated to be confirmation of the findings in other studies. However, comparison of such findings is far from straightforward, for example, the date for the 2.5°C rise is 2100 while in Nordhaus 3°C was reached by 2050. Fankhauser supplies a breakdown of per centage impacts on GNP for five regions as follows: European Union 1.4, US 1.3, former Soviet Union 0.7, China 4.7 and OECD 1.4. This implies worse impacts for China due to the losses in the agricultural sector which account for 47 per cent of Fankhauser's estimate (although see discussion of Tol's work below). Greater regional refinement aims to explore the inequity of impact distribution but in this case the calculations seem too aggregate and their basis extremely abstract. There are also questions over the meaning of the same losses in different regions, their comparability, and measurability. Besides lack of data, this is perhaps why analysts generally prefer to discuss only highly aggregated categories and GDP percentages.

At the same time as this work was being conducted, Nordhaus moved on to combine a traditional optimal growth model with climate and an enhanced Greenhouse Effect damage component, called the Dynamic Integrated Climate Economy or DICE model (Nordhaus, 1994). According to Fankhauser (1995: 61) this model recognised and corrected earlier shortcomings, although he states the damage estimates remained 'in the same order as Nordhaus' previous results', i.e. the new best-guess estimate of $10.03 per ton by 2025 compares to $7.33 per ton in the earlier work (see Nordhaus, 1994: table 5.7). In fact, Nordhaus (1994: 131) states the new estimates use a 6 per cent discount rate declining to 3 per cent, as growth slows, whereas the old figure, with which Fankhauser is encouraging us to compare, used a rate of 1 per cent above the growth rate. A similarly misleading comparison of several studies is made in chapter 6, table 6.11 of the IPCC SAR (Pearce *et al.*, 1996). Variations in baseline case, scenarios and assumptions across studies make any direct comparisons difficult. Attempts at standardising the results of different studies show the extent to which variations exist (e.g. Smith, 1996). Perhaps the closest estimate in Nordhaus' earlier work is for a 4 per cent discount rate which gave an estimate of $0.31 per ton (this is without ad hoc adjustment which is apparently absent from DICE). Loss of GNP under the DICE base run is 1.3 per cent compared to the previous 0.25 per cent from doubling of CO_2 equivalent. Thus, Nordhaus appears to have dramatically increased his estimate of damages. This also seems apparent from the DICE sensitivity analysis where a base run with a 3 per cent pure time preference results in a 12.5 per cent reduction in GHGs and a carbon tax of $13.68 per ton by 2045, while a 1 per cent rate requires a 25.2 per cent reduction and $52.58 per ton tax (Nordhaus, 1994: 109).

Interestingly, despite an apparently more rigorous model, both the earlier work and DICE produce a recommendation of an 11 per cent control of GHGs in the first half of the twenty-first century. Indeed in several respects the DICE model fails to adequately address earlier critiques and maintains restrictive constraints. The upper boundary for losses by a country with 'a great deal of coastal activity and a large part of the economy in agriculture' is 4 per cent of GNP (Nordhaus, 1994: 53). In fact the model continues to extrapolate from the US economy using the same coefficients as in the 1991 studies, although adding some weightings for global estimates, and, as Nordhaus (1994: 55) notes, his results are heavily dependent on these choices. On using the DICE model himself Cline concluded that parameter choice was a cause of underestimating damages. Cline shows estimates of damages from DICE could range between $11.80 to $221.00 per ton of carbon by 2025 (cited by Fankhauser, 1995: 61), which compares with the optimal $10.03 of Nordhaus (1994: 94). The results vary in particular due to the choice of discount rate and size of damages allowed in the model. The range of damage categories also remains limited with the previous three types being supplemented by the addition of a fourth major category of 'other' impacts accounting for over 50 per cent of the total (this appears to have replaced the ad hoc adjustment).

In addition, there are a range of issues which bring into question the construction of the model (Spash, 1996). These, as discussed in chapter 4, relate both to the simplification and representation of both scientific understanding and the economy, as well as the reduction of strong uncertainty to weak uncertainty. Choices affecting the base case are crucial in such modelling and there is a lack of clear reasoning as to the treatment of various GHG emissions scenarios in this regard (e.g. several gases are treated as exogenously determined rather than by economic activity). The treatment of the sinks for CO_2 (e.g. ignoring the 'missing sink', unrealistic assumptions about ocean uptake) also mean the benefits of control are underestimated at low discount rates by a factor of four (see Price, 1994). The DICE model is particularly unrepresentative of any real economy, with its perfectly competitive markets and production assumptions which would in fact result in no world trade. The continued use of GNP figures bounded by historical estimates ignores the impact of climate change on relative prices, i.e. the impact of agricultural losses and flooding will be felt through land and commodity price changes. Past sector importance is a poor guide to the future under the type of changes being forecast.

As in Fankhauser, the treatment of uncertainty is brought to the fore, but again this is in order to reduce surprise and partial ignorance to probabilistic known outcomes. Nordhaus makes use of a survey of an unknown number, group and class of US 'experts' to bound the range of uncertainty on climate impacts and provide support for his own work. On this basis catastrophic impacts are characterised and this work has been used to inform further models (Nordhaus, 1998). The deviation of mean and median in these results shows clear divergence of opinion. Overmuch has been made of this survey work – it appears as substantive data in the IPCC report on damages which also notes the sample size as 19 (Pearce *et al.*, 1996: 205, 208–9). Regardless of the validity of this particular study the approach itself is highly questionable as a way to address strong uncertainty. Similarly, Nordhaus uses a survey of resource and environmental economists (with very few details supplied) to support his choices on discounting (Nordhaus, 1994:155) as if this could bound the uncertainty relating to the choice. The thrust of the survey approach to uncertainty is to obtain subjective probabilities so standard economic models can avoid having to address partial ignorance and indeterminacy. Similarly, Tol (1995: 360) is correct to point out that uncertainty is no reason for neglecting information, but then argues that '... a more rational option is to assess carefully what is known, translating uncertainties into probabilities, and to evaluate the value of the consequences of the enhanced greenhouse effect'. However, he has then to admit that in trying to apply this approach: 'most of the analysis is based on educated guesswork and heroic *ad hoc* assumptions'.

Tol (1995) has also conducted benefit estimates for a 2.5°C warming and 50 cm sea level rise. As in the case of Fankhauser, the research of Tol informed chapter 6 of the IPCC SAR. The work of Tol offers greater regional representation than other calculations of damages, including nine regions.[5] He includes seven main categories of impact as compared to the five in Fankhauser. As with Cline and Fankhauser sea level rise is broken down into three additional sub-categories.

The overall estimates are argued to be in line with other studies for the US while those for world damages are regarded as 'considerably higher' based upon new literature. In fact the estimate of a net 1.9 per cent loss of GDP is within 0.5 per cent of Fankhauser and 0.6 per cent of Nordhaus, while his US estimates are within 0.3 per cent and 0.5 per cent of the same respectively. One substantive difference is in terms of showing large regional disparities in net benefits. Thus, while the US loses 1.5 per cent of GDP, in the African case the loss is 8.7 per cent of GDP and for the former Soviet Union and Eastern Europe there is a net gain of 0.3 per cent.

The case of China is an example worth considering further as this was also analysed by Fankhauser (1995) and appears in Nordhaus (1998). As shown in table 6.2, Tol and Fankhauser's overall net figures for GDP loss are relatively close – within 0.5 of each other – and Nordhaus is the outlier. There is a bias convergence in Fankhauser and Tol (and other studies) due to use of the same base sources and extrapolation from the US to other countries and the world. Yet agreement within the regional rankings of the two studies was taken as significant by the IPCC SAR (Pearce *et al.*, 1996: 205):

> The similarity of estimates should therefore not be interpreted as evidence of their robustness. A substantial degree of uncertainty remains. Nevertheless, the relative ranking of regions appears reasonably robust, with the most severe impacts to be expected in Asia and Africa, and northern and developed regions suffering less.

The point that is being missed here concerns the relative importance attributed to different impacts within such studies. Chinese agriculture is a major loser according to Fankhauser and a major winner according to Nordhaus. Human health and loss of life are the overwhelming impact for Tol. In Nordhaus the willingness to pay for avoiding the risk of an unspecific major GDP loss is the largest category which, due to being an ad hoc and vague calculation, seems best classified as under miscellaneous (as in table 6.2). Clearly there is a large divergence in opinion as to the nature of impacts and their relative sizes, and much detail and information is lost by aggregation and the presentation of net GDP figures (as favoured by the aforementioned IPCC report).

In this latter regard the regional analysis presented by Nordhaus (1998) in his RICE model, a development from the DICE model, is also of particular concern.

Table 6.2 Benefits of GHG control for China as weighted by CBA studies

	Fankhauser 1995 China (%)	Tol 1995 Centrally Planned Asia (%)	Nordhaus 1998 China (%)
Losses avoided			
Agriculture	47	0	0
Forest	0	0	0
Species/ecosystem	13	5	0
Sea level rise	4	5	8
Energy consumption	4	0	0
Human morbidity/mortality	17	73	10
Migration	4	12	0
Hurricanes	1	0	0
Leisure	0	5	0
Water supply	10	0	0
Urban infrastructure	0	0	6
Tropospheric ozone	1	0	0
Miscellaneous	0	0	76
Total[a]	100	100	100
Gains missed (as % of losses avoided)			
Agriculture	0	−14	−43
Energy consumption	0	0	0
Outdoor recreation	0	0	−30
Temperature °C	2.5	2.5	2.5
Measurement basis	$1000 m	$1000 m	GDP
Net GDP loss %	4.70	5.20	0.22
Base year	1988	1988	1995

Data source: Fankhauser (1995) table 3.15; Tol (1995) table A1; Nordhaus (1998) table 10.

Note: a May not add to 100 due to rounding errors.

This follows the trend for including regional breakdowns by estimating impacts on eight regions and five regional income groups. The 2.5°C by 2100 seems to be the consensus scenario amongst this group of studies. What is different here is the inclusion of major gains from global warming. Those from agriculture have already been extensively discussed and their uncertainty was emphasised in earlier chapters. However, there is a large new category which substantially alters the net GDP figures.

The new group here is what Nordhaus calls 'non-market time use', but which in essence consists of recreational and sport activities specified as camping, golfing, walking and hiking. How value is meant to be added by future climatic changes is unclear, but presumably the characterisation of climate change is of a world much as today but a bit warmer with fewer rainy days. If so, the scientific scenarios have been totally neglected. In addition, the main constraint on such recreation would seem to be time and thus the need to work, and for most the world's population to survive, rather than a lack of sunny days. This characterisation of gains from a changing climatic regime seems rather parochial. The concept is doubtful for the US, but stretches credulity for most of the world. However, as in his earlier studies, the characterisation of the US is used as representative of the entire world to produce net GDP figures. The new recreational gains then play a major role. Hence the losses to agriculture in Europe are almost matched by recreational gains and in China are three times the size of mortality and morbidity. In other words even with three times the amount of morbidity and mortality the recreational and sports gains would compensate for the loss. The result for the US is that Nordhaus reduces damages by 38 per cent due to recreational gains and has returned his net GDP figure to 0.45 per cent. Nordhaus believes the enhanced Greenhouse Effect is only a real problem for the likes of India and Africa whose recreational opportunities are expected to worsen.

This picture seems to fit closely with the US political stance on emissions control, and who should pay. The message is that other countries, besides the US, especially the industrially developing countries, had better get involved because the main polluter has little incentive to act. Unfortunately, this neglects the rising damages and distributional consequences faced within the US. The 'wait and see' approach then means that awaiting exceedance of these estimates would mean irreversible commitment to further damages, which become greater the longer the delay. Any extra recreational opportunities seem likely to prove inadequate and ethically questionable compensation for loss of life, flooding, ecosystems damage and crop failure.

Overall, the CBA studies of the enhanced Greenhouse Effect show no consistency in their development of damage estimates over time, as evidenced by including or dropping categories without reason. Thus, the idea that a process of development of economic assessment is moving towards some consensus is clearly false. Attempts to standardise the various studies by correcting the variation in scenarios show the wide variation in assumptions. Initially standardising estimates to a 2.5°C increase and 50 cm sea level rise seems to show convergence (Smith, 1996). However, this requires accepting studies at face value, and ignoring the wide variation in the weighting of categories. Even after standardising the estimates, wide variation is clear if the worst case is calculated on the basis of the highest damages across categories and the best case the lowest figures. The results of doing so for five US case studies shows damages ranging from 0.35 per cent of GDP to 2.16 per cent or $17.6 to $108.4 thousand million in 1990 dollars (Demeritt and Rothman, 1998). Standardisation of available studies seems to reduce the aggregate values but does little to address the range of variation due to author choice of variables and their relative importance (Smith, 1996). In addition, there is variance of estimates across the work of the same authors so that the specific version of their work being used will affect such calculations.

Cost-effectiveness studies

The major advantage of cost-effectiveness is regarded to be the avoidance of debated ethical and political issues surrounding the setting and acceptance of a target for emissions reduction. Most economic studies of the enhanced Greenhouse Effect have centred around the cost efficiency of achieving a given reduction in CO_2 emissions, thus avoiding benefit estimation altogether. For example, a common initial target used in studies was the Toronto agreement's 20 per cent cut in CO_2 emissions by 2005. Cost-effectiveness analysis has been generally regarded as more robust and less susceptible to criticism despite many of the points already made concerning the conduct, methodology and validity of benefit estimation being equally applicable.

A cost is a monetary value placed upon objects in the same way as a benefit. The main difference is one of defining a status quo position from which to discuss a specific policy. Thus, for example, planting a forest creates benefits in terms of reducing CO_2 concentrations, creating recreational opportunities and wildlife habitat. Logging a forest creates costs in terms of releasing carbon emissions and loss of habitat. The control of GHGs regards planting forests as a cost of CO_2 control which has negative costs (secondary benefits) in terms of recreation and wildlife. Thus, categories of costs and benefits are defined by the policy position, i.e. what the action is under consideration. In the market place one person's cost is another person's benefit; you pay for a product and the supplier accepts your payment as fair exchange. The basic rule is to choose the status quo, or in the market the property rights, and define costs and benefits accordingly.

The current literature on the enhanced Greenhouse Effect tends to confuse status quo positions. Some studies merely suffer from inaccurate and sloppy use of terminology, but others make an implicit statement about who should pay for emissions control. Thus, the use of the term 'damage costs' rather than 'benefits' from emissions control can be symptomatic of a fundamental difference and more than a matter of semantics. Those who phrase the question as one of 'gaining the benefits from global warming' and warn against overemphasising 'the costs from damages' are in fact assuming a specific position with regards to what is 'normal'. The policy action required is deliberate climatic warming which costs a certain amount in terms of, say, African droughts and allows the benefits of, for example, reduced winter heating bills in the Northern Hemisphere and cheaper energy (i.e. avoiding emissions control). Despite the unknowable consequences, such authors may discuss climatic 'engineering', such as shooting particles into space or seeding the oceans with trace iron, as a cost-effective strategy to reduce damage, because their presumption is against emissions control. The concept of cost is then being used for that category of outcomes which would be described as benefits under an emissions control strategy, that is damages avoided under emission control are the benefits of that control but when taking deliberate emissions as the status quo these same damages are regarded as the costs of failing to continue to emit. Whether harm created is a cost or benefit is dependent upon choice of status quo position and the analysts perspective. In addition, there is clearly a moral context to the idea of regarding environmental damages as either costs or benefits, which is a point to be discussed further in the next chapter. More generally, an emphasis on the costs associated with any action is far from neutral and will convey specific moral and social connotations under different circumstances.[6]

The setting of parameters in all cost-effectiveness studies is crucial to the outcome. This includes making assumptions about underlying economic growth rates, and the method by which emissions reductions or concentration stabilisation are to be achieved. A base-case 'policy off' scenario is required for comparison with the 'policy on' scenario. For example, a no-intervention growth rate of GDP might be compared with the growth rate under a 20 per cent CO_2 reduction by a specific date. An obvious concern, expressed by those countries trying to achieve or maintain fast rates of material growth, is that GHG control may limit GDP growth. Modelling cost-effectiveness also requires background assumptions concerning energy supply and demand, expectations from research and development, and the cost of low-carbon backstop technologies. The method for achieving the target is crucial to the cost, with the general expectation in the pollution control literature that market mechanisms (e.g. tax or tradable permits) will be the lowest cost options. As Ekins (1995: 290) points out, an increase in the price of energy on the basis of carbon content would have a variety of effects: reducing demand for carbon-based fuels; improving fuel efficiency; encouraging development of less carbon-intensive technologies, products and processes; generating energy saving via improved efficiency of buildings and transport systems. There would also be several substitution effects: a reduction of carbon-insensitive fuels and the introduction of non-carbon fuels; switching between other factors of production and energy; a decline in the carbon intensity of products and processes. How the possibilities for substitution, efficiency improvements and technological change are modelled will determine whether energy price rises are predicted to reduce or increase GDP.

Manne and Richels (1991) used a dynamic optimisation model (Global 2100), which divided the world into five regions with nine energy sectors. This model predicted CO_2 emissions from fossil fuel sources through to the year 2100, and has been used to examine the cost of various policy options. A 20 per cent reduction of CO_2 emissions by 2020, with that level maintained until 2100, was compared to a 'do nothing' scenario where GDP grew at around 2 per cent a year, while energy efficiency grew at between 0.5 to 2.0 per cent depending on the region (making total energy demand per unit of GDP fall). The model had CO_2 emissions in the absence of action rising at 0.7 to 2.1 per cent per year. The principle policy simulation was of a tax levied on the carbon content of fuels. In the model this hit a peak of

$400 per ton carbon, then fell to $250 per ton by 2100. The costs in terms of reduced GDP per annum peaked at approximately 3 per cent for the US by 2030, 1–2 per cent for other OECD countries by 2010, 4 per cent for the former Soviet Union and Eastern Europe by 2030, and 10 per cent for China by 2100.

Just as benefit studies by Nordhaus were influential in the US debate so were the control cost estimates of Manne and Richels (1990). They argued that a 20 per cent CO_2 reduction by 2020 would cost the US economy between $800 thousand million and $3,600 thousand million. These costs were cited by the 1990 *Economic Report of the President* (Paterson, 1996: 81). The upper scenario calculates the present value of costs from 1990 to 2100 discounted at 5 per cent and means 5 per cent of annual GDP would be committed to emissions control by 2030.[7] These figures have aided the US perception that even small reductions could be very costly. This is despite the fact that Manne and Richels (1990: 70) themselves state:

> Experience has shown that energy forecasting, even over decades, is a highly inexact art. At best, one can ask a series of 'what if questions' in the hope of gaining some insights into the relative attractiveness of various means of reducing CO_2 emissions.

As with the benefit estimates, guessing the future is a crucial part of the game.

Whalley and Wigle (1991) considered a wide range of possible taxes, all aimed at a 50 per cent reduction in global CO_2 emissions. A production tax high enough to hit this target produces much larger losses in developing countries than in Europe or North America. The loss of GDP in present value terms over the period 1990–2030 was estimated at 7.1 per cent for industrially developing countries, 4 per cent in Europe and 4.3 per cent in North America. The cost of CO_2 reduction in this model has been criticised as resulting from low supply elasticities for energy (Nordhaus, 1991a: 45). Bergman (1991) used a computable general equilibrium model to calculate the costs of reducing CO_2 emissions in Sweden using a carbon tax. For a reduction in annual emissions from 88 million tons to 63 million tons (28.4 per cent) by the year 2000, the costs are given as 4.5 per cent of GDP. Bergman also found that tax rates needed to rise with the level of cuts in CO_2 because the marginal control cost schedule is rising.

Conrad and Schroder (1991) have argued that the cost, in terms of loss of GDP, depends upon the structure of any tax. They used a general equilibrium approach to estimate costs of hitting the Toronto target for Germany, which – to have met the target by 2005 – would then have required an annual reduction of 1.17 per cent in CO_2 emissions. If only the 'energy intensive industries' were taxed (such as iron and steel, and refining) the cost increased compared to taxing all sectors, because restricting the tax base reduces the possibility for substitution across energy uses. Ingham and Ulph (1991) have raised the issue of how industry responds to carbon taxes, in terms of deciding whether to scrap plant that becomes inefficient to operate under a carbon tax. The need to phase out technologies as new capital investments are required has been seen as a key to keeping costs low, although this locks in a delay between the implementation of a carbon reduction policy and emissions reduction while the capital stock turns over.

Many modelling exercises, such a those mentioned, predict that tax rates will need to increase with the level of emissions reduction, and that even quite small reductions in CO_2 emissions could require large rises in fossil fuel prices. In the case of the UK, for example, Ingham and Ulph (1991) have predicted oil prices would need to rise by 57–128 per cent in real terms, depending on underlying assumptions, for a 20 per cent reduction in CO_2. The proposed carbon tax in Manne and Richels (1990) is $250 per ton carbon which was estimated to increase coal prices by a factor of five. However, both the implicit and explicit assumptions about energy elasticities in such models have been criticised (see Barker, Ekins and Johnstone, 1995).

Contrary to the thrust of the above work, Ekins (1995) has questioned the assumptions being made and concluded that even substantial reductions in fossil fuel use could be achieved without a net cost even if there are only moderate benefits from preventing global warming. He argues that the assumptions and techniques used predetermine the outcome and in particular that the following factors should be scrutinised: the treatment of unemployed resources, revenue recycling, distortions in the economy due to the tax system and dynamic effects of a carbon tax. Some of the points made by Ekins (1995) are worth considering in more detail.

Although perhaps obvious, the way in which the revenues from a carbon tax are used has a major influence on estimated impact on GDP. Saving tax revenues results in contraction of the economy and reductions in GDP, while reducing other taxes could increase GDP. Modelling a carbon tax as a cause of contractionary pressure led the US Congressional Budget Office to claim that a 2 per cent loss of GDP would be the result. Thus, a revenue-neutral modelling approach is called for, although many models have failed to do so. Reducing payroll taxes can reduce unemployment, and positive employment effects will also occur due to the lower relative price of labour and the relative labour intensity of non-carbon sectors. In a study by Barker and Lewney (cited by Ekins) the reduction of value added tax (VAT) in the UK by revenues from a carbon tax to achieve 20 per cent CO_2 reductions meant GDP effects were so small the authors state they should be ignored. Other studies show that such revenue recycling leads to GDP gains as distortionary taxes are removed.

This raises another problem with the conduct of economic modelling. General equilibrium models assume that deviations from the base run are distortions. Thus, introducing a carbon tax appears as a distortion, reducing efficiency. This is despite the fact that the tax is reducing an economic distortion, i.e. correcting the failure to price a production input at its social cost. The approach can be worse still if models allow for revenue recycling but do so by removing non-distortionary taxes. This means such models are biased by assuming that:

- the economy is in equilibrium with all resources fully employed
- the carbon tax introduces a distortion while raising revenue
- revenue is recycled by replacing non-distortionary rather than distortionary taxes.

Taxes can cause welfare losses (deadweight loss) and their size can determine the impact of revenue recycling. For example, using the DICE model, Nordhaus (1994: 120–1) found annual GDP gains of $137 thousand million (1989 dollars) when taking this into account, and that the optimal emissions reduction rose from 8.8 to 32.0 per cent, which was associated with tax moving from $5.24 to $59.00 per ton of CO_2 equivalent. These results were for a deadweight loss of $0.3 per dollar of revenue, although Nordhaus notes estimates for the US are $0.5 to $1.0. Hence the entire outcome of the model is reversed from GDP losses to GDP gains. For some reason these results failed to get any emphasis.

The above discussion on policy has been in terms of a tax on CO_2 generation. Tradable permits for CO_2 emissions have received less attention but are increasingly on the agenda since the Kyoto Protocol. However, there are many questions over their equity and practicality. Schelling (1992) even casts doubts over whether trades would actually occur.

Some other commonly cited alternatives are reforestation, preventing deforestation and cutting CFCs. Tropical forests are estimated to store about 60 per cent of total carbon held by forests. Deforestation, particularly in the Amazon, is a major source of CO_2 emissions, at around 3 billion tons a year. This occurs due to the burning of felled timber releasing CO_2, the oxidation of carbon in soil and a reduction in carbon absorption in following years.

Reddy and Price (1999) note that mitigation policies involving forestry fall into four categories: increasing the inventory of standing forest to sequester carbon, increasing storage in long-lived wood products, replacing non-wood products with long-lived wood products, and utilising biomass energy crops for fuel. The concentration has been on the first option. In this regard they find good reasons for supporting carbon sinks in tropical plantation forestry, which include rapid growth, availability of waste and fallow lands, low establishment costs and relatively low opportunity costs of land (subject to the impacts of population growth). However, forestry can be negative in several respects and to produce social benefits requires appropriate management. For example, plantations in the UK have been criticised for reducing biodiversity compared with traditional forests. As Brown and Adger (1994: 218) explain, over the past 50 years, UK afforestation has caused a net emission of carbon because of the replacement of old growth forests and use of drained peatland.

Thus, reforestation is offered as a method of sequestering CO_2 from industrial sources which, under appropriate management, can deliver multiple benefits. However, there appears to be wide disagreement over the costs of reducing CO_2

emissions by increasing tree cover. Nordhaus (1991a) estimates the cost of preventing further deforestation as much lower than costs of reforestation, although his cost figures are very partial and exclude secondary benefits. For reforestation, Nordhaus (1991a: 59) estimates the cost at $40 per ton of carbon in tropical areas and $115 in marginal areas of the US. This contrasts with Bloc, Hendriks and Turkenberg (1989) at $0.7 per ton of carbon. A more detailed analysis is offered by Dixon *et al.* (1993) for a large number of countries, and shows a range of dollars per ton of carbon sequestered from $0.5 in Nepal to $77.9 in Egypt with most countries nearer the bottom end of the range, e.g. the US at $5.5, the former Soviet Union $4.6, Australia $5.9, China $5.2, Thailand $1.7. Brown and Adger (1994) cite several actual projects financed to achieve international carbon offsets and report the following costs per ton in various countries: $5.6 Ecuador, $1.0–2.0 Russia, less than $1.5 Paraguay, $1.16 Guatemala.

Finally, cutting CFC emissions is the most cost-effective way of achieving reduction in GHG emissions because the marginal control costs appear low and banning CFCs is essential to preventing further depletion of the stratospheric ozone layer. Nordhaus finds that the marginal costs of cutting CO_2 equivalent emissions by reducing CFCs are about $5 per ton of CO_2 up to a 60 per cent reduction in CFC use. Note, 1 ton of carbon equals 3.67 tons of CO_2 (Brown and Adger, 1994: 217), so this estimate is equivalent to $1.4 per ton of carbon. Thereafter, marginal control costs rise steeply. However, the UNEP (1991) reported that CFCs could be completely phased out, along with other halocarbons, by 1997, at little or no cost.

Conclusions

There have been claims of consensus over assessment results each time a new study produces a figure within the 1 to 2 per cent net GDP loss range despite the wide variation in assumptions across studies which makes any comparability at best difficult. Information on different assumptions is often absent from studies, e.g. the assumed date of a temperature change and the related date at which impacts will be felt (the two are distinct and expected to be delayed by decades). As Tol (1995: 354) notes, the estimates throughout the 1990s have been 'at a highly aggregated level, based on the literature on case studies, and educated guesswork and extrapolation'. There was some movement toward increasing the number of damage categories. Cline offered fourteen but others have persisted with only four and employing 'catch all' groupings such as 'other'. Regional analysis has been slow to arrive and crudely performed while distributional analysis has been lost in excessive aggregation.

The estimates of emissions reductions would be greater if distributional weights were included in benefit calculations in order to reflect damage suffered by low GHG emitters, and Ekins (1995: 300) has argued in favour of such weightings. He notes that because high GHG emitters are also likely to be richer they will have a higher willingness to pay and so the damages they suffer actually gain greater weight in a CBA calculus. The poor low GHG emitters should be weighted more highly and he believes this would also help correct an unfair intergenerational distribution due to suffering damages without having been responsible for their cause.

Cost-effectivness requires macroeconomic modelling to understand the impacts of changes in the fiscal system. Revenues raised from a carbon tax could be used to reduce distortions in the tax system at net GDP gains. Such revenues might also be used to remove imperfections in the transport and energy sectors. Changes in capital stock will be important but are beyond the control of consumers, e.g. vehicle purchase versus road construction. Government policy can easily affect substitution possibilities, although models based upon market responses find this difficult to take into account, e.g. the impact of policy on elasticities of demand for fuels. Yet this may be very significant for an aggressive abatement strategy (Barker, Ekins and Johnstone, 1995: 312). Thus, GHG reduction will operate on energy markets through behavioural factors on the demand side, and institutional, structural and technological factors on the supply side. However, Barker, Ekins and Johnstone (1995: 311–12) emphasise that macroeconomic and general equilibrium models operate through monetary values and are not designed for analysis of such fundamental changes as implied by a carbon tax. They state that 'the basic assumption of most models is that the future is nothing more than a continuation of the past'.

The critiques and scepticism concerning benefit estimation are generally absent from cost-effectiveness analysis but without good cause, and even the meaning given to control 'costs' can prove fallible. The fact that a 'cost' seems to convey greater credibility and appear as a factual statement has affected the use of terminology, where 'damage costs' is preferred to 'benefit' estimation. There is also a moral perspective here because avoiding damages as a benefit of control is fundamentally different from incurring a 'damage cost' in order to benefit from greater material throughput. The latter phrasing is used to pass the moral burden on to future generations (and other countries) who are assumed to benefit from GDP growth and must accept damages as another production cost.

The problems outlined here show how economic assessment fails to provide an answer as to what should be done. The costs of reducing CO_2 emissions may be quite high or there may be net gains depending upon the options chosen by the analyst. The benefits of reducing emissions are beyond economists' ability to estimate so the extent to which control options should be adopted, on efficiency grounds alone, is unknown. That political debate is unavoidable, disputes over values normal and ethics inseparable from economic analysis is explained further in the next chapter.

Notes

1 As Ingham and Ulph (1991) note, the optimality condition requires that, in each time period, the present value of marginal control costs and benefits should be equal; present value is calculated using the social rate of discount plus the natural rate of pollutant decay.

2 Also sometimes called national income. GDP is, in theory, a measure of the total flow of goods and services produced by the economy over a year. The value of goods and services is aggregated at market prices. The term 'gross' means no deduction has been made for capital depreciation. Income from foreign investment is excluded, but if added the measure becomes gross national product (GNP).

3 Willig described the conditions under which a consumer's surplus could be used to approximate a change in their underlying utility. See Willig (1976).

4 Gross national product is gross domestic product (see endnote 2) plus the income accruing to domestic residents arising from investment abroad less income earned in the domestic market accruing to those residents in foreign countries. Although different measures, the two terms are often used loosely and interchangeably as a reference to a country's output. This seems to be the case in several of the works reported in this chapter. The distribution of regional differences could be important and create a divergence. Of course at the global level there is no difference, and indeed the idea of foreign investment becomes meaningless, hence some authors use the term world income. In this chapter, where referring to the work of others, usage in the original source is followed.

5 Note that table A1 in this reference which presents the damage estimates has several errors in the summation columns. The most significant is the absence of $100 thousand million, which is 30 per cent of the total net loss for the world, from the life/morbidity category.

6 Some examples may help here. When giving gifts, the social practice is to remove the price label rather than emphasise to the recipient how much the item cost. When seeing a person drowning, the expected action of a potential rescuer in a nearby boat is to spontaneously go to their aid rather than sit down to consider the costs in terms of, say, the petrol used, their time and the inconvenience.

7 In the comment following this article Hogan notes that the 1987 US military expenditure was $282 thousand million or 6.2 per cent of GNP as cited by the *Economic Report of the President* for 1989.

References

Ayres, R.U. and J. Walters (1991) 'The greenhouse effect: damages, costs and abatement', *Environmental and Resource Economics* **1**(3): 237–70.

Barker, T., P. Ekins and N. Johnstone (eds) (1995) *Global Warming and Energy Demand*. Global Environmental Change Series. London: Routledge.

Bergman, L. (1991) 'General equilibrium effects of environmental policy: a CGE modelling approach', *Environmental and Resource Economics* **1**(1): 43–62.

Bloc, K., C. Hendriks and W. Turkenberg (1989) 'The role of carbon dioxide removal in the reduction of the greenhouse effect', in *Energy Technologies for Reducing Emissions of Greenhouse Gases*, edited by IEA, Paris: International Energy Authority.

Boero, G., R. Clarke and W.L. Winters (1991) *The Macroeconomic Consequences of Controlling Greenhouse Gases: A Survey*. London: Department of the Environment.

Brown, K. and W.N. Adger (1994) 'Economic and political feasibility of international carbon offsets', *Forest Ecology and Management* **68**: 217–29.

Brown, P.G. (1988) 'Policy analysis, welfare economics and the greenhouse effect', *Journal of Policy Analysis and Management* **7**(3): 471–5.

Bruce, J.P., L. Hoesung and E.F. Haites (1996) *Climate Change 1995: Economic and Social Dimensions of Climate Change*. Cambridge, England: Cambridge University Press.

Cameron, L. (1993) *Reducing Carbon Emissions: A Comparison of Models*. Presented at New Zealand Association of Economists Conference, University of Otago, Dunedin, August, Electricity Corporation of New Zealand.

Cantor, R. and G. Yohe (1998) 'Economic analysis', in *Human Choices and Climate Change: The Tools for Policy Analysis* 3, edited by S. Rayner and E.L. Malone, pp. 1–104, Columbus, OH: Battelle Press.

Cline, W.R. (1991) 'Scientific basis for the greenhouse effect', *Economic Journal* **101**(407): 904–19.

Cline, W.R. (1992a) *The Economics of Global Warming*. Harlow, Essex: Longman.

Cline, W.R. (1992b) *Global Warming: The Benefits of Emission Abatement*. Paris: OECD.

Conrad, K. and M. Schroder (1991) 'The control of CO_2 emissions and its economic impact: an AGE model for a German state', *Environmental and Resource Economics* **1**(3): 289–312.

Cumberland, J.H., J.R. Hibbs and I. Hoch (eds) (1982) *The Economics of Managing Chlorofluorocarbons: Stratospheric Ozone and Climate Issues*. Baltimore, MD: Johns Hopkins University Press.

Daily, G.C., P.R. Ehrlich, H.A. Mooney and A.H. Ehrlich (1991) 'Greenhouse economics: learn before you leap', *Ecological Economics* **4**: 1–10.

d'Arge, R.C. (1975) *Economic and Social Measures of Biologic and Climatic Change*. Washington, DC: US Department of Transportation, Climate Impact Assessment Program.

d'Arge, R.C. (1979) *Climate and Economic Activity*. Presented at Proceedings of the World Climate Conference, Geneva, WMO Report.

d'Arge, R.C., W.D. Schulze and D.S. Brookshire (1982) 'Carbon dioxide and intergenerational choice', *American Economic Association Papers and Proceedings* **72**(2): 251–6.

d'Arge, R.C. and C.L. Spash (1991) 'Economic strategies for mitigating the impacts of climate change on future generations', in *Ecological Economics: The Science and Management of Sustainability*, edited by R. Costanza, pp. 367–83, New York: Columbia University Press.

Demeritt, D. and D. Rothman (1998) 'Reply to Smith on "Standardized estimates of climate change damages for the United States"', *Climatic Change* **40**: 699–704.

Demeritt, D. and D.S. Rothman (1999) 'Figuring the costs of climate change: an assessment and critique', *Environment and Planning A* **31**: 389–408.

Dixon, R.K., J.K. Winjum and P.E. Schroeder (1993) 'Conservation and sequestration of carbon: the potential of forest and agroforest management practices', *Global Environmental Change* **3**. 159 73.

Dlugolecki, A.F. (1996) 'Financial services', in *Impacts, Adaptations and Mitigation of Climate Change: Scientific-Technical Analyses*, edited by R.T. Watson, M.C. Zinyowera, R.H. Moss and D.J. Dokken, pp. 439–560, Cambridge, England: Cambridge University Press.

Ekins, P. (1995) 'Revisiting the costs of CO_2 abatement', in *Global Warming and Energy Demand*, edited by T. Barker, P. Ekins and N. Johnstone, pp. 283–304 London: Routledge.

Fankhauser, S. (1995) *Valuing Climate Change: The Economics of the Greenhouse*. London: Earthscan.

Fankhauser, S., J.B. Smith and R.S. Tol (1999) 'Weathering climate change: some simple rules to guide adaptation decisions', *Ecological Economics* **30**(1): 67–78.

FitzRoy, F.R. (1992) 'Economic aspects of global warming: a comment', *Green Values* **5**: 4–7.

Funtowicz, S.O. and J.R. Ravetz (1994) 'The worth of a songbird: ecological economics as a post-normal science', *Ecological Economics* **10**(3): 197–207.

Grubb, M., C. Vrolijk and D. Brack (1999) *The Kyoto Protocol: A Guide and Assessment*. London: Earthscan and Royal Institute of International Affairs.

Hanley, N. and C.L. Spash (1993) *Cost–Benefit Analysis and the Environment*. Aldershot, England: Edward Elgar.

Hoeller, P., A. Dean and J. Nicolaisen (1991) 'Macroeconomic implications of reducing greenhouse gas emissions: a survey of empirical studies', *OECD Economic Studies* **16**: 45–78.

Hourcade, J.C., K. Halsnaes, M. Jaccard, W.D. Montgomery, R. Richels, J. Robinson, P.R. Shukla and P. Sturm (1996) 'A review of mitigation cost studies', in *Economic and Social Dimensions of Climate Change*, edited by J.P. Bruce, L. Hoesung and E.F. Haites, pp. 297–366, Cambridge, England: Cambridge University Press.

Hourcade, J.C., R. Richels and J. Robinson (1996) 'Estimating the costs of mitigating greenhouse gases', in *Economic and Social Dimensions of Climate Change*, edited by J. Bruce, L. Hoesung and E.F. Haites, pp. 263–96, Cambridge, England: Cambridge University Press.

Ingham, A. and A. Ulph (1991) 'Carbon taxes and the UK manufacturing sector', in *Environmental Policy and the Economy*, edited by F. Dietz, F. van der Ploeg and J. van der Straaten, pp. 127–239, Amsterdam: Elsevier.

International Energy Agency (1989) *Energy and the Environment: Policy Overview*. Paris: International Energy Agency.

Lave, L.B. (1982) 'Mitigating strategies for carbon dioxide problems', *American Economic Association Papers and Proceedings* **72**(2): 257–61.

Lawson, T. (1997) *Economics and Reality*. London: Routledge.

Manne, A. and R. Richels (1990) 'CO_2 emissions limits: an economic cost analysis for the USA', *The Energy Journal* **11**(2): 51–74.

Manne, A. and R. Richels (1991) 'Global CO_2 emission reductions: the impacts of rising energy costs', *The Energy Journal* **12**(1): 87–102.

Nordhaus, W.D. (1982) 'How fast should we graze the global commons?', *American Economic Association Papers and Proceedings* **72**(2): 242–6.

Nordhaus, W.D. (1991a) 'The cost of slowing climate change: a survey', *The Energy Journal* **12**(1): 37–65.

Nordhaus, W.D. (1991b) 'A sketch of the economics of the greenhouse effect', *American Economic Review* **81**(2): 146–50.

Nordhaus, W.D. (1991c) 'To slow or not to slow: the economics of the greenhouse effect', *Economic Journal* **101**: 920–38.

Nordhaus, W.D. (1992) 'Economic approaches to greenhouse warming', in *Global Warming: Economic Policy Responses*, edited by R. Dornbusch and J.M. Poterba, pp. 33–66, Cambridge, MA: MIT Press.

Nordhaus, W.D. (1994) *Managing the Global Commons: The Economics of Climate Change*. Cambridge, MA: MIT Press.

Nordhaus, W.D. (1998) *New Estimates of the Economic Impacts of Climate Change*. New Haven, CT: Yale University Press.

Pachauri, R.K. and M. Damodaran (1992) '"Wait and See" versus "No Regrets": comparing the costs of economic strategies', in *Confronting Climate Change: Risks, Implications and Responses*, edited by I.M. Mintzer, pp. 237–51, Cambridge, England: Cambridge University Press.

Paterson, M. (1996) *Global Warming and Global Politics*. London: Routledge.

Peake, S. (1998) *Adaptation to Climate Change: An International Policy Perspective*. Presented at Adapting to Climate Change, Emmanual College, Cambridge, England, 3 December 1998.

Pearce, D.W., W.R. Cline, A.N. Achanta, S. Fankhauser, R.K. Pachauri, R.S.J. Tol and P. Vellinga (1996) 'The social costs of climate change: greenhouse damage and the benefits of control', in *Climate Change 1995: Economic and Social Dimensions of Climate Change*, edited by J.P. Bruce, H. Lee and E.F. Haites, pp. 178–224, Cambridge, England: Cambridge University Press.

Pearce, F. (1995) 'Price of life sends temperatures soaring', *New Scientist* **1 April**: 5.

Peck, S.C. and T.J. Teisberg (1992) 'CETA: A model for carbon emissions trajectory assessment', *Energy Journal* **13**(1): 55–77.

Peck, S.C. and T.J. Teisberg (1993) 'CO_2 emissions control: comparing policy instruments', *Energy Policy* **21**(3): 55–77.

Perman, R. (1994) 'The economics of the greenhouse effect', *Journal of Economic Surveys* **8**(2): 99–132.

Price, C. (1994) *Emissions, Concentrations, and Disappearing CO_2*. Bangor: University College of North Wales.

Reddy, R.C.S. and C. Price (1999) 'Carbon sequestration and conservation of tropical forests under uncertainty', *Journal of Agricultural Economics* **50**(1): 17–35.

Reilly, J. (1996) 'Agriculture in a changing climate: impacts and adaptation', in *Impacts, Adaptations and Mitigation of Climate Change: Scientific-Technical Analyses*, edited by R.T. Watson, M.C. Zinyowera, R.H. Moss and D.J. Dokken, pp. 427–67, Cambridge, England: Cambridge University Press.

Rosenberg, N.J., P. Crosson, W.E. Easterling, K. Frederick and R. Sedjo (1989) *Policy Options for Adaptation to Climate Change*. Washington, DC: Resources for the Future.

Rowlands, I.H. (1995) *The Politics of Global Atmospheric Change*. Manchester, England: Manchester University Press.

Schelling, T.C. (1992) 'Some economics of global warming', *American Economic Review* **82**(1): 1–14.

Smith, J.B. (1996) 'Standardized estimates of climate change damages for the United States', *Climatic Change* **32**: 313–26.

Smith, J.B. and D.A. Tirpak (1989) *The Potential Effects of Global Climate Change on the United States*. Washington, DC: US Environmental Protection Agency, GPO.

Spash, C.L. (1996) 'Human-induced climate change: the limits of models', *Environmental Politics* **5**(2): 376–80.

Symons, E.J., J.L.R. Proops and P.W. Gay (1994) 'Carbon taxes, consumer demand and carbon dioxide emissions: a simulation analysis for the UK', *Fiscal Studies* **15**(2): 19–43.

Tol, R.S.J. (1995) 'The damage costs of climate change: towards more comprehensive calculations', *Environmental and Resource Economics* **5**: 353–74.

Tol, R.S.J., S. Fankhauser and J.B. Smith (1998) 'The scope for adaptation to climate change: what can we learn from the impact literature?', *Global Environmental Change* **8**(2): 109–23.

UNEP (1991) Montreal Protocol: 1991 Assessment. *Report of the Technology and Economic Assessment Panel*. Nairobi, Kenya: United Nations Environment Programme.

Watson, R.T., M.C. Zinyowera and R.H. Moss (1996) 'Technical summary: impacts, adaptations, and mitigation options', in *Impacts, Adaptations, and Mitigation: Scientific-Technical Analyses*, edited by R.T. Watson, M.C. Zinyowera and R.H. Moss, pp. 19–53, Cambridge, England: Cambridge University Press.

Watson, R.T., M.C. Zinyowera, R.H. Moss and D.J. Dokken (eds) (1997) *The Regional Impacts of Climate Change: An Assessment of Vulnerability; Summary for Policymakers*. IPCC Special Report. Geneva: IPCC.

Whalley, J. and R. Wigle (1991) 'The international incidence of carbon taxes', in *Global Warming: Economic Policy Responses*, edited by R. Dornbusch and J.M. Poterba, pp. 233–62, Cambridge, MA: The MIT Press.

Whiteman, A. (1991) *A Comparison of the Financial and Non-Market Costs and Benefits of Replanting Lowland Forests*. Presented at Forest Valuation, Stirling University, Scottish Environmental Economics Discussion Group.

Willig, R.D. (1976) 'Consumer's surplus without apology', *American Economic Review*, **66**(4): 587–97.

Yohe, G., J. Neumann and H. Ameden (1995) 'Assessing the economic costs of greenhouse-induced sea level rise: methods and application in support of a national survey', *Journal of Environmental Economics and Management* **29**: 78–97.

7 Loading the dice?

Values, opinions and ethics

Economists and natural scientists often seem to perceive their role as filling an information vacuum. Yet the process of learning requires restricting the focus of understanding and accepting limitations. That is, partial ignorance is part of the methodology, but the hope is that central issues will be included in any analysis rather than excluded by assumption. A fundamental method of trying to prevent such exclusion of relevant alternatives is peer review. In this chapter examples of disputes over the calculation of costs and benefits are used to reflect upon the content and character of the academic debate. The tension in this debate has already been touched upon.

The parameters of the debate are set by the economic model. Thus, Nordhaus (1991b: 936) states:

> The efficient degree of control of GHGs would be essentially zero in the case of high costs, low damages, and high discounting; by contrast, in the case of no discounting, and high damages, the efficient degree of control is one-third of GHG emissions.

In this framework the key issues of economic concern are valuing costs and benefits and deciding upon the appropriate discount rate.

There is a clear desire to produce calculations which can be regarded as 'rigorous', 'scientific' and 'objective' while still maintaining relevance to a subject which is complex, uncertain, politically charged and raises numerous moral questions. Rather than becoming too immersed in technical debates over fine points of models and mathematical calculations, the aim in this chapter is to draw out some of the (often implicit) judgements lying behind apparently objective scientific choices. In doing so the debates over discounting and the value of life are used to exemplify underlying value conflicts. The relevance of strong uncertainty is then explored in the context of the numbers being produced by economists as estimates of the damages due to the enhanced Greenhouse Effect.

Inconsistency and disputed values

A typical practice when facing complex value issues is to note the many possible critiques and drawbacks of work in the area while then going on to employ a methodology which denies the relevance of those same critiques. This may be accompanied by a statement of faith in future research somehow resolving the difficulties. Thus, for example, Fankhauser (1995) raises many of the problems discussed in the last chapter while going on to produce damage estimates he regards as 'fairly robust' (p. 56). Similarly, different authors raise concerns over the results of others but then draw comfort from the proximity of those same results to their own. There is then a tendency to seek validity by comparing results, although the basis for doing so is doubtful. These inconsistencies in research seem to indicate an underlying tension over fundamental values. Purely from the statements made by various authors, their predisposition to certain world views can be discerned.

Perhaps the clearest expression of the underlying conflict and uncertainty over the expression of values can be seen in the exchanges between Nordhaus and Cline. The statements of Nordhaus in response to Cline's work show the antithesis of value commitments. In reply to Cline's critique of the agricultural damage estimates given by Mendelsohn and Nordhaus (1996: 1,315) the authors refer to Cline's own work as unlikely 'gloomy prognostications'. Nordhaus (1994: 57–8) states that Cline's 'extensions outside the marketed sectors are extremely tenuous', that he is 'over-estimating the impacts', relying on 'ambiguous' information and is giving 'a generally pessimistic cast'. This despite the fact that the estimates are then noted to be 'only marginally above those used here at the low end' and actually 'marginally lower' for 5°C or more.

In his own earlier work Nordhaus (1991a: 148) was clear about reliance upon hunches, and on that basis alone was prepared to increase his final results fourfold to account for the 'unmeasured and unquantifiable factors'. Yet the adjustment of net damage estimates upwards is regarded as something of a bias in other studies. In this regard, Nordhaus (1994: 59) believes that the problem with 'many studies of climate change is that people look for problems and ignore opportunities; it is as if there exists an unconscious impulse to find costs and ignore benefits of climate change'. He gives examples of benefits as being leisure activities such as camping (Nordhaus, 1994: 57), space heating, construction, and agriculture (Nordhaus, 1991b: 932). Potential savings from a warmer climate are recognised by Cline (1992b: 55) with regard to non-electric heating. However, he is more sceptical of net gains elsewhere and, for example, notes that the impacts on construction may be either net costs or net benefits. As discussed in chapter 3, where there appear to be benefits they are usually offset by costs, adaptation is costly, the possibility of net benefits seems transitory, and those who benefit are different from those that lose.

There is a very different view of the future between these authors and their expectations as to the impact of global climate change on future generations. For Nordhaus the impact of global warming is apparently expected to be of minor importance compared to other changes and he dismisses long-term implications as follows:

> Simply put, humans live, move, and die faster than climatic impacts are likely to be noticed. This point can be seen by asking what the effect today would be if one's grandparents or great-grandparents had contemplated a warmer globe. Many of them would have given the prospect a loud hurrah.
>
> (Nordhaus, 1994: 59)

Interestingly he goes on to question the sense of talking about future health impacts. He asks rhetorically: 'Can one sensibly talk about health effects when we don't even know what the next century's major health problems will be or what the population distribution will look like?'

The concern here may have arisen because he neglected health impacts while others have pointed out their size and potential importance. Cline estimated them at about 10 per cent of total damages. Fankhauser is cited by Nordhaus (1994: table 4.3) as attributing just under 50 per cent of damages to 'health and amenity' (although Fankhauser's published work gives less weight). The derision in the above quote with regard to health impacts is interesting given the speculative character of all CBA estimates. The difference between projecting future health impacts and predicting carbon taxes, various damages and control costs for a hundred years is hard to fathom. Nordhaus happily recommends that future generations respond to disasters by accumulating capital in 'normal times', and states that his 'DICE model is well designed to examine the appropriate degree of consumption smoothing' and can specify consumption losses and utility functions for different generations (Nordhaus, 1994: 173). In fact, a change of position seems to have occurred four years later when potential health impacts became one of the seven areas included in the calculated damages of his models, and is then stated to be 'one of the major concerns about global warming' (Nordhaus, 1998: 8) Estimates there are given for health impacts from a 2.5°C warming with a breakdown by regions of the globe. The next two sections take a closer look at the debates over how to treat the future and the valuation of mortality and morbidity.

Addressing the future

Many regard the key variable for considering the future to be the discount rate. Cline is described as employing an empirical estimate because it 'fits neatly into his philosophical stance'. 'Hence, from both empirical and theoretical points of view, Cline's argument for the extraordinarily low discount rate is unsupported and unrealistic' (Nordhaus, 1994: 133). This rate is based upon the rate of growth of per capita income and in the order of 2 per cent per annum (Cline, 1992a: 5). In the DICE model the rate settles at 3 per cent. Elsewhere, Nordhaus has employed discounting scenarios at 0 and 1 per cent above the growth rate (e.g. see Nordhaus, 1991a; 1991b; 1992). In fact, Nordhaus (1991b: 926) explains his own use of these rates 'that are very low (either 0 or 1 per cent per year) to reflect the possibility that the future equilibrium will come in a low- or no-growth economy with a low rate of time preference'. His (preferred) middle level of damages in that study were given for a discount rate 1 per cent above a growth rate which, as stated, may be 0, i.e. a 1 per cent discount rate is then required. Price (1994: table 2) notes the lowest discount rate used by Nordhaus as 0.25 per cent.

The real dispute appears to be over the way in which these discount rates are justified. Cline (1992a: 74) follows the argument, used by many, that a discount rate which includes pure myopia should be rejected due to the impact on future generations, and he cites work by both E.J. Mishan and Amartya Sen (Nobel Laureate in Economics). Nordhaus rejects the argument on the basis that such philosophy should be kept out of economic analysis, or in his own words:

> While this argument may be compelling to ethicists from a philosophical point of view, it is completely unrealistic from an economic point of view because it ignores the difficulties of imposing a discount rate that does not correspond to market pricing ... What if a philosopher argues that it is unethical and indefensible to pay royalties to rich people or oil companies? Does that imply that we should use $2 per barrel in our cost–benefit calculations for energy policy though it will cost us ten times that to buy oil? If we consider all the ramifications of this issue, we quickly see that if we decide to override market prices because of ethical objections, this raises countless paradoxes and contradictions.
>
> (Nordhaus, 1994: 132)

Despite the poor wording in the last sentence the message is clear, i.e. ethics and philosophy have no place in economics. This tension between two fundamentally different approaches to economics is apparent in the IPCC SAR when addressing discounting. Here the argument is stated to be a 'conflict' between a descriptive approach from mainstream economics and the prescriptive approach of authors such as Cline (one of the chapter's co-authors). The case of the defenders of the mainstream neo-classical position is that:

> The alternative – over-riding market prices on ethical grounds – opens the door to irreconcilable inconsistencies. If ethical arguments, rather than the revealed preferences of citizens, form the rationale for a low discount rate cannot ethical arguments be applied to other questions?
>
> (Arrow *et al.*, 1996)

As should be clear, the ethical questions fail to disappear just because a market price and economic analysis are substituted for ethical debate and public discourse. Economists are, no more than moral philosophers, in a position to dictate policy in this area or resolve the paradoxes and contradictions, and, as will be explored in the next chapter, ethics is inseparable from the subject. The contradiction is that economics takes a very specific philosophical and ethical position and then, as above, tries to deny the relevance of ethics in economics. The conflict of values remains despite the attempts to remove their explicit discussion from the economic debate.

The value of human life

Studies in economic valuation of environmental impacts have over many years developed various measures for placing a value on life or, more precisely, the risk of death (for an early contribution see Jones-Lee, 1976). Pollution can lead to premature death (mortality) and impacts on health (morbidity). Thus economic studies try to associate a monetary amount with life and health in order to assess the optimal level of resources to be diverted to preventing morbidity and mortality. For example, the willingness to pay to avoid illness is calculated from a contingent valuation survey to estimate the level of air pollution control in an urban area (e.g. see Dubourg and Rodriguez, 2001). Such results are used in transportation assessment to decide upon road building programmes and the installation of safety equipment.

There are two main methods for assessing the risk of death or value of a statistical life. First, an individual may be directly asked their willingness to pay to avoid a risk or their willingness to accept compensation for incurring a risk. Contingent valuation surveys have been most commonly applied in this area but have also been severely criticised in this specific context (Jones-Lee and Loomes, 1997). Contingent valuation also remains more generally controversial (see Spash, 1998). There is in addition an on-going debate concerning the divergence between willingness to pay and willingness to accept and which is the appropriate measure of a welfare change. Willingness to accept, which is normally larger, is the theoretically correct measure when damages are imposed on individuals, although a US expert panel has ruled that willingness to pay should be used as a 'conservative' measure (for a discussion see Knetsch, 1994). The other main alternative for valuing a statistical life is to use measures related to earnings. This approach might, for example, use actual wage differentials in jobs with a range of risks.

As shown earlier, the estimates of mortality and morbidity could swamp other values if the hunch of those such as Tol is correct. Thus, if a CBA approach is being employed, analysts will find themselves either trying to include all values in monetary terms, or stating that a category is impacted but is impossible to value in monetary terms. The obvious problem with the latter route is that the validity of the resulting numbers is brought into question and they then have a doubtful meaning, e.g. stating that GDP loss is 2 per cent but that there is an additional unknown amount to add. Economists using environment CBA have therefore often given a monetary value to loss of life, preferring to have what is regarded as an 'uncertain' positive number rather than nothing in their calculations. They often express the belief that this is necessary because the institutions of government will otherwise neglect these aspects of the decision, which suggests the actual problem lies in the institutional structure, but the tendency is also to avoid questioning the institutional context that deeply.

The result is the philosophy of valuing everything in monetary terms even if individuals refuse to make such trade-offs. In transport policy the public rejection of this monetary approach is exposed when there is a train crash, people are killed and the public discover that the lack of safety equipment is due to the calculation that providing it cost more than expected fatalities times the value of a statistical life. Politicians rarely defend the numbers in such circumstances, although their transport departments may continue to use them on a daily basis.

The GHG control literature has also employed estimates of mortality and morbidity. Cline (1992b: 44–5) briefly reviews some of the options. He calculates the value lost in the US from an increased number of deaths under a doubling of CO_2 at $595,000 per person on the basis of lifetime wages. That is, he takes the lifetime earnings as reflecting the amount society is willing to pay the individual and therefore a reflection of their social worth. He also explains the value could be much greater using a value for a statistical life on the basis of the relationship between wages and the risk of death by occupation and industry. The range might then be $2–$6 million per person. Contingent valuation studies that ask workers how much they would be willing to accept in order to take on more dangerous work result in values between $2–$3 million. Lower estimates arise from actual behaviour with regard to hazard avoidance.

Fankhauser (1995: 47) also includes an estimate for mortality and in doing so states the need to elaborate because this is 'a potentially controversial issue'. He cites estimates from willingness-to-pay studies in the range from $0.2–$16.0 million with an average of $3 million, and then adopts $1.5 million for developed countries, although the basis for the choice of the final estimate seems rather unclear. He goes on to note this estimate is dependent upon various contextual factors, including income. While no adjustment is made for most of these contextual factors, one is made for income to give 'an arbitrary value of $300,000 for middle-income and $100,000 for low-income countries'. The outcome is carefully qualified with emphasis as follows:

> This of course does *not* mean that the life of, say, a Chinese is worth less than that of a European. It merely reflects the fact that the *willingness to pay* for increased safety (a lower mortality risk) is higher in developed countries.
>
> (Fankhauser, 1995: 47)

As has been remarked earlier, this work informed chapter 6 on economic benefits under the SAR by the IPCC. The result of using this arbitrary differential of a factor of 15 between high- and low-income countries was to create considerable controversy.

The storm that raged over the numbers presented in the IPCC chapter can be judged by various letters and short editorial pieces which appeared in journals such as *Nature* (Bruce, 1995; Masood, 1995; Masood and Ochert, 1995; Meyer, 1995b) and *New Scientist* (Meyer, 1995a; Pearce, 1995a; Pearce, 1995b). Representatives from industrially developing nations, led by India and China, refused to accept the report due to the differential weighting given to the value of a statistical life (Masood, 1995). The Indian Environment Minister, Kamal Nath, wrote to other heads of delegations at the first meeting of the Conference of the Parties rejecting:

> ... the absurd and discriminatory Global Cost/Benefit Analysis procedures propounded by economists in the work of IPCC WG-III ... we unequivocally reject the theory that the monetary value of people's lives around the world is different because the value imputed should be proportional to the disparate income levels of potential victims ... it is impossible for us to accept that which is not ethically justifiable, technically accurate or politically conducive to the interests of poor people as well as the global common good.
>
> (Quoted in Grubb, Vrolijk and Brack, 1999: 306)

Nath called for industrially developing countries to veto all discussions under the Framework Convention on Climate Change until the offending calculations were removed from the process (Pearce, 1995b).

A short news item in *Nature* on the issue expressed the common interpretation of the numbers in the report as reflecting a case for little or no action because costs outweighed benefits (Masood, 1995). The Secretary to the IPCC, Narasimhan Sundaraman, wrote in response, objecting to their interpretation of his views on valuing life, and the co-chair of Working Group III, James Bruce, did likewise to explain where he regarded their coverage as erroneous (Bruce, 1995; Sundaraman, 1995). A month later a much fuller piece appeared (with cartoon) explaining how the Working Group III report might appear without the offending chapter 6 (Masood and Ochert, 1995). The politically negotiated policymakers summary for Working Group III proposed to make statements rejecting the basis of the calculations and the authors demanded a right of reply which the IPCC rules did not allow. Critics of chapter 6 were raising questions over the claim that the IPCC report could be an objective scientific document. Shortly afterwards, a letter petitioning removal of the chapter signed by about 40 scientists and academics, including some IPCC lead authors and one from Working Group III, was published in *Nature* (Meyer, 1995b).

IPCC procedures require that the Summary for Policymakers is approved by country representatives and the text therefore needs to be politically negotiated.

Government-nominated experts from Brazil, China, Cuba, India, Colombia and the Alliance of Small Island States, amongst others, objected to the Policymakers' Summary of the work. The result of the dispute was for the Summary to diverge from the underlying chapter. The preface to the report states that during negotiations 'some of the draft text recommended by the Working Group III Bureau was deleted' and that where disagreement persisted differing views are presented. The disclaimer continues: 'Although the country representatives of the Working Group accept the underlying technical report, it is not reviewed in detail and its contents remain the responsibility of the lead authors'. The policymakers summary then states that monetary valuation should avoid obscuring the consequences of climate change and that 'the value of life has meaning beyond monetary considerations' (p. 10).

There were suggestions that a willingness-to-accept approach would produce higher values and should have been used for the calculations (Meyer, 1995a). Certainly a willingness-to-accept measure would be the theoretically correct one to use in this case. However, this would seem unlikely to address the differential issue or the ethical concerns underlying the use of monetary valuation in this context. Respondents might be expected to protest against the valuation method where rights or justice are involved in the decision being considered, or their monetary valuations may be inherently based upon ethical motives. Contingent valuation has also proven unable to address refusals to make trade-offs on ethical grounds in other environmental policy areas which many would regard as less controversial (Spash, 2000b; Spash, 2000a).

Fankhauser, Tol and Pearce (1997) have attempted to explain their position and show how welfare economics provides their calculations with 'consistency and rigour'. In essence they argue that ethical issues are partially separable from those which concern the derivation of the benefits of GHG control.

> Much of the confusion seems to have arisen from the fusion of the two separate issues: the valuation of environmental damages at an individual level, which is a matter of empirical analysis, and the comparison and aggregation of these effects, which is a political process involving ethical judgements on, among other things, the socially desirable distribution of income.
>
> (Fankhauser, Tol and Pearce, 1997: 250)

Their defence is then that distributional concerns should be kept separate from GHG abatement policy and dealt with as an independent policy issue (a point also made in Fankhauser and Tol, 1999). This approach is clear in chapter 6 which, following the same approach as found in the IPCC chapter on discounting, separates valuation of a statistical life into 'descriptive' and 'prescriptive'; the authors claim they perform only empirical investigation under the former approach while the latter would mean employing moral judgement.

Strong uncertainty revisited

The main approach to addressing uncertainty over information content remains scientific peer review and the IPCC has placed much faith in this process (Houghton, 1997: 157–60). This process runs into difficulty because of the pervasive ignorance associated with global environmental problems (Dovers and Handmer, 1995). In order to control for complexity, boundaries are drawn around knowledge and peer review aims for a consensus as if there were an underlying truth to be discovered. Peer review can then become self-reinforcing and the boundaries of partial ignorance heavily defended. Thus, for example, Demeritt and Rothman (1999: 390) question the credibility of the work in chapter 6 of the IPCC Working Group III SAR because the lead authors review and present their own work – in particular, the PhD work of Fankhauser and Tol, whose respective supervisors, Pearce and Villenga, are also lead authors. More generally the economic perspective throughout the report can be seen as suffering from social and disciplinary insularity, which prevents critical thought about the boundaries drawn and taboos of the discipline.

When explaining how the IPCC handles uncertainty, via the peer review process and negotiated policymakers summaries, John Houghton, Co-Chair of Working Group I, totally ignores the entire episode concerning the value of life (Houghton, 1997: 157–60). This may be because moral value conflicts are generally regarded as unscientific. Interestingly, as mentioned previously, Houghton has raised the personal importance of his own religious beliefs as a motive for research into environmental problems, while defending an ability to dissociate these values from scientific research. Similarly, many economists claim that economic values and scientific research are separable from the moral and ethical dimensions of the problems they study. However, whether discounting or valuing damages, ethical and distributional issues are central to discussing the enhanced Greenhouse Effect. That there are contested social values and multiple perspectives on these issues means the boundaries drawn around research agendas are central points of debate and concern.

The dispute over values for loss of life described above is a clear sign of the partial ignorance and indeterminacy involved in this problem. There is general agreement that the issues being discussed here are highly uncertain but there is a general failure to adequately address that uncertainty. For example, uncertainty over future damages is meant to be addressed by insurance markets, although how they should operate in the absence of knowledge of the potential impacts is unclear (as noted in Bruce, Hoesung and Haites, 1996: 15). Distribution is meant to be politically decided, although the time and geographical scale of potential damages and gains mean distribution is the defining problem for economic analysis. An economic assessment of the enhanced Greenhouse Effect which ignores the impact of income, costs and benefit distribution on the analysis would appear to have withdrawn from the realm of relevance.

The desire to refute strong uncertainty has lead to excessive faith in the numbers being produced from economic assessments. That these numbers produce rankings

Table 7.1 Author weighting of impacts in CBA studies of GHG control for the US

	Nordhaus 1991b (%)	Cline 1992 (%)	Cline 1992 (%)	Nordhaus 1994 (%)	Fankhauser 1995 (%)	Tol 1995[g] (%)	Nordhaus 1998 (%)	Max
Losses avoided[a]								
Agriculture	6	28	28	12	12	13	8	28
Forest loss	0	5	2	0	1	0	0	5
Species/ecosystem loss	0	6	5	0	12	7	0	12
Sea level rise	72	11	10	21	13	11	15	72
Energy consumption	22	19	20	4	11	0	0	22
Human morbidity/ mortality	0	9	10	0	16	51	3	51
Migration	0	1	1	0	1	1	0	1
Hurricanes	0	1	2	0	0	0	0	2
Leisure	0	3	1	0	0	16	0	16
Water supply	0	11	16	0	22	0	0	22
Urban infrastructure	0	0	0	0	0	0	14[e]	14[e]
Tropospheric ozone	0	6	6	0	10	0	0	10
Miscellaneous[d]	0	0	0	63	0	0	60	63
Total[c]	100	100	100	100	100	100	100	
Gains missed[b]								
Agriculture	0	0	0	0	0	0	0	
Energy consumption	−16	−2	−1	0	0	0	0	
Outdoor recreation	0	0	0	0	0	0	−38	
Temperature rise °C	3.0	2.5	10.0	3.0	2.5	2.5	2.5	
by year	by 2050	by 2025	by 2280	by 2050	by 2100	by 2100	by 2100	
Measurement basis	$1,000 m	$1,000 m	$1,000 m	$1,000 m	$1,000 m	$1,000 m	GDP	
Net GDP loss %	0.25[f]	1.10	6.00	1.00	1.30	1.50	0.45[f]	
Base year	1981	1990	1990	1981	1988	1988	1995	

Data sources: Nordhaus (1991b) table 6; Cline (1992) table 5; Nordhaus (1994) table 4.1; Fankhauser (1995) table 3.15; Tol (1995) table A1; Nordhaus (1998) table 10.

Notes: a   All figures rounded hence some small positive values of some studies appear as zero, e.g. hurricanes.
     b   Calculated as a percentage of total loss avoided.
     c   May not add to 100 due to rounding errors.
     d   Categories of 'other' and in the Nordhaus 1998 a loosely defined WTP for avoiding 'catastrophic impact'.
     e   Nordhaus includes biodiversity and ecosystem loss.
     f   Significant gains reduce net GDP reported but actual damages still occur with losers differing from gainers.
     g   Includes Canada, also note summation error in original corrected in these calculations.

of countries in a certain order of net GDP losses, or all fall within a few per cent of GDP, is little sign of robustness or validity. For example, consider the assessments conducted for the US, which is the most studied country. Table 7.1 shows the main assessments by categories of loss and gain. Concentration on net GDP losses ignores the wide variety of weightings being given to different categories of impacts. Thus, water supply impacts vary from zero weighting to 22 per cent of damages avoided, outdoor recreation and leisure forms 16 per cent of damages avoided or a 38 per cent gain missed. Variation across studies by the same individual are also notable. Within these categories a range of other assumptions hide along with distributional impacts. For example, the ski industry is expected to suffer severely so the designation of large net gains masks this economic disruption and social change.

When calculations are then transferred to global studies there should be no surprise that similar inconsistencies arise, as shown in table 7.2. Loss of life here accounts for anything from 52 per cent of damages to nothing. Categories of gain appear to be a personal preference of the analysts as are the appearance or otherwise of catastrophic events. Given enough thought the categories of gains forgone might easily be shown to outweigh the losses, and while ignoring both uncertainty and distribution the lobbyist might then claim the enhanced Greenhouse Effect is good for world economic growth.

As Nordhaus (1994: 56) repeatedly informs us: 'It should be noted, again, that, because of infirmities in the underlying estimates of damage, these projections are subject to large margins of error'. In producing parameters for the DICE model a 'precautionary guess' is used to set the magnitude of surprise events (Nordhaus, 1994: 53). While the relative size of the guess categories appear large in this work the general approach is typical of how the estimates are obtained. Other researchers have been unable to obtain the data or calculations upon which Nordhaus has based these numbers and therefore they suffer irreproducibility (Demeritt and Rothman, 1999: 394).

Cline also uses a great deal of guess work and speculation in deriving his numbers, although he at least provides the details of his calculations. For example, species loss is valued by multiplying the opportunity cost estimates for forest land used to preserve the spotted owl by 25. Nordhaus (1994: 58) has criticised this on the grounds of using the spotted owl case which he regards as having been very costly. On reading Cline's reasoning behind this calculation (1992b: 36–7), some more fundamental questions are why he chose a factor of 25, what does 'measured in some intrinsic sense' mean, and on what basis are these 'conservative' estimates? Fankhauser (1995: 34) very loosely bases his own species loss estimates on some highly context-specific mean willingness to pay numbers from contingent valuation surveys on a few species and derives another highly speculative figure. Willingness to accept is the theoretically correct measure and the original studies (e.g. paying for a hunting licence in Wyoming) bear no relationship to the current question. Numbers are in fact being transferred without regard to their original content or meaning and final net estimates produced regardless.

Once numbers are produced they begin to take on their own importance regardless of any lack of rigour or meaning; they begin to grow legs. For example, the estimates of the cost of resettling environmental refugees produced by Cline (1992b: 46–7) are based upon the $3,000 per capita US local government spending on public services in 1989. He assumes this cost will only be incurred for 18 months as the refugees will by then have jobs and be taxpayers (i.e. $1.5 \times 3,000 = 4,500$). On the

Table 7.2 Author weighting of benefits in CBA studies of GHG control at the world level

	Nordhaus 1991b US/World %	Ayres and Walters 1991 World %	Nordhaus 1994 DICE World %	Fankhauser 1995 World %	Tol 1995[g] World %	Nordhaus 1998 RICE World %	Max
Losses avoided[a]							
Agriculture	6	0	20	15	17	7	23
Forest loss	0	0	0	1	0	0	1
Species/ ecosystem loss	0	0	0	15	6	0	15
Sea level rise	72	95[h]	23	17	11	18	95
Energy consumption	22	0	3	9	0	0	22
Human morbidity/ mortality	0	0	0	18	52	6	52
Migration	0	5	0	2	4	0	5
Hurricanes	0	0	0	1	1	0	1
Leisure	0	0	0	0	11	0	11
Water supply	0	0	0	17	0	0	17
Urban infrastructure	0	0	0	0	0	9[e]	9[e]
Tropospheric ozone	0	0	0	6	0	0	6
Miscellaneous[d]	0	0	53	0	0	60	60
Total[c]	100	100	100	100	100	100	
Gains missed[b]							
Agriculture	0	0	0	0	−13	0	
Energy consumption	−16	0	0	0	0	0	
Outdoor recreation	0	0	0	0	0	−16	
Temperature rise °C	3.0	3.0	3.0	2.5	2.5	2.5	
Measurement basis	$1,000 m	$1,000 m	GDP	$1,000 m	$1,000 m	GDP	
Net GDP loss %	0.25[f]	2.25[h]	1.34	1.40	1.90[f]	1.50[f]	
Base year	1981	1981	1988	1988	1988	1995	

Data sources: Nordhaus (1991b) table 6; Ayres (1991: 245); Nordhaus (1994) table 4.2; Fankhauser (1995) table 3.15; Tol (1995) table A1; Nordhaus (1998) table 10.

Notes: a All figures rounded hence small positive values of some studies appear as zero, e.g. hurricanes.

b Calculated as a percentage of total loss avoided.

c May not add to 100 due to rounding errors.

d Categories of 'other' and in the Nordhaus 1998 a loosely defined WTP for avoiding 'catastrophic impact'.

e Nordhaus includes biodiversity and ecosystem loss.

f Significant gains reduce net GDP reported but actual damages still occur with losers differing from gainers.

g Numerous summation errors exist in Tol and all figures were recalculated, the largest error being for morbidity/mortality given as $88 instead of $188 thousand million.

h Central estimate calculated and used here.

basis of current immigration figures he plucks 100,000 new immigrants from the air as the climate induced impact for the US. Fankhauser (1995) uses both figures, although the former is called a 'guesstimate' and the latter unconvincing. He claims the Cline dollar value is matched by that of Ayres and Walters by an alternative method which he however also notes to be unconvincing. In fact Ayres and Walters (1991: 245) mention resettlements for 1988 having cost the US $4,000 per person on the basis of a report in the *Economist*, which would be costs in additions to those of Cline. They also recommend adding to this an amount for lost output, which depends upon job and country, but which they decide as $500/yr for two years based upon 1981 income levels and use this number in their calculations for all countries. On the basis of these researchers the cost of an environmental refugee to the US around 1988 should include resettlement ($4,000), plus infrastructure costs ($4,000/unemployed year), plus loss of earnings (> $500/unemployed year, the figure requiring inflation adjustment from 1981 to 1988). Fankhauser (1995: 50–1) takes $4,500 as the OECD country cost and $1,000 as that for the rest of the world, and using Cline's 'guesstimate' of migration now applied worldwide gets 2.7 million refugees and produces a table of costs totalling $4.3 thousand million.

As if the circulation of dubious figures through economic assessments were not enough, the next layer of their use is by non-economists. For example, Houghton (1997: 134), Co-Chair of the IPCC scientific assessment group, states 'the cost of resettling 3 million displaced person [sic] per year has been estimated at between $1,000 and $5,000 per person, giving a total of about $4 thousand million per year' and cites the source; as Adger and Fankhauser (1993). Unfortunately, Houghton has referenced the wrong source; Adger and Fankhauser only give the aggregate costs of Fankhauser's work referenced therein and no per capita estimates or refugee numbers. Thus, guessed at original numbers, once in the literature, seem to achieve independent validity, passing from one source to the next and soon losing all contact with their original context or factual basis.

Economic analysis of the enhanced Greenhouse Effect shows how value judgements are presented as apparently precise and rigorous scientific numbers often with two and sometimes three decimal places being specified. Funtowicz and Ravetz (1994) have conducted a careful examination of such work using the example of Nordhaus (1991b) to show how such precision is unjustified and the numbers are swamped by the uncertainties reflected in adjustment factors based on the authors' beliefs. As they note:

> By the time that the author has admitted the manifold oversimplifications and uncertainties in his analysis, and has shown how strong are the ad hoc adjustments and hunches which are needed to bring his numbers back into the realm of plausibility, we might ask whether the statistical exercises are totally redundant except for rhetorical purposes.
>
> (Funtowicz and Ravetz, 1994: 201)

Conclusions

This and the previous chapter show how economic assessments of the enhanced Greenhouse Effect fail to address environmental and social complexity. Specific problems are the treatment of uncertainty in the estimation of benefits and cost, the value of morbidity and mortality, the distribution of costs and benefits, the moral standing of future generations and the very size of the problem (there is a point at which marginal welfare analysis loses its theoretical basis). There are many areas of uncertainty, for example, concerning regional impacts of climate change, how people and natural systems will adapt, and the character of the world's economies in the distant future. There are the standard problems of valuing non-market effects such as the displacement of wildlife, the human misery of environmental refugees and loss of life. These are areas which pose moral and political questions. Another challenge, which has received little attention, is how to treat long-term damages incurred by future generations who will suffer damages but may themselves contribute little in terms of GHG emissions.

Implicitly the regard given to future generations plays an important role in the value placed upon climate change projections, because future generations are expected to suffer the worst consequences and delaying action is largely justified by this intergenerational 'externality'. Current models tend to perpetuate the myth that the consequences of our actions will be felt by those on the other side of the world and living in the distant future and then encourage discounting any concerns. Externalising the harm created by individual actions can be viewed as having led to the dramatic potential damages faced by the world under the enhanced Greenhouse Effect. Economic analysts depending upon modern welfare economics are in the uncomfortable position of justifying any actions if society or individuals can potentially (but not actually) transfer resources to those harmed, i.e. the benefits could potentially compensate for the losses. The rising popularity of global climate change as a matter for economists to consider will either force these matters into the debate or show how strong the dominant approach to economic assessment remains by relegating them to the sidelines.

The idea that economists (or scientists) cannot, do not or should not make moral judgements in these cases is clearly false. The fact that they do so implicitly and these moral judgements may be regarded as objectionable when exposed explains much of the aggression and emotion in the debate over valuation, as exemplified here with regard to the valuation of life. The pretence persists that ethical issues can be meaningfully separated from economic analysis of the enhanced Greenhouse Effect, and that such analysis can then be performed in seclusion.

In regard to benefit assessment, the IPCC SAR of Working Group III states that:

> The level of sophistication of climate change damage analysis is comparatively low. Damage estimates are generally tentative and based on several simplifying

and often controversial assumptions ... This low level of sophistication implies
that climate change damage analysis is a particularly worthwhile area for further
research.

(Pearce *et al.*, 1996: 184)

Fankhauser and Tol (1999) have argued that the CBA studies in the 1990s were at
fault largely because they were the first generation of such attempts. They suggest
that the 'second generation' of models will be more sophisticated and offer superior
results. While there is certainly much room for improvement the fundamental issues
will remain regardless of how sophisticated the modelling.

Perhaps the meaning of 'sophisticated' modelling is worth considering. The idea
that models and estimates may become more sophisticated is meant to instill faith in
estimates and be a sign of scientific rigour. The roots of this word lie in the
characterisation of the Greek sophists as those who were prepared to enter into
debate on any matter using whatever arguments no matter how unsound. Sophistry
is a method of argument that is seemingly plausible though actually invalid and
misleading, using an argument known to be false to persuade. Thus, we may worry
that future analysis of the enhanced Greenhouse Effect using economic models may
indeed prove to be more sophisticated.

The methodology of economic investigation is failing. From a sceptical point of
view the models can be seen as hiding as much as they reveal, and their growing
technical jargon and detail as creating more layers of protection from casual scrutiny.
The honesty of early work is self-evident because 'ad hoc' and 'hunch' estimates
were actually called just that, although the guess numbers then were taken to possess
far more meaning than this implied. More recently the same guess categories seem
to have shifted into more technically correct language such as 'vulnerable markets'
or 'willingness to pay for avoiding the risk of a catastrophic impact'. Similarly, the
treatment of uncertainty in the next generation of models remains firmly within the
school of converting strong uncertainty (unknowns) into weak uncertainty (probabilities). Much emphasis is placed upon applying various probability distribution
functions and obtaining subjective probabilities. Credence is then given to the
surveying of 'experts' as to their beliefs and these 'data' are used as key coefficients
of the models.

As Fankhauser (1993: 23) has stated: 'Although there appears to be a strong
tendency in the results to favour more moderate action, it seems similarly true that
through the choice of appropriate parameter values almost any abatement policy can
be justified'. His solution is to call for more research which should in particular
focus upon the slope of the benefit function and threshold effects. However, contrary
to other defenders of mainstream economic logic he recognises the need for
interdisciplinary thought on the subject and the specific importance of philosophy:
'On the economic side questions of discounting and intergenerational equity in general
will have to receive more prominence than they did so far, and this will naturally also

include other disciplines such as philosophy'. In the next two chapters some of these philosophical issues are explored with regard to the treatment of future generations.

References

Adger, N. and S. Fankhauser (1993) 'Economic analysis of the greenhouse effect: optimal abatement level and strategies for mitigation', *International Journal of Environment and Pollution* 3(1–3): 104–19.

Arrow, K.J., W.R. Cline, K.-G. Maler, M. Munasinghe, R. Squitieri and J.E. Stiglitz (1996) 'Intertemporal equity, discounting, and economic efficiency', in *Economic and Social Dimensions of Climate Change*, edited by J.P. Bruce, L. Hoesung and E.F. Haites, pp. 125–44, Cambridge, England: Cambridge University Press.

Ayres, R.U. and J. Walters (1991) 'The greenhouse effect: damages, costs and abatement', *Environmental and Resource Economics* 1(3): 237–70.

Bruce, J.P. (1995) 'Impact of climate change', *Nature* 377(12 October): 472.

Bruce, J.P., L. Hoesung and E.F. Haites (1996) *Climate Change 1995: Economic and Social Dimensions of Climate Change*. Cambridge, England: Cambridge University Press.

Cline, W.R. (1992a) *The Economics of Global Warming*. Harlow, Essex: Longman.

Cline, W.R. (1992b) *Global Warming: The Benefits of Emission Abatement*. Paris: OECD.

Demeritt, D. and D.S. Rothman (1999) 'Figuring the costs of climate change: an assessment and critique', *Environment and Planning A* 31: 389–408.

Dovers, S.R. and J.W. Handmer (1995) 'Ignorance, the precautionary principle, and sustain-ability', *Ambio* 24(2): 92–7.

Dubourg, R. and M.X.V. Rodriguez (2001) 'Calculating morbidity benefits from reducing air pollution: a Spanish case study', in *Evaluating the Impacts of Pollution: Applying Economics to the Environment*, edited by C.L. Spash and S. McNally, pp. 55–73, Cheltenham: Edward Elgar.

Fankhauser, S. (1993) *Global Warming Economics: Issues and State of the Art*. Norwich: CSERGE, University of East Anglia.

Fankhauser, S. (1995) *Valuing Climate Change: The Economics of the Greenhouse*. London: Earthscan.

Fankhauser, S. and R.S.J. Tol (1999) 'Figuring the costs of climate change: a reply', *Environment and Planning A* 31(3): 409–11.

Fankhauser, S., R.S.J. Tol and D.W. Pearce (1997) 'The aggregation of climate change damages: a welfare-theoretic approach', *Environmental and Resource Economics* 10: 249–66.

Funtowicz, S.O. and J.R. Ravetz (1994) 'The worth of a songbird: ecological economics as a post-normal science', *Ecological Economics* 10(3): 197–207.

Grubb, M., C. Vrolijk and D. Brack (1999) *The Kyoto Protocol: A Guide and Assessment*. London: Earthscan and Royal Institute of International Affairs.

Houghton, J. (1997) *Global Warming: The Complete Briefing*. Cambridge, England: Cambridge University Press.

Jones-Lee, M.W. (1976) *The Value of Life*. London: Martin Robertson.

Jones-Lee, M. and G. Loomes (1997) 'Valuing health and safety: some economic and psychological issues', in *Economic and Environmental Risk and Uncertainty: New Models and*

Methods, edited by R. Nau, E. Gronn, M. Machina and O. Bergland, pp. 3–32, Dordrecht: Kluwer Academic.

Knetsch, J.L. (1994) 'Environmental valuation: some problems of wrong questions and misleading answers', *Environmental Values* **3**(4): 351–68.

Masood, E. (1995) 'Developing countries dispute use of figures on climate change impacts', *Nature* **376**(3 August): 374.

Masood, E. and A. Ochert (1995) 'UN climate change report turns up the heat', *Nature* **378**(9 November): 119.

Mendelsohn, R. and W. Nordhaus (1996) 'The impact of global warming on agriculture: reply', *American Economic Review* **86**(5): 1312–15.

Meyer, A. (1995a) 'Costing calamity', *New Scientist* **30 September**: 64.

Meyer, A. (1995b) 'Economics of climate change', *Nature* **378**(30 November): 433.

Nordhaus, W.D. (1991a) 'A sketch of the economics of the greenhouse effect', *American Economic Review* **81**(2): 146–50.

Nordhaus, W.D. (1991b) 'To slow or not to slow: the economics of the greenhouse effect', *Economic Journal* **101**: 920–38.

Nordhaus, W.D. (1992) 'Economic approaches to greenhouse warming', in *Global Warming: Economic Policy Responses*, edited by R. Dornbusch and J.M. Poterba, pp. 33–66, Cambridge, MA: MIT Press.

Nordhaus, W.D. (1994) *Managing the Global Commons: The Economics of Climate Change*. Cambridge, MA: MIT Press.

Nordhaus, W.D. (1998) *New Estimates of the Economic Impacts of Climate Change*. New Haven, CT: Yale University Press.

Pearce, D.W., W.R. Cline, A.N. Achanta, S. Fankhauser, R.K. Pachauri, R.S.J. Tol and P. Vellinga (1996) 'The social costs of climate change: greenhouse damage and the benefits of control', in *Climate Change 1995: Economic and Social Dimensions of Climate Change*, edited by J.P. Bruce, H. Lee and E.F. Haites, pp. 178–224, Cambridge, England: Cambridge University Press.

Pearce, F. (1995a) 'Global row over value of human life', *New Scientist* **19 August**: 7.

Pearce, F. (1995b) 'Price of life sends temperatures soaring', *New Scientist* **1 April**: 5.

Price, C. (1994) *Emissions, Concentrations, and Disappearing CO_2*. Bangor: University College of North Wales.

Spash, C.L. (1998) 'Contingent valuation', in *The Elgar Companion to Consumer Research and Economic Psychology*, edited by P. Earl and S. Kemp, pp. 128–34, Cheltenham, UK and Northampton, MA, USA: Edward Elgar Publishing

Spash, C.L. (2000a) 'Ecosystems, contingent valuation and ethics: the case of wetlands re-creation', *Ecological Economics* **34**(2): 195–215.

Spash, C.L. (2000b) 'Multiple value expression in contingent valuation: economics and ethics', *Environmental Science and Technology* **34**(8): 1,433–8.

Sundaraman, N. (1995) 'Impact of climate change', *Nature* **377**(12 October): 472.

Tol, R.S.J. (1995) 'The damage costs of climate change: towards more comprehensive calculations', *Environmental and Resource Economics* **5**: 353–74.

8 Dividing time and discounting the future

This and the next chapter turn to how economists treat future consequences of current actions and future generations. The economic approach to the enhanced Greenhouse Effect relies upon the neo-classical theory of the efficient allocation of resources between generations. The two phrases 'intertemporal' and 'inter-generational' are used synonymously by economists to refer to distinct time periods into which society is thought of being split (e.g. the present and the future). A third phrase 'intratemporal' refers to the space within such a period while that between groups is referred to as intergenerational. Most political discussions are intratemporal, concerning resource distribution within and across countries amongst those currently existing, while the environmental movement has equally emphasised those as yet unborn, e.g. under the concept of sustainability.

Following this logic, economic modelling of intergenerational resource allocation tends to divide time by generations, e.g. past at time $t - 1$, current at time t, future at time $t+1$. In doing so, economists commonly assume uniformity within each generation, for example, that consumption is split equally among the members of any one generation (Solow, 1974; Page, 1977: 153). While this avoids intratemporal (within a generation) distribution and aggregation issues, the result is to treat generations as if they were distinct individuals.[1] The division of time into separable units then isolates the current from the past or future,[2] and restricts possible relation-ships to intergenerational transfers (e.g. man-made capital, technology and resource transfers).

Resource distribution is discussed in economics as a technical choice of an efficient allocation guided by market prices, among which the price placed upon goods at different time periods is key, i.e. the discount rate.[3] Discounting alone, as a mathe-matical calculation, actually assumes no absolute dividing lines because benefits and costs are reduced toward an asymptotic limit. However, effectively the future becomes insignificant as future values tend to zero so that any given positive rate produces an important now and unimportant future (the past rarely being entered as an economic consideration). Figure 8.1 shows how four different discount rates reduce the weight given to future events rapidly to near zero. The 10 per cent discount rate does so

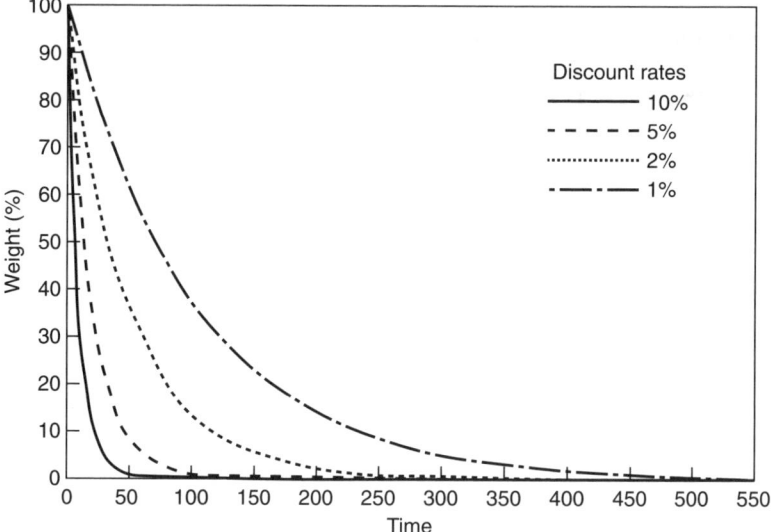

Figure 8.1 Reducing the weight of future events

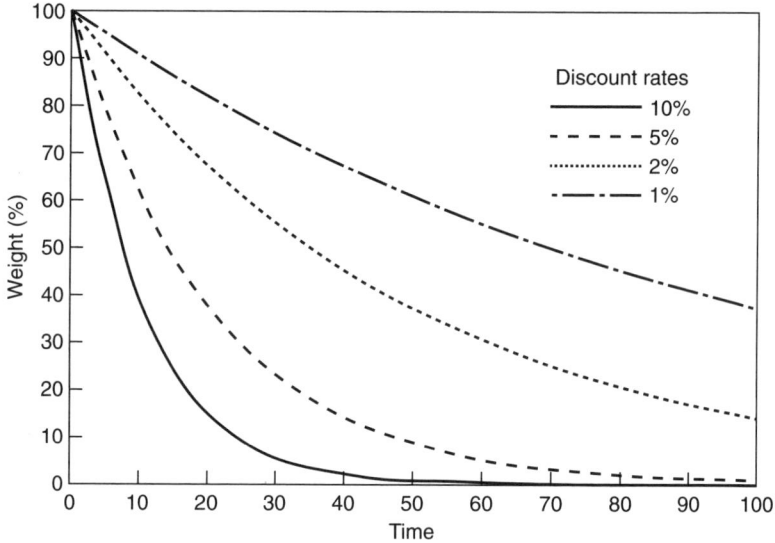

Figure 8.2 Weighting for 100 years of disounting

within about 40 years, at which point values (flows of costs or benefits) would add almost nothing to the summed discounted value arising from a project. Even the lower rates of 1 or 2 per cent limit time horizons to a few hundred years with events then having little or effectively no weight in decisions. Figure 8.2 shows the impact within a 100-year time horizon. For example, under the 10 per cent rate half the discounted value of a flow in perpetuity has accrued within seven years. Rates between 5 and 10 per cent effectively weight any impacts on future generations as unimportant. In the TAR of IPCC Working Group III (2001: 4) the control costs for GHGs were estimated using discount rates between 5 per cent and 12 per cent on the basis of consistency with public sector practice. The thrust of the economic approach, both in modelling and evaluation exercises, is to divide present from future (with respect to values, interests, generations).

This approach disturbs many non-economists and some economists with ethical objections being raised, but in practice discounting is used regardless of such qualms. Economic debates upon resource distribution and discounting are regarded as issues which need to be kept separate from ethics. This chapter takes a different approach by drawing upon literature from both economics and moral philosophy and then further pursuing the moral implications of imposing environmental degradation upon our descendants in the following chapter. The idea of neatly separating out all ethical considerations as suggested in the last chapter by the likes of Arrow, Nordhaus and those defending inequitable treatment of the loss of human life, will be seen as actually defending a very particular ethical position rather than being free of all such considerations.

Discounting is explained in the next section along with several problems in the divergence of practice from theory and debates over technical issues. In the following sections, choosing the discount rate is shown to be an ethical position about the claims of future generations (regardless of basis in consumer or capital theory), but one which economists prefer to treat as a technicality. This is disingenuous because a range of supplementary justifications are found in the economics literature for discounting, although these prove inadequate in several respects.

Discounting the future

Discounting is used to help aggregate the monetary value of an ongoing stream of costs and benefits associated with a project. This produces a present value, which represents the amount of money that must be borrowed, at a given interest rate, to supply the same stream of net returns as would be obtained through the project, assuming perfect capital markets. If benefits exceed costs in every time period the present value is positive for any discount rate. Generally, costs exceed benefits in earlier periods (e.g. due to project construction) and benefits exceeds costs in later periods (e.g. as revenue streams grow). The choice of the discount rate is then crucial in determining whether the present value is positive or negative, and a project deemed viable. Private projects use a commercial rate while public projects and economic efficiency require planning on the basis of a social discount rate (which aims to remove various perceived distortions).

Economists commonly defend such discounting of the future on the grounds that this is the way people actually behave and value events over time. Individuals are assumed to prefer benefits now rather than later while costs are regarded as better delayed as long as possible. Such attitudes are what economists call a positive rate of time preference. Both consumers, via this positive rate of time preference, and producers, via the social opportunity cost of capital, are then characterised as treating the future as less important than the present. In the former case, consumers who lend money expect to be rewarded (e.g. savings account interest) because they have abstained from consumption, while someone else uses their money. In the latter case, producers earn more interest on earlier cash receipts by loaning them to others in the economy and tying into their productivity, making earlier profits more valuable. Missed consumption today requires compensation with more consumption tomorrow, and profits today are better than the same profits tomorrow.

Neo-classical economists have shown how, in a simplified world, a unique discount rate is determined by a free market system. Individuals make decisions about their rates of present consumption versus savings (the marginal rates of substitution between present and deferred consumption). Aggregated, these savings provide a supply of loanable funds. Deferring current consumption increases future income if invested because of the returns on physical capital (e.g. machinery, buildings) via the marginal productivity of capital. Under perfect competition, savings and investment schedules intersect to define a unique equilibrium, where the marginal rate of return on capital equals the marginal rate of time preference (Krutilla and Fischer, 1975: 61). The outcome is a single discount rate, just as in other theoretically perfect markets there is a single equilibrium price.

Some authors maintain that discounting future streams of costs and benefits (on the grounds of consumer preference or capital productivity) is widely accepted by economists (Simpson and Walker, 1987: 221), and unanimously so by those dealing with long-term policy issues such as the enhanced Greenhouse Effect (Schelling, 1995: 395). If so, the only problem lies in practising the technique. Arguments then typically revolve around finding the appropriate consumer discount rate and which rate of return on capital to employ (for example, see the studies and debate in Lind *et al.*, 1982). Consumer discount rates observed in the market are employed as part of a short-cut attempting to avoid directly assessing time preferences. Unfortunately only the loosest empirical justification of a given rate seems necessary in practice. For example, a major environmental valuation study in the UK justified the use of a 25 per cent discount rate on the basis that some credit card companies charged this rate (Department of the Environment, Transport and the Regions, 1999). Others argue the marginal rate of time preference should be only a few per cent or even zero, because anything else is myopic or akratic.[4] Yet, even when the time preference rate is conceded to be zero, a diminishing marginal utility of benefits or a positive return on capital are assumed and used to provide independent arguments in favour of discounting.

The role of diminishing marginal utility is to reduce the weight given to additional units of consumption. Consuming more of the same ('normal') good means the satisfaction from each additional unit diminishes. Thus, consumers who increase consumption over time are assumed to find that the utility derived from additional units falls compared to when they were consuming less. The consumer discount rate is then composed of both the pure rate of time preference and diminishing marginal utility. Such an argument is often applied loosely to intergenerational problems where economic growth is presumed to make future generations better-off. Hence, under diminishing marginal utility, wealthier future generations would be expected to derive less utility from the same unit of consumption than current generations. Whether marginal utility diminishes, stays the same or increases, depends upon the level of consumption, so that if future generations are worse-off in terms of units of consumption their marginal utility will actually be increasing.

The validity of the diminishing marginal utility argument in discounting assumes that economic growth will continue in the future, that such growth increases utility and that the negative consequences of growth (such as pollution) will fail to override the positive effects (Lagerspetz, 1999: 152). This presupposes what should be proven and accepts the past as a good guide to the future. Interestingly, the choice of discount rate, and decisions to ignore long-term pollution, will actually determine future well-being and so believing the marginal utility will be positive can result in making it become negative. Negative marginal utility may also occur amongst sub-sections of the population. As pointed out in earlier chapters, the impacts of the enhanced Greenhouse Effect appear worst for those least able to adapt. Thus, regardless of aggregate consumption levels, there will be disparities amongst groups within future society so that some are better-off while others are worse-off and this means analysts should (but do not) disaggregate their calculations (Schelling, 1995). In addition, there are a range of objects for which diminishing marginal utility appears inapplicable, e.g. human lives saved.

More generally, a market-determined discount rate may prove unsuitable for long-term, public policy decisions due to the reliance on individual preferences. Private preferences determine the marginal rate of time preference. Individuals with finite life expectancies are likely to act differently in their private consumption decisions from a society that has a collective commitment to life in perpetuity. An individual may believe that because they will be dead in 30 years there is no point in considering the needs of a sustainable society 300 years hence in forming their preferences. Thus, the supply of loanable funds for investment is influenced by private time preferences that diverge from a collectively determined rate of social time preference. This divergence occurs for two reasons. First, preferences formed collectively (e.g. via a formal deliberative process) may diverge significantly from those derived as an individual (Niemeyer and Spash, 2001). Second, only the time preferences of the present generation enter into the process. The fear is then that a higher discount rate than is socially optimal will occur and the level of investment will be too low to make adequate provision for future generations (Ramsey, 1928).

Controversy over the consumer discount rate has indeed led to many objections. Broome (1992) identifies seven separate objections to an aggregate consumer discount rate, which are observed in the market, and are being used to provide a short-cut practical tool for evaluating long-term projects. Each point is summarised here with additional references and comments where appropriate.

First, he states his main concern is that the absence of future generations from the valuation process means the outcomes of projects with long-term implications cannot be correctly evaluated on the basis of current market prices. This is a problem for both savings and investment markets as well as commodity markets. Schelling (1995: 398) makes a similar argument, pointing out that optimisation models 'incorporate an irrelevant "time preference"', i.e. that of the current generation alone. As he goes on to note, such models also incorrectly assume that increments in other people's utility can be treated as if they were our own.

Second, in theory, every commodity should be discounted at its own rate of interest (i.e. rate of change in value over time) but, in practice, use is made of a single rate for all commodities. This can seriously distort project evaluation. In particular, benefits which fail to diminish with extra units should be discounted at the pure rate of discount, not the consumer rate. For example, the life of a 20-year-old saved today as opposed to next year appears to have the same benefit, making standard discounting practice unacceptable (a more detailed discussion of this point is given in Broome, 1994: 147–51). The value of environmental entities can also be expected to appreciate over time as they become scarcer, as people become better informed about ecosystem structure and diversity, and as real incomes rise (Hanley and Spash, 1993). Arguments have been put forward that the increasing value of the environment, or non-reproducible parts thereof, can imply either a zero discount rate (Philbert, 1999) or a decreasing rate (Rabl, 1996). Hasselmann (1999) advocates a variation where climate change damages have a zero net discount rate because they rise in value at the same rate as discounting would make them fall, but mitigation costs are subject to a positive discount rate.

Third, deeming a project as good on the basis of profit in terms of consumer prices ignores concerns over compensation (the potential for compensation being all economists tend to require). As all projects create some welfare loss, how or whether to compensate cannot be dismissed. Indeed projects failing a potential compensation test may be deemed worthwhile (e.g. small gains for the poor at the expense of larger losses for the rich), while conversely those passing it can be rejected. Judgements are required about people's gains and losses, and how they are valued. There is no short cut around the issue of compensation, a topic to which I return in the next chapter.

Fourth, the consumer rate varies over time and projecting a short-term rate to the long-term for convenience is theoretically incorrect. For example, if the enhanced Greenhouse Effect causes the economy to contract then consumption will fall and marginal benefits rise making a negative consumption discount rate possible. The dominant presumption in the second half of the twentieth century became one of increasing material consumption on the basis of material throughput in industrially developed economies and neglecting degradation of intangible benefits (e.g. the environment). Aggregate consumption rates also ignore wide disparities within society and across space as well as time.

Fifth, people's myopia means their preferences can diverge from their well-being, e.g. failing to plan for the future. As noted above the same applies in the case of akrasia (Lagerspetz, 1999: 150). This apparently irrational behaviour is an example of the ways in which human behaviour diverges from economic assumptions. Such behaviour then raises questions as to the extent to which economists are prescribing appropriate ('rational') behaviour as opposed to merely observing and describing general laws.

Sixth, market rates are inappropriate because a collective social rate of discount differs from an aggregation of individual rates. Broome explains this as being the public goods character of saving resulting in free-riding and an undersupply of funds. That is, self-serving individuals acting alone assume others will fulfil a social commitment, allowing their contribution to be smaller or non-existent. Such an argument can be used to support government intervention in savings just as in the supply of other public goods. Broome equates this argument to the isolation paradox where individual and collective rates diverge, but the isolation paradox need not be reduced to public goods and free-riding. Individual calculations can differ from collective ones for various psychological and social reasons for which the self-serving free-rider explanation fails to allow. For example, group action may be associated with positive or negative norms which add to or reduce the value of that behaviour

Seventh, the theory only applies to small (marginal) changes and the extension to large-scale or global projects is unfounded. This last point is equally applicable to arguments for both capital and consumption discount rates. Discounting is misused as a concept of value by general application beyond its theoretical limits. A marginal rate is applied to consumption within the margin, total consumption and even to the value of life (Price, 1993: 93). The market rate of interest is merely the value of the units at the margin, i.e. the marginal rate of substitution for increments in consumption over time, and the marginal rate of transformation over time for increments in investment.

As far as discounting at the capital rate is concerned, the appropriate rate of return has been debated, with some arguing all projects should achieve the same rate as for private investments. Others argue that rates must be project specific and take into account the activity displaced and in particular investment versus consumption (Lind, 1982). If consumption is displaced the opportunity cost is commodity value and the consumer discount rate applies. Where a mix of activities is displaced determining the appropriate rate becomes more complex. The opportunity cost of capital is the return from investing in the next best alternative project which meets similar goals. This may therefore be limited to a small range of similar projects, e.g. investment in solutions to a transportation problem are incomparable with projects increasing electricity supply. In the case of public projects the rate might be a few per cent or zero. In terms of environmental assets (e.g. mountain vistas, ecosystems functions and other forms of 'natural capital') again the growth rate may be zero. For the economy as a whole the rate is argued to relate to economic growth which could in practice also be zero or even negative. Technical arguments favouring a universal positive discount rate on grounds of the opportunity cost of capital are therefore found lacking.

In addition, Price (1993) has given a detailed range of arguments as to why technical justifications for capital discounting are flawed when applied in practice. Among his arguments the investment rate of return is seen to be inapplicable because full reinvestment fails to occur and the rate will then vary over time. Examples of failing to reinvest include depletion of North Sea Oil without adequate provision for the decline in natural capital, and cut-and-run logging which has destroyed forests while realising only a small fraction of their potential value (Price, 1993: 82). Exponential growth via reinvestment (a precondition for investing at the rate of return on capital) also faces limits to growth in terms of the resource base and pollution absorption capacity of the planet (Meadows *et al.*, 1972; Meadows, Meadows and Randers, 1992). That is, even where feasible reinvestment may be undesirable, human and material resources need to be complemented by natural resources which are strictly limited, e.g. land capacity, reproductive rates of animals and plants. Thus a sustainable economy in balance with Nature may well avoid reinvestment.

In summary, there are good reasons to question the technical basis for discounting. In fact the choice is far more than a technical formality and many economists, aware of this, call upon various non-technical arguments to justify different practices. Commodity discounting is strictly different from discounting well-being but, as Broome (1992) notes, is regarded as a 'short cut' to the latter. The danger here is the way in which discounting utility from consumption (i.e. the material effects of future events) leads to associated concepts being unwittingly discounted (e.g. the moral importance of future events). As Price (1993) points out this problem is in evidence across a range of issues. Thus, for example, discounting aesthetic experience is confused with beauty, income distribution with equity, labour output with the value of human life. More generally, the attempt to focus on practical discounting methods (i.e. consumer or producer rates) tries to avoid judgements about gains and losses of well-being and the form of the value function, but this proves impossible. The next section explores ways in which empirical and theoretical justifications are employed, and sometimes merged, in order to support the diminution of the interests of future generations via positive discounting of long-term projects. The aim is to reveal some of the underlying issues which often remain concealed in the economic debate.

Can the future be treated as less important?

The literature supporting the discounting of long-term future events can be split by attempts to support two distinct arguments. First, there is the strictly neo-classical economic position, that concern over future events diminishes smoothly over time, or at least approximately so, in accordance with discounting at a given rate of interest. This is particularly unrealistic but remains the maintained position of standard economic approaches. Second, a broader viewpoint is that future events are in general less important than present events and some method is required to reflect this. Discounting is then recognised as a crude and oversimplified approach which is only supported on grounds of pragmatism. The latter often amounts to an admission that how intergenerational events are regarded varies with circumstance and how they should be treated is unclear. The former position tends to concentrate on technicalities and theoretical models while the latter leads into open debate over the treatment of future generations.

Several arguments can be found which have been used to support the treatment of future interests as less important than those of the present (Kavka, 1978; Williams, 1978; Attfield, 1983; Turner, 1988; Broome, 1992; Price, 1993; Spash, 1993). A range of justifications relate to risk and weak uncertainty; issues such as the welfare loss from wasting resources by leaving them undepleted, risks relating to future project returns, and uncertainty over the consequences of our actions. Most often the simple intuition that 'this is how humans behave' is put forward as a self-evident truth and empirical fact. However, once a little thought is given to this proposition, and the empirical evidence investigated, the complexity and variety of human behaviour and relevance of different motives become apparent. A more philosophic complication concerns the uncertain identity and context-dependent existence of future people. This section explores each of these sets of arguments in turn, i.e. the treatment of future events under uncertainty, the empirical-temporal argument and the non-identity problem.

Appeals to uncertainty

Various attempts have been made to relate discounting to the uncertainty of future events and this has also been put forward in the context of the enhanced Greenhouse Effect (e.g. Philbert, 1999). Where the uncertainty concerns the demand for a depletable resource, this is assumed to be positively related to the distance in time from the depletion decision. The further off we try to imagine, the less sure we are that future people will want or need a particular resource. Resource economists aim to model the most efficient consumption of resources and thus human extinction is used to argue that consumption today prevents potential resource wastage tomorrow. For example, Heal (1986) has argued that if human extinction is exogenous (for example due to the cooling of the sun) and the date could be predicted, then the intergenerational distribution of world resources could be arranged to ensure nothing was left. The intellectual game is how to use resources if their ultimate loss is inevitable.

One conventional answer to a possible loss of a resource is to reflect such uncertainty in a higher discount rate, resulting in a faster rate of depletion. For example, if an oil-rich country runs the risk of invasion then oil companies extract the resource faster. However, Fisher (1981: 45–69) has shown how the type of uncertainty under consideration can produce either increased or decreased depletion rates because, sometimes, uncertainty can result in resources being preserved for the future rather than depleted faster. Where assimilative capacity is being depleted, with uncertainty as to the stock, risk aversion would favour reducing the rate of depletion. For example, the rate at which GHGs are presently released should be reduced, if this is now degrading the future absorptive capacity of the atmosphere, and depletion delayed until a future date to maintain a buffer in line with atmospheric systems. In contrast to the type of argument exemplified by Heal, the spaceship Earth[5] literature also sees resource redistribution towards the future as necessary in order to allow higher consumption to balance environmental degradation (d'Arge, 1971; d'Arge and Kogiku, 1973). A key difference between these two conclusions is that extinction, or ultimate resource loss, becomes endogenous in the spaceship, i.e. created by human activity. That is, consumption (assumed to be the sole source of happiness) produces pollution and reduces essential resources. Overall then, in terms of treating the future as less important due to uncertainty, this resource-related literature provides no clear support due to the importance of specific contextual assumptions.

The presence of risk is also used in project appraisal to justify discounting. Thus, the risk of environmental damages occurring from a project may be regarded as diminishing over time so that any associated costs become less important in CBA calculations the further into the future they occur. There is some probability that no damages will occur and this probability may be thought to increase over time. However, again, except under special circumstances, there is no well-defined way to adjust the discount rate such that it will make the appropriate adjustment for risk in the present value of uncertain future benefits and costs in each period. This is explained at length, in the context of energy-related projects, by Lind (1982). In addition, such discussions fail to take into account strong uncertainty (as explained in chapter 5).

Similarly, the moral aspects of treating the risk of future environmental harm as prescribed above is neglected. A positive risk of damages is reduced in weight to equate with a diminishing commodity price. This means that undertaking actions which can harm others is justified because there is a chance they will remain unharmed. My loosening the nuts holding the wheels on your car is acceptable because I am uncertain as to whether they will fall off and you will crash. More specifically, in the context of uncertainty discounting additional comfort is taken from the argument that the chance of harm becomes more uncertain over time. I am less sure what factors might intervene to prevent the wheels falling off three years from now as opposed to three days from now.

Another variation on the uncertainty argument concerns future preferences. As modern economics is built around taking individual preferences into account, the preferences of future generations need to be known.[6] If there is uncertainty as to preferences over time then the beneficial or harmful consequences of an action appear to become less important. However, while the preferences of the unborn are unknown their general interests upon which such preferences are predicated can be identified. The interests behind preferences can be regarded as relatively certain and stable in several general respects as opposed to their specific manifestation in, say, market choices. Thus, there are certain human needs which require fulfilment, regardless of more contextual factors, and a range of desirable states can be defined, e.g. uncontaminated food and water, a liveable climatic regime, opportunity for self-fulfilment and flourishing. In these ways we today differ little from the ancient Sumerians living 6,500 years ago, nor will those thousands of years hence differ from us. Human society has in many such respects remained unchanged over millennia.

In summary, the arguments based upon weak uncertainty prove inadequate, both as technical justifications for discounting and as ethical criteria for treating the future as less important. Weak uncertainty has no simple time trend which would correspond to smooth discounting at a single rate. That future outcomes are uncertain fails to provide adequate justification for undertaking actions with harmful potential and such harm can be recognised as impacting interests which are stable over time.

Treatment of future generations as an empirical fact

Perhaps the most commonly cited reason for discounting is that there is a natural and observable human tendency to divide and separate events by time and then differentiate their treatment. For example, Fankhauser (1995: 116–17) describes the pure time preference rate as being an unquestionable fact due to 'impatience at the level of personal preference', and specifies 3 per cent as the empirical finding. Neumayer (1999) believes observed current behaviour in the form of savings rates supplies a valid reason for positive discounting. There are two problems with these sorts of statements. First, the empirical evidence being called upon is extremely selective and used in an unscientific fashion. This raises questions as to the hidden potential support for preconceived political theories. Second, the grounds for taking what humans do as guidance for what should be done in society are at best weak, e.g. humans also murder, rape, torture, enslave, fight wars and commit genocide. Human preferences, in particular, appear a particularly weak basis for guidance as to moral action (O'Neill, 1993). The first point is explored further here while the second is left for the next chapter.

There is certainly a psychological division between the importance given to events occurring now, in the future and in the past. Yet experimental evidence shows a range of behaviour some of which supports negative discounting (Lowenstein and Prelec, 1991), and all of which reveals a far more complex picture than that portrayed by standard economic discounting. In terms of negative discounting, for example, rather than delaying costs and reaping benefits as soon as possible the opposite may occur. Empirical evidence shows a cost or unpleasant experience can be treated as best out of the way as quickly as possible, while a pleasant experience may be delayed allowing contemplation of the event. One explanation is an anticipation effect which can operate on behaviour in a variety of ways (Lowenstein, 1987). The problem for discounting is then that there is no simple time path to such anticipation which might allow some adjustment of rates, e.g. some pleasurable events may be continually postponed, others only for a short time (for a summary explanation of the anticipation envelope see Price, 1993: 108–9). There are indeed a variety of human behaviours which undermine conventional discounting, even as a descriptive theory, and, while economists have struggled to make these compatible with their behavioural model, psychologists have sought an array of alternative explanations increasing the richness of their own models (see Price, 1993: 103–5). In effect economic appeals to observed human behaviour have been used in a pseudo-scientific empiricism to reinforce the predictions of theoretical market efficiency.

Empirical evidence on human behaviour shows there is no simple relationship, of the sort standard discounting would require, but also no obvious dividing point at which the future should be ignored. Factors such as age, temperament, or affinity affect where any divide of the time-line into present and future is placed, and how events occurring at various points in time are treated. Any psychological separation of the present from the future may then be regarded as somewhat arbitrary (Dower, 1983), and ignores interests of silent voices (e.g. children, past and future humans). Such interests can be identified as of a general type continuing through time but with complex psychological associations for any given generation. Yet a different difficulty arises in taking those interests into account because whoever exists at a given time is contingent upon preceding actions and therefore has no claim for having been harmed by those same actions, a point that is explained further below.

Identity and possible future people

Moral considerability is often defined in terms of the individual and therefore linked to personal identity. Under these circumstances, hypothetical intergenerational contracts can only be made intelligible if personal identities are known (Norton, 1982; Parfit, 1983). Strangely enough, because identity is founded upon existence, the past might then have a place above that of the future, i.e. an identity and existence being definable for past individuals. That the future is only a potential raises the problem of identifying what obligations might exist towards those who will only exist contingent upon current decisions.

Parfit (1984) has pointed out that no coherent sense can be given to an action making the world better-off or worse-off if the specific persons who exist are different as a result, i.e. an action *ex ante* and *ex post* produces two possible future worlds with different people. Individuals are then argued to be unable to claim harm due to the actions of their predecessors if their very existence is contingent upon the events causing that harm. For example, this would be like a child complaining to his parents about the poverty he or she suffers, when the parents poverty is a direct result of making the child's existence possible. The couple might have had a child when wealthier but this would no longer be the same child. The reasoning then runs that, as long as future individuals prefer to live, any action is justified regardless of the related undesirable consequences because the future identity of individuals is determined by the action.

In the context of the enhanced Greenhouse Effect the problem might be characterised as follows, borrowing from Page (1999). Society can either abate emissions (ABATE) or continue business as usual (BAU). The policy choice leads to a different set of people coming into existence in the future. The possibility of all human existence ending is excluded and a future generation is assumed under both scenarios but they are different sets of people. This means the BAU people have no claim for harm because if the policy were ABATE they would not exist (the ABATE people would do so) and BAU people are therefore better-off with climate change and their lives (as long as they prefer to be alive). Under such circumstances Page (1999) asks on what grounds could a BAU strategy be rejected? He identifies three aspects of the problem:

- an 'Intergenerational Harms Claim' that adoption of BAU is wrong because it harms future persons
- a 'Worse-Off Claim' that an act (such as BAU) harms only if a particular person is worse-off as a result
- an 'Identity Dependence Claim' that BAU is a remote but necessary condition for BAU people to exist.

One of these three aspects needs to give in order for the non-identify problem to be removed.

Parfit believes the intuition that creating deliberate harm, as above with BAU, is wrong and should be rejected regardless the non-identity problem. He suggests the need for impersonal principles. For example, given two states with the same number of different people in each, then whoever exists should be no worse-off than those who would have otherwise lived. A minimum quality of life is effectively being defined. As Page (1999) points out, this approach runs into problems when the number of people do vary between states because then, for example, total utility can be higher with more people who are much worse-off. There is no clear reason for rejecting BAU.

Yet the thrust of Parfit's reasoning seems correct – that is, to counter the non-identity problem requires the identification of various impersonal interests. Thus, the argument under the 'Worse-Off Claim' neglects harm to future persons despite present indeterminacy concerning their identity or preferences, or because their lives are being determined by current actions. Whoever comes into existence in the future can reasonably be expected to have the same biological and social needs as those now existing and violating these general interests seems problematic regardless of how the specific identity of individuals may change as a result. Along these lines Baier (1984: 233) has concluded that:

> ... the wrongs we can do a future person are usually restricted to injuries to interest fixed before the identity of future persons are fixed (and to such frustrations and pain as is consequent upon the injury to such interests), and cannot include injury to interests not yet fixed or frustration of wants and concerns not yet fixed or hurts to sensibilities not yet fixed.

Such interests may include basic human needs, for food, shelter, health, and security, which will also remain a prerequisite for the satisfaction of other, more specific and now unknown interests. Thus, a range of fixed interests could be recognised as requiring our protection. In a similar vein Richards (1983: 141) has argued that the relevant moral issue is to determine how persons will fare under different policies, without any attention to the particularities of exactly who exists in the future. Many aspects of choice about creating potential harm in the future can therefore be decided without concern as to personal identities.

One way in which the above argument might then be taken forward is to recognise a 'Specific Rights Approach'. The BAU is then objectionable because many people are brought into existence with specific rights which have been violated and cannot be fulfilled or protected. A problem arises if future people under BAU would waive their violated rights because otherwise they would not exist. The counter argument is that these specific rights are inalienable so that they cannot be waived by individuals (more of a natural rights position). The Specific Rights Approach may also need to be supplemented by the interests of collectives (e.g. future generations) in order to provide rights to environmental public goods, such as clean air, because individual interests in such cases are too weak.

Page (1999) takes a slightly different tack which builds upon some of the preceding arguments. He recognises that an act can be wrong without affecting any particular person, but requires that an alternative 'carrier of value' then be identified. He specifies two carriers of value which actions can affect in order for them to be judged wrong: particular non-human individual entities such as the biosphere (an individual token-affecting view); and particular human collective entities such as generations or nations (a group token-affecting view). This second category then means 'communities which future people belong to are deserving of concern and respect *in their own right*' (Page, 1999: 123). Such communities can be nations or culturally specific groups within society. Page believes this approach can be supplemented with both specific rights and impersonal principles, although how different principles are prioritised (e.g. lexically) would need to be addressed. Page's approach is also complementary to the Specific Rights Approach.

Solutions to the non-identity problem seem to move well beyond the standard debate in economics. Specific future individual interests in terms of personal utility are found to offer an inadequate basis for consideration in current policy because of their contingency upon that policy. Rights appear to be one possible reason for including future harm in current policy decision, and have independent reason for consideration, as will be discussed below. Actions affecting groups such as generations and communities also provide reasons for considering future harm. This has additional interest because of the attempts which some economists have made to consider the implications of various ethical rules by focusing upon the comparative welfare of different generations (as will be discussed in the next chapter).

Conclusions

People forming their present and short-term preferences as consumers and investors in markets simply ignore the consequences in the remote future. Thus, the standard application of discounting, to long-term environmental damages, means that the distant future is almost valueless. In addition, the fact that net costs are distributed across the future, and net benefits received now, means discounting makes acting to degrade the future environment highly attractive.

Many economists wilfully fail to confront the ethical implications of discounting. As a result, intergenerational damages are accepted without much apparent concern. Where long-term damages are acknowledged and taken into account they are weighted as less important than present benefits. If, after weighting, damages are still significant enough to warrant compensation, modern economics can dispel the concern by either the potential compensation criteria or the existence of economic growth. The hope appears to be that the negative consequences of our actions will be felt by those on the other side of the world and living in the distant future so even the need for potential compensation can be dismissed. As Page (1977) noted some time ago, an unavoidable moral judgement is required concerning future generations in order to accept discounting and a given discount rate.

Indeed, the various ethical positions which result from an economist's choice of different discount rates can be categorised as shown in table 8.1, regardless of their empirical or theoretical basis as consumer or producer rates (Spash, 1993). On the philosophic side Lemons (1983: 31) has placed viewpoints on whether a duty to posterity exists into three categories: no moral obligations beyond the immediate

Table 8.1 Positions defining economic and philosophic treatment of the future

	Economic positions	Moral positions
1	An infinite social discount rate should be used	No moral obligations exist beyond the immediate future
2	Intergenerational (between generations) discount rate should be greater than zero but less than infinity	Moral obligations to the future exist, but future is assigned less weight than the present
3a	Intragenerational (within a generation) and intergenerational discount rates should be the same	The rights and interests of future persons are limited by those of contemporary persons
3b	Zero social discount rate	The rights and interests of future persons are given the same weight as those of contemporary persons
4	Negative intergenerational discount rate	Moral obligations to the future exist, and the future is assigned more weight than the present

Source: Adapted from Spash (1993).

future exist; moral obligations to the future exist but the future is assigned less weight than the present; and the rights and interests of future persons are the same as those of contemporary persons. This is an incomplete classification and should include the case where moral obligations to the future exist and the future is assigned more weight than the present.[7]

Only at the extreme of an infinite discount rate would no future effects of current actions be taken into account. More commonly an arbitrary but positive rate is used in the range 5–10 per cent. This effectively divides an important now from an unimportant future, which may diminish quickly to having little or no weight in current decisions, e.g. within 40 years at 10 per cent. The economic debate on discounting has then concentrated upon the short-cut consumer rate and the opportunity cost of capital as if the choice were in some sense 'objective'. Thus, the future is held to matter, but how far this is so is hidden behind the technical debate over the rate chosen. Rarely does the discussion turn to any obligations we may violate by adopting the procedure of discounting regardless of how the rate was derived. A more direct and open approach to the treatment of future generations seems desirable.

A position of equal, fair or equivalent treatment across time might be adopted. Thus, Lemons' third viewpoint can be split into two under an economic approach by considering what 'same' implies. As members of the current generation we may weigh our own welfare differently over our own lifetimes, treating the future as less valuable. If future generations are to be treated in the 'same way', then some may argue for intertemporal and intergenerational discounting at the same rates. Yet weighting the present more heavily than the future is often a myopic policy even when we choose it for ourselves. For example, intratemporally, people fail to provide adequately for their retirement, leading to government support for the elderly. Similarly the problem remains that any standard positive discount rate will cause catastrophes that take place in the further future to be reduced to insignificant factors in the present decision-making process (d'Arge, Schulze and Brookshire, 1982).

The alternative approach to treating future generations in 'the same way' is a zero rate. Fankhauser (1995: 129) believes the question is a political one that academic debate is unable to solve, but (in the absence of intergenerational compensatory transfers) supports the 'good arguments in favour of a zero pure time preference as a second best rate for intergenerational projects'. A zero social discount rate, where intergenerational decisions are involved, would prevent future environmental damages being ignored, counting every future effect as if it had to be borne immediately. There are disputes over the environmental impacts of zero discounting because of the argument that more investment and resource use would take place so leading to higher pollution, although this results from failing to account for pollution externalities in production and has nothing to do with discounting (Broome, 1992: 101–2). Broome favours arguments for zero discounting in the context of the enhanced Greenhouse Effect. A zero social discount rate effectively rejects discounting for impacts of the enhanced Greenhouse Effect but leaves open many questions as to exactly how future generations should be treated, to which I now turn.

Notes

1 Even though economists work within a utilitarianism that is supposedly individualistic (that is, all interests and benefits are those of single individuals) such assumptions effectively aggregate whole generations into single agents having utilities. This approach is also a means of avoiding a range of ethical issues, e.g. treatment of the current poor when making the future better-off and their position relative to the future rich.

2 O'Neill (1999) raises problems which arise for public policy in assuming such separability. He explains how CBA employs additive separability so that value in each time period is independent of other time periods and these values can be summed to give a total value. He also notes that what occurs in the past is ignored by economics and this is a point to which I return in the next chapter.

3 For an in-depth introduction to and critical discussion of discounting see Price (1993). This is the most comprehensive single source on the subject.

4 A myopic person erroneously evaluates the future making choices which systematically overvalue earlier benefits at the expense of later ones. An akratic individual suffers a weakness of will and chooses an outcome they themselves regard as inferior. Such decision-makers are regarded as irrational because they have good reasons to make choices other than those they actually do and would indeed do so if they could see clearly (Lagerspetz, 1999: 150).

5 The spaceship Earth literature developed in the late 1960s and early 1970s described the Earth in terms of a confined system similar to a spaceship. That is, a system with limited finite resources and where consumption produces waste and pollution which is immediately problematic. This simile was felt helpful for explaining the importance of physical laws and ecosystem functions. See Boulding (1966).

6 While the individual is meant to be the centre of value this is qualified when dealing with intergenerational issues. See note 1 (above) and the section on ethical rules in the next chapter.

7 This fourth category is an historical reality, e.g. the Russian people making extreme (though often involuntary) sacrifices after the revolution in order that their descendants might be better-off. In addition, the drive for economic growth, if taken at face value, implies the future should be made better-off than the present.

References

Attfield, R. (1983) *The Ethics of Environmental Concern*. New York: Columbia University Press.

Baier, A. (1984) 'For the sake of future generations', in *Earthbound: New Introductory Essays in Environmental Ethics*, edited by T. Regan, Philadelphia: Temple University Press.

Boulding, K.E. (1966) 'The economics of the coming Spaceship Earth', in *Environmental Quality in a Growing Economy: Essays from the Sixth RFF Forum*, edited by H. Jarrett, pp. 3–14, Baltimore: Johns Hopkins University Press.

Broome, J. (1992) *Counting the Cost of Global Warming*. Cambridge, England: White Horse Press.

Broome, J. (1994) 'Discounting the future', *Philosophy and Public Affairs* **23**(2): 128–56.

d'Arge, R.C. (1971) 'Essay on economic growth and environmental quality', *The Swedish Journal of Economics* **73**(1).

d'Arge, R.C. and K.C. Kogiku (1973) 'Economic growth and the environment', *Review of Economic Studies* **40**: 61–78.

d'Arge, R.C., W.D. Schulze and D.S. Brookshire (1982) 'Carbon dioxide and intergenerational choice', *American Economic Association Papers and Proceedings* **72**(2): 251–6.

Department of the Environment, Transport and the Regions (1999) *The Environmental Costs and Benefits of the Supply of Aggregates: Phase 2*. London: Department of the Environment, Transport and the Regions.

Dower, N. (1983) 'Ethics and environmental futures', *International Journal of Environmental Futures* **21**: 29–44.

Fankhauser, S. (1995) *Valuing Climate Change: The Economics of the Greenhouse*. London: Earthscan.

Fisher, A.C. (1981) *Resource and Environmental Economics*. Cambridge, England: Cambridge University Press.

Hanley, N. and C.L. Spash (1993) *Cost–Benefit Analysis and the Environment*. Aldershot, England: Edward Elgar.

Hasselmann, K. (1999) 'Intertemporal accounting of climate change: harmonizing economic efficiency and climate stewardship', *Climate Change* **41**: 333–50.

Heal, G. (1986) 'The intertemporal problem', in *Natural Resource Economics Policy Problems and Contemporary Analysis*, edited by D.W. Bromley, pp. 1–36, Boston: Kluwer Nijhoff Publishing.

IPCC Working Group III (2001) *Climate Change 2001: Mitigation of Climate Change; Summary for Policymakers*. Geneva: Intergovernmental Panel on Climate Change.

Kavka, G. (1978) 'The futurity problem', in *Obligations to Future Generations*, edited by R.I. Sikora and B. Barry, pp. 180–203, Philadelphia: Temple University Press.

Krutilla, J.V. and A.C. Fischer (1975) 'Further analysis of irreversibility: discounting, intergenerational transfers, and uncertainty', in *The Economics of Natural Environments: Studies in the Valuation of Commodity and Amenity Resources*, edited by J.V. Krutilla and A.C. Fischer, pp. 60–75, Baltimore, MD: Johns Hopkins Press.

Lagerspetz, E. (1999) 'Rationality and politics in long-term decisions', *Biodiversity and Conservation* **8**: 149–64.

Lemons, J. (1983) 'Atmospheric carbon dioxide: environmental ethics and environmental facts', *Environmental Ethics* **5**(1): 21–32.

Lind, R.C. (1982) 'A primer on the major issues relating to the discount rate for evaluating national energy options', in *Discounting for Time and Risk in Energy Policy*, edited by R.C. Lind, K.J. Arrow, G.R. Corey, P. Dasgupta, A.K. Sen, T. Stauffer, J.E. Stiglitz, J.A. Sockfisch and R. Wilson, pp. 2–94, Washington, DC: Resources from the Future.

Lind, R.C., K.J. Arrow, G.R. Corey, P. Dasgupta, A.K. Sen, T. Stauffer, J.E. Stiglitz, J.A. Sockfisch and R. Wilson (1982) *Discounting for Time and Risk in Energy Policy*. Washington, DC: Resources from the Future.

Lowenstein, G. (1987) 'Anticipation and the valuation of delayed consumption', *Economic Journal* **97**: 666–84.

Lowenstein, G. and D. Prelec (1991) 'Negative time preference', *American Economic Review* **81**: 347–52.

Meadows, D.H., D.L. Meadows and J. Randers (1992) *Beyond the Limits: Global Collapse or a Sustainable Future*. London: Earthscan.

Meadows, D.H., D.L. Meadows, J. Randers and W.W. Behrens III (1972) *The Limits to Growth*. New York: Universe Books.

Neumayer, E. (1999) 'Global warming: discounting is not the issue, but sustainability is', *Energy Policy* **27**: 33–43.

Niemeyer, S. and C.L. Spash (2001) 'Environmental valuation, public deliberation, and their pragmatic synthesis: a critical appraisal', *Environment and Planning C* **19**(4): 567–85.

Norton, B.G. (1982) 'Environmental ethics and the rights of future generations', *Environmental Ethics* **4**: 319–37.

O'Neill, J. (1993) *Ecology, Policy and Politics: Human Well-Being and the Natural World*. London: Routledge.

O'Neill, J. (1999) 'Self, time and separability', in *Self and Future Generations: An Intercultural Conversation*, edited by T.-C. Kim and R. Harrison, pp. 91–106 Cambridge, England: White Horse Press.

Page, E. (1999) 'Global warming and the non-identity problem', in *Self and Future Generations: An Intercultural Conversation*, edited by T.-C. Kim and R. Harrison, pp. 107–30, Cambridge, England: White Horse Press.

Page, T. (1977) *Conservation and Economic Efficiency*. Baltimore, MD: Johns Hopkins University Press.

Parfit, D. (1983) 'Energy policy and the further future: the social discount rate', in *Energy and the Future*, edited by D. Maclean and P.G. Brown, pp. 31–7, Totowa, NJ: Rowman and Allanheld.

Parfit, D. (1984) *Reasons and Persons*. Oxford, England: Clarendon Press.

Philbert, C. (1999) 'The economics of climate change and the theory of discounting', *Energy Policy* **27**: 913–27.

Price, C. (1993) *Time, Discounting and Value*. Oxford, England: Basil Blackwell.

Rabl, A. (1996) 'Discounting of long-term costs: what would future generations prefer us to do?', *Ecological Economics* **17**: 137–45.

Ramsey, F.P. (1928) 'A mathematical theory of saving', *Economic Journal* **38**(152).

Richards, D.A.J. (1983) 'Contractarian theory, intergenerational justice, and energy policy', in *Energy and the Future*, edited by D. Maclean and P.G. Brown, pp. 131–50, Totowa, NJ: Rowan and Allanheld.

Schelling, T.C. (1995) 'Intergenerational discounting', *Energy Policy* **23**(4–5): 395–401.

Sen, A.K. (1982) 'Approaches to the choice of discount rates for social benefit–cost analysis', in *Discounting for Time and Risk in Energy Policy*, edited by R.C. Lind, pp. 325–76, Washington, DC: Resources for the Future, Johns Hopkins Press.

Simpson, D. and J. Walker (1987) 'Extending cost–benefit analysis for energy investment choices', *Energy Policy* **15**(3): 217–27.

Solow, R. (1974) 'Intergenerational equity and exhaustible resources', *Review of Economic Studies* **41**: 29–45.

Spash, C.L. (1993) 'Economics, ethics, and long-term environmental damages', *Environmental Ethics* **15**(2): 117–32.

Turner, R.K. (1988) 'Wetland conservation: economics and ethics', in *Economics, Growth and Sustainable Environments*, edited by D. Collard, D. Pearce and D. Ulph, pp. 121–9, London: Macmillan.

Williams, M.B. (1978) 'Discounting versus maximum sustainable yield', in *Obligations to Future Generations*, edited by R.I. Sikora and B. Barry, pp. 169–85, Philadelphia: Temple University Press.

9 Economics, ethics and future generations

The contrast between focusing on efficiency and paying attention to moral issues and social context is apparent from the last chapter. In particular, modern economists' concerns over defining discount rates can be seen to largely miss the point with regard to the content of the arguments of non-economists. The extent to which economic efficiency can meaningfully be pursued while neglecting other social goals seems particularly limited in the case of the enhanced Greenhouse Effect. Greater clarity is then required over the content of the economic debate and in particular the meaning of concepts of harm and compensation. However, before going further some introductory qualifications and comments are required concerning the impacts of human activity due to population growth and the interests of future versus current generations.

Population growth has often been regarded as a primary concern when debating long-term futures. In this chapter the size of future generations is regarded as having no substantive impact upon the main arguments. This could be equated to assuming that some stable population has been achieved at a level which leaves the potential for long-term damages unaffected. The possibility of an increasing population which exacerbates the enhanced Greenhouse Effect, and other problems, might then provide separate economic and moral arguments in favour of population control. However, the enhanced Greenhouse Effect is a function of chemical and energy-intensive lifestyles, rather than purely the scale of human activity. A larger world population could, through appropriate production and consumption choices, live without sizeable GHG emissions. Alternatively, a world population of only one billion could still choose to perturb atmospheric chemistry by using a range of fluorocarbons which have a longer lifetime than CO_2 and are thousands of times more effective at climate forcing. Indeed, the historical creation of the enhanced Greenhouse Effect has been due to the lifestyles of a minority of the human population living in industrially developed economies. Contrary to the statement of Solow (1992: 6) 'the largest single danger to sustainability' is not rapid population growth which we should regard as 'fundamentally a Third World phenomenon'. High per capita resource consumption means one average American or Australian contributes much more to the enhanced

Greenhouse Effect than those in the less industrially developed or materially orientated countries. For example, per capita carbon emissions of those two countries are 4.8 and 4.3 times the world average respectively, while Africa emits 0.26 of that average (Marland, Boden and Andres, 2001). Thus, abstraction from the population scale and growth debate is seen as an acceptable simplification for current purposes where a range of other issues are more relevant.[1]

This chapter also largely abstracts from interregional disparities, which have their own ethical implications. This may be derided as being concerned over the potential future poor and harmed while ignoring those currently in such positions. However, we must recognise that the future soon becomes the present and failing to look ahead is a recognised policy problem. A sole concern with the present results in spending all our time fire fighting and none on fire prevention. There is also implicit in this criticism the idea that the interests of the currently and future disadvantage must be in conflict, whereas analysis from these two perspectives provides a set of reinforcing but different reasons for redirecting policy in the same way. The aim here is to focus upon a key aspect of the enhanced Greenhouse Effect which is hidden in most economic analyses and has gained less political attention. Unjust resource distribution and placing the burden of pollution on the poor within the current generation are genuine concerns under the enhanced Greenhouse Effect (as earlier chapters have highlighted). The difference is that the current poor or harmed can have a direct voice and can choose or endorse representatives to argue their case.[2] At the same time the ethical treatment of those distant in time has lessons of direct relevance to our treatment of those distant only in space, social standing or culture. The more general concern is for how humans choose to act, as members of a community, across all divides.

A final qualification concerns the actual existence of future generations and their exact demographic constitution. The basic assumption throughout the chapter is that a human population will exist into the future, although the enhanced Greenhouse Effect itself may bring this into question (Broome, 1992: 23–4). However, who exists and their life expectancy is conditional upon current decisions. There are then questions over the responsibility of current humans to people who have only the potential to exist in the future and whose existence depends upon our choices (i.e. the non-identity problem). This matter was considered in the last chapter with resolutions including the importance of inviolable rights and the recognition of duties to collective entities such as communities and generations. In the following sections closer attention is given to the meaning of such ethical obligations.

The implications of various ethical principles have been explored by some environmental economists and these are reviewed first. This raises the need for clarifying the meaning of intergenerational transfers. Two types of intergenerational transfer can then be identified (Spash and d'Arge, 1989; Spash, 1993; 1994a; 1994b). First are the basic distributional transfers which have been the central intergenerational concern of economists and which have been given attention by the sustainable development literature. That is, distributional transfers are concerned with the standard of living and avoiding unfair treatment across space and time. Second are compensatory transfers which emphasise a category of often disregarded obligations. These are transfers directly related to a moral duty to make reparations for harm.[3] Yet compensation is also morally questionable as a carte blanche for creating long-term environmental damages. If harm has intrinsic significance then rights may follow. Obligations to future generations defined in terms of rights reveal a very different set of appropriate actions under the enhanced Greenhouse Effect. Thus, some of the fundamental tenets of the current political economy of GHG control are brought into question.

Intergenerational ethical rules

Perhaps due to the rather doubtful and sometimes strained set of justifications called upon to support discounting, some economists have explored ethical rules more explicitly. That is, ethical rules have been employed in economic models of resource allocation to see under what circumstances unequal treatment across generations can be legitimated. The models used compare the impact of various ethical rules on the welfare of different generations, where generations are treated as distinct aggregate units (Schulze, Brookshire and Sandler, 1981; Schulze and Brookshire, 1982; Kneese *et al.*, 1983; Kneese, Ben-David and Schulze, 1983; Pearce, 1983; Kneese and Schulze, 1985; d'Arge, 1989). In most instances these rules have been defined under assumptions which simplify the relevant ethical principles to mathematical formulae for use in optimisation models. Four ethical rules can be found in this literature and are discussed here with a view to their implications for the treatment of the enhanced Greenhouse Effect.

The four rules are: the elitist, the egalitarian, the neo-classical utilitarian, and the libertarian or Paretian. The elitist rule requires that the welfare of the best-off be improved: actions that decrease elitist welfare are wrong. The egalitarian rule is the exact opposite, requiring the welfare of the worst-off be increased or maximising the minimum welfare, often termed the max–min principle. Both rules focus entirely upon the relative level of well-being, without concern about quantifying the sizes of welfare gains or losses. The Paretian rule reallocates resources until no generation can be made better-off without making another worse-off. The neo-classical utilitarian rule reallocates resources in order to maximise total utility across all generations. These last two rules focus upon the relative size of gains and losses while ignoring absolute levels of welfare (e.g. whether the gainer is rich and the giver poor).

The egalitarian rule requires that the welfare of different generations count equally with each other. The max–min rule has also been equated to Rawls' approach to justice, although he himself explicitly avoided applying his intragenerational rule across generations due to the complications this entailed. Under the egalitarian approach, making the future better-off relative to the present (the presumed goal of economic growth) would make the present the least well-off generation and hence is prohibited. If we take an indefinitely large (an infinite) time horizon, and assume finite resources, a policy of mere subsistence in each generation follows. In order to spread a finite amount of resources across infinite generations, and maintain equity, all generations must be committed to living at a subsistence level. However, the move to such a subsistence level is also prohibited, because the future would then have lower welfare than otherwise and welfare lower than that of the present generation (i.e. making the future the worst-off). So while the intuition of equity may be straightforward, trying to determine the implications of egalitarianism leads to complications. Egalitarianism is then often interpreted as the maintenance of the welfare level inherited. Thus, any harm passed on would need to be countered by a corresponding increase of good. However, harm is only considered in terms of impacts on the relative welfare level of each generation. Hence, an egalitarian option (from an original position) is to create harm spread equally across time without any compensation. Indeed deliberately creating good and harm in equal amounts would meet the requirement to pass along the same welfare as that inherited.

Elitism only considers future generations if their welfare is a concern of the elite (selfish altruism) or the future comprises the elite. Resource transfers will only be made if this increases the welfare of the elite, which is the best-off generation. Injuries caused to future generations will be uncompensated as long as the welfare of the elite is unaffected. More than this, changes that improve the welfare of the elite at the expense of others will be undertaken so that harm to the relatively poor is justified. While such elitism appears fanciful and morally unacceptable, there is some resemblance with actual conduct in human society where resources are extracted from less industrially developed economies, with low material consumption, to further supply the materially rich who already have the highest consumption levels.

Neo-classical utilitarianism (maximising total preference-based utility) focuses upon the gains and losses that comprise personal welfare, without any concern about welfare levels. This requires that any generation sacrifice one unit of utility when another generation can, as a result, gain more than one unit. Intergenerational redistributions are made according to the respective marginal utilities of consumption, where utility is dependent upon own consumption alone.[4] A utilitarian ethical system would require reallocating resources to the future to boost welfare as long as future generations have a marginal utility greater than the current generation.[5] Harm which leads to the equating of marginal utilities is justified. Compensation for the effects of long-term pollution will occur when the marginal utility of the current generation's loss, from the compensation payment, is less than the future generations' marginal utility gain. Compensation is excluded if, for whatever reason, the marginal utility of the victims is lower than that of the polluters. This argument is invoked for the enhanced Greenhouse Effect by claiming future generations will be better-off and therefore have lower marginal utility. An act involving the infliction of deliberate harm is then never wrong per se.

The Pareto criterion is the fundamental rule supporting welfare economics. Under a Paretian ethical rule the status quo is reinforced. No redistribution of welfare is allowed unless at least one person is made better-off and none worse-off. Further, the Pareto criterion is commonly applied in the same way to both intragenerational and intergenerational contexts. That is, for intergenerational analysis, an initial endowment is allocated to each generation and then redistributions are allowed if they are Pareto improvements.

The outcome of the rule will depend upon the definition of the starting point (initial endowments). If the initial endowment is entirely allocated to the present generation (as is in fact the case), whether the future gets anything is determined by the ability to make transfers. For example, a transfer from the present (e.g. 100 utils, where utils are some measure of utilitiy) which made the future better-off (e.g. being worth 120 utils) and increased total utility across all generations (e.g. by 20 utils) could only occur if the future could then compensate the present exactly for the original transfer (e.g. 100 utils). In the absence of this 'reverse transfer' the present would be made worse-off (by 100 utils) which violates the Pareto rule.[6]

The creation of long-term environmental damages which would make the next generation worse-off will require full compensation if the initial position is taken to be an unpolluted world. However, if the status quo is taken to be a world with existing pollution (i.e. part of the initial endowment) then pollution abatement is the policy to be considered. Such a pollution control investment is regarded as making the future 'better-off' while reducing the welfare of the present, in exactly the way exemplified above. In this case reverse compensation is required or no abatement can take place. This is in part a failure of mainstream economics to have any conception of history, the past or process, so that the present is taken as the definitive point. Some time ago, Mishan (1971) made a similar point with respect to the way in which transactions costs can lock society into either a pollution-permitting or pollution-prohibiting world. As he explained, under these circumstances, modern economic rationality always finds the current state is optimal.

Indeed, whether and under what circumstances redistributions in light of harm should occur are avoided in modern welfare economics by invoking the principle of 'potential compensation'. Thus, Freeman (1986: 221) states that the basis of CBA is the hypothetical compensation criterion, which 'is justified on ethical grounds by observing that if the gains outweigh the losses, it would be possible for the gainers to compensate fully the losers with money payments and still themselves be better-off with the policy'. Beneficiaries could compensate losers but the action is an economic improvement regardless of whether compensation is actually paid. If compensation is actually paid the principle is nothing more than the Pareto criterion. This leads to the bizarre argument that claims that, while the Pareto criterion has been widely rejected by economists as a guide to policy, and plays no role in 'mainstream' environmental economics, the potential for the same criterion is accepted (Freeman, 1986). The potential for Pareto improvements is invoked to justify policy based upon CBA while rejecting actual Pareto improvements! The only use of the potential compensation criterion is then, in effect, to deny the need for compensation to be discussed. Hypothetical compensation is, for example, consistent with making the poor yet poorer. The ethical implications of such a definition and use of efficiency seem hardly acceptable (Mishan and Page, 1982: 46), let alone ethically justified.

Indeed, the potential compensation criterion has been employed to separate efficiency from equity, and equity has then taken on a catch-all character for 'other' factors. This has meant that discussions of actual compensation have been avoided on the grounds that this is one of the 'equity' issues outside of the economists' realm. There are, of course, exceptions. Spash and d'Arge (1989) have reasoned that actual compensation for the impacts of the enhanced Greenhouse Effect is ethically required and explored different mechanisms by which this might be achieved. Howarth (1996: 269) has shown that actual compensation for reducing resource endowments is a necessary condition for meeting principles of intergenerational fairness. However, the tendency has been in the opposite direction with the need to discuss (let alone plan for) actual compensation being regarded as an unnecessary complication.

This raises a more general concern affecting all the ethical rules discussed above. A persistent modern view, especially among adherents of the positivist program in economics, has been that economists should avoid evaluation and prescription. Page (1988) points out that applied welfare economists have largely limited themselves to one normative idea, efficiency, which is often regarded as so universally appealing and analytically tractable that they scarcely think of it as normative at all. He has argued persuasively for the consideration of equity and other normative concepts besides efficiency, especially where intergenerational issues are involved. Compensation is one of those other normative concepts but the treatment in economics (as above) fails to recognise this as a different moral concern than just equity or living standards.

Distinguishing basic and compensatory transfers

Part of the problem with the economic approach to intergenerational welfare is the sole focus upon allocating resources to achieve a certain standard of living. The discussion of intertemporal allocations has evolved over time from the idea of splitting a fixed, finite cake to one of productivity and opportunity maintenance. This moves the emphasis from a dividing up of a particular resource stock toward asking what welfare can be generated from some economic and political system, given available resources and technology. Solow (1986: 142) puts it this way:

> The current generation does not especially owe to its successors a share of this or that particular resource. If it owes anything, it owes generalised productive capacity or, even more generally, access to a certain standard of living or level of consumption.

As long as all resources are commensurable, substitutable and malleable then anything is expendable and nothing need be preserved for its own sake or because it is essential or irreplaceable.[7]

From that perspective, the problem posed by non-renewable resources is that future generations will have fewer options, other things remaining the same. This is because a given technology and capital stock output will be lower and environmental degradation higher. Barry (1983) believes failing to endow future generations with 'a slice of the pie' as readily obtainable as ours means that their reduced access to easily extractable and conveniently located resources needs to be 'compensated' via improved technology and increased capital investment. Compensation in this sense provides support for a basic standard of living, what economists view as the maintenance of utility, or what we might more generally call productive opportunities. The difference from the mainstream economic attempts at incorporating ethical rules is a move towards identifying certain rights to a standard of living.

However, the level of 'compensation' being referred to under opportunity maintenance is best recognised and termed as a basic distributional transfer (Spash, 1993). Basic transfers are concerned with distributional justice. There is no particular reason to limit compensation for damages to calculations about distributional transfers of this or that resource. Compensation can be defined as making amends for loss or injury and implicitly involves an asymmetry of loss and gain. Long-term environmental damages under the enhanced Greenhouse Effect entail an asymmetric distribution of loss and gain over time. Intergenerational compensation is the attempt to counter-balance negative consequences by creating positive welfare in the same proportion (e.g. as measured by a common metric such as utility). This requires the use of transfer mechanisms, but all transfers need not be compensatory. The reference point for compensation is the level of damages caused to the victim (e.g. an individual, community, generation). The reference point for basic transfers is the welfare level, difference in welfare, or opportunity set of the current generation compared to future generations.

Consider an egalitarian ethical system and assume this is taken to mean the welfare level received from the previous generation should be maintained for the next generation. The current generation would need to maintain the same welfare as that with which it starts. If deliberate substantive harm were inflicted upon future generations, a separate ethical case for transfers exists on grounds of compensation and there will be a need to consider what is adequate compensation for that harm. A focus upon aggregate welfare alone fails to make such a distinction. Thus some regard egalitarianism as spreading the damages of climate change equitably across generations so as to maintain a common welfare level (see Crosson, 1989). The enhanced Greenhouse Effect could then be justified if sea level rise, crop losses and unmanaged ecosystem disruption affected everybody equally in welfare terms. More and more damages could deliberately be created as long as they were spread evenly. However, even if such a designed set of consequences were possible, the outcome appears morally objectionable because creating harm is different from good and compensation for injury is a separate moral issue from concerns over welfare distribution.

An example in the intratemporal context may help clarify the distinction being made here. Assume there is an individual who receives government payments because he or she is unemployed and has no means of support. The government provides for him or her a minimal standard of living. Without these government payments the individual's welfare will be at subsistence level. Assume that this individual lives next to a weapons factory run by the government. Unfortunately, there is on site a toxic waste dump that has been leaking materials into the local environment. The leak is discovered; there is proved a cause–effect relationship between the releases and the local high incidence of cancer cases. The welfare-recipient has also developed cancer since living in the area. Can the government now say to this individual that he or she is so much better-off already, due to the welfare payments that provide a minimal standard of living, that they require no compensation for the cancer? No, because the two kinds of payment cannot be morally linked. The welfare payments are made on the grounds of equity while the liability payments are founded upon grounds of injury. This is a simple and common distinction which has seemingly failed to make any impact on economic analysis.

A common economic argument is that the current generation need be unconcerned over the loss or injury caused to future generations because they will benefit from general advances in technology, investments in capital, and direct bequests of resources or consumption goods. For example, Adams (1989: 1,274) has raised this as a defence of his position against action to control for the enhanced Greenhouse Effect. As he states, while fossil fuel combustion implies forgone opportunities for future generations, they 'typically benefit (in the form of higher material standards of living) from current investments in technology, capital stocks, and other infrastructure' There is no attempt here to designate investment with the express purpose of compensating future generations. Indeed, such a compensation scheme would require assessing the extent to which the future can be made better-off by economic growth being balanced against all long-term environmental problems on a case-by-case basis, e.g. enhanced Greenhouse Effect, ozone depletion, nuclear waste, toxic chemical dumps, loss of species, habitat destruction. Each incidence of harm requires separate consideration of compensation. However, such details are often ignored on the grounds that a generally wealthier future can take care of itself. Indeed, making the future too well-off has recently become more of a concern for some authors (e.g. Lind, 1995; Neumayer, 1999; Marini and Scaramozzino, 2000).

Relative wealth is used as an argument to mitigate against claims for damages. Thus, Lind (1995: 384) defines the enhanced Greenhouse Effect in the following terms:

> The real disagreement between the environmentalists who advocate an all out programme to reduce greenhouse gas emissions, and economists and others who may be more sceptical, is a disagreement over whether future generations will be better off even with global warming than the present one.

A belief that economic growth will continue exponentially and that such growth is linked to human well-being then leads to the conclusion that the current generation is the worst-off. The outcome is the type of conclusion which so shocked John Houghton when he heard it from a UK government minister (see chapter 3), that basically the future can look after itself. In the words of Lind (1995: 382): '... in all likelihood future generations will be much richer than the present one and if they (future generations) want lower levels of greenhouse gases and lower temperature levels they should pay for them'. If irreversible events can only be avoided by action now, or earlier control is more cost-effective, then future generations will need to achieve reverse compensation.

> to implement such a programme of control where future generations would pay the cost, we would need to implement a scheme whereby the future generations would compensate the present and near-term generations for their investments in emissions abatement programmes.

For Lind then the choice is one of the willingness to pay off the victims of pollution, which is contrary to the polluter pays principle and also leads towards the world of pollution as a means of extortion. This is, for example, equivalent to saying Mexico can dump toxic pollutants on the USA and expect either the USA to pay to prevent this or Mexico can just ignore the resulting harm because it is relatively poor.

There are then three questions being raised. Do basic transfers negate any obligations for compensation? If compensation is required can it practically be achieved in an intergenerational context? What is adequate compensation for deliberate harm? The first has already been answered in the negative. That is, basic transfers being provided on grounds of general rules of distributive justice are an inadequate basis for dismissing compensation. Economists cannot ignore future environmental damages due to the enhanced Greenhouse Effect purely because they expect economic growth to increase future welfare. A focus on aggregate welfare ignores distinctions between compensatory and basic transfers.

Second, actual compensatory transfers require consideration as to what might be feasible and the methods available for making such transfers over time. The adequacy of compensation means determining whether all harms can be rectified. Mechanisms for achieving intergenerational transfers are normally taken to include research and development, man-made capital, consumption goods and trust funds. Debating whether the trust fund/cash transfers approach is preferable to abatement of GHGs seems to miss the point but has been seriously put forward as an option (see Lind, 1995). The future possesses all resources so paper entitlements add nothing in terms of real well-being. As redistributive instruments amongst future members of a given generation they require institutional structures which many believe have no prospect of surviving into the medium or distant future, or at least cannot be guaranteed to do so.

Other transfers mechanisms are concerned with increasing well-being rather than merely transferring paper property rights. In general all transfer mechanisms suffer similar problems in terms of being difficult to target on those requiring compensation, and suffering from strong uncertainty as to their outcomes due to the unpredictable nature of future preferences and the state of society. Recognising that transfers are meant for compensation as opposed to being part of basic transfers creates specific problems because the transfers must be targeted and get to their target. This has led to the suggestion that compensation via physical projects may be most appropriate because they can be located where compensation is required. Care is required to avoid confusing such physical compensation with actual abatement and prevention of harm. For example, power companies being required to maintain carbon sinks are preventing not compensating for harm, as suggested by Crowards (1997). Building infrastructure or other man-made capital might be seen as benefiting the future. Alternatively, investment in education may be regarded as improving human capital which may have long-term benefits. However, these are general speculations about actions rather than defining specific characteristics required of an intergenerational compensating project or any compensatory transfer.

Clearly intergenerational transfers are more easily discussed in economic models as means of raising aggregate welfare by economic growth rather than as practical tools to compensate for harm. This problem means that even when the literature turns to abatement as a practical alternative to compensatory transfers the issues become muddled. Thus, Schelling (1995: 400; 2000: 836) argues that 'Abatement expenditures should have to compete with alternative ways of raising consumption utility in the developing world'. He apparently assumes pollution and the creation of harm is the accepted norm and then asks whether this position should be altered (a problem noted earlier with regard to Paretian rules). The abatement policy is described as creating good rather than preventing harm. Abatement in this context is merely one way of raising future welfare, and the only consideration is the aggregate welfare of different groups (i.e. recognising regional disparities in terms of harm). This argument means that if education gives a better rate of return than GHG abatement, as a capital investment, then, on grounds of efficiency, future generations should be well educated and have climate change. There is no consideration here as to the difference between deliberate creation of harm and the maintenance of a standard of living. The only consideration is once more basic transfers to achieve some level of aggregate welfare (resulting from the type of objective function specified). As Neumayer (1999: 34) states, 'it does not matter whether the current generation uses up non-renewable resources or dumps CO_2 in the atmosphere as long as enough machines, roads and ports are built in compensation'. The only moral duty for these authors is to pass on some aggregate level of welfare and so avoid much of the debate on the practical requirements of compensation, e.g. who is to be compensated, how much compensation is required, what form should this take and is such a transfer feasible in practice?

Such positions also assume compensation can be an adequate response and so reject the possibility of incommensurability. For example, Schelling (1995) assumes that abatement (e.g. CO_2 reduction), aiming to prevent damages and harm, be regarded as commensurate with humanitarian aid (e.g. education), creating benefits and good. This might, for example, result in trading off loss of life due to GHG emissions with higher educational attainment. Many may reject the concept of such a comparison. That different values may exist which can neither be measured in meaningful terms by a common unit, nor compared, is a pluralism beyond standard economic approaches (see O'Neill, 1993). Whether categories of harm can be regarded as commensurable and traded off is discussed in the next two sections.

Harm and trade-offs

Economists confronted by ideas of incommensurability, and associated refusals to make trade-offs, counter with the argument that every action implies a trade-off even if only implicitly.[8] The problem with this approach is that everything is a trade-off for something else by the very definition of the term. This means that any human concern can then tautologically be described as involving an action which has an opportunity cost. In this way even ethical judgements become just another commodity to be bought and sold in the market place. Thus, Hasselmann (1999) believes the willingness to pay off current generations to abate GHG emissions gives the monetary value of ethics relating to the issue, and more generally that 'ethical values become monetized in the unavoidable competition with market goods and services' (p. 341). All ethics then are merely matters of how much people are prepared to pay or trade off consumption. From a philosophic viewpoint such arguments appear farcical; unfortunately, in economics they are too often taken seriously. This is in part because of the desire, since the enlightenment, for universal scientific rules which might explain all phenomena.

Such universal application of the concept of trade-offs seems to conflict with both the existence of incommensurable values and rights-based ethics. Hence, Neumayer (1999) derides concerns over the difference between compensation as creating good and environmental damages as deliberate harm, on the grounds that economic growth is founded upon trading off the harming of some people for the benefit of others. The stated fear is that recognising values that lie outside the dogma of trade-offs (e.g. inalienable rights, intrinsic values) means an end to economic growth as many economists prefer to view it. Thus, Neumayer (1999: 340) believes that recognising a right preventing deliberate harm to future generations means 'a virtual standstill in economic actions of present generations' and that 'we are doomed for inactivity'.

The concept of trade-offs is so ingrained within modern economics that it is seen as an unquestionable necessity. In fact trade-offs may explain very little and often nothing of human action because to describe the 'trade' requires bounding an open choice set.[9] The tendency amongst economists opposed to GHG control is to describe GHG abatement as a trade-off between the long-term uncertain benefits of action to help future generations and the benefits of action now to alleviate current poverty. The moral dilemma is made implicit by bounding the choice set so that the current poor must suffer if the future poor benefit. An alternative is to view the problem as the current rich needing to have a little less material consumption to benefit the future poor and avoid creating victims of harm. Thus, why one action is described as a trade-off for another often tells as much about the analyst as the actual decision problem. For example, should lost educational investment in less industrially developed economies be regarded as the cost of GHG abatement (as some authors suggest), or perhaps missile defence schemes and urban four-wheeled drive trucks? Such trade-offs are certainly not the widely publicised aspect of economic growth promoted by politicians, who prefer to talk of the cake getting bigger so nobody loses, e.g. the Bruntland Report (World Commission on Environment and Development, 1991).

The general concern underlying these various trade-offs is that preventing significant harm to future generations means current economic activity may be limited dramatically. This is then argued to mean a reduction in the rate of economic growth and the welfare of future generations from higher material consumption. The fallacy here is that economic growth can only be achieved by deliberately causing significant harm (e.g. loss of life, physical injury, loss of human rights, damage to cultures). Economic growth is being described as if it cannot be achieved via socially and environmentally beneficial production and consumption processes. Of course the concern should, in any case, be for human well-being rather than economic growth per se and the two often diverge widely in practice. If a class of economies can only survive by the deliberate and routine creation of significant harm of the innocent then the time is long overdue for its extinction.

Economic discussions in terms of welfare prove an inadequate basis for issues of the intrinsic value of harm as opposed to good or concerns over liberty. Human tragedy due to the infliction of deliberate harm is soon recognised to involve more than neat calculations of welfare losses and gains. Rights and duties then seem an integral part of human social structure which require explicit attention.

Rights versus consequences[10]

Discussions of potential injustice to the future because of uncompensated long-term damages, or the failure to provide adequately for their survival via basic transfers, do seem akin to arguments over the rights they may hold and our obligations to them. This is an active area of ethical debate with strong policy implications. However, the ethical debate of applied philosophers tends to be caricatured by economists while ethical concepts are reduced to mere shadows of their original. For example, the process of incorporation into economic models transforms all ethical concerns into variations on a utilitarian theme. Preference utilitarianism underlies much of modern economic thought and its central facets go unquestioned.[11] Yet when attempting to explore alternatives (such as different intergenerational ethical rules) economists begin to probe the validity and relevance of that tradition. Trying to incorporate different philosophical ideas shows the restrictions of the framework being used, but the analysts appear unprepared for the challenge mounted against their basic training and too often beat a hasty retreat.

Welfarism, teleology and deontology

In order to understand the nature of this challenge the characteristics of utilitarianism need to be considered. Utilitarianism relies upon two main principles: consequentialism and the location of intrinsic value in utility. Consequentialism determines the rightness or wrongness of an act by the results that flow from it. The utility principle holds some resulting state (e.g. pleasure, happiness, welfare) as intrinsically good. Modern normative economics locates intrinsic value in human welfare and this has been termed 'welfarism'.

The appearance of open ethical debate in modern economics can then be misleading. For example, the egalitarian max–min rule, discussed earlier, has been equated to Rawls' contractarian theory of justice although the reinterpretation in economics means there is no deviation from the two utilitarian principles.[12] The egalitarian and elitist rules only deviate from neo-classical utilitarianism in their concern over the welfare levels of specific groups (the elite or the poor), as opposed to the welfare of all social levels aggregated as if they were one. The use of welfare levels is but a variation on the neo-classical utilitarian concern for good consequences (Sen, 1982; Page, 1983). There is rarely any conception of alternative ethical theories outside these narrow confines.

Yet there is a major confrontation in philosophy between a teleological perspective and a deontological one. Teleological ethical theories, which include utilitarian ones, place the ultimate criterion of morality in some value (such as welfare) that results from acts. Such theories see only instrumental value in the acts themselves but intrinsic value in the consequences of those acts, i.e. an act is instrumental to the creation of a valued outcome. Thus, a teleological argument would be that the enhanced

Greenhouse Effect is justified if material wealth can be created as a result and, if necessary, the wealth might be used to compensate any people harmed. In contrast, deontological ethical theories attribute intrinsic value to features of an act itself. Thus an act (e.g. lying, adultery, murder) is wrong even when it produces better consequences than any of the alternatives. In the context of the enhanced Greenhouse Effect this might mean deliberately harming others (e.g. future generations, the poor, the innocent) in a significant way would be wrong regardless of the material wealth it created.[13] Under deontology the consequences no longer determine what is right or wrong but rather the act itself is either right or wrong.

The economic debate assumes that the relative merits of social states depend uniquely upon the personal welfare characteristics of those persons who live in such states, without attention to considerations of rights. Under welfarism, if two states generate the same personal welfare they must be treated in exactly the same way. Intergenerational efficiency as defined under these ethical rules allows for the violation of human rights (Sen, 1982). The idea of a right to remain unharmed by others can easily conflict with these rules. For example, the present generation might be well-off and future generations starving and disease-ridden due to the enhanced Green-house Effect, yet under the Pareto criterion (without reverse transfers) this situation would be optimal because the future could only be made better-off by making the present worse-off. Conversely, rejection of welfarism means compensatory transfers cannot be decisively and justifiably denied even if a future generation were richer and enjoyed a higher welfare level than the present generation, and even if its marginal utility from the consumption gain is less than the marginal welfare loss of the present generation. Welfarism then appears as an inadequate reflection of moral concerns over the treatment of future generations.

Welfarism assumes that a harm can be corrected perfectly by a 'good' and that the direction of changes in units of welfare is irrelevant (i.e. gains versus losses). This standard approach in economics can be traced back at least as far as Bentham (1843: 438):

> to the individual in question, an evil is reparable, and exactly repaired, when after having sustained the evil and received the compensation, it would be a matter of indifference whether to receive the like evil, coupled with the like compensation, or not.

However, compensatory transfers aimed at creating 'good' may be unacceptable as an attempt to correct for loss or injury. As Barry (1983: 21) has stated, doing harm is in general not cancelled out by doing good. For example, saving two lives provides no justification for killing a third person and calculating a net gain. There is an incommensurability in the attempt to conduct such calculations.

This distinction between doing harm and bringing about good is most apparent where the right to human life is involved, but can be extended to other areas where rights are accepted to exist. For example, assume individuals of a nation are accepted to have a right to live in their own homeland. Sea level rise due to climate change floods the Maldives and violates this right. As a collective the Maldavians may have their cultural values undermined which would represent the type of intergenerational harm specified as relevant under the non-identity solution of Page (1999). Of course the Maldavians can be relocated and compensated but this approach at mitigation assumes a commonly rejected commensurability and as a deliberate act violates the aforementioned right.

If compensation from this generation to that fails to buy moral absolution for a range of harms created under the enhanced Greenhouse Effect (e.g. sea level rise, crop loss, melting Antarctic ice sheets) then the economic approach becomes inoperative. Economic efficiency is used to argue in favour of polluting as long as the damages created are less than the amount of compensation required. Indeed Neumayer (1999) believes that 'whether future generations will accept an increase in the rate of skin cancer or not depends upon what they get in exchange for it'. Compensation is then accepted as a means to deliberately harm others as well as a licence to pollute. Recognising the issue as one of the rights of future generations means avoiding acts which deliberately harm the innocent.

Defining intergenerational rights and duties[14]

The question may then turn to the characteristics of such rights and whether they are inviolable in different respects. Inviolability may be defined as consisting of being imprescriptible, inalienable and indefeasible. These in turn refer to rights persisting through time, persisting regardless of any individual's desire to the contrary and never being overridden.

The justification for rights across time might be equated to those across space today. Consider the export of toxic wastes from country A to country B. Country A wants to be rid of toxic wastes and therefore pays country B to accept them. The right of B's citizens to have an environment free from toxic wastes is bought and sold. Should A act in this fashion? If A's citizens have rights to a toxic-waste-free environment, no matter how much A's citizens may wish to have the benefits of the chemicals produced and to rid themselves of their wastes, this cannot be bought by violating the same rights of B's citizens. The same argument extends to future citizens of B or future citizens of A. Thus, Lagerspetz (1999: 158) has argued that:

> an 'equal treatment' of future generations means only that we have no right to make decisions which would, according to our present knowledge and values, impose on them such costs and risks as we would not be willing to assume ourselves.

Such an imperative can be described as a negative right, i.e. a right correlative with a negative duty to refrain from certain acts.

Respecting rights with a correlative duty to avoid deliberate harm of the innocent would mean that compensatory transfers could no longer be used to justify serious environmental degradation.[15] However, there could still be a role for compensation. Irreversible damages, already underway, which cannot be prevented by stopping pollutant emissions, or other actions, would still require compensation. This is analogous to tort law, where compensation mitigates the wrong when rights, which ought not to be violated, have been violated.[16]

Many economists will object to such reasoning, which would, for example, ban the international trade in toxic wastes and bring into question the drive towards tradable pollution permits. This is in part because the contracting parties are regarded as entering into agreements of their own free will. An additional twist might then be added to the earlier story about the Maldavians by arguing that they believe themselves to be as well-off, or even better-off, in their new homeland so who is to deny them the change. As Bentham (1843: 438) also pointed out:

> What is manifest is – that to no person, other than the individual himself, can it be known whether, in this instance, between an evil sustained, and a benefit received on account of it, any compensation have place or not.

In contrast to those who are present now, future generations are in a class of silent voices unable to give their consent in the way deemed necessary by Bentham. Thus protection is offered by, for example, defining a duty to avoid harm. Indeed Bentham's position might itself be regarded as advocating the inviolable right of individuals to self-determination in order to protect individuals from other powers such as those of government.

In practice there are many cases where intrinsic human values are protected from violation by even voluntary contractual agreement. For example, individuals are prevented from selling themselves or others into slavery regardless of whether or not all parties freely consent. There are various rights which society protects, such as freedom of speech, freedom from torture, and the right to sue another party. Freely contracting children are protected from working in coal mines despite the potential economic gains. There will from time to time be those who would, and do, accept the loss of their rights if they can trade these for enough money but this no more diminishes their intrinsic value than the existence of slavery or torture. Certainly there are a class of rights which appear inviolable by economic compensation. Thus there appear to be reasonable grounds for supporting an inalienable character to any right of future generations to be free from deliberate intergenerational environmental damages.

The question that then arises is the extent to which such rights are 'natural' as opposed to merely attributed by society. A 'natural right' can be defined as a right based upon intrinsic value (Nash, 1989). Natural rights can also be recognised as existing outside of specific legislation attributed to a society at a particular time and place, i.e. by definition imprescriptable. Rights must be valid in this sense if there is to be any universal moral imperative. The United Nations (UN) charter of human rights is representative of such a position. Violations of human rights fail to diminish their importance. Yet the extent to which future generations are recognised to possess inviolable 'natural' rights has still to be clarified in law and, under the UN charter, the future only gains indirect protection via articles intended to protect the current generation.

Conflicting values and moral dilemmas

The failure of social institutions to recognise moral imperatives towards future generations may be justified by some on the grounds that the move to environmentally benign production and consumption processes is too costly. The dramatic change in current human activity required is then seen as good reason why the costs should override any rights. Similarly the prevention of future harm is sometimes described as violating other (more important?) rights, such as the right of current generations to maximise their welfare. Both these arguments question the extent to which such rights are indefeasible or absolute in the sense of never justifiably being infringed.

Moderate deontology: consequences reconsidered

A strong right with a duty to avoid deliberate serious harm challenges conduct in modern industrial economies. As a result such a position is likely to be regarded with scepticism and as too dogmatic because it ignores the consequences of action. That is, the banning of substances is normally restricted because the benefits are argued to be large. This is also the standard argument used to introduce new technologies with unknown but potentially threatening long-term consequences, e.g. nuclear power, genetically modified organisms. The relevance of these consequential and empirical discussions is rejected where the imperative is to avoid serious harm.

Some have therefore explored the importance of a middle ground where neither consequences alone nor rights alone determine the goodness of an act. The appeal to a 'safe minimum standard' can be viewed as an example of constraining economic trade-offs by introducing rights. This standard advocates the protection of species, habitats and ecosystems as long as the costs avoid crossing a threshold and becoming unacceptably large. In the case of the enhanced Greenhouse Effect, Batie and Shugart (1989) argue that the safe minimum standard would support emissions reductions, despite estimates of high control costs. Such a position could be described as moderate deontology.

A moderate deontological position employs rights as the basic mode of operation except where the consequences become extreme (see Kagan, 1998). The moral imperative might therefore be to avoid deliberate harm except where there are overwhelming beneficial outcomes which go beyond a consequential threshold. An extreme asymmetry of benefit relative to harm is then required for the justification of a harmful act. In contrast fairly frivolous forms of material and energy-intensive consumption today (e.g. urban four-wheel drive vehicles, electric toothbrushes, disposable phones and cameras) are being regarded as good cause for creating potentially dramatic future damages (e.g. dislocating and killing tens of thousands due to flooding and climatic change).

Thus, while moderate deontology allows for the introduction of consequential arguments the position is fundamentally similar to rights-based theories except in extremes. In the case of the enhanced Greenhouse Effect no substantive case has been made that controlling emissions would do more than reduce the rate of growth of material consumption for industrially developed economies.

Rights and absolutism

A standard criticism of rights is that there may be conflicts between different rights which then require resolution. This then brings into question the validity of discussing rights as prescriptions for action. Jones (1994: 193) paraphrases Burke as follows:

> Government decisions call for a delicate balance of competing considerations. One interest will compete with another, the pursuit of one good might require the sacrifice of another, we may be able to avoid one evil only if we endure another, and so on. To suppose that the conduct of government can be dictated by a simple catalogue of absolute rights is morally naïve and politically dangerous.

There is indeed good reason for concern over where moral absolutism might lead. Excessively rigid moral systems can themselves be a cause of harm. For example, those who led their countries into the First World War made an absolute moral code of national honour, regardless of human consequences (Glover, 1999). The trench warfare which followed was the result of cold-blooded indifference rather than an unavoidable part of the conflict. The moral codes of many military men and the worst dictators of the past century have been absolute. Thus, the extent to which moral principles should be modified in response to feelings about humane and reasonable outcomes must be high on the moral agenda (Brittan, 2000).

Rights, even when absolute, can be limited in several respects. In general rights operate as only part of moral thinking. The way we implement our rights can be criticised and this must be done from an alternative basis of judgement. Duties can extend beyond and be unrelated to rights. Acts of benevolence, generosity, mercy and kindness by definition have no associated rights (i.e. if they were rights they would no longer be such acts). Interpersonal relationships can no more be reduced to rights and duties than to utilitarian calculations. Thus, friendship and family relationships are poorly described when limited to such terms. There is more to moral life than rights alone.

Rights may also be absolute but conditional in that there are requirements for their fulfilment. They may be conditional upon material circumstances so that, for example, there is no right to a standard of living which cannot be achieved or to non-existent physical goods or services. Rights to socio-economic goods are conditional in this sense so that there are rights to goods today which humans did not possess in the past. Yet the moral standing of such rights remains despite their being conditional upon circumstances (see Jones, 1994).

Rights may also be limited in another respect. A given right may be justifiably overridden by another right or moral consideration. This has been termed 'prima facie' rights.[17] Obviously if a right gives way all the time to other consideration then it loses all meaning as a right. This is why utilitarianism is so difficult to reconcile with rights because social utility could regularly override rights (e.g. the costs of controlling pollution always being deemed too high). Rights which are overridden in order to resolve a moral dilemma imply an injustice will result. Stating that something has a right, even an inviolable one, can still mean being unable to always accede to that right. The key point is that in overriding such a right there will be some moral residue (e.g. guilt at having done something wrong) and this can lead to a moral case for compensation.

Thus, while activities that create long-term environmental damage violate a right to be free from harm, the present generation may be argued to have some right to the socio-economic benefits acquired in the process. For example, chlorofluoro-carbons provide benefits as deodorant propellants and as refrigerants. While linking the demand for aerosol deodorants to rights seems unlikely the provision of refrigeration is (at least potentially) less frivolous. Those in less industrially developed countries may claim that they have as much right to such benefits as do those in Europe or the USA and that this right to basic material commodities outranks any right of future generations to be free from harm.

In this regard the distinction between positive and negative rights is relevant. Positive rights are claims to specific goods and services and require a reciprocal response from those who bear the corresponding duty. Examples include rights to compensation, protection and welfare benefits. Negative rights require only restraint on the part of others and are rights to non-interference. Examples include the right not to be assaulted, libelled or have property taken away. A right to be free from harm due to environmental pollution is clearly in the second category and only requires that we refrain from certain activities. Correlative negative duties need never conflict if they are respected because they only require restraint. A duty to avoid harm can be respected by society using benign consumption and production processes along with a duty to avoid taking goods and services away from those in less industrially developed economies. Positive duties can create conflict as can violation of negative rights, with both leading to moral dilemmas. Thus, where harm is already being conducted, or is threatened, interference is required to rectify the situation leading to possible conflicts with other rights.

An approach to moral decision-making which recognises rights must, if it is to be equipped to resolve conflicts, be able to assign priorities. Rules may be imposed to achieve this so that some argue negative duties are always superior to positive ones. In such situations the choice of which duty to perform means deciding which is the more 'stringent' and this requires judgement. The use of judgement here is different from and makes no call upon trading off various goods in a consequential manner. Thus, a non-consequentialist deontological ethic can allow for defeasible obligations that, in a particular context, can be overridden by others.

When two rights do come into conflict this may be far less problematic than sometimes suggested. The prevalence of conflicting rights will depend upon how extensively rights are asserted. The greater the number and scope the more often there will be conflicts. On the contrary, adequately defining the scope of rights may remove many apparent conflicts. Thus the discussion of harm here has been loose and largely unbounded but on occasion has been qualified by terms such as 'significant', harm of the 'innocent', 'deliberate' harm. These are all ways in which the scope of a right to avoid harm may be limited. As Jones (1994: 199–200) notes, the definition of a right might extend to several pages, although the tendency is to be short in definition to allow popular appeal. He goes on to point out that there may be two substantive causes of rights conflict. First, moral rights may conflict because there are limits to our ability to be totally comprehensive and cover every eventuality. Second, instability in world affairs means no rights structure can expect to be defined so as to avoid conflict. In particular, when people violate the rights of others, rights can conflict and moral dilemmas arise. Jones cites the examples of how to deal with murderous regimes and aeroplane hijackers. These instances often confront society, with tragic choices concerning individuals and their rights.

Limits of value systems[18]

More generally, problems affecting rights as a value-based system of obligations also affect other value systems such as utilitarianism. The general emphasis on the socio-economic benefits of growth often explains why a ban against harmful pollutants is consistently resisted and the right to trade pollution permits is put forward. Yet this requires interpersonal comparisons of welfare where no common metric exists. Problems also arise where there is a stated refusal to trade, as under lexicographic preferences, and such occurrences must be denied or diminished in importance if the economic calculus is to survive. A related problem is when an infinite willingness to accept occurs and so exposes a moral dilemma. In practice even large stated amounts are routinely excluded as 'outliers' because they upset the calculations. Zero bids for protest reasons are another such complication. In effect economists are already working in the realm of conflicting moral considerations. Such conflicts are the essence of moral dilemmas and fail to simply disappear because they are assumed away (e.g. by assuming all values are commensurable and can be traded).

Moral life is complicated and at least instances of conflicting rights make this clear. If future generations are to be the losers then an explicit judgement to that effect is required and the consequent moral regret and case for compensation must be considered. Instead the current economic argument depends entirely upon the interests of the current generation being strong enough and correctly located.

The idea that future generations will be protected on the basis of human interests seems at least as problematic and in general false. Human motivation to act fails to include the interest of all humans and hence there are starving people and gross inequities in resource distribution. Reflection upon what is in the interests of other humans appears to be a weak motivation to act and only operative with regard to what is in the interests of some humans (e.g. family and friends) while excluding others. As Schelling (1995) has argued, making sacrifices now for people in the distant future is similar to doing so for those distant geographically or culturally; he goes on to note the self-obsession of Americans who prefer looking after other Americans to anyone else either present or future. Appeals to self-interested utility-maximising behaviour without recognition of other values merely reinforces such attitudes.

Indeed destruction of the environment may be in the interest of current humans (just another trade-off) and hence the appeal to utilitarian arguments to support concepts such as sustainability prove ill-founded.[19] For example, Wade-Benzoni (1999) cites the destruction of fisheries by short-sighted behaviour restricted to profit-seeking, within one generation, rather than planning across generations. Perversely, this type of behaviour turns out to show how environmental protection and long-term business sustainability are compatible. Unfortunately, even though the burden of self-restraint is often small compared to the prevented loss for future generations, there is a lack of motivation to act on behalf of people who are imaginary, whose lives lack detail and with whom there are few or no ties of reciprocity. Motivation to consider future generations is stronger amongst those who feel a shared fate with other users of a resource (and therefore show self-restraint in their own use). In addition, the behaviours of previous generations are liable to be passed on to future generations, for example affecting intergenerational transfers (Wade-Benzoni, 1999: 1,403).

Rights analysis preserves the sense of tragedy in the world with regard to our treatment of the environment, other humans (current and future) and non-humans. The sense of value portrayed under the preference utilitarian approach is one where humans choose those bits of the world to value and throw away those bits they regard as of no value. This seems to seriously misrepresent the relationship of humans to each other and to Nature.

Economics too readily assumes that value conflicts are resolved when a decision is taken. The necessity of a choice due to practical constraints and political reality is misleadingly represented as a carefully weighed-up trade-off. Indeed human psychology is misrepresented by the idea that because a decision is taken all conflict has been removed. The point is made with regard to the importance of conflicting duties by Jung (1989: 345–6):

> By no means every conflict of duties and perhaps not even a single one, is ever really 'solved', though it may be argued over, weighed, and counterweighed till doomsday. Sooner or later the decision is simply there, the product, it would seem, of some kind of short-circuit. Practical life cannot be suspended in an everlasting contradiction. The opposites and the contradictions between them do not vanish, however, even when for a moment they yield before the impulse to action. They constantly threaten the unity of the personality, and entangle life again and again in their dichotomies.

Conclusions

Four ethical rules as incorporated into economic models were discussed in this chapter. Each could be given an interpretation under which no compensation for long-term damages is deemed necessary.[20] For example, the current generation can be:

- elitist with welfare dependent upon current consumption alone and themselves defined as the elite
- egalitarian and merely spread harm equally across generations including their own
- utilitarian with the belief that the marginal utility of future generations will be lower
- Paretian with reverse intergenerational compensatory transfers reckoned impossible and long-term pollution regarded as the status quo norm
- Paretian with only potential compensation required.

Indeed elements of most of these arguments have appeared in the literature on the economics of the enhanced Greenhouse Effect. That deliberate substantive harm of the innocent can be so easily ignored raises serious questions as to the failure of economics to distinguish between compensation and other transfers.

Compensation was argued to be a distinct and separate concern from basic transfers and an issue which cannot be circumvented by economists. A fundamental step forward would be to question when actual compensatory transfers are both feasible and adequate. If actual compensation proves difficult or impossible to target, or is an inadequate moral justification for deliberately creating harm, then GHG abatement is the best option. That such compensatory transfers may be impracticable across generations leads Lind to recognise that a political decision is required to deal with the ethical issue of abatement, although he sees the issue as one of whether future generations should be 'subsidised' by an abatement programme.[21] Whether compensation can ever be regarded as adequate recompense for the deliberate infliction of a harm was seen to drive straight into the philosophical conflict between teleology (e.g. utilitarianism) and deontology (e.g. rights).

Advantages of the latter appeared in terms of addressing intergenerational well-being. However, both philosophies might also prove too extreme. In the former case only the outcome matters regardless of process or the characteristics of instrumental acts. For example, releasing GHGs is justified by material wealth creation which is often frivolous. In the latter case the context within which acts may occur has no implication. For example, if the act of killing the innocent is intrinsically wrong then deliberately releasing GHGs knowing they will kill an innocent future person is to be prevented regardless of the potential positive results forgone or the costs of pollution control. An alternative to these two extremes is to allow for deontological rules subject to specified constraints either in consequential or non-consequential terms.

Thus, harming an innocent human or non-human can be forbidden up to a certain threshold defined in terms of the good which results from the act. For example, killing an innocent person to save five lives may be rejected but not so if a thousand or a million lives would be saved. As Kagan (1998: 78–84) explains, the moderate deontologist holds a position distinct from the consequentialist because the latter believes that goodness of results is the *only* factor with intrinsic significance and therefore they must *always* regard as permissible the act which leads to the best results. In contrast moderate deontologists are pluralists who believe in the intrinsic significance of acts of doing harm as well as good and will therefore forbid harming someone regardless of the best results overall, as long as they are within the threshold for a constraint on consequential motives to action. 'Moderate deontology is thus a genuine alternative to consequentialism' (Kagan, 1998: 80).

Philbert (1999) quotes Paul Ricæur as describing the realm of human action requiring a trade-off between the short-term focus upon foreseeable consequences and the long-term view of unlimited responsibilities. This sentiment may be taken as being similar to a moderate deontological position in recognising that responsibilities must sometimes be bounded by consequences. However, the extent to which responsibilities are unlimited is often exaggerated. There are then a variety of ways in which we might address the issue, e.g. institutional design, safe-minimum standards, defining rights or specifying duties. Indeed the duty to avoid harming others and the right to be free from harm are already in practice both present and restricted.

Serious consideration of the well-being of future generations has been argued here to require redefinition of the rights structure as realised in society and this may indeed be detrimental to the current generation's selfish interests. The dictatorship of the current generation over the future allows the imposition of damages regardless of how small or frivolous the gain now and how significant or large the extent of future harm. Utility-maximising individuals and profit-maximising firms which lack any moral or social responsibility will push costs onto those distant from them in time and space. That is, the typical agents in a neo-classical economic model are driven by incentives to pass harm onto innocent others and benefit themselves.

The motive to perform moral action may be divided by three types of obligations (Lumer, 2000: 98). A formal moral duty exists when there are morally advanced legal standards. These are largely absent with regard to future generations. An informal moral duty requires following morally advanced non-legal standards. These may appear as social and ethical norms which are followed within society. An imperfect moral duty requires recognition of moral good on the part of the individual who must strive to implement and improve upon socially beneficial norms.

Definitions of harm due to environmental degradation may need to take the form of constitutional rights and the UN charter on human rights (see Eckersley, 1998). This would move the debate over action into the legal and institutional realm and away from 'free' market approaches. Page (1982) has made a point worth considering in this context. Even for the promotion of intertemporal efficiency; institutions are required which honour the wishes of the past and anticipate the needs of the future. The market, as shown by discounting, fails as such an institution which is why there are traditions of common law, the law of wastes, contract law, legislative acts and constitutions. Such institutional arrangements aim to bridge time and connect current to future behaviour.

The task of defining harm is difficult and has only been loosely addressed here. Preference utilitarian models tend to supply a very broad definition in terms of any welfare loss, and, as a result, risk trivialising the issue by equating a large number of minor income losses to a major humanitarian disaster. In as far as welfare losses are individual specific they also run foul of the non-identity problem. There is further complexity in deciding when an action with uncertain consequences is deemed to be in violation of such rights, although uncertainty is rejected as a reason for undertaking actions where harm is a potential outcome. In the case of the enhanced Greenhouse Effect there are strong reasons to believe numerous major contraventions of basic human rights will occur. The point of the current discussion has not been to offer a codified system of law or some constitutional amendment but rather to emphasise a fundamental basis for human action in morality and show the weakness, in this regard, of current economic approaches.

That there are alternative ways of conceptualising the moral dilemma confronting us under the enhanced Greenhouse Effect means there is a need for open debate and a plurality of values. Instead the problem has been characterised as a scientific technical issue with economic consequences. Thus, the Kyoto negotiations which are immersed in ethical considerations about resource distribution, rights and compensation have been treated as legal and economic discussions over technicalities. The most inadequate part of the IPCC information process has been the reporting on economics because of the desire by many of those involved to divorce the subject from ethical judgements, which they then make implicitly.

Many of the concerns raised in this chapter with regard to future generations apply equally to morally significant others. That is, the separation of one human from another happens across space, social class, race, religion and cultural affectation. The role of civic virtue in producing moral decisions and just constitutions is lost in the reduction of all motives to preference utilitarianism. Deliberation is required as to what is right and just if humans are to maintain any status as ethical beings. Yet that deliberation is absent from the development of policy on the enhanced Greenhouse Effect.

Notes

1 The enhanced Greenhouse Effect is also only one cause of extensive and expanding long-term environmental damages, thus the arguments presented here can easily be applied to other activities (e.g. nuclear power generation). Many wastes, freely or inadequately disposed of, are highly toxic, and/or in amounts exceeding the assimilative capacities of ecosystems, so that they can accumulate and persist for decades, centuries, or longer (e.g. polycarbonated biphenols (PCBs), radioactive materials, chloro-flurocarbons). Such pollutants share, with the enhanced Greenhouse Effect, damages which are significant, potentially irreversible, long term, and asymmetrically distributed over time. The net benefits of associated activities accrue now; the net costs accrue in the future.

2 Future generations require representation but are unable to confirm the legitimacy of those individuals or institutions which do so. Representation of future generations, and Nature, is therefore justified on different grounds than that of current humans. Both raise concerns over how democratic institutions can and should operate to represent the weakest in society (O'Neill, 2001). While concentrating upon the interests of future generations can prove more controversial, giving voice to such silent groups is no less important.

3 Such a moral duty can be utilitarian or deontological. That is, current neo-classical theory could be associated with a duty to compensate for harm given a simple rule such as the Pareto criterion discussed in the next section.

4 An egalitarian argument can follow from the utilitarian approach. This requires an appreciation of the law of diminishing marginal utility (additional income yields less than previous additions, though the total continues to rise), and assuming that all individuals are fundamentally alike in their preferences and capabilities for enjoying goods. In the strict form, the utilitarian argument for egalitarianism depends crucially upon the identity of the utility of income across generations. At the opposite extreme, an elitist argument can be made if the marginal utility of income of the elite is higher than that of others; the rich get richer and the poor poorer (see Culyer, 1973: 64–90). The ultimate extreme, under increasing marginal utility, is where one person should be given all the world's resources in order to maximise total utility for society (see Mishan, 1981: 122).

5 Of course, determining the marginal utility of future generations poses a practical barrier to making this requirement operational.

6 Such a reverse transfer of utility could be argued to arise from selfish altruism, i.e. the current generation enjoys making the future better-off.

7 A problem apparent in Solow's writing on this subject is how to treat intrinsically valuable natural and cultural entities. He recognises their existence (Solow, 1992: 3; Solow, 1993: 168), but dismisses the relevance of this constraint by assuming such intrinsic value is rare and exceptional (Solow, 1993). Interestingly, one of his examples of an object with intrinsic value is the Lincoln monument!

8 Refusals to trade in neo-classical economics are usually regarded as instances of lexicographic preferences. That is, an absolute ranking of alternatives exists, as for words in a lexicon. While recognised as a theoretical possibility economists tend to reject the practical relevance of such preferences. However, there is empirical evidence for the significance and relevance of refusals to trade (whether lexical or otherwise) for environmental policy. For a review of relevant literature and empirical results see Spash (2000).

9 The trade-offs you made to read this text may be described as limited (e.g. another reading activity) or open (e.g. any alternative activity and its consequences for your life). The trade-offs you made in choosing your job could be described as another similar job or an alternative life path.

10 My thinking in this area has benefited from numerous discussions with John O'Neill over the past decade. In particular, personal communications during 1997, while conducting joint empirical research into environmental values, aided my understanding on several specific points discussed here. That research was funded by the European Commission, DGXII, Environment and Climate Programme. Of course, I am solely responsible for what is written here.

11 As Arrow (1973: 323) states: 'At no time in the history of economic thinking has there been a thoroughly agreed-on criterion, but at least among the more philosophic circles of economists a utilitarian criterion has been more or less accepted'.

12 The treatment of Rawls' contractarian theory of justice provides a good example of how economists take liberties with philosophical theories. Arrow (1973) reduces Rawls to the max–min criterion and in so doing admits 'I ignore the richness of Rawls' discussion, some other constraints he imposes on the allocation of resources (particularly setting an infinitely higher value on liberty than on goods)' (p. 323). The latter would imply a lexicographic preference which is hard for neo-classical economists to accept or meaningfully operationalise within standard theory. In the same article Arrow notes Rawls informed him personally that 'he did not intend to supply any form of the maximum principle to intergenerational justice' (p. 325). Solow (1974) uses the same interpretation although he again recognises this was not advocated by Rawls. Binmore (1989) discusses Rawls as if he were a utilitarian by putting aside any arguments he put forward as to the rejection of orthodox decision theory, and as he admits his approach 'entails a very substantial re-evaluation of Rawls' approach' (p. 84).

13 Harm can refer to many types of injury, from minor loss of a material object to death. Harm is used here in a generic sense to make a general argument, although implicitly certain significant categories are held in mind. In practice only certain categories of harm would be deemed absolutely wrong. This may lead into ontological difficulties and certainly does so if extended to non-humans.

14 There is no pretence here to provide a comprehensive coverage of issues surrounding rights and their classification, and indeed the treatment here is only superficial. The aim is limited to showing the relevance of rights-based thinking for addressing the enhanced Greenhouse Effect. The text is mainly concerned with claim-rights which have correlative duties without precluding the existence of other rights and rights without duties, or duties without rights. The interested reader is referred to Jones (1994).

15 This is similar to the US Clean Air Act where in 2001 the Supreme Court ruled (in response to challenges by industry) against the weighing-up of costs and benefits in setting air quality standards.

16 The intergenerational context putting this into practice would prove difficult because the polluters are long since departed. This has already proven problematic for cleaning up chemical and industrial waste from the past where firms have sold their polluted lands and/or been liquidated.

17 The distinction of prima facie duties is due to Ross (1930). He calls upon an 'objective fact' about acts, i.e., the characteristic which an act has, in virtue, of being 'an act which would be a duty proper if it were not at the same time of another kind which is morally significant'. He outlines seven categories of prima facie duty: fidelity, reparation, gratitude, justice, beneficence, self-improvement and non-maleficence.

18 I am grateful to Alan Holland for increasing my understanding of several aspects of rights philosophy. In particular some of the points presented here are based upon his input to a workshop held in Zurich, Switzerland under the EC-funded concerted action on Environmental Valuation in Europe (EVE) in 1999. As Alan stated at that time, he has no strong views about the rights position, but his exposition was most enlightening. Of course what is written here is my sole responsibility.

19 This can be clearly identified in the discussion of optimal extinction rates which are accepted as economically rational. Thus, the argument over biodiversity is about what to destroy and when, rather than conservation or preservation. A prime example of this approach is Swanson's *The International Regulation of Extinction* (London: Macmillan, 1994). In contrast the necessity of overriding economic preferences to achieve sustainability has been shown by Common and Perrings (1992).

20 Interestingly none of the rules will typically lead to a recommendation that welfare be continually increased over time, as economic growth recommends or as possible under weak sustainability (i.e., non-declining welfare). Such a rule makes the first generation the worst-off and each succeeding generation better-off than its immediate predecessors. Addiction to material consumption under neo-classical utilitarianism comes closest to providing an explanation, with greater consumption increasing marginal utility so that the more that is consumed by later generations the more value there is at the margin. However, the logic of an addictive allocation is to give all consumption to one generation to maximise utility.

21 For Lind (1995) the overall argument remains that current generations have no obligations if the future is better-off. This is again a failure to draw any distinction between compensation for harm and basic transfers aiming to achieve a certain standard of living. In particular, damages inflicted on a relatively wealthy person are to be regarded as less important because of that relative wealth.

References

Adams, R.M. (1989) 'Global climate change and agriculture: an economic perspective', *American Journal of Agricultural Economics* **71**: 1,272–9.

Arrow, K.J. (1973) 'Rawls's principle of just saving', *Swedish Journal of Economics* **75**: 323–35.

Barry, B. (1983) 'Intergenerational justice in energy policy', in *Energy and the Future*, edited by D. MacLean and P.G. Brown, pp. 15–30, Totowa, NJ: Rowman and Littlefield.

Batie, S.S. and H.H. Shugart (1989) 'The biological consequences of climate changes: an ecological and economic assessment', in *Greenhouse Warming: Abatement and Adaptation*, edited by N.J. Rosenberg, W.E. Easterling, P.R. Crosson and J. Darmstadter, pp. 121–31, Washington DC: Resources for the Future.

Bentham, J. (1843) 'The psychology of economic man', in *The Economic Writings of Jeremy Bentham* **3**, edited by W. Stark, pp. 421–50, London: Allen and Unwin.

Binmore, K. (1989) 'Social Contract I: Harsanyi and Rawls', *Economic Journal* **99**(395): 84–102.

Brittan, S. (2000) 'Men behaving badly', *Prospect* **January**: 60–1.

Broome, J. (1992) *Counting the Cost of Global Warming*. Cambridge, England: White Horse Press.

Common, M. and C. Perrings (1992) 'Towards an ecological economics of sustainability', *Ecological Economics* **6**: 7–34.

Crosson, P.R. (1989) 'Climate change: problems of limits and policy responses', in *Greenhouse Warming: Abatement and Adaptation*, edited by N.J. Rosenberg, W.E. Easterling, P.R. Crosson and J. Darmstadter, pp. 69–82, Washington DC: Resources for the Future.

Crowards, T. (1997) 'Discounting and sustainable development: adjusting the rate, abandoning the process, or extending the approach', *International Journal of Sustainable Development* **4**: 28–39.

Culyer, A. (1973) *The Economics of Social Policy*. New York: Dunellen Company.

d'Arge, R.C. (1989) 'Ethical and economic systems for managing the global commons', in *Changing the Global Environment: Perspectives on Human Involvement*, edited by D.B. Botkin, M.F. Caswell, J.E. Estes and A.A. Orio, pp. 325–38, Orlando: Academic Press.

Eckersley, R. (1998) 'Environment rights and democracy', in *Political Ecology: Global and Local*, edited by R. Keil, D.V.J. Bell, P. Penz and L. Fawcett, pp. 353–76, London: Routledge.

Freeman, A.M. (1986) 'The ethical basis of the economic view of the environment', in *People, Penguins and Plastic Trees: Basic Issues in Environmental Ethics*, edited by D. van der Veer and C. Pierce, pp. 218–27, Belmont, CA: Wadsworth Publishing Company.

Glover, J. (1999) *Humanity: A Moral History of the 20th Century*. New Haven and London: Yale University Press.

Hasselmann, K. (1999) 'Intertemporal accounting of climate change: harmonizing economic efficiency and climate stewardship', *Climate Change* **41**: 333–50.

Howarth, R.B. (1996) 'Discount rates and sustainable development', *Ecological Modelling* **92**: 263–70.

Jones, P. (1994) *Rights*. Basingstoke: The Macmillan Press Ltd.

Jung, C.G. (1989) *Memories, Dreams, Reflections*. New York: Vintage Books.

Kagan, S. (1998) *Normative Ethics*. Boulder CO: Westview Press.

Kneese, A.V., S. Ben-David, D.S. Brookshire, W.D. Schulze and D. Boldt (1983) 'Economic issues in the legacy problem', in *Equity Issues in Radioactive Waste Management*, edited by R.E. Kasperson, pp. 203–26, Cambridge, MA: Oelgeschlager.

Kneese, A.V., S. Ben-David and W.D. Schulze (1983) 'The ethical foundations of benefit–cost analysis', in *Energy and the Future*, edited by D. MacLean and P.G. Brown, pp. 59–74, Totowa, NJ: Rowman and Littlefield.

Kneese, A.V. and W.D. Schulze (1985) 'Ethics and environmental economics', in *Handbook of Natural Resource and Energy Economics* **I**, edited by A.V. Kneese and J.L. Sweeney, pp. 191–220, Amsterdam, The Netherlands: Elsevier.

Lagerspetz, E. (1999) 'Rationality and politics in long-term decisions', *Biodiversity and Conservation* **8**: 149–64.

Lind, R.C. (1995) 'Intergenerational equity, discounting, and the role of cost–benefit analysis in evaluating global climate policy', *Energy Policy* **23**(45): 379–89.

Lumer, C. (2000) *The Greenhouse: A Welfare Assessment and Some Morals*. Osnabruck: University of Osnabruck.

Marini, G. and P. Scaramozzino (2000) 'Social time preference', *Population Economics* **13**: 639–45.

Marland, G., T.A. Boden and R.J. Andres (2001) Global, Regional, and National CO_2 Emissions. *Trends: A Compendium of Data on Global Change*. Oak Ridge, TN: Oak Ridge National Laboratory, Carbon Dioxide Information Analysis Center, US Department of Energy.

Mishan, E.J. (1971) 'Pangloss on pollution', in *The Economics of Environment*, edited by P. Bohm and A.V. Kneese, pp. 66–73, London: Macmillan.

Mishan, E.J. (1981) *Introduction to Normative Economics*. Oxford, England: Oxford University Press.

Mishan, E.J. and T. Page (1982) 'The methodology of benefit–cost analysis with particular reference to the CFC problem', in *The Economics of Managing Chlorofluorocarbons: Stratospheric Ozone and Climate Issues*, edited by J.H. Cumberland, J.R. Hibbs and I. Hoch, pp. 114–56, Washington, DC: Resources for the Future.

Nash, R.F. (1989) *The Rights of Nature: A History of Environmental Ethics*. Madison, WI: University of Wisconsin Press.

Neumayer, E. (1999) 'Global warming: discounting is not the issue, but sustainability is', *Energy Policy* **27**: 33–43.

O'Neill, J. (1993) *Ecology, Policy and Politics: Human Well-Being and the Natural World*. London: Routledge.

O'Neill, J. (2001) 'Representation', *Environment and Planning C: Government and Policy* **19**(4): 483–500.

Page, E. (1999) 'Global warming and the non-identity problem', in *Self and Future Generations: An Intercultural Conversation*, edited by T.-C. Kim and R. Harrison, pp. 107–30 Cambridge, England: White Horse Press.

Page, R. (1982) 'A Kantian perspective on the social rate of discount', in *Coal Models and their use in Government Planning*, edited by J. Quirk, K. Terasawa and D. Whipple, pp. 139–57, New York: Praeger.

Page, T. (1983) 'Intergenerational justice as opportunity', in *Energy and the Future*, edited by D. Maclean and P.G. Brown, pp. 33–58, Totowa, NJ: Rowman and Allanheld.

Page, T. (1988) 'Intergenerational equity and the social rate of discount', in *Environmental Resources and Applied Welfare Economics*, edited by V.K. Smith, pp. 71–89, Washington, DC: Resources for the Future.

Pearce, D. (1983) 'Ethics, irreversibility, future generations and the social rate of discount', *International Journal of Environmental Studies* **21**: 67–86.

Philbert, C. (1999) 'The economics of climate change and the theory of discounting', *Energy Policy* **27**: 913–27.

Ross, W.D. (1930) *The Right and the Good*. Oxford, England: Clarendon.

Schelling, T.C. (1995) 'Intergenerational discounting', *Energy Policy* **23**(4–5): 395–401.

Schelling, T.C. (2000) 'Intergenerational and international discounting', *Risk Analysis* **20**(6): 833–7.

Schulze, W.D. and D.S. Brookshire (1982) 'Intergenerational ethics and the depletion of fossil fuels', in *Coal Models and Their Use in Government Planning*, edited by J. Quirk, K. Terasawa and D. Whipple, pp. 159–78, New York: Praeger.

Schulze, W.D., D.S. Brookshire and T. Sandler (1981) 'The social rate of discount for nuclear waste storage: economics or ethics', *Natural Resources Journal* **21**(4): 811–32.

Sen, A.K. (1982) 'Approaches to the choice of discount rates for social benefit–cost analysis', in *Discounting for Time and Risk in Energy Policy*, edited by R.C. Lind, pp. 325–76, Washington, DC: Resources for the Future, Johns Hopkins Press.

Solow, R.M. (1974) 'Intergenerational equity and exhaustible resources', *Review of Economic Studies* **41**: 29–45.

Solow, R.M. (1986) 'On the intergenerational allocation of natural resources', *Scandinavian Journal of Economics* **88**(1): 141–9.

Solow, R.M. (1992) 'Sustainability: an economist's perspective', *National Geographic Research and Exploration* **8**(1): 3–9.

Solow, R.M. (1993) 'An almost practical step toward sustainability', *Resources Policy* (**September**): 162–71.

Spash, C.L. (1993) 'Economics, ethics, and long-term environmental damages', *Environmental Ethics* **15**(2): 117–32.

Spash, C.L. (1994a) 'Double CO_2 and beyond: benefits, costs and compensation', *Ecological Economics* **10**(1): 27–36.

Spash, C.L. (1994b) 'Trying to find the right approach to greenhouse economics: some reflections upon the role of cost–benefit analysis', *Analyse und Kritik: Zeitschrift für Sozialwissenschafen* **16**(2): 186–99.

Spash, C.L. (2000) 'Ecosystems, contingent valuation and ethics: the case of wetlands re-creation', *Ecological Economics* **34**(2): 195–215.

Spash, C.L. and R.C. d'Arge (1989) 'The greenhouse effect and intergenerational transfers', *Energy Policy* (**April**): 88–95.

Wade-Benzoni, K.A. (1999) 'Thinking about the future', *American Behavioural Scientist* **42**(8): 1,393–405.

World Commission on Environment and Development (1991) *Our Common Future*. Oxford, England: Oxford University Press.

10 Science, economics and policy

The clear message from studying the science of the enhanced Greenhouse Effect is that a substantial change in atmospheric chemistry is now taking place due to human activity. Human-induced climate change is a consequence of unintentionally playing around with global systems. Failure to take action speedily and to curtail emissions affecting the atmosphere has already committed the planet to climate forcing. That forcing has started to impact and will continue to do so affecting future generations.

Observations confirming human-induced climate change are becoming more prevalent. Examples of observed changes given by the IPCC Third Assessment include: shrinking of glaciers, thawing of permafrost, later freeing and earlier break-up of river and lake ice, lengthening of the mid- to high-latitude growing seasons, poleward and altitudinal shifts of plant and animal ranges, declines in some plant and animal populations, earlier flowering of trees, earlier insect emergence and earlier egg-laying by birds (IPCC Working Group II, 2001: 3). This wide range of impacts is merely indicative of the complexity and scale of the problem. Where identifiable climatic factors are limiting specific processes (e.g. economic production, ecosystem function) clear advantages and disadvantages may be specified (e.g. in arid regions, low-lying areas). However, determining in any detail who will lose and who will gain is an impossible task open to speculation. What remains clear is that the longer action is delayed in terms of reducing atmospheric concentrations the more substantial and dramatic will be the results. Yet, despite the consensual scientific support for action, no control of climate forcing is planned.

As far as the Kyoto Protocol is concerned, even without the USA dropping their commitment, the emissions reductions proposed are too small to prevent increasing atmospheric concentrations of GHGs and effectively signal that the international community (as represented by political and legal negotiators) prefers to wait and take what comes. Contrary to media interpretation there is no control of the enhanced Greenhouse Effect on the current agenda. The Kyoto Protocol is seen as a first step of a long process by those who regard emissions control as necessary and international negotiation as the only route to that control. On this basis the planet will be committed to a considerable amount of global climate change due to the enhanced Greenhouse Effect before proposals for serious action even reach the negotiating table. There is then little surprise that the new language, as exemplified by the IPCC, is of mitigation and adaptation rather than control and prevention.

That a major threat to human activity can be so easily put to one side raises several questions over the conduct of research and the role of scientific information. The oft-referred to dichotomy between facts and values seems far more blurred than statements relying upon these philosophical concepts might lead us to believe. Yet trying to separate science from society and economics from politics remains an active endeavour. A short journey through the pages of IPCC reports helps show some of the problems and resulting confusion. The desire to be part of an objective truth-seeking scientific methodology extends uneasily into social and behavioural research where values are disputed more explicitly and multiple perspectives essential to understanding. Hence economics finds itself trying to describe human decision-making in a rigid model of rationality where value conflict is reduced to risk-taking and trade-off. The study of economics in association with environmental policy leads to serious concerns over that approach and the extent to which key concepts, such as ethics, uncertainty and choice, are even understood.

This concluding chapter brings together some of the general points raised by these issues. No comprehensive summary or overview is offered of all the specific arguments which have been covered in other chapters. Instead the aim is to reflect upon some of the implications arising from the preceding analysis for economic inquiry and more generally the conduct of science and policy in the context of the enhanced Greenhouse Effect. A broad concern is the basis upon which knowledge is gathered, legitimised and employed to justify or deny the necessity of environmental policy. The following sections therefore cover the role of scientific information in relation to economic and political power; how economic theory has been characterising and reinforcing a specific and narrow view of decision-making; the way in which this approach has affected the policy process as evidenced by IPCC reports; and the need for changing the approach being taken to the study of economics both in terms of uncertainty and in relation to value theory. Examples from the IPCC Second and Third Assessment Reports (SAR and TAR) are used to help illustrate key points and highlight areas of controversy.

Science and political economy

The discovery, interpretation and acceptance of scientific 'facts' seems strongly connected to beliefs about economic and political 'reality'. Identifying the need for substantial reductions in a range of emissions common within modern industrial economies is an uncomfortable exercise because this also brings into question the scientific method which helped design that economy and supply those technologies. There is a distinct resistance to accepting constraints on economic activity. Like an addicted gambler trying to win back losses, the possibility of more and faster innovation is offered to supply the 'techno-fix'. Specific ideologically bounded solutions (e.g. technically advanced, end of pipe) described as the best available technology are meant to also be the best option. At the extreme, geo-engineering offers the promise of total human control of global systems. Under the TAR this is seriously discussed in terms of 'engineering the earth's climate system by large-scale manipulation of the global energy balance' (Kauppi *et al.*, 2001: 333). Some qualifications are given such as concerns over unexpected environmental consequences, ethics and legal implications, and the treatment of symptoms rather than causes. Such approaches are supported on the basis of a particular world view of human interaction with Nature. Yet the scientists with engineering 'solutions' fail to address the implicit values they employ and the need for open debate to question the boundaries being drawn around knowledge. The political economy of that knowledge is then highly relevant. Research on the enhanced Greenhouse Effect must operate in a world of competing perspectives and power blocks disputing the unknown outcomes resulting from pushing ecological systems beyond their limits.

The ideal of a value-free perspective on the enhanced Greenhouse Effect remains encapsulated in the international approach. Scientific discovery and the resulting delivery of information (e.g. IPCC reports) are largely presented as 'objective' processes so that 'decision-makers' can receive neutral (i.e. value-free) information. The idea of consensus in reporting information also then flows from this concept of truth which is revealed by investigation. This neglects the importance of different cultures and value systems in the development and implementation of research agendas, why specific approaches are adopted (e.g. atmospheric modelling with super computers) to the exclusion of others and the emphasis given to different aspects of knowledge in the presentation of findings (e.g. chemistry versus ecology, equilibrium versus extreme events). Extending the objective and consensual approach to socio-economic research creates even more problems because of the importance of different perspectives in creating understanding. Thus, an apparent consensus upon future economic impacts is bought at the cost of removing alternative values and viewpoints. Yet economics has joined in the scientific methodology in trying to reduce decision-making down to a single analytical process and in supplying single numbers meant to represent changes in global economic and environmental systems.

Thus the enhanced Greenhouse Effect raises questions over the role of science in society and how scientific research is employed in policy. The thrust of the scientific case for substantive control of GHGs appears no more nor less convincing than in the late 1980s, although the research since then may serve a variety of other purposes.

Certainly much detail has been added by the voluminous IPCC reports, and other scientific research programmes, and scientists themselves appear to be more self-assured on the topic. Some may argue the imminent arrival of new reports keeps the political process rolling. However, that global average temperatures have continued to rise has been of far greater political importance. Local evidence and signs of climatic warming and the occurrence of extreme weather events also prove more convincing for the general public and politicians, few of whom are likely to ever open an IPCC executive summary let alone lift a full IPCC report from the shelf. That short-term local observation is an unreliable predictor and climate is not expected to uniformly become warmer are typical points which research has failed to communicate. Public and media consciousness tends to remain disconnected from scientific understanding. Indeed the process of scientific discovery, with respect to the enhanced Greenhouse Effect, seems to have resulted in little actual change in the conduct of society as confirmed by 'business as usual' with the expectation of the need to adapt to whatever comes.

The idea of adaptation is to see what happens and then respond. Adaptation is the risk-taking strategy in terms of weak uncertainty. The arguments for adaptation as a preferred policy option rely upon bounding the decision problem in a specific way. This assumes human and natural systems are robust enough to adapt and are able to respond ex post. Little confidence can be placed in that ability given the lack of analysis of, and belated attention to, rates of climate change and extreme events. Those now being born will live in a world where GHGs have been increased enough to commit the planet to substantial climate change and where average temperatures have risen well beyond those of the last 10,000 years (i.e. 2°C higher) and will continue to rise. This places great faith in technology and neglects impacts on unmanaged systems.

Faith in technology is strongly linked to 'business as usual' in modern industrial economic systems. While there are a range of important GHGs the currently most important are directly linked to fossil-fuel-intensive production and consumption. Much of the attention has then been focused upon CO_2 alone, which is responsible for just over half the current climate forcing.[1] This means large industrial concerns within society have strong vested interests in preventing controls which would reduce their sales, profits, market share and political power. For example, US business has been cited as spending up to $100 million in the late 1990s to fight the Kyoto Protocol (Grubb, Vrolijk and Brack, 1999: 112). Oil and gas suppliers were also large financial backers of the Bush campaign with the return being an anti-Kyoto declaration as one of the first acts of the new president. In this light BP Amoco's admission of the existence of the enhanced Greenhouse Effect proved a dramatic change in position from other oil companies and was politically important. As Rowlands (2000) has shown, by comparing BP Amoco with Exxon, explanatory factors include company interests, management structure and nationality.

Table 10.1 Top twenty CO$_2$ emissions by country

	Total CO$_2$ (metric tons 000s)	World proportion (percentage)	Per capita (metric tons)
USA	1,486,801	23.8	5.43
China (mainland)	848,266	13.6	0.68
Russian Federation	391,535	6.3	2.66
Japan	309,353	5.0	2.45
India	289,587	4.6	0.29
Germany	225,208	3.6	2.75
United Kingdom	148,011	2.4	2.51
Canada	127,517	2.0	4.17
Italy	113,238	1.8	1.97
Mexico	102,072	1.6	1.07
France	100,951	1.6	1.72
Republic of Korea	99,260	1.6	2.64
Ukraine	96,510	1.5	1.90
South Africa	93,808	1.5	2.38
Australia	90,470	1.4	4.88
Poland	87,807	1.4	2.27
Brazil	81,758	1.3	0.49
Iran	79,119	1.3	1.20
Saudi Arabia	77,237	1.2	3.83
Spain	67,468	1.1	1.70
All twenty	4,915,976	78.7	2.35
World	6,243,592	100.0	1.13

Source: Marland, Boden and Andres (2001).

Countries are also divided by their own narrow interests which then affect their treatment of evidence which supports the necessity of controlling GHGs. Table 10.1 shows the top 20 CO$_2$-emitting countries (Marland, Boden and Andres, 2001). The USA heads the league due to high per capita consumption levels. China, with 10 per cent less emissions, comes second but, as with India, large populations drive total emissions levels. Among the second ranking of emitters are the industrialised economies of Russia, Germany, Japan and the UK. The nations most strongly opposing controls at present are the high per capita emissions countries of the USA, Canada and Australia. For such countries the energy-intensive lifestyles of their citizens are directly implicated, but also seen as an individual choice which is sacrosanct.

The potential for controlling emissions by changing behaviour is large, but unpalatable in Western-style market democracies where 'choice' is the mantra. For example, research by the Fraunhofer Institute shows energy conscious behaviour could dramatically reduce German CO$_2$ emissions (*Cordis*, 13 August 2001). In business and trade sectors emissions could be halved by cuts of 23 million tons, while households could further reduce emissions by 61 million tons, about a third for that sector. Similar findings have been cited in IPCC reports. The TAR states:

> Engineering studies suggest 20 to 25 per cent of existing carbon emissions could be eliminated (depending upon how the electricity is generated) at low cost if people switched to new technologies, such as compact fluorescent light bulbs, improved thermal insulation, heating and cooling systems, and energy-efficient appliances.
>
> (Markandya *et al.*, 2001: 474)

Further changes could be made if individual and group behaviour were seen in context and as requiring change. Indeed this is recognised within the TAR by IPCC Working Group III (2001: 46):

> *Current lifestyles, behaviours, and consumption patterns* have developed within current and historical socio-cultural contexts. Changes in behaviour and lifestyles may result from a number of intertwined processes, such as:
>
> • scientific, technological, and economic developments;
> • developments in dominant world views and public discourse;
> • changes in the relationship among institutions, political alliances, or actor networks;
> • changes in social structures or relationships within firms and households; and
> • changes in psychological motivation (e.g. convenience, social prestige, career, etc.).

Individual agents can therefore take substantive independent action but are also locked in to certain types of behaviour by social, psychological and institutional factors. The role of economic incentives and markets is then also limited and the IPCC has used the language of 'barriers' to describe such factors. This language is also criticised within the TAR as 'an impediment to finding socially viable solutions' (Sathaye *et al.*, 2001: 367), and there is indeed a need for conceiving of behaviour within a social context and as a process, rather than merely constrained utility maximisation based upon well-formed and fully informed preferences which are easily aggregated. Indeed energy efficiency programmes show people neither cost minimise nor operate according to welfare maximisation (Sathaye *et al.*, 2001: 367). However, emphasis has been placed upon reaching international agreements which require that all countries divide up responsibility and design complex reduction procedures prior to even addressing any of these issues. The processes have been summarised in the TAR as following three phases: the formation of

Table 10.2 CO_2 emissions by region, 1998

	Per capita (metric tons)	Total CO_2 (metric tons 000s)	World proportion (percentage)
North America	5.30	1,614,318	25.9
Germany	2.75	225,208	3.6
Oceania/Australasia	2.64	410,937	6.6
Eastern Europe	2.05	790,337	12.7
Western Europe	1.99	662,287	10.6
Middle East	1.48	338,858	5.4
Central and South America	0.73	365,419	5.9
Centrally Planned Asia	0.68	924,062	14.8
Far East	0.38	688,802	11.0
Africa	0.30	223,364	3.6
World	1.13	6,243,592	100.0

Source: Marland, Boden and Andres (2001).

national preferences and policy positions for international negotiation; the translation of national preferences into international collective action; and the implementation of international agreements at the national level (Toth *et al.*, 2001: 631). This perpetuates the myth that preferences are the basis for action and that the enhanced Greenhouse Effect must be treated as a technical matter for 'experts' and top-down international negotiation.

The top-down process has been slow to recognise the ethics and justice perspectives. Drawing the link between who will bear the brunt of climate change and who is historically culpable leads to the realisation of distinct asymmetries as a central issue. As has been made clear in earlier chapters the poor, both as nation states and within nations, will be most likely to suffer due to their inability to adapt and their lack of spare resource capacity. On a per capita and total percentage basis table 10.2 shows that North America is the region contributing the most to the enhanced Greenhouse Effect via CO_2 emissions, and this is because of high material consumption levels, cheap fossil fuel pricing policies and inefficient energy use. European nations come second, although they only have about half the per capita emissions levels. Japan and Australia combine to bring Oceania/Australasia up to the second rank. At the opposite end of the scale is Africa with low per capita and total emissions levels. The poorest in that society and in the Far East, Asia and Central and South America seem set to suffer the most while being the least responsible. As Grubb (1995: 465) has stated:

in climate change, the core issues of how to share out responsibility for coping with the impacts, and for keeping global greenhouse emissions within tolerable limits, raise problems that relate to the nature and ethical basis of international and political relationships in the next century, in ways that have never before been faced.

Yet the economic debate on the subject takes a particularly restricted view of these issues. Traditional economic appraisal prefers to avoid explicitly addressing ethical concerns and would rather emphasise the costs of end-of-pipe approaches to pollution control and the risk of taking decisions without 'full information'.[2] In the latter regard, Smith *et al.* (2001: 945) in the IPCC TAR describe the timing of the 'resolution of key uncertainties' as 'critical' while noting that international economic modellers have assumed the resolution of all uncertainty can be realistically expected by 2020. This position implies decisions are only problematic because of a lack of information and once this has been rectified optimal choices will be straightforward. Indeed: 'The analysis shows the optimal hedging strategy when uncertainty is not resolved until 2020' (Toth *et al.*, 2001: 611). That such assumptions are given serious attention raises questions as to exactly how economists draw boundaries around their understanding of the world.

Choices and decisions

The standard economic approach to decision theory is more than a matter of theoretical interest and has, for example, appeared prominently in IPCC reports. Economic 'choice' theory, operating under weak uncertainty, assumes strict comparability of values and that all outcomes are expressed in the same units, normally money. Under this approach, the mythical 'decision-maker' uses the monetary value of final outcomes as a substitute measure of their utility which allows their preferences to be ranked and the most 'valuable' option (in utility terms) to be chosen (Arrow *et al.*, 1996: 63). The 'decision-maker' is assumed to be completely informed about all possible options and consequences. Clearly the preceding chapters have shown this will never be the case for human-induced climate change and the idea of making 'a decision' is a complex matter of political economy involving different socio-economic groupings across space and time. Even those who still have faith in standard risk analysis accept the relevance of a wider political economy. Thus Schneider (1989: 219) states that:

> Regardless of the real risk or benefit of an energy system, or even the best calculated values of risks or benefits, it is the public's perception of these that will determine the political acceptability of an energy option. It is thus imperative that the public and its leaders be familiar with the basics of risk analysis and the issues of fact and value are as clearly and distinctly stated as possible.

This raises issues of how disputed fact-value dichotomies are meant to be addressed in public forums. More generally the question arises of how to deal with conflicts and derive policy.

The economic model is based upon a single agent, the 'decision-maker', and the expansion of this concept to larger groups requires the existence of an aggregate social welfare function, which in the case of the enhanced Greenhouse Effect would be global. Arrow (1951) has denied the existence of such an aggregate preference function without breaking what he regards as basic rules (e.g. avoiding dictatorship). Yet if such a function could exist (and there are suggestions as to how this might be so), the method of construction remains unclear. That is, there are numerous possible ways in which an aggregate function might be constructed, so affecting the outcome.

In practice, social decisions are commonly made by imposing institutional or expert sovereignty, often without public conflict (Cantor and Yohe, 1998). However, such dictatorship is in principle against the ideal of democracy. Collective decisions are also made without either dictatorship or the atomistic-reductionism which centres on the individual. For example, social norms can operate in a way which diverges from the individualistic model of mainstream economics. That is, shared values exist as part of the individual but are irreducible to an individual. Thus, rather than Arrow's world of individualistic preferences, an alternative is inherently relational preferences which are expressions of solidarity (Rayner and Malone, 1998: 6). This changes the problem from one of aggregating individual preferences to decomposing communal values in order to discern social structure.

The standard economic model also assumes all outcomes can be expressed as commensurable values. That is, consequences are measurable in common units which allow them to be compared with each other. This leads to contentious issues such as comparing the value of human life lost due to climate change with consumer items or money or other lives. Those who argue there are great net gains to be made from climate change, by exploiting the opportunities, also assume sweeping comparability. Thus economic 'winners' are described as being those selling services and technologies needed to remedy or mitigate adverse impacts due to climate change, e.g. new pollution control sectors offering employment. That economic growth may be boosted by disasters and enrich some sections of society has little to do with gains in terms of human well-being (e.g. oil spills, wars and military rearmament also appear 'good' in the same way). Measuring changes in quality of life and well-being across diverse cultures is far from adequately addressed by imposing a single numeraire, such as economic throughput.

Divergent values amongst multiple 'decision-makers' mean that quantification becomes meaningless (Arrow *et al.*, 1996: 64). This was noted as follows in a workshop organised by NCAR and the UNEP (see Glantz, Price and Krenz, 1990):

The lack of comparable ethical systems among and within countries will prevent consistent and acceptable application of the methods and criteria and consequently prevent consistent and acceptable assessment of gains and losses or winners and losers. The final perceptions of themselves based on their value systems will determine whether groups see themselves as winners or losers.

If this is so, the cultural relativism of perceptions seems highly relevant in the current period of speculation over possible impacts, so affecting the urgency given to GHG emissions control. Certainly whether and how value systems include strong sympathy for neighbours or future generations will lead to wide variations in assessment. However, this conceptualisation of net losses or gains as being a matter of perception requires some qualification. The occurrence of dramatic climatic impacts will soon start to clarify winners and losers, and can be expected to lead to crisis management. Extreme physical impacts can be expected to override merely perceptual differences. In addition, obligations to others distant in culture, space and time can be based on universal values. As discussed in chapter 9, inviolable rights are advocated by the UN itself in the Charter on Human Rights, and such rights can be recognised with respect to future generations. The challenge is in getting acceptance that these are categorically different values from those in standard economic models and that they are highly relevant to the enhanced Greenhouse Effect. The intergenerational asymmetry of costs and benefits raises questions over respecting the interests of those as yet unborn, and questions how economics treats time. The interregional impacts appear clearly to be worst for the poor and less industrially developed economies, which raises questions of equity and fairness, as well as the divergence of those people's world view from that of the dominant governments amongst the industrially developed countries.

Even when recognising such problems the general economic model of decision analysis and choice is still applied to climate change and has, for example, formed a central focus of economic work by the IPCC, which has been at pains to justify CBA in particular (Bruce, Hoesung and Haites, 1996). There seems little fundamental change in this position in the TAR of 2001 although more space is given to alternative ways of formulating the problem and CBA is more heavily qualified than before.[3] Morita *et al.* (2001: 160) include in their recommendations for future research: 'Explicit cost–benefit analysis of the impacts of timing and burden sharing on mitigation costs and targets'. Markandya *et al.* (2001: 486) give support for estimating 'the social value of biodiversity and culture' via the use of contingent valuation with the caveat that this lacks 'market discipline'. Such monetary valuation is described as provision of hard evidence.

It is suggested that hard evidence is needed to prove that the biological and cultural preservation benefits dominate those from development. It is then logical to compare the costs and benefits when resources are scarce, and an attempt should be made to balance the costs and benefits so that funds are allocated to their highest valued use.

(Markandya *et al.*, 2001: 486)

However, this same IPCC chapter is rather a tortured struggle between strongly pro-CBA economists and those who see alternative viewpoints as valuable and desire a broader approach. For example, the standard approach of economics regarding willingness to pay (WTP) and willingness to accept (WTA) is followed by this statement:

The above analysis of welfare focuses on the narrowly economic dimension. Even within this framework there are complexities that make a full assessment difficult. In addition, however issues of DES {development, equity and sustainability} need to be taken into account.[1]

(Markandya *et al.*, 2001: 460)

This statement has a footnote which reads as follows: '1. Other issues that may need to be considered include incomplete information, perceptual biases, and learning'. This footnote appears as if it were a reply to the paragraph and wishes to limit any interpretation of 'other factors'. There is then a statement noting that 'the authors' believe in converting other dimensions into monetary values; this is presumably to clarify in case the reader was getting confused. In the same paragraph a single reference from 1984 is given with regard to those disputing the validity of CBA, but a footnote then qualifies this omission by noting: 'Indeed, many of the comments on earlier drafts of this chapter took different positions on this issue'. Thus, statements of a neo-classical economic nature are followed by qualifications and counterstatements, and then these are in turn countered by another standard economic argument. However, the executive summary largely ignores all but the standard economic viewpoints.

That disputes over the narrowness of the economic approach fail to get into the executive summaries seems to evidence the same basic position as under SAR. That is, a belief that the economic approach provides 'a valuable framework for identifying the essential questions that policymakers must face when dealing with climate change' and that standard economic analysis 'forces decision makers to compare the consequences of alternative actions … on a quantitative basis' (Munasinghe *et al.*, 1996: 149). Yet this argument sees the process as the main advantage rather than the outcome, i.e. the numbers may be meaningless but thinking about adding up the consequences is meant to be useful. If indeed the process is central then economists (like scientists) need to pay far greater attention to the institutions within which they operate and with which they interact. A similar point does appear in the TAR if only in passing. When reflecting upon the limited nature of economic valuation Banuri *et al.* (2001: 81) state that 'some notions of cost incorporate behavioural, institutional, or cultural responses that can be missed by economic analyses'. The importance of institutions and their functioning is noted along with impacts on individual 'attitudes, values, or preferences' as well as relationships. Costs need not be a mere aggregation of individual measures but this opens rather than closes the problem space. Most CBA practitioners are producing numbers for government bureaucracies with the express purpose of simplifying the choices they face. That is, the CBA process is one in which the analyst learns about the complexity of the consequences of alternative actions, and actually excludes information in order to make the problem manageable. Policymakers have little or no involvement in this process, although they can commission new studies if the numbers prove 'unsatisfactory'.

An alternative process would be to expand upon the values being expressed but this would require a different model of policy formation. The main economists compiling the IPCC reports seem to have been extremely reluctant to take a more realistic approach. The IPCC's economic report under the second assessment, with an economic Nobel laureate as lead author, states: 'Decision analysis uses quantitative techniques to identify the "best" choice from among a range of alternatives' (Arrow *et al.*, 1996: 57). The authors go on to cite some of the problems with applying this analysis to 'the real world', namely: the lack of a single decision-maker means no universally preferred solution, quantitative comparison of decision options is meaningless for climate change due to the incomplete and inconsistent utility valuation of outcomes; and probabilities are unquantifiable. There is then a contradictory set of statements which tell us that on the one hand decision-makers cannot make rational choices without decision analysis, which is needed to prevent information from becoming 'cognitively unmanageable', and on the other hand decision analysis has such unrealistic assumptions as to make it useless for the climate change problem. The authors of this decision-making frameworks chapter of the IPCC SAR themselves note that:

> The treatment of uncertainty in decision analysis is quite powerful, but the probabilities of uncertain decision outcomes must be quantifiable. In climate change, objective probabilities have not been established for many outcomes, and subjective probabilities would be controversial, so climate change decisions cannot fully satisfy this requirement.
>
> (Arrow *et al.*, 1996: 57)

So, basically, this is a reluctant admission of strong uncertainty. Despite this the wish is to stay within the economic paradigm and the authors are at pains to protect the model. Indeed, as long as ignorance is only partial: 'It is inappropriate, therefore, to sacrifice the power of decision analysis to address uncertainty simply because some uncertainties are not quantifiable' (Arrow *et al.*, 1996: 65). The model is more important than the observed nature of the world. Thus, partial ignorance is reduced to weak uncertainty and 'the authors denote surprise scenarios as those where the true value of a parameter appears at least 2.6 standard deviations away from its current "best guess" value' (Arrow *et al.*, 1996: 67). Similar logic for avoiding strong uncertainty is found elsewhere in the SAR. For example, Banuri *et al.* (1996: 101) claim there is 'some idea of plausible outcomes and their relative probability', which they then take to 'increase the appropriateness of approaches based on subjective probabilities'.

Qualitative information on confidence levels in the SAR of Working Group II seems to have helped avoid the kind of disputes which arose over the quantitative assessments attempted by economists doing monetary valuation in Working Group III. However, under TAR the qualitative information relating to confidence ranges (e.g. very high confidence) are linked to probabilities (e.g. 95 per cent or greater) and so to a quantitative subjective risk approach. This gives a false sense of precision and reintroduces the idea that weak uncertainty is the only relevant concept. Elsewhere concepts relating to strong uncertainty arise but are once more reduced down to subjective (if troublesome) risk analysis (Banuri *et al.*, 2001: 79):

> Decision-analytic methods can still be applied, but the process of eliciting subjective probabilities is much more complicated. The experts must factor in assessments about the likelihood of each of the alternative theories being correct, on top of assessments of the probabilities for alternative parameter values within the methods suggested by that theory. In addition, the experts need to provide some estimate of the uncertainty in outcomes caused by factors not incorporated into any existing theory.

More blatantly contradictory and misleading passages relate to the work of Wynne, Funtowicz and Ravetz, and Westra in the chapter on decision-making frameworks. Key issues are stated paraphrasing these authors' work and highlighting uncertainty as being irreducible, and the importance of public discourse. However, this is then followed immediately by a paragraph stating that uncertainty can be reduced to risk. To quote the passages in full (Toth *et al.*, 2001: 619):

> The issue here is not the problem of a 'deterministic version of scientific uncertainty' – a temporary matter of imprecision which will be eradicated when

enough research has been devoted to the questions (Wynne, 1994). The starting point is the acknowledgement that uncertainty emerges not only from the long time-scales involved and/or the ability of models to predict long-term events, but mainly from endemic uncertainty, indeterminacy, and ignorance related to the co-evolution of natural and social systems. Furthermore these methods stress the relevance of values, ethical and social, and thus introduce the need for public discourse and debate (Westra, 1997).

A central concern in adaptive approaches is with the plurality of value systems and how multiple perspectives can inform the decision process. Various attempts have been made to incorporate a variety of perspectives in relation to uncertainty and to make uncertainty more explicit by expressing it in terms of risk.

Perhaps then unsurprisingly the executive summary fails to mention adaptive management, strong uncertainty or public participation but rather states the following:

> Finally, large uncertainties or in some areas even ignorance characterize many aspects of the problem and require a risk management approach to be adopted in all DMFs [decision-making frameworks] that deal with climate change.
>
> (Toth *et al.*, 2001: 603)

Typically there is some tension within such reports because claims of robustness appear but are countered by qualifications which in turn are ignored as models are applied or recommended regardless. Practical implications then arise due to overconfidence in the standard economic models due to the dismissal of qualifications and alternative viewpoints. For example, flaws in the operation of markets lead to a warning against 'over-reliance on insurance mechanisms' in the increasing dependence upon adaptation as the policy response to calls for GHG control (IPCC Working Group II, 2001: 8). In practical terms insurance markets have their limits, they are imperfect, they can collapse with insurers going bankrupt and claims being left unpaid, while the realisation of large disasters previously thought unlikely or ignored can suddenly lead to uninsurable risks. Yet the fire insurance analogy appears under Working Group III (Banuri *et al.*, 2001: 83–4) with the conclusion that: 'In any case, policies that help build or strengthen mitigation capacity are consistent with the insurance approach'. This is related to the belief that '... subjective probabilities can be utilized effectively when empirical data are not available or are inconclusive' (Banuri *et al.*, 2001: 84). The insurance industry itself is much more cautious, over its abilities to address global climate change, than theoretical economists. However, overall there is a reluctance to accept the paucity of standard economic models under such circumstances.

Clearly 'optimal choice' approaches are of limited use when addressing the enhanced Greenhouse Effect because the social commitments are large and partial ignorance and indeterminacy swamp the decision space. Yet, instead of addressing this head-on, the preference is for noting 'surprise' as a possibility and then making it a probability, or relegating the whole issue to the background. Houghton (1997: 165), the co-chairman of IPCC Working Group I, recognises that surprise events cannot be ruled out and that 'the risk posed by such possibilities is impossible to assess'. Unfortunately, rather than making the link between the 'possible impossible' and the concepts of partial ignorance and indeterminacy he uses the inappropriate insurance analogy borrowed from economists and states that 'although the possibility of surprises should not be ignored, neither should they feature as the main argument for action'. The standard economic analysis proves dominant but has done little to help focus on the actual nature of the problem.

Redefining economic inquiry

In fact the whole economic, and scientific, approach is brought into question by such complex and irreversible problems as the enhanced Greenhouse Effect. That is, repeated experimentation is not an option in order to test the models and hypotheses. For example, if the West Antarctic Ice Sheet melts and sea level rises several metres there is no second chance to try for lower emissions to see if this could have been avoided or to determine how probabilities of such a disaster vary with different emissions levels. Empiricism begins to reduce to scientific speculation and the judgement of the concerned citizen becomes as relevant as that of the specialist. As Wynne (1992: 127) states:

> We cannot, therefore, expect to leave the responsibility for defining the criteria of clean technology to environmental science and risk assessment, nor to any such technical disciplines alone. Nor can we even expect them objectively to discover the different risks and benefits, for policy institutions then to exercise societal values and choices. The natural knowledge which those disciplines generate is already partly a reflection of tacit dominant cultural values and identities, ones which may be part of the problem.

In terms of trying to understand complex environmental issues the acceptance of our ignorance is a necessary and positive step, but one which most scientists and politicians find impossible to express (at least in public). Hence the admission that objective probabilities are impossible to obtain is replaced by the call for subjective probabilities to be used and for a scientific or other elite to provide these speculative numbers so that the pretence of predictability can be maintained.

Rather than accepting our partial ignorance and avoiding stress on systems there is a tendency to explore the potential for systems collapse and react only after disaster strikes. This has been termed the rivet popper problem due to the following metaphor. An aeroplane has far more rivets in the wings than are necessary for safe flight and therefore some rivets can be removed without any adverse consequence. The repetition of this action produces the prediction that the rivets are unnecessary as empirical observation shows pulling them out leads to no adverse impacts and the plane flies as before. Empirical-based policy follows so that rivets are removed without concern. At some point one rivet too many is popped out of the wings and the plane crashes. New empirical evidence allows us to update our predictions but too late for the plane and its passengers. In the case of the enhanced Greenhouse Effect the scientific approach has been used to await the empirical evidence to confirm irreversible climatic change. This is despite the calls by scientists themselves for action without such evidence.

As this discussion implies, the approach of normal experimental science is of limited applicability to complex environmental problems. This has led to the suggestion that a revised approach to the role of scientific knowledge and its use in environmental policy is now required. Yet this is a problem which also lies at the heart of modern economics. The realm of weak uncertainty is the only one considered despite the fact that strong uncertainty surrounds us by the very nature of the way we try to understand the world. Economics fails to address the long term adequately because it fails to account for strong uncertainty and the significance events derive from their place in the passage of time. Long-term prediction, as if certain, is so blatantly misleading that economists sensibly retreat. Yet serious attention to partial ignorance and indeterminacy as a field of research would mean a different approach to economics which moves away from equilibrium theories and states, including dynamic states. In order to take account of time and ignorance a theory of process is necessary (Loasby, 1976: 220). Unfortunately, instead, equilibrium theory conceals ignorance and accentuates strong uncertainty.

Economics, like science, would progress by reclassifying theories into those addressing weak uncertainty and those addressing strong uncertainty. The latter may initially appear to be a largely empty set and, as a start, requires unifying the work of such authors as Keynes, Shackle and Loasby. Weak uncertainty, as explained in chapter 4, covers the standard approach of economics to the unknown. As in natural science, work in this area concentrates upon situations which we can accept as being well-defined. That is, a judgement is required as to whether such a definition is appropriate to a given situation. As discussed in chapter 5, Wynne has argued this acceptance depends upon the level at which the knowledge is intended to be used. For example, making incorrect assumptions in a laboratory experiment may result in temporary damage to the surroundings, doing the same with a nuclear reactor may result in Chernobyl and long-term global consequences. The level of social commitment to knowledge is therefore crucial in defining the relevance of weak versus strong uncertainty. Where weak uncertainty can operate the analyst will assume a set of relevant probabilities ('subjective' or 'objective').

The theories under the weak uncertainty branch of economics would require explicit understanding that their consequences depend upon their assumption. Rather than concentrating on formulating and refining the conditions under which generalisation can be made about economic factors achieving equilibrium, the concern must be for how far conditions can be violated without seriously affecting the results to which they lead. Unfortunately, information is far too readily used without any regard to the assumptions, context or meaning, e.g. monetary values and discount rates. Constrained maximisation is only of use in as far as the assumptions of the analyst, which defined the decision space, are in fact relevant. A clear distinction is required between the assumptions which form the basis of models and information used for practical analyses. Optimality, such as cost-effectiveness, is in fact consistency analysis and the best outcome is not guaranteed by the model, but only the choice that is consistent with the assumptions. Where economists are aware of the unreality of their assumptions any policy advice must be highly qualified. Instead the outcome is to concentrate and refine what we know, and restrict discussion to weak uncertainty. Another metaphor is as follows. A man loses his house keys while walking home across a field. He calls on his neighbours for help in the search, and then proceeds to start searching in their house. When they ask why he is searching here, when he lost the keys in the field, he responds 'because this is where there's light'.

The strong uncertainty approach requires analysis at the organisational and individual level to probe how partial ignorance and indeterminacy interact with decision-making. Here the need is for a reconsideration of the theory of choice used in economics which currently excludes the central concern of the subject which is choice, subject to ignorance and indeterminacy. Institutional analysis, behavioural economics, social psychology and theories based upon process are possible contributors to furthering research in this area.

Decision-making needs to be understood in terms of strong uncertainty. Thus, the process of searching for information might better be understood with behavioural models. Actors in the negotiations on climate change have been noted by Paterson (1996) to have been engaged in a process of developing their ideas as to what policy should be followed. This is in contrast to the models, such as game theory, which assume rational economic agents with preconceived goals and a need only to refine probability estimates. The whole negotiating process can instead be seen as one of generating new courses of action and revealing possible outcomes.

A range of decision strategies can be used to address strong uncertainty. For example, the rent-seeking characterisation of politicians, describing their only concern as being the next election, excludes decision-making under strong uncertainty where making short-term decisions is a reasonable response.[4] Such short-term decision-making has the perceived advantage of avoiding disruption to the stability of existing coalitions and allowing situations to be controlled by surrounding institutional structures. These can be bad strategies in a rapidly changing world where neglected information proves the most important, and radical and rapid reaction is required to prevent catastrophic irreversible events.

Institutional analysis can also prove insightful. Decision-makers exist within organisations designed to respond to specific kinds of information and will accept that information as it proceeds through control systems. Hence weak uncertainty with insurance analogies is discussed in preference to strong uncertainty or endogenous risk, and cost–benefit information is used although ethical values are the central issue. As Loasby (1976: 225) points out: 'The consequences of ignorance, notably the desire to limit ignorance, which show up in organisation and in industry, also affect both the type and content of decisions'.

Basing long-term plans or forecasts on present knowledge or past trends must be highly questionable. Plans must be adaptable taking into account the need to respond to often drastic changes. Investigating and preparing for the consequences of possible future events is often more useful than refining estimates of their probability. In the end the ways in which we deal with strong uncertainty must, by definition, be partial and incomplete. The aim must be to question how and why specific knowledge is bounded and to see problems from multiple perspectives rather than within narrow disciplinary confines.

Scientists and economists tend to ignore evidence which appears incompatible with accepted scientific and economic knowledge. Normal science operates in the short run. As Loasby (1976: 195) notes: 'In academic work as in business, long-run questions, even if no more intellectually taxing, are much less comfortable, because they tend to open up an unpalatable – and sometimes potentially infinite – range of options'. Thus, as in any analysis or decision, many potentially significant factors must be ignored, and institutional mechanisms exist to provide reassurance that the factors ignored are substantively unimportant. This is why the neo-classical economic paradigm is so comforting and weak uncertainty remains dominant. Paradigms restrict the agenda for enquiry, provide reassurance and highlight the need for faith. This faith or belief provides the framework within which logic and evidence then, and only then, can operate.

Preferences, value and time

A major area in which the boundaries drawn around economic knowledge appear most flawed is valuation. Disputes between economic co-authors are clear in the literature but the attempt of the IPCC for consensus tries to brush over all such problems. This clearly failed in the case of economic valuation and discounting as documented earlier (see chapters 6 and 7). In the IPCC SAR the most heated public debate occurred over the monetary valuation of life. As a result most chapters of the economic report of Working Group III, besides that presenting the offending numbers, included some disclaimer as to the value of a statistical life being problematic and/or an ethical issue beyond the scope of their current discussion. Grubb *et al.* (1999: 304) state that:

> The Policymakers Summary in this area was the most convoluted and awkward of all, and the most painfully disjointed from the underlying chapter; it is the only case in the history of the IPCC where authors sought formally to distance themselves from the governmentally negotiated Policymakers Summary.

The TAR chapter on costing methodologies mentions the value of life as having created 'much controversy in SAR' but gives no specifics or references, while suggesting an average value should be used to address 'equity' considerations (Markandya *et al.*, 2001: 483). Generally the type of monetary valuation studies which created controversy have been removed from the Working Group III report and make only a brief appearance in Working Group II in chapter 19 where they are heavily qualified and given low confidence. Unfortunately the value issues raised by the debate following the SAR gain little attention.

The range and type of values in society go well beyond the consequential and utilitarian preoccupation of standard economics. This was shown in chapter 9 with respect to the interests of future generations and how the intrinsic value of harm might be reflected in a rights-based approach. This means a set of values in society which cannot be reduced to welfarism and certainly bear no relation to monetary calculations. Other sets of such values can also be recognised. For example, as a CBA advocate, Freeman has considered the value of organisms which have no link with human consumption or production and concluded there is no basis for establishing an economic value. He goes on to state that:

> Rather than introduce some arbitrary or biased method for imputing a value to such organisms, I prefer to be honest about the limitations of the economic approach to determining values. This means we should acknowledge that certain ecological effects are not commensurable with economic effects measured in dollars. Where trade-offs between noncommensurable magnitudes are involved, choices must be made through the political system.
>
> (Freeman, 1986: 226)

Impacts on such organisms are expected as part of the enhanced Greenhouse Effect but rather than take them into account the tendency is to ignore them. This is in fact a general problem once economic calculus becomes dominant in social decision-making and political life, i.e. what cannot be squeezed into the figures is assumed irrelevant.

The need for an interdisciplinary approach is apparent because of the variety of values held in society, many of which are non-economic and incommensurable. For example the IPCC special report on impacts recognises both the value of goods and services provided by ecosystems and that: 'In addition, natural ecosystems have cultural, religious, aesthetic and intrinsic existence values' (Watson *et al.*, 1997: 2). Clarifying the impact of human activities upon these various values, as well as their content and meaning, goes far beyond standard economic approaches but cannot merely be relegated to an unspecified political system.

At the end of the day economic assessment must accept the role of social norms and fundamental ethical positions in defining how environmental problems are perceived and addressed in society. This means moving away from the pretence that a single dominant value concept can be universally applied or a single philosophy (i.e. preference utilitarianism) will suffice. The issues being grappled with in the context of the enhanced Greenhouse Effect involve contested social and moral values, and strong uncertainty, and must therefore be addressed using theories of political economy built upon explicit moral judgements.

Specific preferences over consumer goods are often whimsical judgements and, as marketing shows, preference-based choices can be manipulated by creating fashions and fads or appealing to social aspirations. Public concern over complex environmental problems are subject to strong uncertainty, and shrouded in a lack of basic understanding.[5] The role of preferences as an input to decision-making is then highly questionable. Social psychologists regard preferences as contextual and constructed although stable attitudes towards objects and issues can still exist (Spash, 2000: 457). The formation of a behavioural response with regard to a given issue is subject to a variety of influences including basic needs, ethical beliefs, social position and attitudes. Public decision-making is then better regarded as a process in which the construction and evolution of preferences takes place rather than an appeal being made to well-formed and well-informed public opinions. Thus, there is far more prescription than description with regard to the role of current and future preferences. As noted by IPCC Working Group III (2001: 46):

> In some situations policy development is based on a model of human psychology that has been widely criticized. People are assumed to be rational welfare-maximizers and to have a fixed set of values. Such a model does not explain processes, such as learning, habituation, value formation, or bounded rationality, observed in human choice.

This raises the concern as to why economists focus upon individual preferences, as opposed to moral judgements or social norms, to form the basis for decisions about the future. The appeal to empirical observation of human preferences has been criticised as a poor basis upon which to make social decisions (O'Neill, 1993). Preferences in the market place seem benign when choosing between different characteristics (e.g. flavour, colour, size) of a standard consumer item (e.g. an ice cream). However, the same approach is also taken to events of environmental degradation which have different time characteristics so that preferences determine which are regarded as unimportant and which close enough to deserve serious attention. This assumes that policy requires no more than observing individuals' tastes for impacts now or later, as if choosing the flavour of an ice cream. In contrast, both social and individual decisions often require reflection upon fundamental ethical beliefs and values held by various social groups to which we as individuals relate as to what is acceptable behaviour.

Amongst the questions over acceptable behaviour is the treatment of future people. Sen has compared the deliberate creation of pollution with torture and found welfarism equally poor at addressing both. In terms of the impacts of long-term pollution on future generations he states: 'Lasting pollution is a kind of calculable oppression of the future generation' (Sen, 1982: 346). He regards this as requiring supplementary non-welfarist analysis arising from considerations of liberty. This leads him to state, with regard to long-term pollution, that: 'The avoidance of oppression of future generations has to be given a value of its own'. This is similar to the position as found under rights-based thinking where harm has intrinsic value. There deliberate harm of the innocent is wrong regardless of the net welfare gains. Thus, deliberate creation of long-term damages as being contemplated under the enhanced Greenhouse Effect must be judged on grounds other than economic welfare.

The rephrasing of concerns over future generations as a moral debate can be contrasted with the economic approach which concentrates upon resource allocation. Rather than say 'equal' treatment (i.e. shares of welfare-generating consumption) the issue might be rephrased as 'fair' treatment. Diminishing fairness with distance in time appears objectionable compared to reducing the weight given to future consumption. This may be taken as indicative of the distinction between commodity discounting in economics and discounting well-being, which Broome (1994) believes has confused philosophers as to the content of the economic debate on the subject. However, as discussed in chapter 8, the two do indeed become confusingly intertwined in economic practice and the technically justified discount rate is applied to reduce the weight of future well-being. The philosophers are correctly worried by discounting.

In the TAR, following the argument of the SAR, discounting is stated to have an ethical and an empirical approach. However, discussion of the former is almost totally neglected. Without explanation a rate of 'around' 3 per cent is stated to follow from 'ethical considerations' (Markandya *et al.*, 2001: 467), but in any case this rate is never recommended and soon forgotten. There is some mention that rates which decline over time might be preferable to a constant rate. However, the supposed 'empirical' method is stated to provide the correct rate which is justified as follows (both in chapter 7 and the technical summary):

> For mitigation analysis, the country must base its decisions at least partly on discount rates that reflect the opportunity cost of capital. Rates that range from 4–6 per cent would probably be justified in developed countries. The rate could be 10–12 per cent or even higher in developing countries.
>
> (Markandya *et al.*, 2001: 455)

This raises a concern over the unequal treatment of future generations between nations with the implicit result that future damages in poor countries are less important than those in rich ones. In addition, the possibility of using private rates of return arises in order to assess the economic potential of a new technology (e.g. for mitigation): '... we would evaluate cost-effectiveness using market prices and the private rate of time discounting, and also take into account consumers' preferences regarding the acceptability of the technologies' performance characteristics' (Metz *et al.*, 2001: 45). Private rates for projects are noted to be in the order of 10 to 25 per cent (Metz *et al.*, 2001: 52). Little attention is given to any problems this might raise. Issues of intergenerational equity are noted with only one reference, and the following footnote:

> Although this issue received attention in the IPCC SAR (IPCC 1996), the discussion was framed in technical terms, namely the determination of the appropriate discount rate, which made little accommodation for philosophical, legal, and sociological perspectives on intergenerational rights and responsibilities.
>
> (Banuri *et al.*, 2001: 87)

Unfortunately there is little sign of progress in TAR which is presumably why this comment appears in a footnote. The policymakers summary for IPCC Working Group III (2001: 6) recommends a rate of 5–12 per cent as being in line with public sectors

The paucity and inconsistent treatment of issues concerning future generations, and ethics in general, is more surprising because of the supposed emphasis placed upon equity and sustainability. Working Group III summarises the major addition of SAR as being to address equity, while that of TAR is meant to be the addition of sustainability. Equity is noted to be a wide-ranging issue so that:

> Considerations of the national, intranational, industrial, and intergenerational distributions of the benefits and burdens of mitigation policies – as well as

considerations of the historical contributions to the accumulation of GHGs – are crucial to develop equitable climate policies.

(Banuri *et al.*, 2001: 84)

Yet when attention turns to decision-making frameworks 'ethical and cultural prescriptive rules' are given the following entry in a classification table: 'Primarily concerned with the implications of alternative social organizations. Has had limited application to climate problem' (Toth *et al.*, 2001: 611). Such rules are described as unable to address most of the characteristics of the enhanced Greenhouse Effect (i.e. global, long-term, pervasive human activity, uncertain, irreversible) whereas CBA, as a sub-category of decision analysis, is stated to address all these aspects. Decision analysis is further stated to have the 'ability to incorporate the full dimensionality of the climate problem explicitly' (Toth *et al.*, 2001), and as such appears prominently along with statements supporting the idea of the resolution of uncertainty. When discussing 'equity and costs' (Toth *et al.*, 2001: 668–73) a strange mixture of statements appears as to what equity might mean combined with a discussion of tradable permits, markets and income distribution. This includes the derision of matters of fairness with the following statements (Toth *et al.*, 2001: 668):

> Others find little evidence that fairness matters much … Even for cases in which fairness seems to play some role, willingness to pay had a stronger role … Fairness might be one criterion, but is probably not the most important.

This contrasts with the coverage of sustainable development and climate change (Toth *et al.*, 2001: 634–51) which is linked to lifestyle choices and technology transfers with a strong emphasis on the need for new decision frameworks which include cultural and social factors deemed irreducible to individual choices. Post-normal science is put forward and the need for participatory decision methods with citations to the work of Renn *et al.* (1993), O'Hara (1996), and van den Hove (2000).

> … extended peer community participation is essential to incorporate into the decision process both the plurality of different legitimate perspectives and the management of irreducible uncertainties in knowledge and ethics, …

(Toth *et al.*, 2001: 648)

> Decisions must be made about which of the systemic possibilities to promote and which to discourage, how to deal with uncertainties, and what risks to take considering irreversible changes and potential bifurication points. These decisions must be informed by science, but in the end they are an expression of human ethics and preferences, and of the socio-political context in which they are made (Kay *et al.*, 1999).

(Toth *et al.*, 2001: 649)

In this set of conflicting passages we find economists trying to distance themselves from what are supposedly the central issues (i.e. equity and sustainability) or at least reduce these to much narrower concepts.

Economics, equity and sustainability are difficult concepts to regard as leading to a scientific consensus and especially so when different methodologies and perspectives appear in direct opposition. Yet Banuri *et al.* (2001: 103) believe 'these three perspectives are complementary in nature, and can be helpful for the policymaker if used in conjunction' despite their producing conflicting goals. Economists persist in a perspective which excludes and downgrades the importance of other perspectives. For example, after recognising equity principles might be applied the following qualification is made:

> However, there is a strong bias towards the principle of efficiency and its underlying utilitarian maxim. Also, it is important to recognise that self-interest plays a crucial role in voting for a specific operation rule, and that self-interest or, alternatively, particular preferences are at the core of economic considerations. Closely related to the concept of preferences is willingness to pay ... Hence economics in terms of efficiency is a major aspect when negotiating emissions-limitation commitments.
>
> (Toth *et al.*, 2001: 670)

There are then diametrically opposed views that either equity can be dealt with separately or that equity is an integral part of the problem. This raises a question as to how such positions are meant to be equated to achieve a consensus report approach (the IPCC stated desire). The apparent practice is to note issues in the body of report chapters but to ignore them when producing executive summaries and to concentrate upon standard economic models of decision analysis. After all:

> In a rational world, the ultimate level of climate and thus GHG concentration stabilization would emerge from a political process in which the global community would weigh mitigation costs and averted damages associated with different levels of stabilization. Also weighed would be the risks of triggering systemic changes in large geophysical systems, like ocean circulation, or other irreversible impacts.
>
> (Toth *et al.*, 2001: 673)

That the world fails to conform to the model is to be lamented and so 'irrationality', as dealt with by non-economists, has to be given some room.

Such economic isolationism requires delegation to political scientists, philosophers or others of all responsibility for determining how to fairly treat those in both the past, present and future, but as a result any meaningful discussion of social well-being over time is also to be removed from economics. In practice economists do make recommendations affecting different generations while bounding their perspective on professional responsibility. One result is that the connection of current well-being to the past and future is a factor largely absent from modern economic analysis.

In human society there is clearly a strong sense of community between generations.[6] Consider how the links across time are ever present and a preoccupation of individuals and society. Events that happen after a person is dead can affect their well-being. For example, individuals wish to be remembered and thought of well, and those with economic power build monuments and endow museums or charitable causes to that end. Historical revision of the past can also destroy the reputation and character of individuals. Thus, the welfare of an individual need not pass from the economic calculus with their death. The impact can be both directly related to the utilitarian value of the individual's existence as well as more indirectly. In the latter regard, descendants of an individual might be expected to care most about their reputation, but even for those from two millennia or more ago, with no such identifiable descendants, some duty of care seems essential. Indeed, slandering the writings of an ancient Greek philosopher may be taken as seriously as if they were alive today, and for religious leaders (e.g. Muhammad, Jesus, Buddha) can be taken far more seriously. There is an unequal treatment in this regard so that some are soon forgotten and others remain in the common psyche. Yet, the main point remains that the interests of an individual can be temporally widely dispersed and there is a sense of community across time.

O'Neill (1999) emphasises how important the narrative order of events is in evaluating those same events and public policy. Actions, places and events have a sense of meaning because of their historical context. Thus actions are undertaken now which aim to make intelligible or redeem past events. The failure O'Neill recognises in economics is the inability to give meaning to either human life or social decisions. 'What is absent is precisely a view of human lives as ones that have a narrative structure – as stories of physical and mental growth and development, of decline, of success and failure of projects and relationships' (O'Neill, 1999: 98).[7] He explains the relevance for environmental policy using conservation as an example; similar points arise from the literature on having a sense of place, e.g. ancestral connections, landscape as embodying cultural history. There are strong implications for how the enhanced Greenhouse Effect is addressed and the seriousness paid to its implications. Historical context must be given to the policies being proposed rather than regarding action as occurring in a vacuum. As O'Neill (1999: 100) explains:

> We enter worlds that are rich with past histories, the narrative of lives and communities from which our own lives take significance. The problem is, or

should be constructed as, the problem of *how best to continue the narrative*, and the question we should ask is: *what would make the most appropriate trajectory* from what has gone before? The value in these situations which we should be seeking to uphold lies in the way that the constituent items and the places they occupy are intertwined with and embody the life-history of the community of which they form a part.

The relevance of looking back seems absent from most modern economic discussions in contrast to observed political economy. On the social and political agenda the unfair treatment of whole peoples is a major preoccupation (e.g. Scottish land clearances, the conflict in Ireland, apartheid in South Africa, extermination of the native Americans and Australians by European settlers, the African slave trade). Numerous wars and conflicts around the world are embedded in perceptions of past injustice and result in the consumption of considerable resources, loss of life and human misery. If the aim of economics is to show how resources can be allocated to create a better society, the past will need to feature far more prominently in the analysis.

A sense of community and moral considerability across time is in stark contrast to the discussion of humanity by division into distinct generational units which become rapidly less important with time. As was shown in the preceding chapter, the tendency in economics is to neglect the past and take current action as the status quo, e.g. describing avoidance of long-term damage due to the enhanced Greenhouse Effect as a benefit to future generations rather than the prevention of a substantive deliberate harm of the innocent. Issues of past injustice and historical resource use are liable to remain high on the agenda in any debates over the enhanced Greenhouse Effect and who is regarded as responsible for control or compensation for impacts.

There is also a basic psychological aspect to humans which makes the neglect of the past worrisome. The human psyche is rooted in the past but modern society rushes forward with technology so that a division is drawn which results in a loss of guiding instincts. As Jung (1989: 236) has explained, our psyches are still embedded in the Middle Ages, classical antiquity and our earlier primitive past.

> Nevertheless, we have plunged down a cataract of progress which sweeps us on into the future with ever wilder violence the further it takes us from our roots. Once the past has been breached, it is usually annihilated, and there is no stopping the forward motion. But it is precisely the loss of connection with the past, our uprootedness, which has given rise to the 'discontents' of civilisation and to such a flurry and haste that we live more in the future and its chimerical promises of a golden age than in the present, with which our whole evolutionary background has not yet caught up. We rush impetuously into novelty, driven by

a mounting sense of insufficiency, dissatisfaction, and restlessness. We no longer live on what we have, but on promises, no longer in the light of the present day but in the darkness of the future, which, we expect, will at last bring the proper sunrise.

He goes on to specifically warn of 'the terrible perils to which the most brilliant discoveries of science expose us' and the fleeting impressiveness of new methods and gadgets which generally fail to increase contentment or happiness. 'Mostly they are deceptive sweetenings of existence, like speedier communications which unpleasantly accelerate the tempo of life and leave us with less time than before.'

Concluding remarks

In effect, if the accumulated science is correct, human induced climate change would have been difficult to avoid with drastic action when first called for 20 years ago and is now inevitable. The international community, led by industrially developed countries, has already shown reluctance to take serious action. Years have been spent to negotiate minimal reductions in GHGs which will have little or no impact on global emissions growth. The calls for 20–50 per cent reductions in the late 1980s have been replaced by an aggregate 5 per cent for a limited range of countries with extensive qualifications.

The option of preventing significant change is no longer available but preventing greater extremes is an option. The immediate policy choices are how much change and how soon, how to adapt, and how and who to compensate? Yet the meaning of continued emissions under 'business as usual' has still to be communicated effectively to most members of the GHG-emitting general public, who seem blissfully unaware of their role in global climate change or at least unconcerned. While the international negotiations roll on from one annual conference to the next, domestic politics almost totally neglects the issue. Implementing control policies would alter this but the impact may be negative because the public debate has been scientific and technical without realisation of the extent to which behavioural change is required. The current path of human lifestyles and economic systems will have to be redirected dramatically if emissions are ever to be controlled to the extent of preventing the perturbation of atmospheric chemistry.

Deciding who should control their GHG emissions, by how much and who pays does involve challenging specific governments and sectors of industry, as well as individual lifestyles. This conflicts with the ideology of free choice in an unregulated market system of political economy. From this perspective there is little surprise that, despite the embellishments, international negotiations have so far totally failed to address the need for substantive reductions in GHGs over current levels and remain minor adjustments to 'business as usual'.

A concern throughout this book has been for how the current state of the world is perpetuated and in particular the role played by economics in doing so. The standard economic approach to decision theory provides a model which, even supportive analysts have to admit, cannot account for central facets of such problems. Still economic models seem able to reinterpret empirical evidence and ignore key issues. For example, the substitution of subjective for objective probabilities aims to maintain a model despite the inadequacies of the resulting numbers. The challenge of understanding and directly addressing strong uncertainty remains unmet both in economic and policy debates. The result can only be surprise events and disasters which provoke knee-jerk reactions and excessive, often inappropriate, responses.

Economics has failed to address key concerns arising from the enhanced Greenhouse Effect. Symptoms of that failure appear in IPCC reports, and elsewhere, and their cause lies within the methodology being adopted. There is a need for an approach to economics which has an explicit research agenda addressing strong uncertainty and multiple values. Recognising the role of tacit dominant cultural values in both natural and social sciences means broadening the basis for environmental decision-making. Planning for the future means accepting and addressing partial ignorance. Economics has tended to narrow rather than broaden the focus of attention. The range of values prevalent in society is far from adequately taken into account. Hence the issue of the intrinsic value of harm, which has specific relevance to the enhanced Greenhouse Effect, has been almost totally ignored. Social norms and fundamental ethical positions are as relevant as economic preferences and in the current context more so. Thus, there is a need to provide for greater pluralism. Part of that broadening of perspective requires that we relate to the sense of community through time and our place within that community. This requires serious attention to our relationship with and treatment of future generations, who are widely accepted to be the main losers from continued GHG emissions, rather than their relegation to a footnote in the debate.

The role of science in policy is also of great concern because of the excessive faith placed in technology during the twentieth century without regard to its drawbacks. Many sections of the public today are much less ready to accept scientific information and reassurance at face value, often to the annoyance of industrial concerns and the political elite. More research to fill information gaps cannot remove the need for moral judgement. There is then also a general inadequacy in the political approach to long-term, complex problems which are subject to strong uncertainty.

The continual call for more research implies a belief in the existing inadequacy of information. If the possibility of new knowledge arising, about courses of action which have never previously been considered, or even suspected, is accepted then the future is unpredictable – an obvious point which has failed to be taken fully on board. Thus, a common reaction to environmental problems is to appeal to unknown technological advances and follow this with reference to a long list of past failures to predict the ever-changing options. Future technologies cannot be predicted and therefore all the worries of environmentalists may be solved by scientists and engineers. The very same analysts fail to see the logic of their argument. If the future is unpredictable we must plan for the unexpected.

To the extent that social institutions also fail to recognise moral imperatives towards current and future victims of environmental harm a greater burden is placed upon individuals to do so. This requires recognising and avoiding actions inflicting or threatening deliberate serious harm of the innocent. Green and socially responsible consumerism, organic food production and ethical investment are signs of behaviour in this direction but only amongst a minority. Actions at the collective level for addressing the enhanced Greenhouse Effect depend upon the institutions of government taking some initiative in opening the debate and leading the way. However, harming the innocent is politically easy when they are removed in space and time. Faith that such institutions will act appropriately seems sorely misplaced in the context of the enhanced Greenhouse Effect and yet they will be required to do so if society is to successfully transform itself. Drastically reducing GHGs in modern industrial and industrialising economies, while avoiding substitution by equally harmful technologies, requires far more fundamental change than has yet been contemplated.

Notes

1   The establishment of an international network for the study of policy issues relating to non-CO_2 greenhouse gases only occurred in 2001 (de la Chesnaye and Vainio, 2001).

2   Thus a standard response to calls for pollution control has been to suggest the need for more research. A political motive may become clear where on-going research programmes are merely renamed to give the appearance of new agendas without any added substance i.e. placing existing research under climate change budgets. At the same time the expected return from further research is often limited in terms the extent to which this will better inform decisions.

3   Note also some key economists advocating CBA under SAR no longer participate in TAR; key topics have been removed from the socio-economics report of Working Group III to the impacts report of Working Group II; there is no mention of the controversy over the valuation of life despite the supposed scientific process which is meant to build upon important issues in the published literature. Valuation of life is mentioned in TAR at various points and in a qualified fashion, but the political and ethical debate is ignored. A similar approach is taken to discounting with superficial note being made of some disputes.

4   The logic of such a short-term approach actually features in the IPCC SAR economics report where it is termed an 'act-learn-act' strategy (Arrow *et al.*, 1996: 67–8).

5   While environmental awareness has increased over the past 20 years there is still much confusion over the meaning of fundamental concepts such as biodiversity or the difference between the enhanced Greenhouse Effect and ozone hole.

6 I am grateful for discussions with Alan Holland for several points made here. He noted that reading say Horace or Shakespeare can be discussed as increasing Horace's or Shakespeare's well-being. Thus, the rhetorical question of Marx: 'What have future generations ever done for us?' while amusing misses the point; the question should be: 'What will future generations do for us?'

7 Similarly, different types of events are treated with greater or lesser significance because of their historical context, e.g. an apple falling from a tree in Newton's garden has more historical importance than one doing so in my garden today. The meaning of even apocryphal events is set within an historical context.

References

Arrow, K.J. (1951) *Social Choice and Individual Values*. New York: Wiley.

Arrow, K.J., J. Parikh, G. Pillet, M. Grubb, E. Haites, J.C. Hourcade, K. Parikh and F. Yamin (1996) 'Decision-making frameworks for addressing climate change', in *Economic and Social Dimensions of Climate Change*, edited by J.P. Bruce, L. Hoesung and E.F. Haites, pp. 53–77, Cambridge, England: Cambridge University Press.

Banuri, T., K. Goran-Maler, M. Grubb, H.K. Jacobson and F. Yamin (1996) 'Equity and social considerations', in *Economic and Social Dimensions of Climate Change*, edited by J.P. Bruce, L. Hoesung and E.F. Haites, pp. 70–124, Cambridge, England: Cambridge University Press.

Banuri, T., J. Weyant, G. Akumu, A. Najam, L.P. Rosa, S. Rayner, W. Sachs, R. Sharma and G. Yohe (2001) 'Setting the stage: climate change and sustainable development', in *Climate Change 2001: Mitigation*, edited by B. Metz, O. Davidson, R. Swart and J. Pan, pp. 73–114, Cambridge, England: Cambridge University Press.

Broome, J. (1994) 'Discounting the future', *Philosophy and Public Affairs* **23**(2): 128–56.

Bruce, J.P., L. Hoesung and E.F. Haites (1996) *Climate Change 1995: Economic and Social Dimensions of Climate Change*. Cambridge, England: Cambridge University Press.

Cantor, R. and G. Yohe (1998) 'Economic analysis', in *Human Choices & Climate Change: The Tools for Policy Analysis* **3**, edited by S. Rayner and E.L. Malone, pp. 1–104, Columbus, OH: Battelle Press.

de la Chesnaye, F. and M. Vainio (2001) 'Initiation of the non-CO_2 greenhouse gas network', *Greenhouse Issues* September: 4.

Freeman, A.M. (1986) 'The ethical basis of the economic view of the environment', in *People, Penguins and Plastic Trees: Basic Issues in Environmental Ethics*, edited by D. van der Veer and C. Pierce, pp. 218–27, Belmont, CA: Wadsworth Publishing Company.

Glantz, M.H., M.F. Price and M.E. Krenz (1990) *Report of the Workshop 'On Assessing Winners and Losers in the Context of Global Warming', St. Julians, Malta*. Boulder, CO: National Center for Atmospheric Research.

Grubb, M. (1995) 'Seeking fair weather: ethics and the international debate on climate change', *International Affairs* **71**(3): 463–96.

Grubb, M., C. Vrolijk and D. Brack (1999) *The Kyoto Protocol: A Guide and Assessment*. London: Earthscan and Royal Institute of International Affairs.

Houghton, J. (1997) *Global Warming: The Complete Briefing*. Cambridge, England: Cambridge University Press.

IPCC Working Group II (2001) *Climate Change 2001: Impacts, Adaptation, and Vulnerability; Summary for Policymakers*. Geneva: Intergovernmental Panel on Climate Change.

IPCC Working Group III (2001) 'Technical summary', in *Climate Change 2001: Mitigation*, edited by B. Metz, O. Davidson, R. Swart and J. Pan, pp. 15–71, Cambridge, England: Cambridge University Press.

Jung, C.G. (1989) *Memories, Dreams, Reflections*. New York: Vintage Books.

Kauppi, P., R. Sedjo, M. Apps, C. Cerri, T. Fujimori, H. Janzen, O. Krankina, W. Makundi, G. Marland, O. Masera, G.-J. Nabuurs, W. Razali and N.H. Ravindranath (2001) 'Technological and economic potential of options to enhance, maintain, and manage biological carbon reservoirs and geo-engineering', in *Climate Change 2001: Mitigation*, edited by B. Metz, O. Davidson, R. Swart and J. Pan, pp. 301–43, Cambridge, England: Cambridge University Press.

Kay, J., M. Regier, M. Boyle and F. George (1999) 'An ecosystem approach for sustainability: addressing the challenge of complexity', *Futures* **31**(7): 721–42.

Loasby, B.J. (1976) *Choice, Complexity and Ignorance: An Inquiry into Economic Theory and the Practice of Decision-Making*. Cambridge, England: Cambridge University Press.

Markandya, A., K. Halsnaes, A. Lanza, Y. Matsuoka, S. Maya, J. Pan, J. Shogren, R. Seroa de Motta and T. Zhang (2001) 'Costing methodologies', in *Climate Change 2001: Mitigation*, edited by B. Metz, O. Davidson, R. Swart and J. Pan, pp. 451–98, Cambridge, England: Cambridge University Press.

Marland, G., T.A. Boden and R.J. Andres (2001) *Global, Regional, and National CO_2 Emissions. Trends: A Compendium of Data on Global Change*. Oak Ridge, TN: Oak Ridge National Laboratory, Carbon Dioxide Information Analysis Center, US Department of Energy.

Metz, B., O. Davidson, R. Swart and J. Pan (2001) *Climate Change 2001: Mitigation*. Cambridge, England: Cambridge University Press.

Morita, T., J. Robinson, A. Adegbulugbe, J. Alcamo, D. Herbert, E.L. La Rovere, N. Nakicenovic, H. Pitcher, P. Raskin, K. Riahi, A. Sankovski, V. Sokolov, B. de Vries and D. Zhou (2001) 'Greenhouse gas emissions mitigation scenarios and implications', in *Climate Change 2001: Mitigation*, edited by B. Metz, O. Davidson, R. Swart and J. Pan, pp. 115–66, Cambridge, England: Cambridge University Press.

Munasinghe, M., P. Meier, M. Hoel, S.W. Hong and A. Aaheim (1996) 'Applicability of techniques of cost–benefit analysis to climate change', in *Economic and Social Dimensions of Climate Change*, edited by J.P. Bruce, L. Hoesung and E.F. Haites, pp. 145–77, Cambridge, England: Cambridge University Press.

O'Hara, S.U. (1996) 'Discursive ethics in ecosystem valuation and environmental policy', *Ecological Economics* **16**: 95–107.

O'Neill, J. (1993) *Ecology, Policy and Politics: Human Well-Being and the Natural World*. London: Routledge.

O'Neill, J. (1999) 'Self, time and separability', in *Self and Future Generations: An Intercultural Conversation*, edited by T.-C. Kim and R. Harrison, pp. 91–106, Cambridge, England: White Horse Press.

Paterson, M. (1996) *Global Warming and Global Politics*. London: Routledge Ltd.

Rayner, S. and E.L. Malone (eds) (1998) *Human Choice and Climate Change: What Have We Learned?* Human Choice and Climate Change, no. 4. Columbus, OH: Battelle Press.

Renn, O., T. Webler, H. Rakel, P. Dienel and B. Johnson (1993) 'Public participation in decision-making: a three step procedure', *Policy Sciences* **26**: 189–214.

Rowlands, I.H. (2000) 'Beauty and the beast? BP's and Exxon's positions on global climate change', *Environment and Planning C: Government and Policy* **18**(3): 339–54.

Sathaye, J., D. Bouille, D. Biswas, P. Crabbe, L. Geng, D. Hall, H. Imura, A. Jaffe, L. Michaelis, G. Peszko, A. Verbruggen, E. Worell and F. Yamba (2001) 'Barriers, opportunities, and market potential of technologies and practices', in *Climate Change 2001: Mitigation*, edited by B. Metz, O. Davidson, R. Swart and J. Pan, pp. 345–98, Cambridge, England: Cambridge University Press.

Schneider, S.H. (1989) *Future climatic change and energy system planning: Are risk assessment methods applicable?* Presented at Risk Analysis and Management of Natural and Man-Made Hazards: Proceedings of a Conference, Santa Barbara, California, 8–13 November 1987.

Sen, A.K. (1982) 'Approaches to the choice of discount rates for social benefit–cost analysis', in *Discounting for Time and Risk in Energy Policy*, edited by R.C. Lind, pp. 325–76, Washington, DC: Resources for the Future, Johns Hopkins Press.

Smith, J.B., H.-J. Schellnhuber, M.Q. Mirza, S. Fankhauser, R. Leemans, L. Erda, L. Ogallo, B. Pittock, R. Richels, C. Rosenzweig, U. Safriel, R.S.J. Tol, J. Weyant and G. Yohe (2001) 'Vulnerability to climate change and reasons for concern: a synthesis', in *Climate Change 2001: Impacts, Adaptation, and Vulnerability*, edited by J.J. McCarthy, O.F. Canziani, N.A. Leary, D.J. Dokken and K.S. White, pp. 913–67, Cambridge, England: Cambridge University Press.

Spash, C.L. (2000) 'Ethical motives and charitable contributions in contingent valuation: empirical evidence from social psychology and economics', *Environmental Values* **9**(4): 453–79.

Toth, F.L., M. Mwandosya, C. Carraro, J. Christensen, J. Edmonds, B. Flannery, C. Gay-Garcia, H. Lee, K.M. Meyer-Abich, E. Nikitina, A. Rahman, Y. Wake and W. John (2001) 'Decision-making frameworks', in *Climate Change 2001: Mitigation*, edited by B. Metz, O. Davidson, R. Swart and J. Pan, pp. 601–88, Cambridge, England: Cambridge University Press.

van den Hove, S. (2000) 'Participatory approaches to environmental policy-making: the European Commission Climate Policy Process as a case study', *Ecological Economics* **33**: 457–72.

Watson, R.T., M.C. Zinyowera, R.H. Moss and D.J. Dokken (eds) (1997) *The Regional Impacts of Climate Change: An Assessment of Vulnerability; Summary for Policymakers*. IPCC Special Report. Geneva: IPCC.

Westra, L. (1997) 'Post-normal science, the precautionary principle, and the ethics of integrity', *Foundations of Science* **2**: 237–62.

Wynne, B. (1992) 'Uncertainty and environmental learning: reconceiving science and policy in the preventive paradigm', *Global Environmental Change* (**June**): 111–27.

Wynne, B. (1994) 'Scientific knowledge and the global environment', in *Social Theory and the Global Environment*, edited by M. Redclift and T. Benton, pp. 168–89, London: Routledge.

Glossary

Biosphere The part of the global carbon cycle including living organisms and their organic litter/detritus.

C3 plants Plants producing compounds with three carbon atoms after the initial stage of photosynthesis, e.g. wheat, rice, soybean and several major weed pests.

C4 plants Plants producing compounds with four carbon atoms after the initial stage of photosynthesis, e.g. maize, sorghum, sugar cane, millet and forage crops. C4 plants are less responsive to CO_2 fertilisation than C3 plants.

Cost–benefit analysis The calculation of the consequences of an action in monetary terms leading to the weighing-up and comparison of positive and negative outcomes.

Double CO_2 A concentration of carbon dioxide twice that of a reference level. Often the reference level is the pre-industrial concentration which is taken to be related to a 'clean' atmosphere as far as the enhanced Greenhouse Effect.

Equivalent CO_2 concentration The concentration of all greenhouse gases, including different radiative properties and residence times, translated into an equivalent concentration of carbon dioxide. This is often referred to as $2 \times CO_2$.

External climatic variability External here means a factor, such as orbital forcing, affecting the distribution of radiation entering the climate system.

Externalities The economic characterisation of pollution as deriving from factors which are external to an economic actors' decision-making, e.g. a household making noise without regard to their neighbours or a firm polluting a stream without regard to others. Internalising externalities as the solution to pollution requires enforcing monetary payments for each and every externality, both positive and negative.

Evapotranspiration Discharge of water from the Earth's surface to the atmosphere by evaporation from bodies of water, or other surfaces, and by transpiration from plants.

Internal climatic variability Internal here refers to a factor, such as the Greenhouse Effect, affecting the distribution of radiation after it enters the climate system.

Irradiance The total flow of radiation received on a unit area of a given surface.

Isostatic adjustment Isostasy is a state where there is equal pressure on every side. In geology the term refers to universal equilibrium in Earth's crust. This crustal equilibrium is maintained due to gravitational yielding of rocks beneath Earth's surface.

Isotope One of two or more atoms that have the same atomic number (i.e. the same number of protons in their nuclei) but have different mass numbers.

Kyoto Protocol The Kyoto Protocol of the Framework Convention on Climate Change was adopted in December 1997. This aims to make operational the mechanisms for achieving the control of greenhouse gases and preventing 'dangerous anthropogenic interference with the climate system' (Article 2). Lack of signatory countries means the agreement remains unratified as of 2001 and has therefore yet to come into force.

Maunder minimum A period from 1654–1714 during which sunspot activity was dramatically reduced. This was coincident with the Little Ice Age leading to speculation over possible links.

Orbital forcing The variation in Earth's rotation or orbit around the Sun which then leads to a change or forcing of climatic conditions.

Photodissociation Breakdown of chemicals by reaction with sunlight.

Pleistocene Geological timescale, epoch beginning 1.5 to 2 million years before present.

Radiative forcing A change in average net radiation at the top of the tropopause because of a change in either solar or infrared radiation. A radiative forcing affects the balance between incoming and outgoing radiation. The radiation balance is the difference between the absorbed solar radiation and the net infrared radiation.

Reflectivity The ratio of the energy reflected from a surface to the energy incident on that surface.

Sink A reservoir which absorbs a gas released elsewhere in its cycle.

Source The pool from which a gas is released to another part of its cycle.

Stratosphere Area of the upper atmosphere extending from a base of 8 km (in polar regions) or 15 km (in the tropics) up to 50 km.

Strong uncertainty A lack of knowledge about the future which involves ignorance. Future possible states of the world may be unknown and unknowable. Attributing probabilities to possible states may be meaningless. Standard scientific methods of risk analysis fail to be applicable to or account for strong uncertainty. See chapter 5.

Subsidiary Body for Scientific and Technological Advice One of the ad hoc subsidiary bodies under the UNFCCC. This body receives the IPCC (and other) reports and interprets the information in order to draw conclusions for consideration by parties to the Convention.

Thermocline A transition layer of water in the ocean, with a steeper vertical gradient than found in the layers above or below. The permanent thermocline separates the warm mixed surface layer of the ocean from cold deep water, occurring at depths between 100 and 1000 metres. The thermocline acts as a barrier to downward mixing of CO_2.

Transmittance The effectiveness with which the atmosphere acts as a medium for the passage of energy.

Transpiration The process in plants by which water is taken up by the roots and released as water vapour by the leaves.

Tropopause The boundary between the troposphere and stratosphere. It marks the vertical limits of most clouds and storms.

Troposphere Lower layer of the atmosphere extending up to 15 km (about 8 km in the polar regions and 15 km in the tropics.

2xCO$_2$ See equivalent CO_2 concentration.

United Nations Framework Convention on Climate Change (UNFCCC) Adopted on 9 May 1992; entered into force 21 March 1994 (90 days after the 50th ratification); ratified by 177 countries by 2001.

Weak uncertainty A lack of knowledge about future events which can be characterised in terms of risk and probabilities. Probability distributions can be constructed from the repeated observation of the same event ('objective' probabilities) or by expert advice ('subjective probabilities'). See chapter 4.

Index

Page references followed by 'f' refer to figures, those followed by 't' refer to tables, and those followed by 'n' (plus a number) refer to notes, e.g. 257t, 44f, 217n4

ABATE (abate emissions) 213
abatement 225, 230, 232, 242–3
Abrahamson, D.E. 50, 81
absolutism 238–40
accelerated policies scenario 114
acidic deposition 3–4, 21, 31, 54
'acting then learning' strategy 159
Adams, R.M. 72, 80, 88, 113, 123, 228
adaptation: GHG control options 154, 185; and impacts 80–4, 89, 216; as policy option 252, 253–4
Adger, W.N. 106, 126, 176, 177, 196
aerosol emissions 30–1, 54, 81
Africa: CBA studies 164, 169, 171; CO_2 emission 257, 257t; impacts 69–70, 73–4, 88
agriculture: CBA studies 163–4, 166, 169; damage estimates 185; impacts 65, 70–5, 79, 83, 123–5, 260; socio-economic models 113; see also crops; wheat
aircraft 39, 48, 158
air pollution: CBA studies and reduction 163; control policy 153, 171, 172–7, 178, 279n1; crops losses 124; economic situation 2–6, 153; ethics and values 20–1; historical background 11–19; scientific approach 6–11; victims and compensation 229
air temperature see temperature
akrasia 204, 207, 217n4
albedo 26, 28–9, 28t
Alexander, V. 76
Alliance of Small Island States (AOSIS) 16; see also islands

alternative energy sources 40, 132
American Economic Association 159
American Economic Review 159
annual variation, atmospheric CO_2 44, 44f
Antarctic ice sheets 66, 84; East Antarctic 87; West Antarctic 85–6, 126–7, 131, 132, 265
anthropogenic emissions see emissions
Arctic regions 64, 138
arid regions 68–70, 69t, 73–4, 126
Arrhenius, S. 25
Arrow, K.J. 187, 246n11, n12, 262
assessment see costs and benefits; impact assessment; risk
atmosphere 8, 44–5, 44f; see also CO_2; stratosphere
attitude(s) xiii, 110, 121, 131, 132, 133, 144, 204, 241, 261, 270
Australia 68–9, 255, 255t, 257
averages and variability 104
Ayres, R.U. 154, 161, 162, 163, 164–5, 196

Baier, A. 214
Banuri, T. 263, 272–3, 274
Barbier, E.B. 126
Barker, T.P. 154, 178
Barry, B. 227, 234
Batie, S.S. 237
behaviour see human behaviour
beliefs: and facts 133–4, 140, 141–4, 147; and values 141, 142, 192, 271
Bellagio (Italy) 64
beneficial impacts, global climate change 78–80, 88–9, 259
benefits: of control 154, 160, 164, 165, 167, 169, 170t (estimation 172, 177–8, 179, 185); secondary benefits ('no regrets') 156; see also costs and benefits; damage
Bentham, J. 234, 236

Bergman, L. 174
Binmore, K. 246n12
biodiversity 75–6, 135, 161, 279n5
biota 75–6
Bloc, K. 177
Bolin, B. 10
Braswell, B.H. 36
Bray, A.J. 110
British Isles 67, 116, 117n1; *see also* UK
Broadus, J.M. 125
Broome, J. 206, 207, 208, 217, 271
Brown, K. 176, 177
business as usual (BAU) 21, 213–14, 254, 277

Callendar, G.S. 78, 137–8
Canada 72–3, 255, 255t
capital discounting 207–8
carbon dioxide *see* CO₂
carbon taxes 88–9, 163, 173–6, 178
Carter, T.R. 71
catastrophes: costs and benefits 156; extreme
    events 90; future, and discount rate 217;
    insurance and risk 264, 265; strong
    uncertainty 126–7, 278
cause–effect relationships 132
CBA (cost–benefit analysis): the 1990s 198;
    CFCs 163, 176, 177; compensation
    criterion 225–6; decision-making 260–2,
    273; discounting 203; estimates 203,
    177–8, 194, 261–2, 279n3; GHG control
    157–8, 159–77, 170t, 188–9, 193t, 195t,
    279n3; moral issues 173; reduction of air
    pollution 163; sea level rise 164–5, 166,
    169; uncertainty 168
cereals 71
CETA (carbon emissions trajectory assessment)
    160
CFCs (chlorofluorocarbons) 32, 33f, 37–8, 47;
    CBA studies 163, 176, 177; damage and
    rights 239; effect of 132, 135
Chen, R. 126
Chichilnisky, G. 129–30, 134
China: CBA studies 166, 169, 170t, 171, 190;
    emissions 254–5, 255t
chlorofluorocarbons *see* CFCs
choice: and decisions 258–65, 273, 277–8;
    emissions control 254–5; indeterminancy
    136
Christian beliefs and values 141, 142, 192
claims, of future generations 213–14
climate change 1–23, 26–32, 44, 48–52,
    60–90; adaptation 80–4, 89; agriculture
    70–5, 79, 83; arid zones 68–70, 68t;
    beneficial impacts 78–80, 88–9, 259;

British Isles 116, 117n1; early signs of 109;
    forcing 28, 49–50, 53, 251; historical
    analysis 61, 148; industrially developing
    countries 126, 164; policy 88, 104–5,
    139–40, 144–6; predictions and
    measurement 46, 107–10, 125, 138; sea
    level rise 66–8, 81–2, 82t, 84–7, 88;
    temperature 31, 48–52, 52f; unavoidable
    significant change 277; unmanaged
    ecosystems 75–6; *see also* countries;
    emissions reduction; impact assessment;
    impacts; local information; regional climate
    change; temperature
Cline, W.R.: CBA studies 154, 161, 163, 165,
    166, 167, 177, 194; impacts and
    adaptations 80, 124; values 185, 186–7,
    189
CO₂: agriculture 70–1, 72, 79, 124–5;
    atmospheric CO₂ 44–5, 44f; carbon taxes
    88–9, 163, 173–6, 178; concentrations
    and temperature 45, 63–4; control costs
    and benefits 160, 254; emissions 42–6, 44f
    (emissions by country and region 254–7,
    255t, 257t; global warming 11, 13, 25, 50,
    165; hydrocarbon deposits 27); fertilisation
    effect 164; as major pollutant 5; non-CO₂
    gases 279n1; predictions and measurement
    165–6, 173–4 (in 1930s 138; in 1970s
    109–10, 158; in 1990s 158–60, 177);
    socio-economic models 114; sources by
    energy type 41t; sources and sinks 32,
    34–7, 35f, 54n2, 168 (forests as sinks 112,
    176; oceans as sinks 111, 114); *see also*
    double CO₂-equivalent scenarios; emissions
    reduction; GHGs (Greenhouse Gases)
coal: efficiency and CBA studies 163, 175;
    pollution 3, 46; production and utilisation
    18, 40–1, 42
Cobb–Douglas production function 114
compensation 221, 223, 234–5, 236, 242;
    economic models 225–6; intergenerational
    issues 206, 227, 229–31; *see also* damage;
    harm; transfers
Conrad, K. 174
consensual approach 145, 253, 268–9, 274
consequentialism 233
consumerism 204–8, 210, 215, 270–1, 279
consumption 41–3, 41t, 206–7, 211, 216–17,
    270–1
contingent valuation 188, 189–90, 191
control: abatement policy 225, 230, 232,
    242–3; CBA studies 160–77; costs and
    benefits 148, 153–78, 155f, 193t, 195t,
    254; damage 172; emissions 10–19,

237–8, 254–5; GHG adaptation 154, 185; optimal level 155; social regulation 122, 139–41, 153–4, 238–9; uncontrolled future 228–9

cooling: predictions and measurement 110, 158; radiative 39

coral 76, 108

cost–benefit analysis (CBA) *see* CBA (cost–benefit analysis)

costs and benefits 148, 154–60, 155f, 184, 185, 254; human welfare 160, 161, 164, 169

countries: CO_2 emissions 254–7, 255t; *see also* developed countries; industrially developed countries; industrially developing countries; less-developed countries; local information; lower-income countries; poor

critical values 105–6

Crocker, T.D. 88

Croll, James 27

crops: genetically modified 7–8; losses and air pollution 124; rainfall 105; regional climate change 70–3, 74, 79, 123–5; uncertainties 132, 137; *see also* agriculture; wheat

Crosson, P. 72, 78, 143

cultural perspectives 253, 259–60, 273–7, 278

Daily, G.C. 128

damage: control 172; estimates 165–6, 167–8, 171, 179n5, 185; long-term and future 185, 197, 210, 215, 245n1, 276 (ethics 225, 228–9, 239, 243–4; irreversible 236); *see also* harm

Damodaran, M. 159

Daniel, M.M. 72

d'Arge, R.C. 6, 12, 158, 159, 226

death (mortality) 186, 188, 189, 192, 194

debate: economic valuation 268–9; emissions reduction 10–19, 129, 173–8; scientific 145–6

decision-making 241–2, 253, 258–65, 267–8, 273, 277–8

deforestation *see* forests

Demeritt, D. 160, 192

deontology 234, 237–8, 243

deserts 68, 73–4

Detwiler, R.P. 36

developed countries 88, 121–2, 174–5, 189–90, 254–5, 272, 279; *see also* industrially developing countries; lower-income countries; poor

DICE *see* Dynamic Integrated Climate Economy

disasters *see* catastrophes

discounting 186–8, 201–8, 202f, 209, 210; ethical implications 215–17, 216t, 271–2; negative discounting 212; objections to 206–8; zero discounting 217

distribution 21, 201–3; ethics 203, 217n1, 222, 279; the future 209–11, 226; impact of global climate change 166–7, 177; intergenerational 223–5; value and ethics 192–3

distributional transfers 227

Dixon, R.K. 177

Doake, C.S.M. 86

domestic politics 277

dose-response approach 7

double CO_2-equivalent scenarios 80, 90n1, 109, 111, 123; agricultural impact 65, 72, 73, 123–4; CBA studies 161–2, 161t, 165–6; ecosystems 75; migration 126; mortality 189; temperature 25, 76, 81; *see also* CO_2

drought: climate predictions and measurement 109; probability of enhanced Greenhouse Effect 103; uncertainty and migration 126; *see also* rainfall

duties, and rights 232–7, 238–9, 241–2, 243, 245n3

Dynamic Integrated Climate Economy (DICE) model 167, 168, 169, 176, 186, 187

dynamic optimisation model 173

East Antarctic ice sheets 87

Easterling, W.E. 79

EC (European Community) 13

Economic Journal 159

economic models 159–77, 264; egalitarian 223–4, 227–8, 233, 242m 245n4; elitist 223, 224, 233, 242; enhanced Greenhouse Effect 5; libertarian (Paretian) 130, 157, 223, 225–6, 234, 242; limitations of 232, 261–2, 273–5, 278; neo-classical 113, 117n1, 201, 204, 209, 233, 268 (intergenerational ethical rules 223, 224, 244); scientific 8, 147; socio-economic 112–15, 114, 116, 121–30, 137–9; strong uncertainty 116, 121–30, 137–9, 141–2, 147; uncertainty 110–12, 115–16; utilitarianism 233, 239, 241, 242, 244; *see also* CBA; economics; economy; GCMs; scientific models; socio-economic models; uncertainty

Economic Report of the President (1990) 174, 179n7

economics: methodology, values and beliefs 140–1, 143, 192, 197, 198; narrow approach of 261–2, 273–5, 278; no concept of history 225, 275–6; positivist program 226; welfare economics 223–6, 261; *see also* CBA; costs and benefits; economic models; economy; GCMs; scientific models; socio-economic models; uncertainty

Economist, The 161, 196

economy: agricultural impact 123–5; air pollution 2–6, 153; CBA studies 163–4, 177–8, 194; climate change impact 158–9, 172–7; energy consumption 42–3; ethics, future generations 221, 222–31, 243–4, 245n2, 260, 269; future generations 232; impact assessment 62, 79, 88, 89; migration 126; new approach of inquiry 265–77; uncertainty 121–3, 129–30, 139–40; *see also* CBA; economic models; uncertainty

ecosystems: discounting the future 206; and ecology 138–9; impact of global changes 60, 161, 166, 269–70; probability of enhanced Greenhouse Effect 105; risk assessment 115; unmanaged 75–6

efficiency: coal 163, 175; energy 21, 156, 162–3; and ethics 226; and human rights 234

egalitarianism 223–4, 227–8, 233, 242, 245n4

Ekins, P. 154, 173, 175, 177, 178

Electric Power Research Institute, US 160

electricity 3, 40

elitism 223, 224, 233, 242

El Niño 44, 116, 131

emissions: anthropogenic 4, 25, 26, 30–1, 30t, 38, 53, 54; industrial 31, 37, 174–5, 279; *see also* climate change; countries; emissions reduction; impact assessment; impacts; local information; regional climate change; temperature

emissions reduction: control 10–19, 237–8, 254–5 (costs and benefits 154–5, 156, 157, 162, 166, 173–8, 259–60); emissions by country and region 254–7, 255t, 257t; enhanced Greenhouse Effect 10–19, 129, 173–8, 254; ethics 20–1, 172, 186–8; global warming 11, 13, 25, 50, 165; hydrocarbon deposits 27; industrially developing countries 16, 47, 279; Kyoto and US commitments 251–2, 254; minimal achievement 277; safe minimum standard 237–8; trends and GHGs 40–8, 54, 80, 177–8; *see also* climate change; countries; emissions reduction; impact assessment;

impacts; local information; regional climate change; temperature

empirical evidence 211, 212, 266, 271–2, 278

employment 175

energy demand and consumption 41–3, 41t

energy efficiency 21, 156, 162–3

energy prices 173

enhanced Greenhouse Effect 25–54; agricultural impact 123–5; CFCs 37–8; economic models 5; emissions reduction 10–19, 129, 173–8, 254; environmental change 60; ethical debate 244–5, 252; future effects of 123–8, 213, 217, 228, 245n1; global warming 49–51; historical overview 11–20, 25; insurance and strong uncertainty 129–30; orbital forcing 28, 49–50, 53; post-normal science 144; probability 98–106; reflectivity 29; scientific models 8; scientific research and policy 253–4, 279n1; sea level rise 123–5, 131, 265; value and ethics 20–1, 253; *see also* GHGs

environment: discounting the future 206; enhanced Greenhouse Effect 60; issues and ignorance 265–6; protection and sustainability 241; social regulation and control 139–41

environmental economics *see* economics

Environmental Protection Agency (EPA) 81, 123–4

environmental refugees 194, 196; *see also* population

'environmental space' concept of 140

EPA (Environmental Protection Agency) 81, 123–4

equilibrium analysis 113, 159

equilibrium changes 60–1, 74, 267

equity 226, 272–4

Erikson, J.D. 124

ethics: discounting 215–17, 216t, 271–2; economics 223–6, 228, 232, 241–2, 258, 278, 279n3; efficiency 226; emissions reduction 20–1, 172, 186–8; impact analysis 62; intergenerational 223–6, 244, 272; monetary valuation 188–92, 197, 231–2, 258, 268–77, 269; resource distribution 203, 217n1, 222, 279; *see also* future; future generations; intergenerational issues; moral issues; rights; values

Europe: CBA studies 163–4, 166, 169, 171, 174; CO_2 emission 257, 257t

European Community (EC) 13

European Summit (Venice, 1980) 40

evidence 7, 8, 11, 12t, 30, 34, 38, 51, 71, 78, 80, 87, 89, 98, 100, 104, 107, 108, 109, 115, 116, 128, 137, 138, 142, 143, 147, 162, 169, 171, 208, 209, 211, 212, 246, 252, 254, 260, 261, 265, 268, 273, 277
empirical 211, 212, 266, 271–2, 278; knowledge 268; observational 109
experiments, scientific 7–8, 71, 265
exports, regional climate change 72, 73, 89
externality theory 5–6, 62
extreme events 90

'facts': and beliefs 133–4, 140, 141–4, 147; false, and 'objective' 133–4; scientific and economic 137–8, 252–3
fairness 273
Fankhauser, S.: CBA studies 154, 165, 166, 167, 196, 198; doubling of CO_2 126; the future 211, 217; probability approach 106; values and opinions 185, 186, 189, 191, 192, 196
feedbacks and complexity 109–10, 185
fertilisation effect of CO_2 164
fertilisers 5, 37, 46, 124
Filchner-Ronne ice shelf 86, 127
financial institutions 163–4
fingerprints, of human climate change 51, 108–9
Firor, J.W. 141–2
fish 78, 136
Fisher, A.C. 210
Fitzharris, B.B. 78
Fitzroy, F.R. 164
floods 65, 109, 125
food supplies: CBA studies 164; ethical production 279; regional climate changes 65, 73, 74, 89
forcing, climate 28, 49–50, 53, 251
Forestry Commission, UK 163
forests 34–6: costs and benefits 162, 166, 172, 176–7; regional climate changes 64, 65, 83–4; as sinks 54, 112, 176
fossil fuels: beneficial impact 78; control costs 155, 156; control of GHGs 228; GHG emission 40–2, 43, 46, 87, 173–7; as hydrocarbon deposits 27; source of GHGs 5, 25, 34, 37; vested interests in 254; *see also* coal
fossils, measurement of climate change 108
Freeman, A.M. 225, 269
Friends of the Earth, Scotland 140
Fukui, H. 105
Funtowicz, S.O. 144, 145, 146, 196

future 201–17; discounting 186–8, 201–8, 202f, 209, 210; enhanced Greenhouse Effect 123–8, 213, 217, 228, 245n1; harm 215, 244–5; importance of 209–15; long-term damage 185, 197, 210, 215, 245n1, 276 (ethics of 225, 228–9, 239, 243–4; irreversible 236); long-term predictions 266, 278–9; moral issues 210, 211, 212, 215–16, 216t; uncertainty 209–11, 266, 278; *see also* ethics; future generations; history; human behaviour; human welfare; intergenerational; intergenerational issues; moral issues; rights; predictions and measurement; social issues; time scales; values
future generations 211–17; damage 185, 197; discounting 205, 206, 209; economic growth 232; economics and ethics 221, 222–31, 243–4, 245n2, 260, 269; human welfare needs 211, 213–17, 227–8, 243; moral issues 271, 272, 278; policy 213–14, 266–77; rights 213–15, 222–3, 243–4; *see also* ethics; future; human behaviour; human welfare; intergenerational; intergenerational issues; moral issues; rights; social issues; values

Gaffney, J.S. 39
gas 42, 79, 254
GHG gases 53–4, 53t; natural gas 40, 46, 163; non-CO_2 gases 279n1; *see also* CO_2; GHGs
Gaussian distribution 100
GCMs (general circulation models) 8; double CO_2 equilibrium 65; uncertainty 110–12, 115–16; *see also* economic models; scientific models; socio-economic models
GDP (gross domestic product) 162, 163–4, 169, 173–5, 179n2, 179n4, 193
generations *see* future generations; intergenerational issues
genetically modified crops 7–8
geo-engineering 253
Geophysical Fluid Dynamics Laboratory (GFDL) 8, 80, 123
Germany, CO_2 emission 255, 255t
GHGs (Greenhouse Gases): adaptation 154, 185; anthropogenic emissions 4, 25, 26, 30–1, 30t, 38, 53, 54; control costs and benefits 148, 153–78, 155f, 193t, 195t, 254; emissions 40–8, 54, 80, 177–8; global warming 11, 13, 33f, 49–51; infrared fluxes 32; lifetimes 36–7, 46; non-CO_2 gases 279n1; predicted trends 26, 173–4;

principal gases 53–4, 53t; sources and sinks 26, 32–40, 54, 154, 168; uncertainty and risk analogy 128; wheat production 113; *see also* CO$_2$; GHGs

glaciation (ice ages) 27, 28, 49, 50, 108

glaciers 66, 108

glass-house experiments 71

global climate *see* climate change

global economy *see* economy

global engineering (geo-engineering) 23n2

global warming 11, 13, 25, 33f, 49–51, 165; impact 88, 161–2; *see also* temperature

GNP (gross national product) 162, 163–4, 166–7, 168, 169, 173–5, 179n2, 179n4

Goddard Institute for Space Studies (GISS) 8, 72, 80, 123

Goemans, T. 67

Goodess, C.M. 48, 49–50

Greenhouse Effect *see* enhanced Greenhouse Effect; GHGs

Greenland 84, 86

Gribbin, J. 125

gross domestic product (GDP) 162, 163–4, 169, 173–5, 179n2, 179n4, 193

gross national product (GNP) 162, 163–4, 166–7, 168, 169, 173–5, 179n2, 179n4

Grubb, M. 9, 257–8, 269

guess work 194, 196, 198, 263; *see also* uncertainty

Gulf Stream 116, 117n1, 131

Hall C.A.S. 36

halocarbons 37, 47, 177

Hansen, J.E. 45, 50–1, 85, 104, 142

harm: and compensation 221, 230–1, 235, 242; and constitutional rights 244; future 215, 244–5; and 'good' 234–5; intrinsic value of 278; meanings of 246n13; and trade-offs 231–2; *see also* damage

Harrison, S.J 141

Hasselmann, K. 206, 231

Heal, G. 129–30, 134, 209–10

health: impact and effects 3, 6–7, 186; morbidity and values 186, 188, 189

hemispheric temperature changes 51, 64–5, 89, 108, 116

Hendriks, C. 177

history: climate change 61, 148; cultural and social importance 275–7, 280n7; economists lack of historical awareness 225, 275–6; enhanced Greenhouse Effect 11–20, 25; *see also* future; predictions and measurement; time scales

Holland, A. 280n6

Hollinger, C.S. 138

Houghton, J., emissions reduction 10, 46; future generations 62, 196, 229; religious views 141, 142–3, 192; surprise events 265

Hourcade, J.C. 157

Howarth, R.B. 226

Hulme, M. 61

human behaviour: consumption 206–7, 211, 216–17, 270–1; emission control 255–6; empirical evidence 211, 212; interpersonal relationships 238–9; lifestyles 255, 273, 277; self-interest 241; *see also* future; future generations; human welfare; intergenerational issues; social issues

human life, value of 159, 188–92, 269, 275–6, 279n3

human rights, and efficiency 234; *see also* rights

human welfare: costs, benefits and control 160, 161, 164, 169; economic failure to recognise value of 275–6; future needs 211, 213–17, 227–8, 243; impacts 153, 161; intergenerational issues 243; marginal utility 205, 224, 245n4, 245n5; quality of life 259, 275; standard of living rights 227; values 20, 188–92; welfarism 233–5; *see also* future; future generations; human behaviour; intergenerational issues; social issues

humid tropical regions 66

Hunt, E.K. 6

hydrocarbons 38

hydroelectricity 40

hypothetical compensation 225–6

ice, impacts 64, 66, 78–9, 84–6, 265; catastrophic surprise 127, 131, 132

ice ages (glaciation) 27, 28, 49, 50, 108

ice core analysis 42, 48–9, 108, 110

ice sheets, Antarctic 66, 84; East Antarctic 87; West Antarctic 85–6, 126–7, 131, 132, 265

identity and future generations 212–15, 222, 235

Idso, S.B. 141

IEA (International Energy Authority) 40

ignorance: environmental issues 265–6; partial 168, 184, 192, 263, 266, 278; strong uncertainty 122, 129, 135–6, 146, 147

IIASA *see* International Institute for Applied Systems Analysis

impact assessment 61–2, 270; agricultural 79; economic situation 62, 79, 88, 89; ecosystems 270; ethical concerns 62;

extreme events 90; global 61–2; interdisciplinary approach 270; intertemporal 77; regional 61–76, 63t, 166–7, 169–70, 177, 189–90, 222, 260; valuation of damages 166, 189–90, 197–8; *see also* climate change; countries; emissions; emissions reduction; impacts; local information; regional climate change
impacts 60–90; agricultural 123–5; air pollution 3, 6–7; beneficial 78–80, 88–9, 259; by latitude 63t, 64–7; distribution 166–7, 177; economic 158–9, 172–7; ecosystems 60, 161, 166, 269–70; extreme events 90; global warming 88, 161–2; health 3, 6–7, 186; human welfare 153, 161; humid tropical regions 66; ice 64, 66, 78–9, 84–6, 127, 131, 132, 265; industrially developing countries 126, 164; intertemporal 62, 76–87, 77t, 89–90, 148n2; islands 67, 84, 102, 125, 235, 236; observed changes 251; sea level 66–8, 81–2, 82t, 84–7, 88; *see also* climate change; countries; emissions reduction; impact assessment; local information; regional climate change
incommensurability 231
inconsistency, research and values 185–91
indeterminacy 136–7, 146–7, 168
India 171, 190, 255, 255t
industrial emissions 31, 37, 174–5, 279
industrially developed countries 88, 121–2, 174–5, 189–90, 254–5, 272, 279; *see also* industrially developing countries; lower-income countries; poor
industrially developing countries 22; carbon taxes 174–5; climate change 126, 164; contingent valuation 189–90; economics and ethics 222; emission reduction 16, 47, 279; Greenhouse Effect insurance 130; impact 22, 89; sea level rise 67, 88; *see also* industrially developed countries; lower-income countries; poor
information: imperfect and risk 97–117; local 113
infrared fluxes 27, 31–2
Ingham, A. 174–5, 178n1
institutions 163–4, 268, 279
insurance 123, 129–30, 264, 265
intergenerational issues: compensation 227, 229–31; continuity 275–6; distribution 223–5; ethics 223–6, 244, 272; projects 201, 216, 217; rights and duties 234, 235–7; transfers 222–3, 229–31; welfare 243; *see also* future; future generations;

human behaviour; human welfare; social issues
Intergovernmental Panel on Climate Change (IPCC) *see* IPCC
International Energy Authority (IEA) 40
International Geophysical Year (1957) 11
International Institute for Applied Systems Analysis (IIASA) 42
interpersonal relationships 238–9
intertemporal impact: beneficial 78–80, 89; climate change 62, 76–87, 77t
intertemporal impact of global climate change 62, 76–87, 77t, 89–90, 148n2
intertemporal periods 201
intratemporal space 201, 228
investment, and the future 208, 279
inviobility 235
IPCC (Intergovernmental Panel on Climate Change): accelerated policies scenario 114; agricultural impact 79, 123, 125; atmospheric CO_2 concentrations and emissions 2, 44–5, 46; benefits of control 160; CFC's 37–8; climate change predictions 31, 32, 50; decision theory 258, 260; energy supplies and fossil fuels 42; ethical debate 244–5, 252; extreme events 90; GHG emission 13, 54; global CO_2 budget 36; *see also* SAR; TAR
impact assessment 61–2, 270 (costs and benefits 153, 158, 162–3; damages 168; interdisciplinary approach 270); intertemporal impact 77; migration 126; oceans, report on 76, 80; ozone loss 39; policy development 2, 252, 254, 270; probability approach 106; regional impact 75; scientific approach 8–9; scientific modelling 112; sea level rise 81–2, 84, 85, 125, 126–7; socio-economic approach 5, 21–2; Summary for Policymakers 190–1; uncertainty 192; *see also* SAR; TAR
islands 16, 67, 84, 102, 125, 235, 236

Jaeger, C.C. 133, 144
Jaeger, J. 64
Japan 255, 255t, 257
Jones, P. 238, 240
Jones, P.D. 98–9
Jung, C.G. 242, 276–7

Kagan, S. 243
Kahneman, D. 133
Kapp, K.W. 5
Kastings, J. 46
Kattenberg, A. 87–8

Kauppi, P. 253
Keeling, C.D. 44
Kelejian, H.K. 73, 112–13
Kerr, R.A. 34
Keyfitz, N. 126
Keynes, J.M. 121, 148n1, 266
Kimball, B. 79
knowledge 141–4, 147, 268
Kokoski, M.F. 113
Kyoto Protocol 15, 16, 18–19; CBA studies
    159, 176; emissions control 4, 251–2;
    ethical debate 21, 244; impact of sea level
    rise 67; principal GHGs 54; US attitude to
    254

Lagerspetz, E. 235
Larsen A and Larsen B Antarctic Shelf 85, 86
latitude 63t, 64–7
'learning then acting' strategy 159
Lemons, J. 215, 216
less-developed countries 60, 73, 260, 272; *see
    also* industrially developed countries;
    industrially developing countries; poor
libertarianism (Paretian model) 130, 157, 223,
    225–6, 234, 242
lifestyles 255, 273, 277; quality of life 259,
    275
Lind, R.C. 210, 229, 242–3
Little Ice Age 108
livestock production 70
Loasby, B.J. 121, 122, 135, 136, 147, 266, 268
local information 113
logical positivism 140
long-term damage 197, 210, 215, 245n1, 276;
    ethics of 225, 228–9, 239, 243–4; future
    policy 213–14, 266–77; future predictions
    266, 278–9; irreversible 236
lower-income countries 65, 164, 190; *see also*
    industrially developed countries;
    industrially developing countries; poor
lower-latitude 65

Maldives 67, 125, 235, 236
Manne, A.S. 88, 106, 129, 154, 159, 173, 174,
    175
marginal changes 156–7, 207
marginal costs and benefits 155f, 157, 161
marginal utility 205, 224, 245n4, 245n5
marine ecosystems 76
Markandya, A. 260–1, 272
Martinez-Alier, J. 140
materials balance theory 6
Mauna Loa, Hawaii 11, 43, 107
max–min principle 223, 233, 246n12

Mazza, P. 51
mean temperature 101–2
measurement *see* predictions and measurement
Mendelsohn, R. 76
Meteorological Office, UK (UKMO) 8, 29, 31
methane 39–40, 48, 54, 64, 114
mid-latitude 65
migration 126, 194, 196; *see also* population
Milankovitch, M. 27
minimal achievement 277
minimum standard of emissions 237–8
minimum welfare (max–min principle) 223,
    233, 246n12
Mishan, E.J. 187, 225
mitigation 252, 272
modelling, sophistication of 198; *see also*
    economic models; GCMs; scientific
    models; socio-economic models
monetary valuation 190, 231–2, 258, 269
Montreal Protocol 18, 37, 38, 47, 54
Moore, B. 36
moral issues: CBA studies 173; the future 210,
    211, 212, 215–16, 216t; future generations
    271, 272, 278; insurance 130; political
    economy 270, 278; rights, value and ethics
    197, 231–2, 237–42, 244; *see also* duties;
    ethics; future; future generations;
    intergenerational issues; rights; values
morbidity 186, 188, 189
Morita, T., 260
mortality 186, 188, 189, 192, 194
myopia 204, 207, 216, 217n4

N_2O *see* nitrous oxide
National Academy of Sciences, US 13
National Aeronautical and Space
    Administration (NASA) 8, 142
National Center for Atmospheric Research
    (NCAR) 8, 75, 259–60
natural gas 40, 46, 163
Nature 190
Nature (natural world) 115, 135, 245n2
NCAR *see* National Center for Atmospheric
    Research
negative discounting 212
negative rights and duties 239
neo-classical model 113, 117n1, 201, 204,
    209, 233, 268; intergenerational ethical
    rules 223, 224, 244
Neumayer, E. 211, 231–3, 235
Newman, J.E. 74
New Scientist 190
New Zealand 68, 70
niches 105–6

nitrous oxide (N_2O) 32, 33f, 37, 46
nitrous oxides (NO_x) 38–9, 114
NO_x *see* nitrous oxides
noise 108–9, 115
non-CO_2 gases 279n1
non-identity problem, future generations 222, 235
non-renewable resources 227
Nordhaus, W.D.: agricultural impact 123; economic models 113–14, 117n1; GHG control studies 154, 159, 160–2, 163–5, 167, 168–9, 170, 176, 177, 194; recreational benefits 79; values 185–7
Norgaard, R.B. 140
North America 71–2, 83–4, 104
North–South divide 89
Northern Hemisphere 64–5, 89, 108, 116
nuclear power 12, 133, 139
nuclear weapons 39

objective risk 120–1
objectivity 133–4, 253
obligations, and rights 223
observational evidence 109
oceans 34–5, 54, 76, 80, 111, 114
OECD (Organisation for Economic Co-operation and Development) 40, 41, 135, 166
oil 42, 46, 79, 163, 175, 254
O'Neill, J. 217n2, 246n10, 275
optimisation model 113, 114, 159, 173
orbital forcing 27–8, 49–50, 53
Oregon State University (OSU) 8, 111
ozone 38–9, 47–8, 53, 54, 136, 163; tropospheric ozone 4, 38, 48, 158
'ozone hole' 38, 132, 135
ozone smogs 6–7

Pachauri, R.K. 159
Page, E. 213, 214–15, 235
Page, R. 244
Page, T. 215, 226
paleoclimatic data 108, 110
Paretian (libertarian) model 130, 157, 223, 225–6, 234, 242
Parfit, D. 213, 214
Parry, M.L. 61, 71, 74
partial ignorance 168, 184, 192, 263, 266, 278
particulate emissions 30, 30t
Paterson, M. 10, 11, 267
Pearce, D.W. 191
Peck, S.C. 159, 160
peer review 192

people *see* future generations; human behaviour; human welfare
Perman, R. 156
Petit, J.R. 42
Philbert, C. 243
philosophy 186–8, 199, 233, 246n12, 271
photodissociation 37
Picket, R.C. 74
polar warming 51
policy: adaptation 252, 254; CBA studies and policymakers 262; global climate change 88, 104–5, 139–40, 144–6; long-term and future generations 213–14, 266–77; pollution control 153, 171, 172–7, 178, 279n1; risk options 254, 258
political economy 252–8, 259, 261–2, 270, 278
political issues: decision-making 259; economic arguments 211; scientific approach 278; social approach 254, 257–8, 261–2, 277–9; stability and regional climate changes 69; temperature 254
pollen 108
pollution *see* air pollution
poor 222, 260; *see also* industrially developed countries; industrially developing countries; less-developed countries
population: impact of global climate change 89, 121, 164 (desertification 73–4; sea level rise 66, 125–6)
positive rights and duties 239–40
positive risk 127
positivist program 226
post-normal science 144–6, 273
potential compensation 225, 226
power stations 3
precipitation *see* rainfall
precursor emissions 4, 38
predictions and measurement: CO_2 in 1990s 158–60, 177; CBA studies in the 1990s 198; climate change 46, 107–10, 125, 138; CO_2 109–10, 138, 158, 165–6, 173–4; future and long-term 266, 278–9; GHGs 26, 46, 173–4; global cooling 110, 158; long-term predictions 266, 278–9; *see also* future; history; time scales
preferences 205, 211, 259, 271
Price, C. 176, 208
probability 98–106, 132–3, 144, 168; global temperature 99f, 100f, 102f, 103f, 104f, 105f
probability density function 98–101, 115, 166; ignorance 135–6; indeterminacy 136–7;

strong uncertainty 121, 131, 132; weak uncertainty 98–101, 131
project evaluation, discounting 206, 210–11
protection, environmental 241
psychology 270–1, 276
public awareness 254, 258, 279n5

radiation 31–2
radiative cooling 39
rainfall: probability of enhanced Greenhouse Effect 103, 105; regional climate changes 64, 65–6, 68, 84
Ravetz, J.R. 144, 145, 146, 196
recreation 79, 161, 166, 170–1, 185
Reddy, R.C.S. 176
reflectivity of earth's surface (albedo) 26, 28–9, 28t
reforestation *see* forests
regional climate change 61–76, 63t, 169–70, 260; agriculture and CO_2 70–1, 72, 79; biota 75–6; CBA studies 164, 166–7, 177; CO_2 emission 257, 257t; coral 76; crops 70–3, 74, 79, 123–5; deserts 68, 73–4; exports 72, 73, 89; floods 65; food supplies 65, 73, 74, 89; forests 64, 65, 83–4; rainfall 64, 65–6, 68, 84; sheep farming 70; stability and political issues 69; temperature 63, 65, 68–9, 81–3, 82t; water supplies 68–70, 69t, 72, 73–4; *see also* climate change; countries; emissions; emissions reduction; impact assessment; impacts; local information; temperature
Reister, D.B. 45
religious beliefs and values 141, 142, 192
renewable energy sources 41, 42; non-renewable resources 227
research and values inconsistency 185–91
resource distribution *see* distribution
Resources for the Future 158
responsibilities *see* rights
Revelle, R. 126
RICE model 169
Richards, D.A.J. 214
Richels, R.G. 88, 106, 129, 154, 159, 173, 174, 175
rights: and absolutism 238–40; constitutional and harm 244; and duties 232–7, 238–9, 241–2, 243, 245n3; future generations 213–15, 222–3, 243–4; intergenerational 234, 235–7; social responsibility 278–9; standard of living 227; UN Charter of Human Rights 237, 244, 260; and utilitarianism 241; and values, moral issues 197, 231–2, 237–42, 244; *see also* ethics;

future; future generations; intergenerational issues; moral issues; rights; values
risk: analogy 128; assessment 115, 127–8, 131; aversion and insurance 129; defined 120; exogenous and endogenous 129, 131, 134; the future 209, 210; imperfect information 97–117; perceptions of 133; policy options 254, 258; strong uncertainty 120–3, 122t, 127–30, 131, 133, 134, 135; uncertainty 135, 263–4; valuation surveys 188
rivet popper problem 266
Rosenberg, N.J. 76
Rosenzweig, C. 72, 80
Ross ice shelf 86, 127
Roth, R. 51
Rothman, D.S. 160, 192
Rotty, R.M. 45
Rowlands, I.H. 104, 161, 254–5
Russia *see* Soviet Union (former)

Sagan, C. 28
SAR (Second Assessment Reports) 8–9, 10, 19; benefits of control 160, 167; CO_2 measurement 44; decision analysis 262; discounting 187, 271, 272; impact assessment 46, 50, 66, 83, 86, 169; peer review 192; valuation of damages 166, 189–90, 197–8; valuation of life 268–9
Scandinavia 3–4
Schelling, T.C. 176, 206, 230, 231, 241
Schneider, S.H. 126, 258
Schroder, M. 174
science issues: air pollution 6–11; costs and benefits of GHG control 153; empirical evidence 266; experiments 7–8, 71, 265; perceptions of 140, 141–7; policy issues 278; political economy 252–8; post-normal science 144–6, 273; social issues 9, 140, 144–7, 146–7, 148, 253
scientific models 8, 110–12, 137–9
sea level rise: CBA studies 164–5, 166, 169; climate change 66–8, 81–2, 82t, 84–7, 88; enhanced Greenhouse Effect 123–5, 131, 265; glaciation 50; islands 16, 67, 84, 102, 125, 235, 236; strong uncertainty 125–6, 131
seasons 78–9, 104–5, 106
sediment 108
semi-arid tropical regions 65–6, 73, 74, 88
Sen, A. 74–5, 187
Seneft, D. 79
Senum, G.I. 39
sheep farming 70
Shugart, H.H. 237

signals predicting climate change 108–9
sinks: forests as 112, 176; GHGs 26, 32–40, 54, 154, 168; oceans as 111, 114
Smith, J.B. 61, 258
Smith, V.K. 113
smog 3, 4, 6–7, 38
social issues: decision-making 259; GHG control options 153–4; political awareness 254, 258, 261–2, 277–9; regulation and control 122, 139–41, 153–4, 238–9; responsibility and rights 278–9; scientific approach 9, 140, 144–7, 146–7, 148, 253; uncertainty 266–7; value systems 253, 274–6; *see also* future; future generations; human behaviour; human welfare; intergenerational issues
socio-economic models 26, 112–15, 121–30, 137–9, 147, 268
solar radiation 26, 27–8
Solow, R.M. 226–7, 246n7, 246n12
sources: of alternative energy 40, 132; by energy type, CO_2 41t; of renewable energy 41, 42
sources and sinks: CO_2 32, 34–7, 35f, 54n2, 168 (forests as sinks 112, 176; oceans as sinks 111, 114); GHGs 26, 32–40, 54, 154, 168
Southern Hemisphere 116
Soviet Union (former) 47; CO_2 emission 255, 255t; crop production 73; GNP 166, 169
Spash, C.L. 226
species 105, 161, 166, 194
Spruce 83
Stockholm meeting (1972) 13
storm surges 84, 88, 102, 125
stratosphere 38, 39, 48, 132, 158
strong uncertainty 120–48, 122t; agricultural impact 123–5; alternatives excluded 132; assessment 127–8; catastrophes 126–7, 278; cause–effect relationships 132; CBA studies 168; decision analysis 263; droughts 126; economic models 116, 121–30, 137–9, 141–2, 147; ignorance 122, 129, 135–6, 146, 147; indeterminancy 136–7, 146–7, 168; insurance 129–30; knowledge and belief 141–4, 147; migration 126; new policy approaches 266, 267–8; post-normal science 144–6; precision and 'objective facts' 133–4; probability density function 121, 131, 132; probability estimates 133–4; risk 120–3, 122t, 127–30, 131, 133, 134; science, perceptions of 140, 141–7; sea level rise 125–6, 131; social regulation and control

122, 139–41; subjective probabilities 132–3, 144, 168; value and ethics 192–6; weak to strong uncertainty 134–41; weak uncertainty 128–31; weak uncertainty, how weak is it 131–4; *see also* weak uncertainty
subjective probabilities 132–3, 144, 168
subjective risk 127
sub-Saharan Africa 69–70, 73–4, 88
subsistence agriculture 65
subsonic aircraft 48
sulphate aerosols 31, 81
Summary for Policymakers (IPCC) 190–1
Sundaraman, N. 190
supersonic aircraft 39
surprise events *see* catastrophes
sustainability 9, 22, 241, 272, 273

TAR (Third Assessment Reports): benefits of control 160; CBA studies and decision theory 260; discount rates 203, 271, 272; economics and ethics 257–8; geo-engineering 253; GHG emissions 44, 48; impact assessment 61, 77–8, 81, 89; monetary valuation 190, 269; observed changes 251; policy report 9, 10–11, 19, 22, 23n1; sea level rise 66, 80, 85–6; strong uncertainty 120; temperature increase 50, 54n1; valuation of life 268–9
technology 228, 237, 253, 254, 278–9
Teisburg, T.J. 159, 160
teleology 233–4, 243
temperature: and climate change 31, 48–52, 52f; CO_2 concentrations 45, 63–4; double CO_2-equivalent 25, 76, 81; global, and probability 98–106, 99f, 100f, 102f, 103f, 104f, 105f; global warming 11, 13, 25, 33f, 49–51, 88, 161–2, 165; hemispheric changes 51, 64–5, 89, 108, 116; measurement and prediction 108–10, 138; political importance of changes 254; probability and mean temperature 101–2; regional climate changes 63, 65, 68–9, 81–3, 82t; *see also* climate change; impact assessment; impacts; regional climate change
thresholds 10, 105–6
time preference rate 204, 205
time scales: cultural and social importance 275–7, 280n7; the future 201–17; GHG lifetimes 36–7, 46; impact and global climate change 62, 76–87, 77t; *see also* future; history; predictions and measurement
Tirkkonen, J. 145

Tirpak, D.A. 61
Tol, R.S.J. 154, 168–9, 177, 191, 192, 198
Toronto Conference (1988) 128, 172, 174
Toth, F.L. 273, 274
tourism 79
trade-offs 231–2, 246n9
transfers 222–3, 227–31, 236, 242, 273; *see also* compensation
transmittance 27, 29–31
transportation: aircraft 39, 48, 158; assessment 188, 189; precursor emissions 4, 38
tree rings 108, 110
tropical regions 65–6
tropospheric ozone 4, 38, 48, 158
Turkenberg, W. 177
Tversky, A. 133
Tyndall, J. 25

UK: CO_2 emission 255, 255t; Forestry Commission 163; GHG emission control 3, 18, 176; sea level rise 67; *see also* British Isles
Ulph, A 174–5, 178n1
uncertainty 90, 168, 197, 198; decision analysis 262–4; environmental factors 139–40; the future 209–11, 266, 278; GCMs 110–12, 115–16; social issues 266–7; *see also* economic models; economy; strong uncertainty; weak uncertainty
UNEP: costs and benefits of GHG control 153, 177; cultural relativism 259–60; impact assessment 61; sea level rise 67, 125
United Kingdom *see* UK
United Nations Framework Convention on Climate change (UNFCCC) 15, 16–18, 83, 190
United Nations (UN) 8, 13; charter of human rights 237, 244, 260
United States *see* US
unmanaged ecosystems 75–6
US: agriculture 72, 73, 113, 123; CBA studies 161, 163–4, 169, 171, 174, 193t; climate measurement and predictions 109; CO_2 doubling 123; CO_2 emission 4, 18, 254–5, 255t; Electric Power Research Institute 160; emissions control 4, 18, 251–2; impact assessment 61; Kyoto Protocol 254; precursor emissions 38; sea level rise 67; socio-economic models 113
utilitarianism 233, 239, 241, 242, 244
UV-B damage 124, 135

valuation (economic): costs and benefits 158–60, 184, 185; damages 166, 189–90, 197–8; discounting 206, 210–11; ethics 188–92, 197, 231–2, 258, 268–77, 269; GHG control 154, 158–60, 188–92; surveys and risk 188
values: air pollution 20–1; and beliefs 141, 142, 192, 271; 'carriers of values' 214–15; contingent valuation 188, 189–90, 191; economic valuation 268–77; ethics and distribution 192–3; ethics and enhanced Greenhouse Effect 20–1, 253; GHG emissions 20–1, 184–99, 259–60; harm, intrinsic value 278; human life 20, 159, 188–92, 268–9, 275–6, 279n3; limits of value systems 240–2; natural 236–7, 246n7; rights and moral issues 197, 231–2, 237–42, 244; social and commensurable 259; social issues 253, 274–6; strong uncertainty 132–3, 140, 141–4, 192–6; value-free and cultural perspectives 253; welfarism 233; *see also* ethics; future; future generations; intergenerational issues; moral issues; rights; valuation
variability 44, 44f, 102–5, 107–8, 171–2
Varichek, B.V. 73, 112–13
Vaughan, D.G. 86
vegetation 108
victims, and compensation 229
Villach Conference (1985) 13, 64, 65
volcanoes 29–30, 43, 53
Vostok ice core analysis 42, 48–9

Wade-Benzoni, K.A. 241
'wait and see' 159, 171
Walker, J. 46
Walters, J. 154, 161, 163, 164–5, 196
Warrick, R.A. 127
water supplies: agricultural impact 124; CBA studies 164; regional climate change 68–70, 69t, 72, 73–4
Watson, R.T. 88, 153
Watts, J.A. 108
weak uncertainty 97–116, 122t; CBA studies 168; decision analysis 263; feedbacks and complexity 109–10; the future 209, 211; insurance risk model 123; modelling 110–15; new policy approaches 266–7; predictions and measurements 107–10; probability 98–106; probability density function 98–101, 131; socio-economic models 112–15, 268; strong uncertainty 131–41; weak to strong uncertainty 134–41; *see also* strong uncertainty

weather patterns 98, 253–4
welfare *see* human welfare
welfare economics 223–6, 230–1, 261
welfarism 233–5
West Antarctic ice sheets 85–6, 126–7, 131, 132, 265
Whalley, J. 174
wheat 71, 72, 73, 113; *see also* agriculture; crops
Whorf, T.P. 44
Wigle, R. 174
Wigley, T.M.L. 27, 46

Wilenius, M. 145
Woodwell, G.M. 126
World Climate Conference, First (1979) 12, 13, 158
World Climate Conference, Second (1990) 15, 17t
World Meteorological Organisation (WMO) 11, 64, 153
Wynne, B. 134, 136, 137, 138, 142, 146, 265, 266

zero discounting 217